LICENSED TO KILL

LICENSED TO KILL

HIRED GUNS IN THE WAR ON TERROR

ROBERT YOUNG PELTON

CROWN PUBLISHERS / NEW YORK

Library of Congress Cataloging-in-Publication Data
Pelton, Robert Young.
    Licensed to kill : hired guns in the war on terror / Robert Young Pelton. —
1st ed.
        p. cm.
    Includes bibliographical references and index. (alk. paper)
    1. War on Terrorism, 2001–   2. Iraq War, 2003–   3. Mercenary troops—
United States.   4. Mercenary troops—Iraq.   5. United States—Military policy.
I. Title.
    HV6432.P45   2006
    355.3'540973—dc22   2006016029

ISBN-13: 978-1-4000-9781-4
ISBN-10: 1-4000-9781-9

Printed in the United States of America

Design by Lenny Henderson

10 9 8 7 6 5 4 3 2 1

First Edition

CONTENTS

To the unheralded heroes of the War on Terror,
the contractors who have sacrificed their lives in service to their client

CONTRACTOR'S CREED

---

*I am a U.S. contractor. I look out for myself, the operators to my left
and right, and no one else.
I will always take advantage of the fact that I can finally tell military
officers to pound sand,
and will do so at every opportunity.
I am my country's scapegoat, the "plausible deniability" warrior,
and I love it.
Less than $700 dollars a day is unacceptable.
I am trained to eat things that would make a billy goat puke,
but will refuse anything less than 60 dollars per diem because
I am greedy.
I care not for ribbons and awards for valor.
I do this job for the opportunity to kill the enemies of my country,
and to finally get that boat I've always wanted.
I will be in better shape than 99% of the active duty personnel,
although this is not hard.
I will equip myself with the latest high speed gear,
and will trick out my M4 until it weighs more than 24 lbs, not because
it works better, but because it looks cool in the photographs.
I will carry more weapons, ammunition, and implements of death on
my person than an infantry fire team, and when engaged I will lay waste to
everything around me.
In any combat zone, I will always locate the swimming pool, beer,
and women, because I can.
I will deploy on my terms, and if it ever gets too stupid,
I will simply find another company that pays me more.*

—From an e-mail circulated on contractor channels

LICENSED TO KILL

Prologue

A handsome, blond, youthful-looking man bounds into the lobby of the Ritz-Carlton in Tysons Corner, Virginia. He is thirty-six-year-old Erik Prince, former Navy SEAL, sole owner of Blackwater USA, heir to the Prince family fortune, and perhaps the most controversial proponent of the privatization of security. Though Blackwater's headquarters are located on a seven-thousand-acre training facility in Moyock, North Carolina, it's convenient for Prince to maintain an office in Tysons Corner, since both the Pentagon and CIA are within easy driving distance.

The media has portrayed Erik as shadowy and elusive. He is not, but he has earned the reputation because he's declined numerous interview requests. With major lawsuits having been brought against Blackwater by families of deceased employees, there's a legal need to stay low profile. Yet, Erik's agreed to go on record with me. I can only speculate that my having spent a month running the deadly Baghdad Airport road with Blackwater's security teams, and my occasional encounters with Prince at closed social events, have convinced him of my sincere desire to understand what his world is all about.

In my decades of traversing war-torn regions, I've broken bread with a number of wealthy owners of private armies, but Erik is the first I've gotten to know in the posh setting of an upscale American hotel lounge. Sitting across from him, observing his energetic, optimistic demeanor, I conclude that not a single person in the crowded room would guess Prince's true profession. He interrupts his ever-vibrating cell phone only once, to take a call from "the boss"—his wife.

Erik has plenty of reasons for optimism, because in the past five years, his security start-up has grown from "shooting range and target manufacturer" to one of the world's most successful providers of security training and armed men. Blackwater's operations extend from New Orleans to Afghanistan and from Azerbaijan to Iraq. As of early 2006, Prince had eight hundred men on the ground in Iraq, three hundred in New Orleans, two hundred in Afghanistan, and hundreds more flying planes, running personal security details, guarding facilities, and training soldiers around the world. Erik is especially enthusiastic about his new Blackwater Academy, which will recruit, hire, and deploy the thousand-man army he's touting as his company's "next step." The grueling eight-week program won't charge eager recruits who fail the course and will subsidize successful graduates by guaranteeing them a job with Blackwater. As of fall 2006, Blackwater is on track to train thirty-five thousand men over the next twelve months and has more than eighteen hundred people deployed in seven countries. Prince likes to think of Blackwater's relationship to the traditional military as something akin to FedEx's relationship to the U.S. Post Office—an efficient, privatized solution to sclerotic and wasteful government bureaucracy.

Amid the post-9/11 private security industry explosion, Prince has made the most of his business acumen. He doesn't cite as his hero a famous soldier, mercenary, or privateer, but rather a businessman: Alfred Sloan, the man who originally built GM into one of the world's largest and most profitable corporations. The Prince family empire started small—with Eric's father's company inventing the lighted vanity mirror on sun visors—and ballooned as the patriarch expanded into other endeavors.

Erik is obviously a product of his upbringing: "My family's business was automotive supply—the most viciously competitive business in the world. My father was focused on quality, volume, and customer satisfaction. That's what we talked about around the dinner table." By emphasizing these same values, Erik believes he can deliver a lighter, faster, smarter army, without the ponderous support infrastructure required by the conventional military.

As a result of the major push toward privatization of support services that began in the 1990s, the U.S. government has learned that employing the private sector to solve problems can be more cost-effective than building giant bureaucratic solutions. And, indeed, Erik often finds enthusiastic audiences at the CIA, the State Department, and the Pentagon for his fixed-cost, solution-oriented presentations. At the same time, he's aware of the sometimes tepid public support for what can be viewed as an army of "mercenaries" solving the world's woes. Admittedly hawkish, family-values-stressing, and from a redder-than-red Republican background, Prince understands that not everyone shares his views. He recognizes that when it comes to Joe Everyman, he has some convincing to do.

Erik has a pitch prepared to combat the "mercenary" label and the frequently negative perceptions that spin off from it. He starts by reminding me that the American Revolution would have failed without private militias raised by wealthy landowners. Prince views Blackwater's role in international affairs as akin to that of Baron von Steuben, Kościuszko, Rochambeau, and Lafayette—soldiers-of-fortune who helped the American irregulars fight the well-trained and -armed British Army. He also likes to point out that "contractors" hired by the U.S. military go back to the WWII-era Flying Tigers—a group of secretly funded Americans who flew under Claire Lee Chennault's corporation CAMCO. The Tigers shot down Japanese planes and targeted infrastructure for three times what regular aviators made, plus a bonus for every downed plane.

The examples Prince cites go far beyond the functions private security contractors have so far served in places like Iraq and Afghanistan, and indicate the direction of Prince's ambition. "Security" traditionally means trained men guarding other people, places, or things, but Prince wants to offer more. As his next expansion step, Erik wants to augment the current UN (United Nations) peacekeeping arrangements with his own private military force. The UN, he says, is an organization that spends 70 percent of its $10-billion budget on peacekeeping missions—a task that has doubled over the last ten years. According to him, the peacekeeping arm of the UN is a broken, corrupt organization, "a racket used to fund undisciplined, poorly trained and equipped Third World armies."

Prince has even hired Ambassador Cofer Black, formerly of the CIA and State Department, to tout the newest iteration of Blackwater's private army at rubber-chicken dinners for foreign representatives. In March 2006, Black told his audience at the Special Forces Operations Exhibition in Amman, Jordan, that his company could supply a brigade-sized force quickly and relatively cheaply. "The issue is who's going to let us play on their team," he said, later clarifying that: "We would get the approval of the U.S. government for anything we did for our friends overseas."

Erik has the capability to launch his own brigade of private soldiers, or what he likes to call "Relief with Teeth"—a seventeen-hundred-man privately trained and equipped army that would field its own air force of helicopters and cargo craft. Those with the money could also rent "fire support," complete with a private gunship, intelligence gathering, aerial surveillance, armed helicopters, armored vehicles, remote-controlled blimps, and fast-attack aircraft with JDAMs (joint direct attack munition) or cluster bombs. There would be a construction, medical, supply, and combat group adhering to a ratio of about one Western professionally trained officer to ten TCNs, or third-country nationals—essentially, foreign grunts. Erik stipulates that his clients must be American allies and that Blackwater takes all the high-tech toys home when the contract ends. While Erik has developed this capability, he won't discuss whether he's found purchasers for his newest line of services.

In describing the model he'd use to organize his private force, Erik cites the classic command structure of past mercenary operations like the South African company Executive Outcomes (EO). Erik praises EO for mounting an effective intervention that ended bloody conflicts in Sierra

Leone and Angola. He doesn't mention that EO was not only banned by South African legislation, but also carries a stigma for the perception it was used by its owners and patrons as a tool to capture lucrative natural resources.

There is a vast difference in the moral and legal implications of Executive Outcomes's activities when compared to Blackwater's ambitions, though the two entities are located on the same private military continuum.

Most simply stated, mercenaries are soldiers-for-hire—and private military (or security) contractors are security-guards-for-hire. Mercenaries can be paid to overthrow heads of state, whereas security contractors have protected heads of state, diplomats, Saudi princes, military bases, shipping lanes targeted by piracy, petroleum operations, diamond and other mineral mines, NGO (nongovernmental organization) programs, and post-Katrina New Orleans. However, by far the largest market for security services (and the crucible for events that have essentially created the industry) is post-invasion Iraq. There, attempts to carry on reconstruction while bullets are flying have been largely dependent on the level of security that can be maintained. Security contractors have protected L. Paul Bremer and John Negroponte, CPA (Coalition Provisional Authority) installations, commercial or government reconstruction projects, and oil pipelines. Contractor-protected security convoys have become ubiquitous as diplomats, business leaders, journalists (and the material that sustains them) are shuttled from place to place. Even a run to pick up kitchen equipment can inspire a firefight—as was the case when four Blackwater contractors were very publicly and brutally killed, desecrated, and hung from a Fallujah bridge in March 2004. That incident thrust the role of the private military contractor into the media spotlight, sparking a debate about the role of civilians in a war zone and the difference between security contractors and mercenaries.

Mercenaries *fight*, while security contractors *protect*, firing back only if they or what they're guarding comes under attack, and only until they can make a safe retreat—at least, that's been the dividing line that's supposed to exist. But as entrepreneurs like Erik Prince push to open new markets for their security products, there will almost certainly be a blurring of that already less-than-distinct line. In fact, some critics argue that the line never existed.

I've spent much of my adult life following the activities of mercenaries and soldiers-for-hire. In 1975, I taped three Michelin road maps of Africa to the wall of my apartment and charted the progress of Colonel Callan and his ill-fated band of mercenaries across Angola. In the late 1990s, I met my first professional mercenary turned security contractor, Cobuss Claassens, who'd formerly been employed by Executive Outcomes. What I learned from Cobuss was that the difference between mercenaries and contractors depends on the person, not the job. The ultimate moral leash on these people is how they view themselves, not how the world views them. When I met my first security contractor, who was working on a CIA-paid covert hunt for bin Laden in the border region of Afghanistan, I recognized we could be on the cusp of a dramatic shift in the practice of modern warfare, or perhaps a return to a bygone era of privateers and bounty hunters.

Driven by a desire to understand this new phenomenon, I decided to traverse this closed world, from its most sordid end to its most respectable. What follows is a description of that journey. It is not intended to be en- tirely comprehensive—that is, an academic treatise on the complete range of issues raised by this newest development in warfare. For example, I have no interest in investigating the manipulation of the bidding process; the news media seems to be doing an adequate job exposing such abuses. How- ever, I learned so much in my travels—about the men who choose this kind of career, the type of work they must do, the watershed events in their his- tory, the big-picture problems the rapid growth of the industry has engen- dered, and what this might portend for the future—that it seemed imperative to share my newly acquired insight. In what follows, I try not to tell the reader what to think. Rather, I invite him or her to travel with me and experience a wide array of characters and scenarios. My only agenda is to guide readers to a new understanding of how in the future these individ- uals and corporations could be harnessed as a force for good or evil.

INTRODUCTION

Roll Hard

"Another day, another mission."
— Introduction to daily Blackwater Mamba team briefing

The flies at the airport are irritating. "Fuck!" Griz swears loudly, getting angrier every time he fails to snatch one out of the air. Griz is also pissed because he shaved his head, and it doesn't seem to be growing back. Miyagi tells him to chill. Griz, nicknamed after the grizzly bears of his native Pacific Northwest, is an ex-marine with no talent for catching the insistent flies that probe his mouth and nose. In an unusual tribute to his employer, Griz has tattooed on the back of his impressively large bicep a big-ass Blackwater logo—the familiar bear paw and sniper scope graphic that recalls the black bears that wander the six thousand acres of the Great Dismal Swamp headquarters. It's a logo that often appears in place of the expected American flag on armed men and vehicles in Iraq.

The twelve-man Blackwater security detail has just arrived at Baghdad International Airport (BIAP) to pick up a new rotation of contractors arriving from Amman. With only two flights coming in per day, the monstrous airport complex of boxy, nondescript neo-European architecture has the quiet, eerie atmosphere of an abandoned movie set façade, an isolated oasis situated on the outskirts of the violent reality of Baghdad.

Waiting for a flight always feels like a too-brief peaceful respite sandwiched between the high-intensity trips from and back to the Green Zone along the airport road, better known as "Route Irish" or "IED Alley." Tensions are particularly high today, since the morning briefing announced that a recent forty-eight-hour span saw sixteen attacks along the four-mile route. The Blackwater Mamba team makes the journey almost every day, rolling hard to avoid the daily barrage of gunfire or IEDs (improvised explosive device) insurgents direct at American convoys.

The Mamba team doesn't mingle with the other security details that sit inside the dark parking garage nearby. It's bad juju to not stay focused and is decidedly uncool to fraternize with other security companies. Blackwater's Mamba team trash-talks other private security companies—Triple Canopy, MVM, USIS, and DynCorp—like football players make fun of opposing teams. They all nod to acknowledge the other's presence, often with a muttered insult under their breath, but that's as far as the conversation ever gets.

T-Boy stands off by himself "zoning," as he calls it, staying focused on the dangerous return trip to the Green Zone. T-Boy looks like he has adopted a style of generic death—black helmet, black shirt, black mask, black goggles, with a large skull and crossbones chalked on the back of his armor vest and another drawn on his Kevlar helmet. All the gear covers the skull tattoos. T-Boy mans the lead PKM light machine gun and has to stay tight since the insurgents have started a new tactic of pulling ahead and then slowing down to detonate in front of a convoy. He won't stand down until we get back to the team house.

Baz, a former Kiwi SAS (Special Air Service), breaks out a Macanudo cigar, and Gecko hits the duty-free shop for a soda, while 86, Baghdaddy, Critter, and the others shoot the shit. A tousled blond ex-marine from Mississippi, 86 has gym-built biceps encircled by swirling black tribal tattoos and likes to wear a dirty crushed Yuengling beer ball cap and oversized Ray-Ban aviator glasses. He got the name 86 because he was 86'ed out of the State Department detail when they actually checked his record and pulled his clearance. It's an old joke. As the only good ole boy on the team, 86 always suffers good-natured jibes from his other teammates.

Juan, the dark-haired, ever-smiling fiftysomething Hispanic from El Paso, hangs out with the Chileans, joking and chattering in Spanish. The Chileans are former Pinochet-era soldiers brokered to Blackwater by Grupo Tactico as TCNs, or third-country nationals. They make about $2,400 a month doing "static" work—mostly guarding the Blackwater compound back in the Green Zone. In their late thirties and early forties, the excellent former officers get tapped to do the Mamba run when manpower is short, or when they get bored.

Tool, the redheaded ex-marine and driver/mechanic, uses the wait time to have a Camel cigarette and check out the three-Mamba convoy for any mechanical problems. The Mambas are South African–built leviathans, designed to withstand mine blasts and provide protection from snipers—a definite move up from cramped GMC Suburbans or armored BMW 7 series. The downside is that the Mambas are slow, top heavy, and look like a convoy of white circus elephants bristling with helmeted men and guns popping out of their five hatches—not exactly low-key swimmers in an ocean of sharks.

Miyagi, who got his radio handle because of his resemblance to Pat Morita in the *Karate Kid* movies and his need to wear thick reading glasses, leads the convoy. A former L.A. cop from a tough inner-city beat, Miyagi speaks in a cool-guy Latino riff. For luck, he wears a dark red scarf his wife sent him. Short, with a salt-and-pepper beard, his weapons and gear hang off him with a comfortable look typical of security contractors. As a group, they resemble the actors in a badly cast B movie about mercenaries. "Bro," Miyagi says, describing the look the contractors try to achieve. "We call it CDI—Chicks Dig It. When we pull in to the airport and stare at ourselves in those mirrored windows, all we say is, 'Hey, bro, CDI.'" The team laughs.

Miyagi continues, "We also use the expression 'You're shit hot.'"

Griz answers with an exaggerated pointed finger, "No, you are shit hot!"

Miyagi shoots back, "No, YOU are shit hot!" The others laugh. They know Miyagi is jacking the new guy with the usual cliché of contractors being vain cowboys.

Gecko, a young, square-built, shaven-headed ex-marine, gets back with an armful of duty-free junk food. He rhapsodizes of the days when they could walk through the airport with all their gear. "Now you have to take all your weapons off just to go into duty free," he complains as he passes out Cokes and candy bars.

Griz continues snapping at Iraqi flies, trying in utter desperation to keep them off his Coke can. Miyagi advises him to chill again, though a steady chorus "Fuck! FUCK! Fuck!" underlies the rest of the conversation as the stealthy insects escape Griz's angry grasps. Flies are like insurgents here, omnipresent, persistent, and a part of life and death—just one more thing to make things miserable in the sandbox.

The flight finally arrives. The passengers—mostly well-dressed Iraqis pulling new, wheeled luggage—deplane. The Iraqis meet their local drivers while the few Westerners are greeted by their professional security details and get into unlicensed BMWs and GMCs. Helmets, armor, and a full load of mags and M4 rifles have been laid out for the new rotation of Blackwater contractors the Mamba team has come to the airport to pick up. The newbies and returning friends arrive to a chorus of hellos, hugs, knuckle bangs, and shoulder thumps. They all get a quick briefing from Miyagi while sliding on armor. Weapons are racked back, loaded, and readied. The run is on, but the Mamba team holds back. The insurgents watching Route Irish had been given an hour to marshal their forces in readiness of hitting us on our return journey, so we let the other groups go first to draw the fire that can be expected on the trip back to the Green Zone. The team finds it funny that I wear the gear but prefer to hold a camera instead of a gun. They remind me that if given the chance, insurgents would lay to waste every man in the vehicle and every vehicle in the convoy.

We pull away from the terminal at 2:30 and begin the long southern drive that loops around the runway to the gate. We are "green" here, as in "safe." When we leave the last airport checkpoint, we will go "red," entering the high-danger zone with weapons hot.

At 2:35 we wave to the Gurkhas guarding the exit gate, pass the GBC Logistics sign, and leave the relative safety of the airport. A sign at the exit reminds us, ALL WEAPONS RED, meaning racked back and safety off. No more jokes. Miyagi calls over the radio, "Everyone man their sector." The drivers punch the gas, and like bulls bolting out of a rodeo pen, the Mambas surge through the open gates. Stretching before us is an expanse of charred and stunted date trees, victims of previous blasts. A brightly optimistic Iraqi election sign adds grim irony to the danger of the impending run. A busy feeder road runs parallel fifty yards off to the side, with a wasteland of blackened BMW carcasses and scorched ground between us. Entering the danger zone, input becomes compressed; events play out in slow motion. The radio spits out terse commands and retorts. Continuing to accelerate. No traffic on the main road. "All clear."

Two thirty-seven, approaching first bridge, called "J" for "jihad." The radio crackles: "Remember this morning's briefing. They said watch for explosives under the bridge." Scan for Iraqis dropping grenades, pop-up snipers, bomb throwers. "CLEAR!" Then our first merge. Traffic pouring onto the highway. A notorious hot spot where bombers merge into traffic and detonate themselves.

"*IMSHI!*"—Arabic for "get back"—yells Miyagi, repeatedly punching his fist straight out. One car ignores him. BRRRRT! Puffs of smoke rise from bullets zippering the road. The startled driver and his family look up in shock as we blur by. The acrid scent of gunpowder comes and goes. Another exit, another overpass. Everyone in the top turrets raises his weapons and pivots on the bridge like dancers in a grotesque ballet. "CLEAR!"

Radio crackles: "Cars slowing down!" Approaching another bridge. "Clear the bridge!" Guns swing up and out, then back on traffic in perfect unison. The median now appears a flooded lake of orange Jersey barriers. Possible IEDs? Scan for unusual objects. It's 2:39. More cars pulling onto the highway alongside. The last Mamba keeps them back or pulled off to the side. A whiff of cordite. T-Boy must be firing the PKM machine gun.

"WHAT THE FUCK!" 86 yells over the radio. Up ahead, black-chadored women run across the highway. All guns flick forward. The women look petrified at the sight of three massive white trucks loaded with armed men bearing down on them. They run in terror. False alarm.

Or was it? Insurgents use distractions to slow or stop vehicles so they can be blown up.

Gecko calls off oncoming vehicles like a quarterback calls plays. "Car coming up fast, check out the passenger. Oncoming . . . four people in a taxi." Tool uses the mirrors to watch for any fast movers from the rear. Passing by the Saddam monument. It's 2:40. We enter the Kill Zone. Intel charts with colorful green, orange, and red graphics have shown us that most people die along this stretch. The tone on the radio changes. "CLEAR!" Another exit coming up. Low, stunted, dirty trees block the view. A bullet cracks by my head. No sniper in sight. Focus on the road. We take the off-ramp that will lead us to Gate 12, and from there, into the relative safety of the Green Zone. Over to the left, the twisted shell of a car still burns. No time to stop.

A flat pressure followed by a deep heavy boom comes from behind. Then the rolling gray smoke mushroom ascends to mark yet another Iraqi martyr sent to Allah's paradise in a cheap Japanese import. We missed this one by a good five or six minutes. Focus ahead. High fencing on each side. T-Boy sounds tense. A pile of trash on the side of the road we don't recognize. IED? Keep rolling. Just debris from a blast the day before.

It's 2:41. The "Little Birds," Blackwater's tiny teardrop-shaped Boeing helos, swoop down to a mere few yards above and arc up in tandem like an insane carnival ride. I can see the pilot, Steve, and the two gunners hanging off the skids with their SAWs (squad automatic weapons). They are Blackwater's guardian angels, dispatched without being asked to provide cover for the Mamba convoy.

Gate 12 to the Green Zone. Almost there. Up ahead a car brakes. Another car darts toward us. Guns up. "CHECK HIM OUT!" Gecko barks. Is the driver nervous? Dressed in white? Clean-shaven? No, just a taxi trying to avoid the traffic jam around the gate. Coming off the overpass. It's 2:42. Residential neighborhoods to the right and left of us. Young marines lounging on gray concrete barricades wave us through. Not safe yet. Juan yells to the marines that an Iraqi was stuffing a package in a drainpipe just as we drove in.

We roll through the priority lane and stand down. Exhale. Weapons on safety. Back in the Green Zone. It's 2:43 and we've just completed the most perilous eight-minute drive in the world. When Tool goes over the vehicles, he finds a new spider mark from a high-powered round in the windshield of our Mamba. No sweat. Tomorrow they will do it again. New day. New mission.

Part One

Hired Guns

CHAPTER 1

Kill Them All

"I am here for the money."
—Afghan General Zia Lodin to the CIA

"The solution is to let them kill each other," the small, energetic senior citizen in the Windbreaker tells me over a fiesta omelet with extra jalapeños at a Florida Waffle House. He points upward. "Send up a satellite and take pictures. Keep the Special Operations teams in the hills, fifty miles out of the towns. Then go in at night and do your work. Kill them. Kill like we did in Germany. Flatten the place. You have to not mind killing innocents. Even the women and children."

These are the words of seventy-five-year-old Billy Waugh, Special Forces legend, seasoned CIA paramilitary, renowned assassin, covert operator, and the world's longest operating "Green Badger"—or CIA contractor. Over breakfast we discuss my most recent trip to Iraq with contractors and the deadly and confused situation there. Billy is giving me his frank opinions on what needs to be done in Iraq to stop the ever-mounting toll of dead Americans. His reference to tactics in Germany and other wars is not based on a book but on events in his lifetime.

The best clue to Billy's age comes from the vast historical and geographical area over which he can roam in the first person. Billy Waugh tried to sign up to fight during the closing year of World War II but was

17

sent back to his home in Bastrop, Texas, because he was only fifteen at the time. He finally became an army paratrooper in 1947 at age seventeen; joined the barely two-year-old Special Forces (SF) in 1954; worked off and on with the CIA starting in 1961, fully enjoying his long career in the business of killing and espionage. Waugh is a decorated veteran of Korea, a twenty-seven-month decorated veteran of Southeast Asia during the Vietnam era, an eleven-year Special Forces veteran, and a veteran of a yet-to-be-determined number of CIA operations as either an employee (Blue Badger) or as a contractor (Green Badger). He knows many people and has been to many places—Vietnam, Bosnia, Sudan, Kosovo, Iraq, Yemen, Libya, Afghanistan, and dozens of other countries. Just as an employee and contractor for the CIA, Billy has worked and traveled in sixty-four countries since 1989.

Billy exudes obvious pride regarding his work for the Agency and has not only written a book about some of his adventures, called *Hunting the Jackal,* but also travels around speaking to graduation classes, SF associations, and even football teams. His three-month-old metallic-champagne Lincoln Town Car already has twenty-two thousand miles on it, mostly from driving between Florida and Washington. "I can't fly anymore," he admits. It's not that he is afraid of crashing; he just carries too many weapons. When he gives his motivational speech, he says, "It's all about being shot up and how to keep on going. How to be tough." At his age and with his experiences, Billy Waugh should not be alive. His custom front license plate provides clues. While his rear plate advertises WOUNDED WAR VET, the front plate spells it out in simpler terms: 8 HITS, with an illustration of a Purple Heart medal.

Our waitress at the Waffle House probably assumes this short, compact man with thinning hair and thick glasses is an energetic grandfather. His black Members Only jacket, golf shirt, and nondescript pants wouldn't spark her curiosity, unless she noticed the grinning skull patch on his jacket—a Special Operations Association logo. Billy's culture and style is rooted in the U.S. Special Forces. He wears two large army rings, an SF pendant on a gold chain, and a gold Rolex Daymaster with diamonds around the bezel—not in a decorative fashion, but more like tribal badges common among ex–Special Forces soldiers. Billy Waugh is also a Texan, famously outspoken, and doesn't suffer fools. Despite his age and limping gait—the result of old combat injuries—Billy has the mental and physical vigor of a twenty-one-year-old. He speaks in staccato bursts like machine-gun fire, beginning every conversation with a barrage of questions and finishing up with a few bursts of opinions.

I first met Billy over the phone, and he immediately began interspersing his spiel with questions, like an opening mortar bombardment designed to confuse or narrow in on an opponent. Even in person, Billy likes to sort out the person across the table as friend or foe. If enough names and answers click, he becomes your friend. If not, the conversation comes to an end. His only caveat to the curious is, "I ain't gonna tell you any classified stuff" or make the Agency look bad.

Billy talks about killing like civilians might talk about their golf game. It's what he does, what he did, and what he knows—something the U.S. government trained him and paid him to do for many years. Billy's descriptions of death and killing are not intended to impress but to assure the listener of the difference between good and bad people. Billy must be excused for his blunt talk. He normally seeks out the company of soldiers who understand such things. The Special Operations community lauds him as a living legend, and just the way he refers to himself in the third person, speaking his own name in compressed syllables—"billywaugh"—gives him a ring of uniqueness and celebrity.

In his biography, *Hunting the Jackal*, Waugh describes himself as someone who simply functions in combat, someone who does not spend too much time worrying, complaining, or examining what he does. Billy has killed countless people, has had people try to kill him, been nearly dead, and has lost many friends. He has worn the smell of death, whether by retrieving maggot-infested booby-trapped bodies of comrades killed in battle, or in the private weight of burying dozens of close friends. Despite this, even at his advanced age, he would gladly go anywhere his country would send him under any conditions to kill or help others to kill America's enemies. But his days of killing and hunting America's enemies are over now. Even in America's new "dead or alive" War on Terror, Billy sees a change in how contractors and paramilitaries are allowed to operate.

Billy tells me how Special Forces tactics have changed since his early career. "Closing in and doing hand-to-hand with the NVA [North Vietnamese Army] was not a very bright tactic, but it was the only tactic we knew during the sixties and early seventies. The new tactic is to use Special Forces accompanied by some of the OGA [other governmental agencies] and not allow our friendlies to close with the enemy. The new tactic is to fight a 'standoff' type of war in most cases. Usually a four to five kilometer standoff is the recommended distance to close with the enemy." Today's CIA and Special Forces method of training proxy armies is designed to create a "hands-off" relationship. He explains that the license to kill once accorded special operations has been finessed or outsourced to avoid direct liability. "We don't pull the trigger but we sure as hell give them a gun, bullets, show them the target, and teach them how to pull that trigger. It didn't use to be that way." Given his long career in covert operations, Billy should know how it "used to be."

From its founding in 1952, the mission of Special Forces was to operate behind enemy lines, train insurgent troops, and act as a force multiplier. They were recruited from the more elite airborne units and were usually aggressive, independent-minded men with high IQs and good moral character—men who would follow orders but could think for themselves under great pressure while working in hostile environments. All the early members of the Special Forces had basic foreign language skills, held at least a sergeant's rank, and were willing to work behind enemy lines in civilian clothes. Due to the Special Forces's covert nature and links to the CIA, most people did not know they existed until the early 1960s, when President Kennedy became a major supporter and expanded their role dramatically in the newly emerging Vietnam conflict, first as advisors and later as ground troops. Their close relationship with the CIA was kept in the background.

The CIA also had their own paramilitary teams, some of them contractors, others seconded from the military. I ask Billy what the difference was.

Billy rubs his thumb and finger together. "Money. The CIA had money, lots of it. We [Special Forces] did the legwork."

The concept of Special Forces was not new, but America was confronting an unfamiliar style of warfare in Southeast Asia—a communist insurgency that did not stand and fight in big battalions, but rather sent agents in plainclothes to recruit, train, and equip insurgents. What the CIA and the Special Forces did in Southeast Asia was modeled on what the OSS (Office of Strategic Services) did in occupied France with the Jedburghs, whose mission was to drop in covert operators to coordinate supply efforts and provide communications and intelligence. The training and operational efforts of Special Forces were greatly expanded from the simple tactics taught by the Jedburghs in World War II.

Billy joined the Special Forces in the mid-1950s and began working occasional covert assignments for the CIA starting in 1961. At the time, Billy didn't really think of himself as a covert operator, though in March of 1965, Waugh was asked to form an "A" team and to set up an operational base from which to run the northeast section of the Binh Dinh Province in South Vietnam. Billy's mission was to recruit and train up an army of mercenaries—a Civilian Irregular Defense Group, or CIDG—to disrupt the NVA's movements within enemy-controlled territory. The CIA's Combined Studies Division would supply the funding, and the Special Forces would do the legwork.

Billy and his team built a rudimentary fort along the An Lao River and an airstrip using the labor of about a hundred mercenaries recruited from the lowlands. Once set up, his team was to coordinate efforts to harass the enemy in a twenty-kilometer circle around their base. The North Vietnamese Army had full knowledge of the base but did not try to overrun it. Unlike the Jedburghs, who would work inside cities or out on farms in occupied France, the Americans were running a covert war from fixed military bases.

On June 18, 1965, Billy, a small team of three SF, and eighty-six South Vietnamese mercenaries left their roughly hewn A-team fort and hiked along a trail that followed the An Lao River on a seventeen-kilometer recce to a small NVA camp. They planned a stealthy brutal attack in darkness to convince the Vietcong that the area was too dangerous for a base camp. Billy and his group had killed over one hundred sixty sleeping soldiers when they heard a bugle sound a call to arms for the approximately four thousand NVA troops who had just landed the day prior.

Nearly all of the Vietnamese mercenaries were gunned down as they fled across a rice paddy. As Billy ran, a bullet shattered his right knee and another destroyed his right foot. A third bullet penetrated Billy's left wrist, knocking his watch off. Waugh lay on the ground, soaked in blood, his leg bones glistening white through his ripped uniform, left for dead. It should have been the end of Billy Waugh. He remembers counting how long the green tracers of bullets glowed as he tried to judge the distance of NVA troops, and smelling and feeling the heat of kerosene from napalm dropped by American reinforcements, until a final bullet clipped him in the head and knocked him out cold.

Thirty-five-year-old Master Sergeant Billy Waugh awoke a few hours later to find himself stripped naked by the enemy. The sun burned down on his exposed body, crusting his blood in sticky patches, as the pain from his wounds exploded in his head. Around him the fighting continued. A helicopter arrived under fire to lift him out, but the soldier who tried to carry Billy in was shot twice through the heart and lungs. Waugh crawled the final few feet and was helped onto the helo. As Billy lay there on the floor of the slick, he looked up in time to see a bullet hit the helicopter gunner's arm, almost severing it. Billy made it to a hospital in a heap of the dead. When the battle stopped raging, the enemy had lost six hundred men, and out of Billy's eighty-six mercenaries, only fifteen had escaped. One American from the A-team had been killed, and three, including Billy, had made it out alive.

For the next few months, Waugh lived in a hazy painkiller-numbed world. It would take over a year for his wounds to begin to heal. At the other end of this dark tunnel, he realized his ultimate calling: Waugh wanted to get back into not just what he calls the "vanilla" SF, but the "blackside" SF who worked directly with the CIA. He had already died once and so had no fear of death. His injuries meant he might never again function in normal special operations, but Billy wasn't about to let injury end his lifelong dream of being a soldier. Most soldiers would accept that they had used up their luck, but Billy wanted back in, demonstrating a tenacious pit-bull approach that would be the hallmark of his combat career and scare off others whenever Billy asked for volunteers on missions. It is no surprise that in the future, Billy would take great pride in working alone.

Despite being barely able to walk, he talked his way into being assigned to a CIA-funded group called Military Assistance Command Vietnam–Special Observation Group (MACV-SOG), and by doing so took the journey from the overt "white" side of military operations to the "black" side of warfare—deniable TOP SECRET–level covert and clandestine operations that were never intended to be revealed to the American public. His knowledge of Special Forces and his eagerness to go into combat got him accepted with friends who put him up in an aircraft to do forward air controlling, observation, and rescue. When the pus stopped oozing out of his legs and they began to mend, he started working on the ground.

The MACV-SOG was created in 1964 as a clandestine, unconventional warfare joint-operations group working in Vietnam, Laos, and Cambodia. Although essentially a military project, the joint military and intelligence program reunited two halves of what used to be combined under the World War II–era OSS. The MACV-SOG combined CIA, Special Forces, mercenaries, counterinsurgents, independent contractors, and private front and legitimate corporations in the war against the North Vietnamese. The joint operations made use of both CIA officers and active military that both funded and directed the actions of hired indigenous paramilitaries. The use of mercenaries provided an element of deniability not allowed uniformed U.S. troops, particularly in countries not considered part of the hostilities, like Cambodia and Laos. MACV-SOG operated until April 30, 1972, and the successor agency, the Strategic Technical Directorate Assistance Team 158, ended all U.S. covert and paramilitary activities in Vietnam on March 12, 1973. At the end, MACV-SOG had comprised approximately two thousand Americans and over eight thousand indigenous troops.

Private contractors involved in MACV-SOG were typically ex-military retirees hired by the old-boy network, men who had military skills; who knew how to keep quiet; and who could carry out the necessary tasks of hiring and managing mercenary armies. The mercs typically came from indigenous groups and would be hired with CIA money and trained by "sheep dipped" Special Forces teams, meaning active military with security clearance working directly for the CIA. In the 1961 to 1975 secret war in Laos, for example, forty to fifty CIA employees worked with several hundred hired "civilian" (mostly former or serving military) contractors who flew spotter aircraft, ran ground bases, and operated radar stations in civilian clothing. The idea was to wage war using private contractors with logistics and supplies provided by CIA proprietaries—Agency-owned and funded commercial companies. It was warfare conducted by a convoluted web of intelligence officers, paramilitaries, civilian contractors, and the military, all with deniable links and calculated absence of accountability to the American taxpayer. Covert action has always been a dirty business done in faraway places that furthered the aims of American interests.

Although the CIA's major focus was against the expansion of postwar Communism, they could not turn the tide in Vietnam. The Agency also began to be attacked on the home front, beginning with Seymour Hersh's accusation in his December 22, 1975, article that the CIA had been spying on Americans inside the country. President Ford created the Rockefeller Commission to investigate possible spying on antiwar and civil rights activists, and Congress created the Senate's Church and the House's Pike committees to study CIA abuses.

A destructive rampage against the U.S. intelligence community ensued. What began as an investigation of wrongdoing ended up exposing many of the CIA's numerous failures. The investigations also revealed that the CIA hid funds among numerous government agencies, with even the GAO (Government Accountability Office) not knowing the exact amount spent on covert activities. Pike soundly criticized the ability of the intelligence community to predict conflict and took a dim view of the success of the previous ten years of covert actions. The Church Committee's report detailed CIA plans to assassinate the leaders of Cuba, the Congo, South Vietnam, Indonesia, Haiti, and the Dominican Republic. It made clear that no American finger pulled the trigger, but weapons, support, and/or training were provided with that intent in mind.

The Church-Pike investigation dealt a crippling blow to the CIA's ability to operate aggressively and autonomously. Assassinations were specifically banned by presidential findings; the use of dirty tricks, mercenaries, contractors, and proxy agents was reined in. Suddenly, men like Billy Waugh were considered anachronisms, destabilizing and potentially dangerous. Over eight hundred clandestine service operators were fired that year, and the Special Activities Division was almost defunct. Had Billy been working contracts for the CIA at the time, he would certainly have been released or reassigned in the aftermath of Church-Pike and the gutting of the CIA it sparked.

Experiencing a decided lack of opportunity, Billy thought it a godsend when he received a mysterious phone call and request to meet in a hotel room in northern Virginia on July 25, 1977. Waugh was told to pack for a one-year deployment to the desert—the standard preamble for a covert mission. The three other team members were all Special Forces vets. The country was Libya. The mission was to train a Special Forces group that reported directly to Col. Moammar Gadhafi. The training gig had all the style and function of a black mission under deep cover with good deniability. No serious questions were asked; no official background checking occurred. The man in charge was an ex–Agency employee named Ed Wilson. It was not unusual for a former employee or soldier to be working as a freelance contractor under nonofficial cover.

The day before Billy and his team were to leave for Libya, he received another phone call, this time from a former Special Forces operator working directly for the CIA. Credentials were produced; names were dropped. Billy was confident this was a legitimate contact. The mysterious figure informed Billy that the Wilson deal was not an official Agency project, but he took the unusual step of giving Waugh a Pentax camera and told him that if he took photos of anything interesting, there would be money in it for him. His contact gave him a secret code word to use when contacting him. Needing the money, Billy, kept his mouth shut and accepted the offer.

Billy spent a year training Libyan forces on Wilson's contract and photographing various sites for the CIA. In November of 1979, the hostage situation in Tehran began and the Arab world became increasingly hostile to Americans. The U.S. embassy in Tripoli was burned and looted. Given two hours to leave Libya, Billy made it out on a flight to Frankfurt with just the clothes he was wearing and a dozen rolls of undeveloped film.

Ed Wilson was eventually arrested and charged with illegal arms trafficking with Libya. He claimed to have been acting with CIA support, an assertion contradicted by a CIA affidavit read at his trial that stated the Agency had not had contact with Wilson since the early 1970s. Wilson was sentenced to fifty-three years in prison but was released in late 2003 when a federal judge ruled that the CIA had lied in its affidavit by not reporting eighty contacts the Agency had had with Wilson during the time in question. More disturbingly, Wilson was able to document forty jobs the CIA hired him to do after his retirement from the Agency. The line between covert and criminal is often blurry.

After Libya, Billy drifted for more than a decade, spending most of his time working at jobs he hated and drinking a lot. The eighties were lost years, as Billy approached midlife limping from wounds and burdened by a two-decade career of almost continuous combat. A life of intense action and danger had been swapped for mind-numbing boredom. "I drank a lot and they didn't care for that. The CIA said, 'We would bring you on tomorrow if you would stop drinking.' I told them, 'Well, I am not sure I am through drinking yet. I think I am going to have some more to drink.' Then when I stopped drinking, they said, 'Come, come, come.'"

In 1989, Billy received a phone call from a former SF friend inviting him to Washington. "The job was to become part of a hit squad designed to eliminate individuals who posed a significant threat to the United States," he explains. Billy could not believe his luck. He thought this time he would function as an independent contractor with an official mandate to kill—something taken for granted in wartime but rarely permitted outside of combat. Billy had worked as a "Blue Badger"—a CIA employee—and he didn't like it. He didn't like Washington, DC. He liked doing things on the outside, on his own terms, away from the bureaucracy of Langley. Billy was a lone wolf and both the Agency and Billy liked it that way.

Despite his initial enthusiasm, Billy soon learned that the CIA of 1989 was a very different organization from his earlier days with them. His perceived opportunity as hit man for the CIA soon downgraded into an observational role—the equivalent of watching prey through a rifle scope but never being allowed to pull the trigger. He had to replace his sniper scope with a camera, his bullets with a pen. The CIA tasked Billy with finding and tracking the enemies of the United States until such time as when a decision about their fate could be made.

Billy knew that the publicity of the Church Committee had forced President Gerald Ford in February of 1976 to sign Executive Order No. 11905—the twenty-two words that removed assassination from the toolkit of U.S. foreign policy. Successive presidents reconfirmed the same finding. The presidential finding quite clearly covered contractors and mercenaries: "No person employed or acting on behalf of the United States government shall engage in, or conspire to engage in, assassinations." In Billy Waugh's new role as an independent contractor for the CIA in Africa, he could use all of his skills as a covert observer and tracker, except the most lethal. Billy's first years back in covert operations saw him posted to the hotbed of Islamic terrorism—Khartoum, Sudan.

Billy enjoyed the Sudan. He liked Arab countries in general—his basic command of the language and ease with the culture made it enjoyable—and there was plenty to do in Khartoum, or "K-Town," as the Agency called it. Billy soon found he had plenty of bad guys to track, photographs to take, notes to write, maps to draw, and reports to file.

Billy worked out of the embassy under diplomatic cover, giving him some degree of protection from Sudanese legal persecution. Unless the Sudanese caught him doing something illegal, they could harass him but they couldn't arrest or kill him. Billy worked alone, often doing his work as he jogged at night. "I would do six-week to ninety-day rotations between February 1991 and July 1992. If we stayed more than a month, the Sudanese security forces would get antsy." While he was operating in the

Sudan, a rich, exiled Saudi named Osama bin Laden decided to relocate there and became just one of many miscreants Billy was tasked to babysit.

An Islamic government supported by Iranian largesse controlled Sudan. The well-educated Islamist Hassan al-Turabi served as vice president and was responsible for the country's policy of benevolence toward militant Islamic groups, dissident religious figures, and terrorists. He shielded himself behind President Omar Hasan al-Bashir. In 1991, an odd collection of fugitives, criminals, and expats had gathered in the Sudan, including such well-known personalities as Carlos the Jackal, Abu Nidal, and the blind Sheik Omar Abdel-Rahman. Representatives and cells of most major Islamic groups also had offices in Khartoum, including Hezbollah, Islamic Jihad, and others. After bin Laden moved to Sudan following the first Gulf War, he set up ventures like a sesame-seed export business, started large construction projects like the road from Khartoum to Port Sudan, and began to gather around him the nucleus of what would come to be known as al-Qaeda. He also set up a training camp fifteen miles north of Khartoum in Omdurman.

Billy got to know bin Laden's routines and habits very well. He thinks of how things could have been different if he had been allowed to kill bin Laden during the Sudan years. He holds up his fingers as if holding a bullet to make his point. "Before September eleven, lawyers owned the place. If you had to pee, you had to see a lawyer. People were running scared. George Tenet was not doing anything aggressive at all. The problem was the oversight committee. Tenet wanted to do stuff but they wouldn't let him do it. If we wanted to KIA anyone, we had to get the permission of senators and congressmen.

"We could have killed bin Laden innumerable times. Every day I put in fifteen contingency plans for killing him. Our idea was to kill him and dump him over the Iranian embassy wall. Make 'em look bad. As lax as they were in their embassy, we could have just propped him up against their wall. We would just dump him there and call the Sudanese and say, 'Hey, there was shooting out at the Iranian embassy. You better go take a look.' I put that in a plan; they said, 'Are you out of your mind?' There was one guy who loved the idea as soon as it was sent forward—Cofer Black.

He was told, 'We are not going to do that.'" Billy pauses, thinking about the lost opportunity. "Just one damn ten-cent bullet."

This absolute ban against extrajudicial killings would remain in effect until late 1998 when, in reaction to the bomb attacks on U.S. embassies in East Africa, President Clinton signed a carefully worded series of memorandums of notification, or MONs, that would accept the use of lethal force by the CIA and its proxies in their attempts to capture and bring bin Laden to justice. It did not include a direct order to kill bin Laden but was written with the full understanding that his death as an accidental byproduct in a snatch operation was an acceptable risk. Clinton issued further MONs to include bin Laden's associates, but all were very carefully worded to stress that the pretext of any mission would be to bring them to justice, not to simply end their lives. A direct order to kill would have required a "lethal finding," and it wouldn't be until after 9/11 that the legal barriers to presidentially authorized targeted assassination would be removed.

Billy never expected that bin Laden would become any more or less dangerous than the rest of the rogues' gallery found in Khartoum in the early 1990s, and he never imagined that he would finally get his wish and be sent with orders to kill the tall Saudi in the fall of 2001. Then September 11, 2001, changed the perspective on America's willingness to kill its enemies.

"I was in the CIA on September eleven, on the sixth floor getting ready to go to Thailand on a drug thing. Somebody watching TV said, 'Whoa, look at that damn pilot . . . flew that plane right into the building.' Then the second plane hit and the alarm went off. There were two other planes missing. They sent out the word to evacuate the building. I have never seen the CIA move so fast. You should have seen the traffic on Highway 123. All the people were doing ninety miles per hour heading out of DC, and the CIA was trying to join the traffic. People over there really hate the CIA. They don't know anything about the CIA. They really didn't know the manacles we had on our wrists. The CIA wasn't killing anyone. Their people might be disappearing, but it was other governments doing that. They blame the CIA for a lot of underhanded deaths, but it wasn't us."

The chief of the CIA's Special Activities Division called Billy the next day and asked him to start recruiting contractors to be inserted into Afghanistan for paramilitary actions against bin Laden and company. "Cofer Black got his orders from an all-night meeting at Camp David. He flew down there and when he came back, you could tell that things were different. They wanted people killed. They weren't going to fire off some missile and hit some friggin' dust pile. They wanted some dead bodies on the ground."

"No-Good Cheatin' Shithead"

In mid-November 2001, Billy Waugh and his team of hired contractors journeyed to Tashkent, Uzbekistan, in the belly of a massive air force cargo plane. Billy believed he was beginning his last war, perhaps his final mission. At seventy-one, he was the oldest operating CIA contractor with combat experience. The group of men he traveled with intended to find and kill Osama bin Laden and his cohorts. They had little expectation of or interest in taking them alive.

President Bush had signed a secret presidential "finding" that authorized the CIA to kill bin Laden and his lieutenants; however, to make sure there was no ambiguity, Cofer Black asked Gary Schroen, the leader of the first CIA team into Afghanistan, to send back bin Laden's head in a box. Billy remembers those hectic days in September. "Bush told the Agency, 'I want dead bodies.' Cofer told him he would have flies on their eyeballs within a week."

The scale of the 9/11 attacks had forced a dramatic change from Clinton's previous standing orders to allow use of lethal force in operations designed to bring bin Laden to justice. According to Billy, "Bush gave us a license to kill. Did he sign a license to kill? No, but we had the words out of his mouth, and the lawyers just had to fill out the paperwork. You will never see that document. I have a Gamma clearance, and I will never see that document as long as I live."

George Tenet and Cofer Black had promised President Bush they could effectively hunt down bin Laden's group and topple the Taliban by sending in teams from the CIA's Special Activities Division and Special Forces A-teams. The problem was the CIA didn't have enough trained people available to back up that promise, so they turned to their time-honored cohorts: contractors and the mercenary proxy army. CIA operations officer Gary Schroen was pulled out of his retirement prep program and dispatched to the Panjshir Valley in Afghanistan to hire a mercenary proxy army in the form of the Northern Alliance. Billy Waugh signed on to help other CIA officers assemble more teams to join Schroen and his posse of bin Laden hunters inside Afghanistan.

In 2001, no American corporations specialized solely in the provision of trained-up ex-military operators: Blackwater Security, Triple Canopy, and similar firms sprang up only after post-9/11 military deployments— primarily Iraq—created a massive market for this type of service. So instead of being able to recruit through the equivalent of a military services temp agency, Billy had to rely on his own contacts and the old-boy network, drawing some of his team away from active duty and the rest from ex-military independent contractors he knew. "I was hired to recruit sixty-four men around the Fort Bragg area—sixty-four men," he adds for emphasis. "I went down to Delta and got twenty, and then I got ten of the people I had known before that had been in Delta. Then I got some SEALs. I grabbed some from SEAL Team 6. There's big difference between SEALs and SF. That's why now a lot of them don't want the job. They [SEALs] want short missions. They don't want to hang out six months out of the year. My first pick is always SF. I show them a film and I ask them if they can do what they see on this film. Can they not only swim but shoot underwater? Can they do night operations, and jog for seven miles? I remind them that in Afghanistan, O_2 [oxygen] is short above five grand [5,000 feet]. I look for language; the SEALs don't have language. The SEALs just want to go in, blow a lot of people away, talk about it, write it up, and plan for the next mission. SF wants to go in and stay. That's why we recruited SF."

Billy is visibly proud of his accomplishment in such a short period of time. "I got 'em because I talked to Commander Jerry Boykin. I got about twenty or twenty-one. These guys come trained in HALO [high

altitude–low opening parachute qualification], in good shape, and qualified. They all turned Green Badge immediately. They took a shortened
version of the polygraph. I lost three out of thirty, mostly because of
drugs. First, we make sure they are in shape, so they need a PT test. One
of the best guys was over sixty and has worked for the Agency for forty-
five years." After three decades of being restrained, Billy was readying for
his chance to go to Afghanistan and kill America's most lethal foe.

During the initial stages of the war in Afghanistan, the CIA fielded between eighty and a hundred Green Badgers and Blue Badgers. Billy had
managed to round up five dozen independent contractors and sheep-
dipped military; the rest came from the Special Activities Division of the
CIA. They were to carry in an initial infusion of cash to buy loyalty from
warlords and influential leaders, gather intelligence about enemy positions, and search for Osama bin Laden and his associates. They would also
interrogate prisoners, map out the intelligence landscape, and deal with
the ever-changing alliances and allegiances of the Afghan fighters. Billy
Waugh had convinced the higher-ups at the CIA that he could help coordinate between the CIA officers and the SF teams. What the CIA and
Special Forces accomplished in Afghanistan began a new era of joint operations where military, intelligence, paramilitary, indigenous, mercenary,
and even civilian contractors were working in unison with full lethal capabilities, something Billy hadn't seen since his days in Cambodia, Laos, and
Vietnam.

After a week in Tashkent sorting out logistics, Billy's team flew to
Bagram, the military airfield north of Kabul, and headed toward the Ariana Hotel. The Ariana had been used for the Taliban's intelligence services, but with the Taliban gone, the CIA set up headquarters there. Billy's
tools of the trade were both high-tech and low-tech. He had brought one
rucksack with cold-weather gear, an AK-47 with seven magazines, a "shit-
load" of grenades, and an H&K 40 mm grenade launcher. He also carried
the AN/PRC 112 survival radio, digital cameras, a handheld GPS, an old
compass, and a bone-handled Old Timer knife. He also had a few thousand
dollars stuffed in his pockets for personal spending money.

On December 1, Billy's seventy-second birthday, he and his small team of contractors headed south by road from the Ariana Hotel with a small group of newly hired Afghan bodyguards. The CIA team had been given money to hire a thousand or so local fighters when they got near their destination point in the southern Logar Province. They then planned to rendezvous with Special Forces Operation Detachment Alpha (ODA) 594, who would train the new hires for combat and support operations. Special Forces ODA 594 comprised a twelve-man team, plus an air force TAC-P controller to coordinate air strikes. One of Billy's tasks was to make sure the SF team did not mix targets and hit Afghan friendlies by mistake.

Once a target was identified, there was a check for any friendlies or civilians in the area, then deconfliction with other units, and finally the okay to kill was granted. Air strikes using JDAMs, or smart bombs, were called in by using GPS coordinates, laser designator binoculars called SOFLAMs (Special Operations Forces Laser Marker), or by "talking in the pilots"—just giving a series of visual indicators that gave the pilot an accurate visual sighting. Hellfire missiles were mounted on the Predator UAV (unmanned aerial vehicle), giving remote-control kill authority to operators using joysticks and firing buttons, as in a video game. It was all done over the radio, and the man actually pushing the Fire button was sitting in an air-conditioned trailer thousands of miles away.

Even though they were prepared to give effective coordination for surgical air strikes, Billy still did not feel like they had sufficient support, since the bulk of American air power was concentrated around the battle of Tora Bora at that time. "We moved from Kabul to Paktia Province. We stayed there for about twenty days, and then blasted into Gardez. The Taliban had no idea what was happening. We didn't get the air we wanted. The air [assets] were up in Tora Bora. We couldn't do the combat that we wanted."

Heavy combat was thankfully not necessary, since the Taliban was quickly folding up across the country with little resistance. They had already fled Gardez when Billy and his team rolled up in a twenty-five-vehicle convoy on January 4, 2002, and began to settle into a compound east of town. Their job was to create a conveniently titled "Eastern Alliance" mercenary force, even though no such thing existed. The other function was to gather as much intelligence as quickly as possible—essentially setting up a network of intelligence assets, as well as arresting and shaking down Taliban supporters fingered by paid informants. Billy's group set up shop in a large mud-walled compound, and he gave orders to a local strongman to have his Afghans threaten any media that came within three kilometers.

The mountain pass between Gardez and Khost crawled with Taliban, and Billy's team began hunting down groups of fighters. They used phone intercepts, Predators with night vision, old-fashioned turncoats, and night surveillance using the latest in infrared imagery. ODA 594 spent their days training the Afghans in weapons use, as well as infantry and small unit tactics. They all spent much downtime listening to Billy tell war stories about Cambodia and Laos—the good old days when the CIA worked directly with Special Forces and when hunting down enemies and killing them with mercenary armies was standard operating procedure.

By January 15, the Afghan proxy forces were up to three hundred Afghans. General Lodin, a Pashtun commander who had worked with the CIA in the 1980s, had volunteered his son, who showed up with thirty friends. "It's hard to get good information out of these lying-ass Afghan warlords. We worked with a bunch of lying bastards. The old man [General] Lodin was in charge and his son Zia Lodin worked as a captain for us. He was straight up about it: 'I am here for the money. I don't like those people in the Panjshir and I only like my people.'"

The elders in Gardez had supplied about a hundred local men, and two commanders named Kabir and Zaibdullah headed up a contingent of one hundred seventy. Billy describes Commander Zaibdullah as a "no-good cheatin' shithead," a well-paid ally "who was not to be trusted under any circumstances." Almost immediately the Afghans under Kabir had begun to act suspiciously, and the team felt in jeopardy.

Billy was used to dealing with criminals and warlords, but it soon became obvious that they were not going to catch bin Laden in this murky world of shifting and dual allegiances. The CIA estimates that it handed out $70 million in cash to win the initial stages of the war in Afghanistan and considered it a bargain, even though the loyalty the money was supposed to buy did not lead to the death or capture of bin Laden or many of his minions.

The Afghans hired by the CIA and trained by Special Forces also included Zahim Khan and Pacha Khan Zadran, a thuggish-looking warlord who would later call in a U.S. air strike to target a delegation of Pashtun tribal elders on their way to congratulate Hamid Karzai in Kabul. It was the duplicity and character of America's Afghan proxies that ensured that the bulk of the Arab, Pakistani, and Uzbek jihadis would slip away, and that bin Laden would never be found.

Billy remembers the hardships of Afghanistan, but his best memories remain of the new generation of contractors and paramilitaries he got to know. "What I have noticed is that the new lads of the paramilitary are stronger, better-trained, more able with communications, have wonderful gear, can shoot straighter, and generally outshine the old-school lads. . . . However, their on-the-ground decision making has become a non-occurring event. Commo is just too good, and all decisions are rendered up the chain of command.

"In my time before we had all these radios and high-tech communications, decisions were rendered by old-schoolers in the field without fear of wrath from the hierarchy. But these days, decisions are strictly arrived at by the same hierarchy," some several hundred miles from the combat zone.

Much to his disappointment, Billy's time in Afghanistan never did bring him face-to-face with his old nemesis, Osama bin Laden. Even the locals he worked with seemed too eager to take his money and too reticent to root out the enemy. He would have preferred the heat of the Cambodian jungle, as the cold up in the mountains made his joints ache. He smelled bad and began to think that maybe he was, as he puts it, "too old for this shit." After two months in-country, Billy Waugh said farewell to ODA 594, heading home in mid-January. It was going to be up to somebody else to capture Billy's nemesis.

Enter Blackwater

The use of contractors in the War on Terror started with Billy Waugh's five dozen recruits, an ad hoc paramilitary force of firepower and expertise whose rapid deployment filled an important role in helping the American offensive adapt quickly to the unconventional terrain. As it had done in Laos and other covert conflicts, America had effectively "outsourced" aspects of the War on Terror to retired military and local indigenous mercenaries. After the decimation of the Taliban, the CIA would be working to set up an extensive intelligence network in Afghanistan and Pakistan to help hunt down Osama bin Laden and remnants of al-Qaeda and the Taliban. The CIA's decision to hire a corporation to bolster personal protection teams for CIA officers would catalyze one company's first foray into the private security industry. The initial $5.4-million six-month contract began Blackwater's transformation from a minor steel-target manufacturer and shooting-range into a massive security conglomerate.

Before 9/11, Erik Prince was working to make his business profitable. Although Prince had grown up immersed in a world of business acquisition and expansion, the original Blackwater model seemed to cater more to Erik's personal interests than pure profit. In 1997, Erik had broken ground on his Blackwater Training Center, at that time a six-thousand-acre property with a shooting range designed to offer specialized training for military and police. Growth was slow. From 1998 until 2000, only six people worked in the training department, and Prince often had to dip into his own pocket just to make payroll. In early 2001, Prince began Blackwater Target Systems to build an innovative self-resetting steel target. He managed to turn a slight profit, but business conditions were not entirely favorable when one of his first employees, Jamie Smith, initially suggested Erik start a new division specializing in providing security.

Smith has a background in the CIA and had been working as a role player and trainer at Blackwater off and on to make some extra money for law school, but he had quit to start his career as a tax lawyer after graduating in 2001. Prince wanted to retain him as an employee, but Smith had a bigger vision. Jamie saw a market in hiring out men skilled in State

Department–style personal protection skills and wanted to create a division that had potential as a growth industry. It wasn't until after 9/11 that Prince became fully committed to the idea. He called Smith in November 2001 to offer him a position as vice president of Blackwater, and by January 2002, Smith had relocated to headquarters in Moyock, North Carolina.

Having no reason to train a force of security contractors before they had any work to do, Smith suggested they begin by trying to work all of his and Erik's contacts to find an opportunity. Erik told Smith that a friend of his had recently joined the CIA and that he could be in a good position to help move the business plan forward. Buzzy Krongard had been appointed to the position of executive director of the CIA in March 2001. He had quite a few years of experience as advisor to the DCI (Director of Central Intelligence), but further back in his career he had been an investment banker, and it was in that capacity that he had first become acquainted with Erik and the Prince family fortune.

Erik's timing was either fortuitous or calculated, since CIA security resources were soon spread thin. Six months after 9/11, the Global Response Staff, the CIA's security division, was overstretched, and they needed protection for their newly established Kabul station. The CIA had hired corporations for collection and other covert needs before, but they had rarely contracted out their field officers' security to private industry. After Prince called seeking opportunities for his new business venture, Blackwater obtained a $5.4-million six-month contract that specified that it was for an "urgent and compelling" necessity. "Urgent and compelling" contracts eliminate all the competitive bidding requirements, so the contract went straight to Blackwater.

The "black" contract awarded by the CIA to Blackwater required eighteen contractors plus a C1 and C2—the first and second commanders. Although the work would be dangerous, both Blackwater and the independent security contractors Prince hired would be offered enough of a financial incentive to take the calculated risk. Jamie based what to charge the CIA on what DynCorp was charging the State Department for similar work. The contractors would be paid $550 per day—just a slight bump over what Jamie was paying the instructors at Moyock—but Blackwater would bill out at a rate of $1,500 per man per day. That tripled figure not only factors in costs of training, transport, and other overhead, but also includes a fairly healthy profit margin. The individual contractors would earn about $18,500 in a month, but Blackwater would gross $30,000 per day, which would add up to $900,000 a month. Although this was a relatively small contract, it showed that the private sector could bolster capacity in time of need. Within just three years, Blackwater would grow from this tiny ad hoc job to being the second largest provider of private security services, with three quarters of a billion dollars in annual billings.

At the time he won his first contract from the CIA, though, Erik had one problem: His security empire consisted of only himself and Jamie Smith. Smith advertised in the *Washington Post* jobs section and both started working their contacts to put together their first team. The basic requirements were a Sensitive Compartmented Information (SCI) security clearance, experience working in hostile environments, and knowledge of the rigorous requirements of State Department personal security detail (PSD) training. Within weeks, Blackwater had hired, vetted, and trained enough men for the contract.

The team headed over to Afghanistan in May 2002, flying in to Bagram Airbase. Erik Prince, owner, president, and CEO, went over himself for two weeks, ostensibly to work as a contractor, though Smith described Erik's short trip as being closer to "playing CIA paramilitary."

The majority of the team would stay in the capital for the duration of the contract, providing security for the CIA end of Kabul Airport and the "Annex," the CIA's Kabul station based at the Ariana Hotel. The contractors' job as part of the Global Response Staff—the CIA term for extra security help required to operate in a hostile environment—was to guard the compound and to ensure intel officers made it to and from meetings safely. One contractor was briefly dispatched to assist with a specific task in Herat, and the CIA requested two to be stationed at a tiny border post in Shkin to provide security for officers holding clandestine meetings with local leaders. Jamie Smith and Erik flew south from Kabul to begin the contract in Shkin. Jamie would stay for two months, but Erik would leave the mud fort after one week and return to Kabul to "schmooze" the Agency chiefs, as Jamie describes it.

The helo flight to Shkin heads due south of Kabul, ascends to ten thousand feet to clear the mountain pass made famous by Operation Anaconda, descends past an old bin Laden compound and into what some call Fort Apache, a large mud fort complex set in the town of Shkin on a bleak dust-covered landscape just three miles from the Pakistan border. The CIA considered this "Indian territory" and chose the location because it was the farthest their Pegasus Air Mi-17 could fly to and from Bagram without a refueling stop. Shkin's other claim to fame was that it was the first U.S. firebase built since the Vietnam War. A platoon of Rangers provided the firepower and ran night patrols. A Special Forces ODA, a Ranger Force, a British SAS team, and even Delta operated from the base as the secretive joint endeavor, Task Force 11—the group charged with finding bin Laden, Gulbuddin Hekmatyar, Mullah Omar, and other high-value targets. Since rumors persisted that bin Laden roamed freely right across the border in Pakistan's tribal areas, tensions ran high at the base.

Although Fort Apache was the most remote firebase, subject to regular attacks from enemies who would strike and flee back across the border into Pakistan, much of the day was spent exercising, housekeeping, and tanning on the dirt walls. When a call came in from a local informant, the contractors would scramble to set up a safe meeting place—typically a dead-end dry creek bed where one man could watch from the ridge while the other blocked the entrance. The case officer and a translator would then drive out to make the connection and the payoff. When the informant approached, the contractor guarding the entrance would step out to stop him, search him, and then send him on to the meeting.

Most of the work would turn out to be blissfully routine, but the underlying sense of being always surrounded or watched by an unconventional, unpredictable, unseen, amorphous enemy made the job more difficult for the mental endurance it required. Erik and Jamie learned immediately that the locals were not to be trusted, nothing was to be taken for granted, and they were never to let their guard down, since events could turn in a second. Shortly before they had arrived at Shkin, a convoy of SF had been been ambushed and one communications officer killed. The group had obviously been sold out by their duplicitous Afghan guide, since the lead vehicle in the convoy—the one in which the guide was riding—escaped unscathed while the rest were peppered with AK fire.

This environment of suspicion and paranoia kept them constantly on edge and may have played tricks on their minds. As Jamie recalls, one day while out doing recon for a meeting spot, "We drove up the dustiest road on the earth. It was like talcum powder and was so thick that I had to stop at times because I simply could not see the road in front of the truck. As we drove on the older road, I spotted three Toyotas filled with armed men gaining on us and using a new road that paralleled ours. We rounded a corner covered by a building and they were nowhere to be found." They weren't phantoms, and they couldn't have just disappeared, but it made no sense that they didn't attack. Nothing in Afghanistan made sense.

Smith served out the term of the six-month contract, with two months at Shkin and the rest in Kabul. Though Erik's stay had been brief, the experience energized him. He loved the intrigue and excitement so much that the thirtysomething head of the Prince family empire decided he wanted to join the CIA's Special Activities Division and enter the world of covert operations as a paramilitary.

Joining the CIA can take months, but the normally arduous and lengthy interview process must have been expedited for Prince's benefit. By July he was asking Smith for advice on how to pass the polygraph—the last hurdle required before a CIA recruit can accept a job offer. Erik's first test had been "inconclusive," so he had to take it again. Smith advised him that any number of factors could have led to that result and suggested it may have just been nerves. Though Prince had already effectively worked for the CIA in a covert capacity as a contractor, he would be ultimately barred from becoming a "Blue Badger" because he lacked certain hard skills. Erik just had to refocus himself on growing the Blackwater empire.

Prince's first contract was not renewed after the initial six months. The official reason given was that Blackwater had never managed to stay fully staffed up to the required terms of the contract, though rumors have circulated throughout the security industry that the CIA had discovered a conflict of interest relating to Buzzy Krongard. That loss didn't seem to have any long-term impact on the business, though, since according to current president Gary Jackson, Blackwater has settled in to a pattern of doing about 15 percent "black" contracts—assumedly CIA—which these days would add up to nearly $100 million in annual revenue for the company.

That first CIA/Blackwater contract could be considered one of the early watershed events indicating where the private security business was heading, or perhaps it would be more correct to say where the War on Terror was leading the industry. The abrupt state of war that began on 9/11 had stretched the U.S. government's resources beyond what could have been realistically anticipated on September 10, 2001, creating an opportunity for private industry to supplement the government's security resources. In another example of how the industry is exploding, Jamie Smith has since left Blackwater to try and ride the current wave of opportunity by founding his own successful security start-up, SCG International Risk in Virginia Beach.

The two most important long-term government-related sources of employment for security contractors in Afghanistan have been in the hunt for bin Laden and the guarding of President Hamid Karzai. In my quest to traverse the world of the private security contractor, I made arrangements to visit a former Special Forces friend working on the job protecting the life of Hamid Karzai. While in Afghanistan, I also hoped to find out how the hunt for bin Laden was progressing.

Two years to the day after the beginning of the war, I journeyed to Afghanistan to see how the War on Terror had changed.

CHAPTER 2

Edge of the Empire

"I have no fucking idea who we are fighting."
—Task Force 11 member

Somewhere on the border between Afghanistan and Pakistan, a thunderous whup, whup, whup provides the soundtrack for a graceful, intertwining aerial ballet above my head. It's a cold December morning, and two Huey helicopters are circling a hilltop five hundred yards to the east. They zoom in close enough to my perch that I can smell their turbine exhaust and clearly make out a bug-helmeted door gunner gripping his minigun. The flat, deep sound echoes off the mountains as one Huey prepares to land, feeling for the ground as if hesitant to touch down in this hostile place. The other helicopter dives and swoops behind the hills like an angry hawk, looking for attackers.

From my own redoubt atop a steep cliff, I overlook a wide valley across the barrel of a battered antiaircraft gun aimed at Pakistan. Since the end of the active combat phase of the war in Afghanistan, private security contractors have been combing this area with CIA and military operators involved in the hunt for bin Laden. I am sitting on the ramparts of an unnamed American firebase, unmarked on any official map, and manned by what look like Special Operations troops and Afghan mercenaries. Its loaded weapons are pointed toward the border of an ally nation, and its vehicles are left packed for a hasty departure. Similar outposts of hastily constructed Hescoes—five-foot-tall gray cardboard and wire mesh containers filled with gravel—crown a few of the surrounding hilltops. On top of the Hescoes, sloppily stacked sandbags, a clutter of ammunition tins, and silver loops of concertina wire add a touch of paranoid sparkle. At a distance, these makeshift citadels have the look of medieval crusader castles, but up close they appear haphazardly stacked protection against attacks.

As I scan the area through my binoculars, I can see rolling foothills, steep valleys, and widely spaced pine trees. Far below us on the dusty road, colorful and overloaded "jinga" trucks clank and groan as they bring goods from Pakistan into Afghanistan. Off to the left, in the direction of Pakistan, my Afghan hosts point out a mountain from where they say the frequent incoming rocket attacks are launched. Officially, the Pakistani Tribal Police has jurisdiction over the tribal areas on their side of the mountains, while the U.S. military handles things on the Afghan side. Unless my GPS is wrong, however, this American outpost, armed by Afghans, is technically about five miles inside Pakistan.

"Your Americans!" shouts the smiling Afghan soldier manning the "tower" alongside me, pointing to the arriving choppers. Outfitted in U.S. Army–style fatigues and mirrored blue wraparound sunglasses, he is one of about forty hired guns—or "campaigns" as the U.S. military terms them—guarding this firebase, each of whom makes a healthy $150 a month. They live simply in an ancient-looking mud fort slightly down the hill—their only decoration Pakistani advertising calendars, their only furniture ammunition cases and cheap plastic lawn chairs. But this is their home, and they are doing their best to make me welcome.

According to the U.S. military, the main bases in Khost, Gardez, Oruzgan, and Asadabad are the frontlines in the War on Terror. However, the CIA and the U.S. military jointly operate a number of smaller, more remote bases like this one. This base must remain nameless, but from the look of the Afghan guard, it wouldn't last long, anyway. Most media attention in this region focuses on the disturbingly Russian-sounding town of Shkin to the south; this isn't surprising since the picturesque mud fort has just played host to one of the biggest processions of journo junkets in Afghanistan. The tours come with premade clichés and cinematic blurbs to spare. "The most evil place," the military press officers chirp happily back at Bagram. "Something out of *Mad Max*," the base commander tells visiting TV talking heads with a straight face. Even the three hundred or so rank-and-file soldiers at Shkin will trot out "Fort Apache" or "the Alamo" to eager journo junkets. Some journos will tell you privately that the soldiers at Shkin have been ordered in writing by their commander not to mention the cross-border operations or the amount of U.S. artillery, smart bombs, or bullets that are fired toward and into Pakistan. The U.S. military has done the ultimate hat trick: running a covert operation right under the noses of visiting journalists.

Despite the official statistic that nine out of ten U.S. casualties occur here, the mud fort at Shkin may be one of the safer spots along the border with Pakistan. Most of the attacks that have killed or wounded the Americans in the area have been ambushes outside the base. The Americans insist that they are drawing the fire of the Taliban or al-Qaeda, but it may be the other way around. Remote detonated mines wound one soldier, and the easily downed helicopters called for rescue become targets. Forcing Americans to patrol vulnerable routes, and short-burst contacts designed to lure out larger patrols into bigger ambushes, are all textbook examples of eighties-era mujahideen tactics. Though extensively documented and studied in war colleges, the muj strategy seems to have been forgotten by fresh-faced recruits fighting out on the fringes.

The outpost I have arrived at overlooks a well-known mountain pass between the Pakistani city of Miram Shah and its Afghan neighbor, Khost. Miram Shah was a famous supply and R & R base for mujahideen rebels who fought against the Soviet occupation in the 1980s, and it remains a major smuggling center. The U.S. military, the Pakistan government, and others believe Osama bin Laden remains secreted in the mountainous Pashtun tribal areas somewhere between Khost and the northern Pakistani city of Peshawar. Bin Laden worked and fought here with the muj in the eighties, and eventually moved back to the area after leaving the Sudan in the late 1990s. Coordinated attacks against Afghan and American forces not surprisingly continue at their highest rates in this region.

I am back in Afghanistan almost exactly two years after the start of the war in late 2001. At the time of my current visit, the U.S. military has just kicked off Operation Avalanche, which will send some two thousand troops and hundreds of helicopter sorties into the border area around Khost in a futile attempt to eliminate remnants of the Taliban and the al-Qaeda network. A classic low-level insurgency has persisted since the end of major combat operations, with significant swaths of support for the Taliban, smuggling groups, and regional warlords making stability a particularly fleeting prospect in this part of the country. With the post-9/11 focus on bin Laden, current events have superseded the historical memory of nearly unceasing warfare in Afghanistan. This was the edge of the empire for Alexander, for the British, and then the Russians. Like a moving wave that eventually sinks into the sand and disappears, grand ideas and great campaigns have met the reality of resilience in the people, place, and idea of Afghanistan. Now Americans find themselves on the ragged edge looking east, on the opposite side of the Durand Line from where they began peddling money and influence to fight the Russians almost two decades ago.

During the Soviet war against Afghanistan, the Pakistani ISI, or Inter-Services Intelligence bureau, specifically endorsed secretly supporting the Afghan side with money, arms, ammunition, training, operational advice, and safe haven, while maintaining a policy of plausible deniability. A war by proxy or even "a thousand cuts" was the preferred form of aggression. Direct attacks by the Pakistanis, the Americans, or others would have provoked worldwide outrage and possible Soviet retribution, but blaming violence on locally based jihadi groups bolstered the idea that a grassroots movement was fighting back against injustice or persecution.

The Pakistanis created a paramilitary army under a variety of religious-sounding names, supported seven political groups in Peshawar, and laid the tracks for the CIA and Saudi funding train to turn Afghanistan into one of the most expensive covert proxy wars in America's history. The

Americans and Saudis funneled an estimated $6 billion in weapons and aid to the jihadi groups in their efforts to bleed the Soviets in Afghanistan. To do this, the ISI created an internal Afghan bureau charged with setting up secret training camps, moving weapons and supplies through Pakistan to the border, and making sure the thousands of volunteers were fed, housed, clothed, trained, and bundled off to jihad with nary a ripple in the pond of international relations.

The Islamic world sent their angry and idealistic young men, who quickly absorbed the cultlike desire to find purpose through martyrdom and self-sacrifice. Paramount in the cult of jihad was not only the concept of death as the ultimate sacrifice, but also the idea that great princes would serve alongside simple peasants. If one could not actually fight, then supporting these almost saintly men was considered a sufficient fulfillment of doctrinally required jihad. Saudi Arabia had pledged to match U.S. contributions to the anti-Soviet Afghan jihad dollar for dollar, and numerous private Gulf businessmen independently supported the efforts of well-traveled and convincing middle men like Abdullah Azzam and his eager young cohort, Osama bin Laden.

Abdullah Azzam, a Palestinian-born radical Islamist firebrand, worked tirelessly to encourage Muslims to travel from around the world to fight jihad in Afghanistan. Bin Laden, Azzam's protégé and former student from Saudi Arabia's King Abdul Aziz University, came to Peshawar to assist in managing the Arab-speaking volunteers and funneling Saudi money toward radical groups. Together they established the "Services Bureau," Maktab al-Khadamat, to coordinate the recruitment and training of the non-Afghan fighters for jihad against the Soviets, an organization viewed as the forerunner to al-Qaeda. During this period, bin Laden made the contacts and won the supporters he uses today as sanctuary and support.

Bin Laden was reputed to be a pious, intelligent, and generous man who supported the Wahhabist, or more orthodox, groups by arranging funding, transport, and training for thousands of Saudis and Arab-speaking volunteers. Bin Laden had no association with, nor did he have any need of, the CIA to run his organization out of its little guesthouse in Peshawar.

Azzam and bin Laden had ample funding from Muslim individuals and charities, so they had no use of income tainted by the infidels' touch.

In order to keep track of the hundreds of fighters who came to train and fight, and in order to notify relatives of their martyrdom, the group kept a close accounting of the volunteer jihadis who came and went. This bookkeeping, with its copious list of dedicated Islamist fighters from around the world, soon became a great resource for what is now referred to as al-Qaeda—an old-boys network that has disturbing echoes of the lists used by the CIA to recruit former Special Forces as contractors.

The ISI military strategy against the Soviets relied on the assumption that they planned to create and defend a series of major military bases or strategic towns and the routes between them. As expected, the Soviets stayed out of the countryside, keeping their central redoubt at Bagram, north of Kabul. They set up fortified firebases and sent out patrols to choke off supplies and interdict fighters entering from Pakistan. Surveilling the base and estimating troop strength, patrols, resupplies, and time for emergency air support, the muj would regularly besiege and over-run these garrisons. The mujahideen were careful to never expose themselves to traditional battles in which they might lose, only striking long enough for a deadly surprising initial blow, and then disappearing in a safe retreat. They used the lessons of General Giap in French Indochina as their model—the same tactics that defeated the Americans in Vietnam simply by embroiling them in a bloody and expensive guerrilla war. No one battle defeated the Russians, but it was the long, costly, unpopular war that ultimately forced a Soviet retreat.

The mujahideen used these tactics against the Russians as they now use them against the Americans. In this war, the few modern developments on the ground are the Thuraya satellite phone and the remote-control detonator (usually a car key remote or radio transmitter). The funding of the anti-Soviet jihad created much of the system, the funding conduits, the training, the players, and the tactics that are being used to repel and harass the U.S. troops today. The parallels are striking: today, U.S. policy supports a friendly government and trains an indigenous army (like the Russians), and shies away from intensive ground involvement (as did the Russians), preferring to fly from central bases and to stay in fortified compounds (as the Russians did). The major differences currently are the massive number of NGOs operating with Western agendas, the lack of attention to the educational system, the use of security contractors, the absence of an immense influx of covert funds to support the foreign "invader" of Afghanistan, and the deliberate lack of names for the groups that attack Westerners and their proxies. The Americans view their mere presence in Afghanistan as a victory. The insurgents, however, see tying down the Americans and bleeding their resources as winning. After all, every Afghan will tell you, How long did it take for us to defeat the British? How long did it take us to send the Russians packing? Similarly, the war against the perceived American occupation of Afghanistan could become one of generations and timeless revenge.

The basic propaganda elements of jihad were fixed during the war against the Soviet Union. The mujahideen viewed America, Pakistan, and Saudi Arabia as allies but claim full credit for the power of religion and conviction in defeating the Russians and their puppet government. To the Afghans, the war provided one more example of how their country acts as a graveyard for foreign aggressors, even though foreign aggressors supplied the money and weapons to defeat another foreign aggressor. Most Afghan men between thirty and sixty can relate dramatic tales of dead Russians, crashed helicopters, burning convoys, and violent counterattacks. Every Afghan speaks of the jihad with pride, and the experience has provided a wellspring of nationalism. They conveniently forget that in the mid-1990s, after the Russians had left, the same holy warriors destroyed Kabul and massacred its people. Many of these fundamentalist factions provide sustenance for the jihad against the Americans today in Afghanistan, and few locals have forgotten bin Laden's contributions as a mujahideen during the war.

The "Parrot's Beak," or the area of Pakistan that juts into Afghanistan below Tora Bora and above Khost, continues to be the weak spot for American operations. Khost, with its mountain fortresses of Zhawar Khili, has been the traditional center for resistance; Miram Shah, directly across the border in Pakistan, has always been the staging and retreat point for attacks. In the 1980s, Miram Shah was the gateway for 20 percent of the muj's arms needs. Today it offers the fastest route into Kabul and the easiest place from which to launch an attack against Americans and to slip safely back over the border. A number of border posts have been attacked and overrun south of Khost—not once, but multiple times. The Pakistani towns of Wana and Angoor Ada are the main southern staging points for these attacks against the American base at Shkin, farther to the south in Paktika Province.

As a Westerner, to travel to the Pakistani border from inside Afghanistan is easy. To travel to the Afghan border from inside Pakistan seems nearly impossible. Tall, skinny Pakistani soldiers wearing brown sweaters and cheap shoes enforce the famous NO FOREIGNERS ALLOWED signs in the tribal areas. In the eyes of the world community, Pakistani borders geographically contain the tribal areas. However, cartographers deliberately mislead. The tribal areas do not wholly accede to the idea of Pakistan but consider themselves the center of an independent nation called Pashtunistan, an entity falsely divided down the middle by the colonial-era Durand Line.

The Durand Line runs along mountainous ridge tops, a wandering artificial border originally designed to separate India from Afghanistan. A British colonial officer named Sir Mortimer Durand created the 1,519-mile-long border between India and Afghanistan as part of a November 12, 1893, agreement with Amir Abdur Rahman Khan. At the time, area Pashtuns violently opposed its imposition, and this rarely marked or defended border has been ignored as much as possible ever since.

The central government in Pakistan always had trouble developing support in the tribal area, and Pakistani leaders have long recognized that they face a potentially explosive scenario there. Pashtuns make up only 12 percent of the population but control 40 percent of the territory of Pakistan. If these tribally linked Pakistani Pashtuns were to align themselves with Afghan Pashtuns (approaching half of Afghanistan's population) to form a separate entity, Pakistan would become a tiny, mostly Punjabi-populated country—a ripe target for Indian aggression. So Pakistan takes the affairs of Afghanistan, and their influence in them, very seriously.

The jihad against the Russians provided an ideal opportunity to promote universal religious ideals while repressing more traditional Pashtun tribalism. Today, the Pakistanis proceed cautiously by using troops recruited from the local tribes and only interfering in local affairs with the direct permission of tribal leaders.

Despite insistent pleas by the governors of both Gardez and Khost to avoid the border area, I set out from Khost for a day trip with the relative of an elder warlord of the border region acting as guide. I want to see for myself how the hunt for bin Laden is going and to seek out the elusive American contractors I have heard to be participating in the area's operations. The "dangerous" trip to the border turns out to be a bit of a disappointment when I am greeted not with suspicion, but with hospitality. As we approach the last Afghan checkpoint, the border guards do not check for passports, they do not inspect our car, but they do insist we stop for tea. Why do they not suspect us? Their answer surprises me: "If someone wanted to sneak in, they would use any of the numerous other unmanned entry points." I quickly discover that the concept of the border is as illusory as the American concept of controlling it.

At the actual border, no markers or signs differentiate Afghanistan from Pakistan; there literally is no recognizable border. Where my GPS tells me there should be a border, I see only a flat expanse ringed by low scrub-covered hills. There are tea shops, tiny wooden boxes that pass as convenience stores, and clusters of Afghans sitting around on their haunches in typical fashion. Taxi drivers wait for customers, friends wait for friends, and relatives pass the time chatting and laughing.

Toward the eastern side of the valley, I see a group of tall Pakistanis in sweaters and salwar kameez, and behind them a random collection of white minivans and cars. I am told that people are not allowed to drive into Pakistan but must walk across to take a Pakistani-licensed taxi. Vans pull up from both the north and south trailing white clouds of dust; families unload and walk toward us unmolested or even watched by the Pakistani soldiers. Curious as to the complete lack of interest in people crossing both to and from Afghanistan, I walk down to the gaggle of tall Pakistani soldiers to inquire.

I assume the one with the striped stick must be in charge, and I am right. I ask him if Taliban and foreigners are coming across the border and attacking Americans in Afghanistan. "That not true," he says convincingly. "The Afghans are lying." Around me, about seventy Afghans squat while waiting for taxis or just watching the constant flow of people back and forth. Up on a hill on the Pakistani side of the valley is a fortification with a radio tower. The Pakistanis see me videotaping and demand that no pictures be taken, so I step back a few feet across a low gully into what I assume is Afghanistan and keep filming.

I film van after van letting out passengers and groups of men going into Pakistan unchallenged and even unquestioned. It does not even appear that anyone is asked for identity papers by the Pakistani border guards. It makes me wonder how certain the Pakistani with the striped stick could be about his assertion that fighters are not crossing this border to attack Americans on the Afghan side. Later when I have tea with the Afghans sitting around below, they tell me that Arabs and Pakistanis from one or two hills over walk weapons in at night loaded on the backs of donkeys. The Pakistani guards appear to be symbolic and are here simply to bolster their meager wages. They're ultimately beholden to tribal bosses back in the border towns—not to Musharraf's central government—and the need to move or not move people across the border is decided well beyond their level of authority.

The next day back in Khost, I walk up to a young Afghan with a Thuraya and say I want to meet the Americans. When I had asked him about visiting the border a few days before, he had told me not to go there because of the danger. Now he tells me to go there if I want to see my American friends. The difference was a cash incentive. So much for the secrecy of American-supported firebases, since I've now discovered the secret to locating them—just ask any young English-speaking local with an $800 satellite phone. A short cab ride later, poorly disguised as an Afghan, I arrive at the shabby hilltop firebase overlooking the pass leading from Miram Shah toward Khost.

Coming up the hill toward the base are two armored tan Humvees, a beige camouflage pickup with an orange marker panel on top, and a brown-and-green-camouflage Land Rover, all followed by a convoy of Toyota pickup trucks overflowing with Afghan troops who wave to show off their heavy weapons and their new shooting gloves and sunglasses. So here I am watching this seven-truck convoy driving past on its way toward the nearby hilltop landing area, and I'm wondering exactly how I make contact. I jump down the sandbagged stairs to talk to the bearded commander, Shah Alam. In bad Pashto, I point to the gray helos circling around the hilltops and say "friends." Alam squeezes me into a former Talib Toyota truck, and the Afghans and I make the convoluted journey from the hilltop fort to the landing pad on the next hill. In between these hills, I see Afghan "campaigns" filling sandbags and building yet another fortification farther into Pakistan. As expected, the main Hesco barriers were being built facing the Pakistani side. It appears painfully obvious that the enemy, like Ahmed Shah Massoud told me many times, is Pakistan.

As we make it to the landing area, the two Hueys depart, leaving behind a group of silver-haired officers, each wearing a bulletproof vest and carrying a pistol. Their fresh haircuts, spotless armor and helmets, and neatly pressed uniforms are a little too crisp and clean in contrast to the dirty, unshaven look of their Special Forces bodyguards. They load into the convoy, which turns around and heads back over to the hilltop firebase.

Those left guarding the landing pad look like a task force—one of several elite groups composed of U.S. Army Special Forces, Delta Force, Navy SEALs, CIA paramilitaries, and military contractors who hunt for high-value targets (HVTs). This group appears to be comprised of a sergeant from the U.S. Army's 20th Special Forces Group, a unit of army reservists shipped in from Alabama, a young air force close air support controller, and an unshaven American in civilian clothes—khakis, photographer's vest, hiking boots. He wears Oakley shades and keeps a finger-forward grip on a battered AK-47—an unusual weapon for an American, even in this neck of the woods, and the mark of a contractor. In later conversations, the Contractor will confirm my suspicion—that I have encountered the elusive Task Force 11—but for the moment, he turns and walks away as I approach the group.

According to the U.S. government, what I am looking at doesn't exist. There are not only no operations inside Pakistan, Task Force 11 has been dissolved, as have Task Force 5 and Task Force 20. In July of 2003, U.S. Central Command said they had disbanded Task Force 11, described as "an elite group of Delta Force and Navy SEAL commandos who hunted high-value Taliban and al-Qaeda operators in and around Afghanistan" and created Task Force 20, which was moved to the Iraq theater to hunt down Saddam Hussein and former high-ranking Baathists. In November of 2003, General John P. Abizaid disbanded Task Force 5 and Task Force 20, operating in Afghanistan and Iraq, respectively, and created Task Force 121. As the U.S. military describes it, the new global task force was designed to react with greater speed on tips on HVTs (high value targets) and was not to be "contained within the borders where American conventional forces are operating." It is now one of the Pentagon's most highly classified and urgent operations. An air force brigadier general commands Task Force 121. All operations and information remain classified, and the Pentagon refuses to discuss any activities related to the task force—specifically the rules of engagement and whether this force needs permission of a foreign government to operate within its territory.

According to official descriptions, these task forces are made up "primarily" of Delta Force operators and Navy SEALs, supported by the 160th Special Operations Aviation Regiment, and are tasked with finding and destroying high-value Taliban and al-Qaeda elements "in and around" Afghanistan. The word "primarily" masks the other task force members who go by the acronym "OGA" or "other government agencies," and "around" Afghanistan implies they could be operating across the border with official approval under "hot pursuit" or "Amcit under fire" rules. When asked in a press conference who now hunts for Osama bin Laden and Taliban leader Mullah Mohammed Omar, a military officer answered, "Other folks are doing that." The real truth lies somewhere deep in the belly of the American security machine.

After the helicopters take off and the convoy has ferried the older gentlemen over to the base for their meeting, I am left talking to "the other folks." Even the army oddly says it is not actively looking for Osama bin Laden, though here standing in front of me is the army looking for Osama bin Laden. The secrecy of this task force and their direct supervision and direction by the CIA requires the army to disavow their activities. So officially the people I am looking at don't exist.

I walk over, trying hard to act nonchalant as I begin talking to the technically nonexistent American soldiers guarding the landing area. The dark, bearded leader of the Special Forces team listens to my compressed bio, looks me up and down, and says, "Yeah, we'll talk to you. . . . Just wait for these REMFs [Rear-Echelon Mother Fuckers] to go home and we'll come and get you." His message seems to be to make myself scarce until the heat is gone, so I go back and sit on the side of the hill with two other team members to wait out the older officers' visit to the remote base.

"Welcome to the war America forgot," says a Special Forces sergeant in a cynical greeting. He is a big burly man wearing one large earphone and tan camo. Unlike the rest of the team, he doesn't have a beard and seems eager to talk immediately. He was in Iraq for nine months and then was sent directly to Afghanistan for a six-month assignment. "Fuck this one weekend a month shit!" he snorts. He is reserves, part of the 20th Special Forces group from Alabama. He doesn't feel too out of place: "The countryside around here reminds me of southern Utah."

What I quickly learn from him is that in the borderland, the enemy has returned in force. The Americans and Afghans have been attacked and ambushed on a regular basis. The United States had already abandoned one of its four outposts, a firebase in nearby Lawhra. The others have come under increasingly frequent attack and occasionally change hands between the Afghans, the Taliban, al-Qaeda, the Pakistanis, and the Americans. The attacks come from the Pakistani side and almost always happen at night, beginning with rockets, then rocket-propelled grenades, and then three-wave assaults: one waiting to advance, one lying down to fire, and one advancing to repeat the process. Often, the mystery attackers take the base from the Afghan regulars for a few hours, only to be chased out by arriving American air support.

The sergeant seems a little rattled by the recent attacks in the area. "We got hit pretty bad two weeks ago," he tells me, adjusting his dirty Jack

Daniel's cap. "Six guys in our unit got Purple Hearts. They were waiting for us—knew exactly where we were. . . . The Pakistanis watched the whole thing and did nothing."

He points to a spot a little over a mile away. "They fire rockets right from that hill on the Pak side. We meet with the Pak officials every month right on the border. . . . They smile. We smile. They bullshit us and we bullshit them. Then they watch us get attacked without lifting a finger. This place is fucked." I ask him if the men who attacked him were Taliban, Pakistanis, or Arabs. He looks up at me, squints in the sun, and spits again for effect, admitting, "I have no fucking idea who we are fighting."

After cooling my heels for a couple of hours at the landing area, waiting for the officers to depart, I once again bump into the American with the AK-47—the Contractor. He starts off not with a greeting, but with a warning: "They're not gonna let you cross into Pakistan. . . . And don't be surprised when the head Afghan kicks you out."

I ask him who "they" are.

"TF," is his curt reply—task force.

Apparently, some videotaping I had done earlier had not gone over well. "You've filmed their base and vehicles. If the bad guys catch you across the border, they will use it to hit this place."

He seems most curious to know how I got here without getting attacked. "Did you see those antennas on all four corners of that pickup truck? Those are jammers. People around here bury antitank mines and then detonate them with cell phones or car-alarm-detonated triggers. They hire kids to sit at the side of the road and wait for Americans. They tried to kill Musharraf yesterday, and his jamming system was the only thing that saved him. Delta can't figure how you got here in one piece. I am sure they are looking you up right now." He smiles, then walks off.

I head down to the main firebase. The once-friendly Afghan commander, Shah Alam, quickly approaches me with a tone of near-panic in his voice. "You came here to take pictures," he says. "You have enough pictures, now please go." He obviously has orders to get me off this hill and going in the opposite direction of Miram Shah. In a typical Afghan gesture, he then asks me to join them for lunch before leaving.

The Contractor reappears as I am packing up to leave and inquires about my destination. I tell him I have been staying near Gardez with a man I call Haji, whom I had met a week earlier at a gathering of tribal elders. Haji is well known from his days as a mujahideen commander, and before that, a cross-border trucking czar, a former drug smuggler, and a supporter of the Taliban, back when they were better known for crushing warlords than supporting al-Qaeda. He has now retired but remains a man who can be called upon to resolve critical problems and defend the weak. Without hesitation, he had invited me to stay at his home for a week, on the condition that I not reveal its exact location or his full name. With no fear of overextending the elder's endless hospitality, I invite the Contractor to join me at Haji's.

The opportunity to go through Taliban territory with a stranger obviously intrigues him. He is supposed to be heading back to Khost for some R & R, so the idea of taking a taxi instead of going in an OGA convoy has a bizarre appeal. He gets his battered mountaineering backpack and tosses it into the ancient white-and-yellow taxi. We start out on the drive, but first I insist we stop at a small market a few miles from the base. Sixty dollars turns my new American friend into a rough facsimile of a bearded farmer, complete with wool hat, waistcoats, and light blue salwar kameez tunic. Satisfied we both look like idiots—but Afghan-looking idiots—we take off.

Despite his initial bluster, he is not used to being so exposed, so out in the open. As we come up on checkpoints, he drills me on how to evacuate the car from the same side, how to keep a pistol under my leg, and how the windshield will deflect rounds. As we head into the series of switchbacks that mark the start of the mountains, the Contractor starts to loosen up. We have a long time to talk on the ride, bouncing and rattling down the potholed dirt roads. He agrees to answer some questions about his work on the condition that I not reveal anything that might harm his mission and that neither he nor his home base be identified. I agree. His story fascinates me as I type it into my pocket computer.

"What you were looking at was part of TF-11—'JAYSOTUF,' or Joint

Special Operations Task Force [JSOTF]. There were some REMFs in there on a dog and pony, but the team also has a couple of shooters, usually three or four Delta, a vanilla twelve-man SF team, an Air Force CAST, a case officer, an OGA element, and about thirty or forty Afghans for weight. They are the tip of the spear out here—the hunter-killers in this part of the woods.

"I am a contractor. The CIA has been using civilian contractors for decades—guys who are neither officially military, government, or intel. They started in Vietnam. They needed a deniable operator—someone that if he is caught they can say was not part of the U.S. government. These days the CIA has plenty of money, so it's easier just to hire us than train new people. There are the soldier-of-fortune, beer-bellied, raucous, ring-wearing guys you see in town, and then there are us—guys into fitness, in their late twenties to late forties. They have inside and outside guys. Inside are guys who never admit they work for the CIA; outside guys are the ones who for some reason got outed. One guy was outed because the CIA sent him a W-2 with 'CIA' in the space under 'employer.'"

Most of the operators are "sheep dipped," he says, serving in some official capacity to provide a plausible military or civilian cover but actually working "black ops," top-secret CIA operations that are never revealed in their military CV. He tells me, "Most of the paramilitaries come from Delta Force, and I only met one SEAL. . . . They typically are recruited from the serving military and then seamlessly join the Agency as contractors. They get out and are directly flipped. They get recruited with enough time to do the background process early enough so they can go straight in. Guys in the military usually have a clean record, no financial problems, no gaps, no legal problems. By watching them and flowing them into the Agency, there is no explanation time in between. There is no shortage of volunteers. . . . People make fun of the Agency, but all the SF guys are trying to work there. You get whatever you need, you don't get dicked with, you have your own chain of command, and you don't answer to the local military commander. You are not in the federal system, or in the military system."

"Working in Afghanistan is pretty easy," he continues. "You sign up, train up, and fly in. Most of the operators go into Tashkent [in neighboring Uzbekistan] via commercial and then to Kabul on a military flight. You land there, and they pick you up in a truck and check you in at the hotel. Nobody asks any questions. . . . You check in, get a couple days in town, and then talk to the chief of base. You get your walking papers and fly out to Khost, Ghazni, Kandahar, or wherever you're going." The going wage, he says, is $1,000 to $1,250 a day for a contractor with security clearance, slightly better than in Iraq. Three months is the usual tour of duty. "People get freaky if you leave them out here more than ninety days."

Our driver and my translator, Doc, stare straight ahead, looking for freshly disturbed potholes, a place the Taliban like to hide remote-detonated mines. I've told them that the Contractor is my cameraman, and he is enjoying his undercover role as sidekick. He uses his GPS to mark checkpoints and track the road as we travel up into higher altitudes. The checkpoints, manned by Taliban and warlords' foot soldiers, are simply speed bumps guarded by armed men who stare into the front of the taxi. My driver boldly waves them off and keeps going. I try to look as Pashtun as a blue-eyed *feringhi*, or foreigner, can. With his heavy beard, the Contractor looks more like an Afghan than I ever will. I tuck my glasses in my pocket, pull my dirty brown blanket tightly around my face, and stare impassively out the front window as we go through the checkpoints. We somehow easily pass through four more where both trucks and passenger vehicles are being stopped and emptied.

The first base the Contractor was assigned to, he tells me, was set up in the most remote area that could be resupplied by helicopter. "They flew us in after dark on a nighttime resupply mission on a CIA Russian helo—a bird that wouldn't say 'Here come the Americans.'" A four-truck convoy came out to meet them. The new crew hopped off, the old crew hopped on, and the helicopter took off.

"When I first saw the terrain through the NVGs [night-vision goggles], all I could think of was the surface of the moon—talcum-powder dust, rocks, dirt, and low barren foothills rolling into mountains on each side, all in green. There was nothing but stars, rocks, and a medieval mud fort in the distance. Inside there is this big bearded guy with a Western hat warming himself over a diesel fire in a fifty-gallon drum. He sees us, laughs this crazy laugh with his face lit by the fire, and yells out, 'Gentlemen, welcome to the edge of the empire!' Man, I got the crazies when I heard that.

"The outpost used to be someone's compound. You've seen this place in a hundred movies. *Star Wars, Mad Max, Beau Geste,* and a dozen Westerns. It's that last outpost of civilization before you hit the savages. . . . The CIA rented it because it was on a busy infil route for the Taliban and al-Qaeda from Pakistan. I got my first clue when I saw a map in the deputy minister of security's office marked 'Top Secret.' It had little green circles clearly marking where the bad guys were. The problem is that the circles were all in Pakistan in places like Miram Shah and Wana.

"When I got here, they sent two of us to meet with the Pakistani border guards. It was a three- or four-mile drive. Seems like they hadn't seen armed plainclothes Americans before. They swiveled the big gun on us as we were driving up. They were damn hostile to us. They said their head intelligence guy would come to meet us there tomorrow, so the next day we all meet in a little hut with the Waziristan Scouts. We did the initial scout and then the two of us went back to pick up the chief of base, the young case officer, and a translator. The translator told them what we are doing here, why we are here, and what we want to cooperate on—'Can we give you a phone?' 'We might have to chase someone across the border,' et cetera. They said it's not a problem as long as we didn't go too far inside the border. They didn't really say what would have happened if we had hit the town. It was another three miles to the town."

The hunt for bin Laden, he says, is not like the hunt for Saddam, with thousands of troops looking under every carpet and behind every tree. Even the Pakistanis can't operate in the tribal areas without serious backlash.

"Our job is to shake the apple tree," the Contractor says. "We aren't hunting bin Laden from the top. Our strategy is to focus on the little guys—just like how they do drug busts in the States. Put the heat on the runners and little guys until they get nervous and start contacting higher-ups. Then we intercept their calls and the hunt begins. We are just hired killers. Guns with legs. We were there to provide security to the case officer, roll guys up, or do hits. The fort was run by the chief of base, a CIA bureaucrat that wouldn't give us the time of day."

The Taliban, he says, aren't a priority. "Mullah Omar is not an issue. We are looking for al-Qaeda. . . . We hunt al-Qaeda. We are not trying to develop intelligence inside the religious schools. We are looking for people connected to bin Laden.

"We ask simple questions like, where do they sleep at night? Once we can find where they sleep, we can monitor them. When we find the house, we can pick up any electronic communications and send them directly to Langley, [MI5 headquarters in] Cheltenham, or Washington. . . . Once you find their base, you don't want to hit 'em; you let 'em talk and use that intel to roll up the lower-level people. We can do voice-print on them and even know who they are talking to if that person is in the database. If they set up a meeting or give us a GPS location, somebody might get hit the next day. If they still don't contact higher-ups, then you snatch another guy or make him disappear. You do that a couple of times and they will get nervous."

Doc, I notice, has been listening intently. The Contractor adjusts his rust-colored wool hat and admires his Afghan look in the mirror before continuing.

"The trouble is that we are doing this inside Pakistan," he says. "That's why you need a contractor. Our government can say that 'we' are not going into Pakistan. But you can be damn sure that white boys are going into Pakistan and shooting bad guys.

"The chief of base runs the show. The case officers are buried on the base. I had been there a month before the case officer went outside. The base is an Agency operation with enough troops on the outside to make it look like a military base. The Agency is leasing the property the base is on. The army runs their own operations, but they tell the chief of base what they are doing. The CIA is still compartmentalized by country. If you go inside Pakistan, you have to call the chief of station in Islamabad and he can't poach the project."

Most of the contractors at his base spend their downtime working out, running sprints between the helicopter pad and back, and doing triceps presses with big rocks.

"We like to stay in shape. When you're in combat, you want to make sure you're using everything you got. You want to make sure you take a few guys with you, even if you only have your bare hands. Most of us are into steroids big time. D-balls [Dianabol] to bulk you up and Sustanon to help you maintain what you gained. The doctors turn a blind eye to it. We get the stuff across the border in Pakistan. When you see guys bulked up, you know what they are on. We keep control of it, though."

He looks at the arid terrain and high adobe forts around us. He shifts his AK, then smiles. "These days the Agency is looking for Mormons and born-agains. People with a lot of patriotism and the need to do good. At least we start that way. . . . I don't drink, smoke, or eat crap," he says, smiling. "My only weaknesses? Pepsi and women."

As we wind down the backside of the Taliban-controlled mountains, I see the familiar tabletop range that marks the location of Haji's compound. The Contractor seems pleased that he has loaded the road and all of its checkpoints into his GPS. Haji lives in one of the largest compounds in the Gardez area, a good indicator of his importance. Each of its four outer walls stretches over nine hundred feet long and thirty feet high. His compound sits on a barren plain outside of town in front of the dramatic backdrop of Taliban-controlled mountains, just past the U.S. base in Gardez. In the mountains to the south lies the deadly Shah-i-Kot Valley, location of Operation Anaconda in March 2002, and beyond that the mountain redoubt of Zhawar Khili, the massive cave system built by bin Laden to provide shelter against Soviet air bombardment. Extensive poppy fields stretch to the north and east. Inside the compound, Haji has a separate guesthouse and two more walled areas, one for his family and the other for his crops. Designed for maximum defensibility, large square guard towers cap each corner of the compound, and each section has its own full stock of weapons and ammunition. Even the outside toilet, a long walk up a rickety ladder, has three gun ports. Each corner tower used to have an antiaircraft gun, but Haji said he removed them out of fear of being bombed by the Americans. From the early morning until late into the night, the sky above Haji's compound is filled with Apaches, Blackhawks, Chinooks, B-1B bombers, and jet fighters.

Haji welcomes me with the bear hug and double buss of a prodigal son. He immediately senses that my friend is much more than a cameraman. In addition to carrying an AK and wearing Oakleys, the Contractor has the disconcerting habit of pacing twenty yards back and forth as if doing a security sweep, and scanning every room he enters for hostile elements. But since the Contractor is my friend, he is welcomed without question.

Since I had first arrived at Haji's compound a few days prior, we had by now established a pattern of three daily long meals served on the floor, followed by endless cups of tea, and hours of conversation through a translator. It was really all we had been doing since I had arrived. Though it had taken Haji some time to grow comfortable with me, he eventually had opened up about his opinions of the current situation in Afghanistan.

The first night we had engaged in small talk, his stance was neutral. Yes, he supported the Americans, even though he still seemed angry over something they had done in 2001. Yes, he thought the Taliban was finished. The second night we discussed more specific concerns. There is violence here, no government, only one school but no teachers. By the third night, as the remains of dinner were picked up and green tea was poured, Haji had finally become more forthright. I had asked him if the reports of the Taliban's return to the area were true.

"Yes, they come here . . . usually at night. They ask for food or shelter. They do not stay long, and we do not ask them where they are going. In some cases they intimidate people, and in other cases they pay. But they seem to know who to talk to. In every group of twenty or so Taliban, there are about four or five Arabs. They need to be with the Afghans because they do not know the way, and they do not speak the language."

Haji has enough stature to speak his mind about the Taliban, but even he sees the need to be cautious when discussing the Arabs, what Americans call al-Qaeda. "People do not like the Arabs here because they are arrogant and act superior to the Afghans." He laughs. "We like to say they are more interested in taking videos than fighting."

It is clear that al-Qaeda is still here and still intimidates. Back at the tribal meeting before Haji invited me to stay with him, I had asked to stay with another elder who controlled a border region. The long-bearded man had replied, "You are welcome to stay, but the Arabs will leave a letter at my door that unless you leave the next day, they will kill me and my family." I had thanked him for his offer and accepted Haji's invitation instead.

"During the jihad against the Russians, there were people in every village who would cook food and help us," Haji tells me. "No one ever worried about being betrayed or discovered. No one even posted sentries. Now these same people are scared when they see the Talibs or the Arabs. The Arabs have to use sat phones to communicate and sneak into villages at three A.M., usually leaving before light the next day."

Haji first met bin Laden in the 1980s, when bin Laden was a wealthy young Saudi helping the mujahideen in their battle against the Soviets. The Pakistani ISI had given Haji three truckloads of rockets but no way to transport them back to Afghanistan. "What was I going to do with three truckloads of rockets? The ISI told us that Osama had an office near the University of Peshawar and to go and ask him for help. . . . We went to his office and filled out an application so that he would pay for the camels and mules. They wanted to know things like how much the rockets weighed. I didn't know how much the rockets weighed." Since Haji wasn't with one of the Saudi-backed mujahideen commanders, bin Laden said he couldn't help them.

Haji only knew bin Laden as a man helpful to the mujahideen and never expected he would become what he has, but he doesn't think bin Laden will ultimately succeed in Afghanistan because "the Afghans are tired of migrating and fighting." Haji says he thinks bin Laden has taken refuge on the Pakistani side of the border, in a valley town called Chitral. "That is where people traditionally hide from those who seek them. There is little movement there in the winter. The airplanes don't work well [for surveillance] that high up, and you will know when people are coming. Bin

Laden knows the tribal areas very well, and the tribes know him very well." His answer makes sense but doesn't quite ring true somehow. Newspapers in Pakistan have been reporting that bin Laden has visited the tribal areas between Gardez and Khost. I would guess that Haji probably has a pretty good idea of bin Laden's location, but knows that it would be dangerous for an Afghan to possess such information. A close friend of his was sent to Guantanamo Bay for knowing the same people whom Haji knows.

When asked about Mullah Omar, he responds promptly, "Mullah Omar was in Miram Shah during Ramadan and has now moved to Quetta for the winter." This time his tone is matter-of-fact. He won't say how he knows this, but his guess coincides with both Pakistani president Pervez Musharraf's and Afghan president Hamid Karzai's statements about Omar and other senior Taliban being spotted at prayers in Quetta.

Despite having worked with the Taliban, Haji has mixed feelings about their reign in Afghanistan. "I met many times with Mullah Omar and all the other Taliban commanders. They were not educated men. They were not even good Muslims. The Taliban took all the prostitutes to Kandahar, and the Arabs were all screwing around. In time, they considered themselves separate from the people. A foot soldier was more trustworthy than a tribal elder." Now, he explains, "there are two categories of Taliban: the jihadis, who want martyrdom, and the people who fight for money.

"The Taliban are not Pashtun. We have dancing. We sing. We make decisions in jirgas [a democratic-style group of representatives]." The Taliban, Haji tells me, has ignored its Pashtun culture by becoming entranced by Wahhabism, Saudi-backed religious extremism. "Afghans do not like Wahhabis. The Taliban relied on other people and lost touch with the Afghan people. That is why, in the end, the Taliban could never be governors, only occupiers."

Haji has an equally bleak forecast for the Americans: "I can guarantee you the Americans will not succeed. They rely on people they pay money to. Now they are surrounded by people who want money. They have turned away from the tribal elders and made bad friends."

He does not show a preference for either contingency, responding in disgust, "I try not to involve myself with these things." Though he may hold unspoken preferences, clearly neither has earned his full support, perhaps because both seem to view his role as a tribal elder as irrelevant under the new system.

I grow to like Haji, and he treats me like a son. He insists that I sit on his right-hand side and urges me to eat the best part of the sheep, not clearing the vinyl mat until I have eaten to his satisfaction. He makes sure I sit on the warmest part of the floor. He pesters me to grow my beard out and tugs at it every day as if that will speed the process. It was Haji's generosity that had made me want to invite the Contractor to join me for a visit at the compound, though the Contractor's awkwardness ends up trying Haji's hospitality.

At dinner the night we arrive, Haji wants to hear all about my trip. He pushes food directly in front of the Contractor: choice cuts of greasy mutton with fresh bread and a dish—specially prepared by Haji's wife for the guests—of what appears to be curdled milk with oil poured into it. The new guest keeps his arms folded and mumbles, "Gotta get to ten percent body fat." Haji makes several attempts before giving up, staring hard at the Contractor, then looking at me with hurt confusion. "Just pretend to eat something and compliment the food," I tell the Contractor. The Contractor frequently stands up in the middle of the hours-long meal, making excuses about having to shoot some video. When he leaves the room for good, Haji turns to me and asks through the interpreter, "What's wrong with your friend?"

The same scene repeats at each breakfast, lunch, and dinner for three days. Two of Haji's sons and an ever-changing parade of locals who come to ask favors from the elder usually join us. Haji's brother visits with his three-year-old grandson and asks me to come by to try to fix his satellite phone—a phone that still makes free calls courtesy of the CIA. The Contractor mostly stays silent. He seems genuinely interested in the conversations but doesn't seem to know how to interact with Afghans who aren't informers. The Contractor continues to refuse to eat even a grain of rice, and I come to dread Haji's stone-faced looks in my direction. Haji even tries shopping for us himself, apologizing for not having eggs at one breakfast because it is too cold for the chickens to lay. The Contractor, meanwhile, gets by on Atkins Bars and sips of bottled water pulled from his pack at daybreak and before bedtime.

Haji had welcomed the Contractor, but the feeling was different than when I had been staying there alone. It was an official sort of hospitality now, one designed to discharge Haji's responsibilities in order to communicate something to someone most Afghans in the area would consider the enemy. Haji adamantly wanted his opinion of a recent bombing to reach someone at a level of authority inside the American forts. So finally, on the third day with the Contractor, he breaks out of Pashtun protocol, speaking frankly to tell his mysterious American guest about the increasing frustration that the tribal elders have with the Americans. He has received word that a family of eight has been killed in the nearby town of Seyyed Karam. He doesn't explain how he knows the details of their deaths so soon.

"A local thug lived there for eighteen years and has been threatening to rocket the meeting in Kabul," he tells us. "An informer called the Americans, but by the time the air attack took place, the man was long gone. Instead another man and his family were hiding out in the house because the man had killed someone in a property dispute. He, his wife, and his six children were found buried under a wall."

Haji explains that the people in town are upset. Not about the fugitive, since this was perceived as an odd form of justice, but for the man's innocent wife and children who had no quarrel with the Americans or townspeople.

"This man could have been arrested with a minimum of violence, but the Americans chose to attack the house with aircraft and weapons designed to destroy tanks."

What's going on is clear to Haji. "The informers are making money from both sides." The Contractor says he understands, and the meal ends in silence.

After breakfast, I thank Haji for his hospitality. He talks to me like a clucking mother hen, pushing me to get a move on and to stop messing around with my camera. Once we get out in the daylight, he rushes us to get in the car and drive away, lest we are spotted outside of his compound. He trusts the discretion of the locals who have come by to visit over the past few days, but if word had gotten around that he had some unidentified Americans staying with him, unfriendlies could be watching the compound. Across the horizon, the rotors of Blackhawks slice through the crisp morning air.

On our way back toward the border, the Contractor wants to stop in at another base and talk to someone from OGA (other government agencies), a euphemistic term used to describe high-level clandestine operators who don't fit into the traditional military structure. He seems eager to pass along Haji's complaints about the Americans' use of excessive force and reliance on paid snitches. I stay outside.

After just a few minutes, he emerges, shaking his head. "Seems like the OGA guy wouldn't even get off his cot to say hi. He just sent his local peon to say he already had the intel."

The Contractor holds up a stack of dirty Pakistani rupees. "The puke said thanks and here are some rupees for the cab ride." He shakes his head. "Company policy is to always give something to someone bringing intel."

Looking at the pile of grubby notes, he shakes his head again. "That's fucked, man," he says, getting back into the car. What better reason for someone to feed the Americans a bunch of lies than to get a handful of money out of it.

To be fair, the idea that an armed American civilian would just stroll into a military base with relevant information might give any official pause, since the military only works with established intelligence sources. Walk-ups are considered the most unreliable form of intelligence, but being on the other end of a wad of dirty rupees clearly pisses off the Contractor.

Reliance on bad intel and the lack of good relations with the local population has compounded the security problems, he says. "When you do a madrassah hit"—that is, a raid on an Islamic school—"the locals get pissed. You don't always find bad guys, but everyone gets slammed to the ground, zip-tied, bagged, and tagged. You forget to give them a hundred bucks at the door and they'll swear to get you. They will, too. The next time the Americans are on patrol in their Dumbvees, they are set up."

This reminds me of a traditional Pashtun saying Haji told me days before: "If you take your revenge in a hundred years, you are rushing things."

Despite the treatment he just received from OGA, the Contractor insists the folks he works directly with are beginning to catch on and improve their methods of collection. "Now we want to get inside the heads of the people we are dealing with. We want a softer, more personal relationship, instead of basing the transaction on money.

"A while back, Rumsfeld said we might be creating more enemies than we are killing. . . . Duh . . . But things are changing. We don't work with local Afghan commanders so much. We also don't give a shit about what the Paks say, so we are allowed to slide and glide a little more inside Pakistan. . . . For some reason Pakistan is still like the Catholic Church, where it is sanctuary," the Contractor tells me. "The bad guys are inside Pakistan using Pakistani protection to attack Americans inside Afghanistan and then running back knowing they won't be chased. Hopefully, things will change."

For now, though, covert operations continue and task force looks for excuses to cross the border, the Contractor says. An American civilian operating inside Pakistan could need help, which gives the U.S. military a reason to cross the border in support, hot pursuit, or just to call in mortar and air fire on nebulous "bad guys." But until they do, the shadow war depends on men, like the Contractor, willing to work and fight in a no-man's land just beyond the reach of U.S. power. I ask him if there's an extraction plan if a mission in Pakistan gets messy. "The extraction plan is that once you are across the border, you are on your own. There is no uplift. You are screwed if things go wrong." But that vulnerability is essential to the role of a contractor. "You are not in the federal system or in the military system," he says. "You are deniable, disposable, and deletable."

That independence—and the secrecy that goes with it—is part of the Contractor's code. And, as far as he is concerned, it should remain inviolate even in death. "When we get killed, it's usually because we fucked up," he says. "We lost two guys, set up and ambushed. We lost a case officer in a training accident. That, along with [Johnny Micheal] Spann getting killed in the middle of an interrogation, adds up to four CIA operators killed in this war." Traditionally, the CIA does not disclose an operative's identity, even if he is killed. But in Spann's case, the Agency decided that his anonymous star would be going on the Wall of Honor at a time when the Agency desperately needed a publicly identifiable hero. "That's a decision that has been made since September 11 to polish up the CIA's image. You can't shit on a dead hero, so I think the number-two guy at the Agency has decided to grab some glory to counteract all the Agency fuckups since the Bay of Pigs. . . . Tenet got hammered because of 9/11 and wanted to show that we are still working, to show that we are putting out an effort. The problem is that fucks the rest of the guys and their families because this leaves the wives and families dangling in the wind, and you have more tradecraft exposed. . . . I don't know why we have to be the poster boys to fix the CIA's reputation."

Revealing Spann's name made him a hero, but it also exposed his wife, which blew her cover and publicly identified his children as the offspring of two covert officers. When I thought about it later, I understood that the Contractor saw this public celebration of his private tradecraft as a violation of his own tribe's code. The Contractor's willingness to talk to me seemed to be driven by his anger over seeing that code of secrecy begin to crumble. The independent contractors he works with in the covert world of OGA assignments signed on for the job because they could be assured their exploits and identities would be kept under the radar, if for no other reason than for the protection of their families. But now it seems the CIA is willing to sacrifice that commitment to its operators in order to grab a little glory.

The Contractor asked me to leave him off a short distance from his base. He didn't want to have to explain what he was doing driving around in Taliban territory. I said good-bye to the Contractor near his little mud fort at the edge of the empire and carried on in my little yellow-and-white taxi.

CHAPTER 3

The Praetorian Guard

"At the end, we all knew there might be a conflict of interest."
— Contractor working Aristide's personal
security detail during his downfall

The fall of the Taliban did not guarantee American forces a respite from random violence, ambushes, and daily attacks by bombs and rockets. In the new Afghan reality, the number-one target is Hamid Karzai. Karzai is a Westernized "moderate" Pashtun with a noble lineage and diplomatic skills who speaks fluent English along with four other languages. He was an easy choice for the United States to support as leader, but any Afghan who dared to align himself with America became a target of not only the Taliban, but also disgruntled warlords like Gulbuddin Hekmatyar. Afghanistan has a long history of using assassination to change the course of their nation, so a future attempt on Karzai's life seemed a near certainty.

The U.S. government originally began training a team of Afghan bodyguards to protect Karzai but soon recognized the unreliability of the custom-made palace guard. It seemed no amount of training would make the Afghans an effective security force, and the indigenous detail remained vulnerable to infiltration. Other Afghan leaders, like General Rashid Dostum or Ismail Khan, had trusted contingents of hardened fighting men who had fought with them for decades, some having endured prison time and great hardship in the service of their leaders. Karzai had little military experience and no trusted men who could be counted on to take a bullet for him, if necessary. Karzai called the State Department and begged for a security detail.

Dictators avoid ethnic or tribal intrigue by hiring professional mercenaries as palace guards. For example, the Saudi royal family hires ex–Delta and Special Forces independent contractors for their protection. However, it is unusual in modern times for one country to contract and pay for the only protection for a foreign leader (although at one time the State Department managed the security of Haiti's Jean-Bertrand Aristide, before handing it off to a private firm).

As an interim measure before a long-term solution could be formulated, the assignment went to JSOC (Joint Special Operations Command), who assigned a detail from SEAL Team 6, the covert antiterrorism group. Better known as DEVGRU, for Development Group, SEAL Team 6 is the naval equivalent of Delta Force. As one of its specialties, DEVGRU provides personal security for high-ranking military in high-risk environments. The SEALs deployed on June 2, 2002, and their security detail was in place by the fifteenth of that month. This particular team was scheduled for a six-month rotation, to end on December 15.

The SEALs shadowed Karzai much like special operations groups guard U.S. generals and admirals when they visit Afghanistan. The show of force that followed Karzai around may have given the impression of tight security, but it wouldn't be long before an enemy of the new Afghan government would exploit a critical vulnerability to take a shot at the president. While using an American detail may have removed the threat of infiltrators from Karzai's immediate protective force, it did nothing to prevent the same in the security forces of other Afghan leaders.

On September 5, 2002, Karzai traveled to his hometown of Kandahar to attend his younger brother's wedding. After evening prayers, Karzai was leaving the governor's compound in his black American-made SUV when an uniformed member of the palace guard, who had just been hired seventeen days earlier, fired four to eight shots at Karzai with a Makarov pistol. Flying bullets barely missed Karzai, instead hitting Governor Gul Sherzai in the neck. When the assassin fired the first shots, a twenty-three-year-old shopkeeper leapt, pulling him to the ground to wrestle the gun away. A young boy also moved in to help. The SEALs, trained to kill at close quarters, began shooting in the direction of the assassin and killed all three Afghans. Although there was only one assassin, the young boy and shopkeeper were killed for their well-intentioned, if amateur, attempts to save Karzai. The bloody event hit the news and instantly communicated a message that the U.S. military protected Karzai and dealt out violence without regard to the innocent or guilty. The fallout from the incident made it an even greater imperative to devise a new answer for Karzai's protection problem. Luckily, Craige "Mad Max" Maxim had already been working on replacements.

Maxim, a white-haired, compact man in his midfifties, has thirty years in the army, with twenty of those years in Delta. Oakley sunglasses usually mask his no-nonsense facial expression. Craige headed Delta's training program and gained fame in the service for running high-risk PSDs to protect generals and dignitaries in war zones or other areas with a high likelihood of attack. He is up front about his motivations for getting back into the business as an independent contractor after retiring from Delta: "I missed the action. It was my way of doing something after September eleven. It became personal."

Most agreed that the emergency deployment of SEAL Team 6 was overkill and expensive, but the importance of Karzai's survival to U.S. national interests made even extraordinary measures necessary. Using the SEALs bought time until a long-term solution could be devised, which is what Craige had in mind when he pitched the idea to the State Department of recruiting a detail of independent contractors to keep Karzai alive. He had the contacts and experience, and said he could have a crew of three dozen American bodyguards up and running in sixty days.

"I said if I was able to select, hire, and fire, I would take the job. I made a list of how many weapons we needed, what kind, and we had to coordinate that with State. It had to be sanctioned by the DoS, and they were in way over their head." So the State Department supported Craige's idea and added the plan to an existing DynCorp contract, making Maxim and his men subcontractors to DynCorp. "DynCorp already was doing State Department security contracts in Jerusalem and Bosnia, and they had $50 million left over on their contract, so they just shoehorned the Karzai job on their contract." Although some Afghans would be integrated into the Karzai Protection Detail, or "KPD" as it was called, it would remain a foreign-manned and funded detail paid out as a private contract to Dyn-Corp.

Using private contractors could contribute to a slightly more positive public perception than having Karzai constantly accompanied by members of the U.S. military, which only added to the impression that he was an American puppet. Also, if any unfortunate incident occurred, the blame could be shifted away from the American government and military to the provider of services. Further, the contractors' training could be tailored for the special situation in which they would be expected to work, something that Maxim believed could prevent a controversial tragedy such as what occurred in the Kandahar incident. "I have a love-hate relationship with the SEALs. They do things differently. For example, the AIC's [agent in charge] job is to cover and evacuate. You can't do that if you are carrying a long gun. I will just say that the events that transpired were directly related to the SEAL mind-set."

Craige and his advance team spent time in Kabul in July of 2002 doing the initial vulnerability assessment. Craige then spent July and August recruiting. By September 8, he had thirty-nine contractors lined up for the Karzai protection detail, and he continued adding to that as he could. "What we did was spend a lot of money to hire the right people. We hired the kind of people whose safety is between the trigger finger and the brain. People who can read the situation—color, contrast, movement, stuff you either understand or you don't. A good seventy percent of my team were 'white side' SEALs. Forty-six was the total number we ended up with. When I hire a team, it's all about attitude and tactical sensing. That's something you get with experience. Combat veterans have it, but so do cops." State initially requested that all security details be made up of former SF, but Maxim insisted that former police officers would also have the skills necessary for the job. Given the limited recruiting pool of former SF and the ballooning demand for such security details, the concession was an important one.

Craige recruited his Karzai team before the Iraq war, and thus prior to the massive explosion in demand for private security services, so he envisions a day when it won't be so simple to assemble a team of experienced professionals for such an important assignment. "At some point, we are going to have to train people from scratch. . . . We know that the tier-one people are going to be tapped out. It takes ten years to become a professional, ten minutes to dress like one, and ten seconds to talk like one."

A high-risk personal security detail goes to a much greater measure of protection than the standard variety, and operators must be highly trained to anticipate and respond to a virtually unlimited variety of attacks. Craige points out, "There is a big difference between high-risk protection and the kind of protection that the Secret Service provides. The Secret Service and State Department provide executive protection typically in a nonhostile environment. We add to that because of the threats where we work. They provide a two-car motorcade. If it's a high threat, we roll a lot harder. We make sure we have enough spank to get the job done."

When on duty guarding the "principal," or protected individual, an operator must be completely attuned to the possibility of danger behind every car or around every corner, without allowing paranoia to spark overreaction to nonthreats. It's difficult to estimate how many individuals actively seek the assassination of Karzai, but since one lucky bullet could end America's plan for Afghanistan, the State Department was taking no chances. Snipers, sniffing dogs, fortified checkpoints, and many other military elements were combined to create a small armed force similar to the Swiss Guard that protects the Pope.

Craige views the business of PSDs as a cat-and-mouse game—a game he has yet to lose. He also knows that as the protection around the principal increases, so does the level of threat. "When we first arrived, the Taliban were doing 'dog' hits . . . putting out objects with explosive residue on them to see if we would stop. They used a double-layer toolbox once and had a surgical glove with explosives residue just to see if we would find it. The enemy learns and adapts." Not long after the new DynCorp security detail arrived, massive bomb blasts and even surface-to-air missiles would be targeted at Karzai.

Conditions were not ideal. Maxim refused to let his people use the building set aside for their housing because of security issues. The assigned house was abandoned in favor of a hastily constructed "Camp Aegis," a cluster of tents erected a hundred yards away from where Karzai slept. Maxim's team moved into Camp Aegis on December 15, 2002.

Craige delivered his team on schedule, and Karzai stayed alive during his time on watch, but the deal would come crashing down when Dyn-Corp's management style clashed with Maxim's understanding of their business arrangements. Craige is blunt about what happened: "DynCorp fucked with us on our benefits, mostly holiday pay, so we walked as a group when our ninety days was up." The experience left a bitter taste in Mad Max's mouth. Faced with the mutiny of Karzai's entire PSD deciding not to renew their contracts, DynCorp had to scramble to replace the entire team, or risk leaving an important client completely exposed.

When Craige Maxim and his team walked on DynCorp, it was not reported or known to the outside world that Karzai's life could be dependent, not on national security or patriotic loyalty, but on a dispute over holiday pay. For DynCorp, losing a few million dollars on a contract that does not affect the core business does not have much effect, though not being able to deliver on the Karzai detail could risk endangering other government contracts. At the time of the Karzai contract, 95 percent of DynCorp's $2-billion company and 23,000 employees worked on U.S. government business. Much of the personal security work that DynCorp won before September 11 has been subcontracted to aggressive new companies like Blackwater and Triple Canopy.

In DynCorp's scramble to replace Karzai's security detail, Pete Walther, an ex–Special Forces weapons sergeant from South Dakota, signed on with four dozen other ex-police and -military for two back-to-back six-month contracts.

Square-jawed and built low, Pete resembles a real-life white-skinned version of the Incredible Hulk. In his early thirties, he originally hails from the Midwest and spent over a decade in the Special Forces as weapons specialist. He had been in ODA 595, the Special Forces A-team that teamed up with General Dostum in the Dari Suf Valley at the beginning of the U.S. offensive in Afghanistan. He followed Afghanistan with a tour in Iraq, and then returned to his home base at Fort Campbell, Kentucky. He admits that Afghanistan was the World Series for the Green Berets. His time in Iraq taught him that "Big Army" controlled that war and that Special Forces took a backseat to the traditional military. The "Stop Loss" had been lifted on his team, giving him the freedom to make a decision—stay in the Special Forces until retirement, or get out to work as a contractor making three times his normal salary. DynCorp typically paid State Department rates—$450 to $550 a day—but the Karzai contract paid $600 a day and a guaranteed year-long assignment with two six-month contracts. Over $200,000 sounded enticing to a soldier who would typically make less than $50,000 a year in the U.S. military. Pete represents just one of thousands of operators who have decided to leave the military and transfer millions of dollars' worth of training and institutional knowledge to the private sector, where it is repackaged and sold back to the government at a premium. Shortly after his retirement, Pete boarded a plane and headed to Kabul to risk his life in the protection of a foreign leader.

Guarding "the Old Man"

Kabul has changed dramatically in the two years since the Taliban fell. Sandbags block easy access to the oft-shelled palace complex in Kabul. Along the busy road, shipping containers filled with dirt act as blast barriers against truck bombs. Improvised steel plates provide cover for machine-gun positions. The rooftops sprout antennas. Snipers watch through binoculars from makeshift towers. Tajik-Afghans from the ethnic group of the head of the military, General Fahim, have posts outside the perimeter, while mostly Pashtuns help guard the Pashtun president inside the gates. A simple flash of my U.S. passport allows me access to the outside gates, but the Afghans who accompany me must cajole and bullshit their way through to the inner sanctum, even though it is common for foreigners and journalists to have an interpreter and a driver in Kabul.

The Afghan guards at the entrance to the palace appear flummoxed by my request to visit a member of Karzai's protective detail. I had met Pete when I traveled with his Special Forces ODA during the earliest phase of the war in Afghanistan, and we had kept in touch in the two ensuing years. Pete and I had been chatting on his Afghan cell phone since I had arrived in Kabul, and he told me to just stop by the palace for a visit. Outside the small gate office, I could see a group of American contractors standing around behind their sandbags. Frustrated by the Afghans' refusal to allow me entrance, I just politely tell them that I am going to go over to talk to the Americans and that if I am an imposter, the Americans would shoot me before they could.

Calling the Afghans' bluff, I then run into a wall of bureaucracy as the Americans have to radio the command center, check my bags, search me, and figure out what to do. They finally radio to see if Pete is around. He answers back that he is working the "old man's" PSD, "walking the diamond" while Karzai attends meetings. I am supposed to wait until he can break away.

Since the contractors are not allowed to receive packages, I suggest that they check my camera bag and confiscate a suspicious item—a bottle of Johnnie Walker Black Label. A gift of liquor usually earns fast friendship with contractors working in a country that bans its sale. Nick, who is working the gate, is especially appreciative, and we hang out while he gives me a thorough briefing about his job.

Nick, a former Marine Forward Recon from a small town in the Midwest, is at the tail end of his contract with DynCorp. He saw working the Karzai detail as a way to make money, continue his interest in the military, and be part of a unique moment in history. A young, bearded operator, Nick takes me through the mechanics of joining the Karzai detail and the specifics of what they can expect and encounter while on duty.

"To join the detail, a résumé is sent to DynCorp, which is sent to the State Department. If the State Department then decides that the candidate qualifies, a bio is requested and more paperwork is generated. The next step is to pass a psychological test and fill out the forms to get a top-secret clearance. Then DynCorp sends the applicant a class date. The class goes through three weeks of training for close protection; driving; shooting; close-quarter battle, or CQB; hand-to-hand stuff; and other topics related to the State Department requirements for personal protection details. An average of seven applicants are dropped during the classes. Graduates are issued gear; sign a raft of paperwork, including employment contracts, insurance forms; and then are flown to Afghanistan. On arrival the scrutiny continues. When you get to the detail, the newbies are evaluated by all sections: CAT [counterassault team], snipers, PRS [primary ring security], and drivers. Then the team leaders sit down and pretty much choose who they want. If drivers got the first pick from the last class, then CAT or snipers will get the first pick from the next class. Usually the best shooters and guys go to PRS because they are the actual bodyguards."

These days the team consists of mainly ex–Delta Force, Marine recon, Navy SEALs, Army Rangers, Army Special Forces, and air force combat controllers. There are also two active-duty combat controllers assigned for close air support capabilities, which can include A-10s, Apache helicopter gunships, and B-52s. Regardless of any kind of supply shortage the military may suffer, the Karzai detail wants for nothing. According to Nick, "it is amazing the money they spend in this detail. State Department went out and bought all the same gear, radios, weapons, vehicles, that DEVGRU had when they ran the detail, and that is what we use. Today there is a B-1 bomber on station for a show of presence. The pilots decide to buzz the palace and the city of Kabul to remind everyone of America's military might. The Karzai detail still has carte blanche from the Pentagon. Ammunition requests, any type of support, never gets turned down."

All of the autos used for the Karzai detail are fully armored, and Dyn-Corp uses a combination of Lexus and Mercedes-brand SUVs. Contractors on the Karzai detail carry M-4s and Glock 19s and are each issued a personal Motorola radio for communication while on duty. Those operating the PRS have to wear collared shirts or a suit and tie over their body armor, since they're likely to be in the background during media photos, but the rest can wear whatever they want. The style of the detail still echoes the look Craige Maxim created. Some dress OGA-style with distinctive safari vests and outdoor runners, while others sport a casual look that almost says fishing or weekend hunting. They have relaxed grooming standards, and members can wear beards, goatees, and long hair.

A normal day on the detail starts the night before when Karzai returns from his day of meetings. At the front gate of his house, the Afghan chief of protocol asks Karzai when he will be coming to work the next day. That time is passed on to the shift leader of the detail. The shift leader announces the time over the radio for the leaders of the PRS, drivers, and countersniper teams. Then the team leaders from each section check in to let the shift leader know that every element of the detail knows when to be ready the next morning. Much of Karzai's work is local, but when he goes farther afield or when important dignitaries are at the palace, a specialized counterassault team (CAT) is included in the schedule.

Karzai's movements are limited because he is such a high-value target. Most of his movements are inside the secured palace area. No matter where he goes, even inside the palace grounds, he has a full contingent of foreign contractors and Afghan bodyguards walking the diamond. Nick walks me through the daily routine of protecting Karzai from assassination: "In the morning, the drivers and bodyguards . . . get ready on the boardwalk of the camp one half hour prior to the start time. They then get into the Suburbans and drive to the Man's house. The drivers take the vehicles to get washed, and PRS and the two State Department guys [shift leader and agent in charge—AIC] wait in front of the house. Afterwards, the drivers show up when the vehicles are done and stage also in front of the house. The Man comes out, and the personal detail or the 'diamond' walks Karzai to the office in the palace along with some Afghan bodyguards. The drivers follow behind the diamond with the limo and Suburban in case the Man gets ambushed on the way to the office. Snipers are covering from rooftops around the move site. Afterwards, the bodyguard stays with Karzai and rotates through positions at the office building."

Karzai spends most of each day in meetings, making Nick feel privileged for his special position watching the business of running Afghanistan. "I have gotten a chance to meet some very interesting people on this detail, especially working PRS. When you are at position three by the Man's office, you hear and see a lot. I have heard Karzai talking to George Bush, Kofi Annan, CIA and MI6 officials, and many other dignitaries. I have helped protect Pervez Musharraf from Pakistan, Hillary Clinton, Senator McCain from Arizona, president of Albania, prime minister of Belgium, and Colin Powell, plus numerous generals and foreign ambassadors, and Rush Limbaugh. I have also seen BBC, CNN, and PBS do their interviews with him, and a ton of press conferences. When the three UN officials were taken hostage in Kabul, I even overheard American generals and Karzai discuss the rescue of the three hostages, which never took place because the Afghan government negotiated with terrorists and paid the ransom. One of the hostages was the wife of the top UN official here in Afghanistan. I have also seen many jihad leaders.

"During the afternoon, Karzai goes to the mosque to pray. The detail walks him again. Then they take him to lunch in a building where he will typically eat lunch with elders from different provinces of Afghanistan. The elders are there to bitch at him and give him gifts. Snipers work this event, just in case. This is a daily occurrence for this schedule. At times in the evening, Karzai will also go and visit the king of Afghanistan, who lives on the palace grounds. That move also requires the bodyguards, drivers, and countersnipers.

"In the afternoon after his meetings, the bodyguards walk him back to the office with drivers following once again in the vehicles and snipers providing cover from buildings around the area. PRS then takes up their positions again around the office building and continue to work until the Man goes home. Protocol will give the State Department shift leader the time to go home, and he then announces it over the radio again. The Man then gets walked home just like when he was getting taken to the office in the morning. That's a typical day of keeping Karzai alive."

Though Nick may enjoy certain aspects of his position near the circle of Afghan power, he can never forget the ever-present danger in which he operates. Karzai still has a long list of enemies, and attacks can be as random as the time when someone fired two rockets at him as he walked out of his office. The rockets went high and long, and his bodyguards managed to grab him and push him into a building. There are other attempts that Nick remembers: "There are three incidents that have occurred that stick in my mind the most. The car bombing of DynCorp was a huge bomb that killed three DynCorp employees. It rocked everything around us. At the time, Karzai was outside talking to elders from another province. He was obviously nervous, but would not go inside or stop talking, even though a car bomb just went off a few thousand meters from him." The car bomb had targeted the antidrug trainers working for DynCorp and may have heralded the new direction of the war, not with the Taliban or al-Qaeda, but by drug interests against the U.S.-hired companies who aim to shut down Afghanistan's most lucrative business.

The second incident was a firefight in front of the palace. "We were standing there and I heard two sounds like a cap gun. It was rounds whizzing by my head. Then all hell broke loose and about a thousand rounds were fired. People were trying to storm the ministry of defense across the street, and the guards shot into the crowd, killing three people."

The closest call, however, came when Karzai was on a campaign tour in 2003. Despite the difficulty of traveling, Karzai had been under a lot of pressure to campaign, even though the force of U.S. public-relations dollars behind him virtually assured his election. The media was coordinated to document a campaign stop in Gardez, still a hotbed of Pashtun resistance to the U.S.-supported government.

Nick remembers: "We already knew there was a huge threat and tried to talk the Man out of going. He still insisted. We were flying two CH-47s and two Apaches. I was on the helicopter with Karzai and my team. When we approached Gardez, I looked out of the helicopter and saw a mass of people coming out of their houses. We were already on edge. Intel was coming in from our CAT teams and snipers already on the ground. It didn't look good. The first helicopter landed with all of the press. As we came in, we unbuckled and were ready to run out and form a box. We form a box or diamond to protect the Man as he walks from the helicopter to the armored vehicle. I expected to land softly, but about fifteen feet off the ground, the helicopter just dropped. A rocket went right over the top of our helicopter. The State Department shift leader yelled 'SAM!'—surface-to-air missile—over the radio. One of the vehicles on the ground also took a single shot from somewhere. Our helicopter tried to do evasive maneuvers to get us out of the area. We grabbed on to anything we could. We thought we were dead. The pilot got us onto our side, and we dropped so fast I thought we were going to crash along with everyone else. I threw my seat belt on and waited for the impact that never came. The pilot pulled it up and got us out of there. There was a rocket, maybe two fired at us. When we got back to the palace, the pilot landed, we got off, and he took off as fast as he could. You could tell he was scared shitless. Karzai was also a little shook up.

"The next day Karzai wanted to go back, but State said hell no, even though George Bush was pushing him to get out and campaign before the elections. One reporter asked Karzai why he would not go back, because most presidents would have. The press is so fucked up sometimes."

Though one might expect DynCorp to have learned a lesson after having to manage a crisis of losing their first Karzai detail because of a pay dispute, it appears that old ghosts still haunt the system. Nick has decided to leave for a job with Blackwater in Iraq, and Pete has decided to leave as well and work for his old SF captain doing training in Arizona. One of the team members mentions, "DynCorp is trying to screw our new guys out of the pay increases. DynCorp is notorious for fucking their people when it comes to money. I have been here a year and half and we threatened to walk twice. The whole detail just said they would quit because they try to screw us out of money. They have given in a few times, but it looks like they won't this time for these new guys. Most of these guys are thinking about going to other companies and breaking their contracts because of this. The State Department will blackball them from going to other companies like Blackwater that have State Department contracts if they quit. It is really screwed up."

DynCorp's contract to provide the palace guard is just one of many contracts with the U.S. government, ranging from $600 million to eradicate drugs in Colombia to $500 million to train police in Iraq. The contract to protect Karzai is only one part of a $43-million contract related to Afghanistan, a minuscule line item in DynCorp's $1.8 billion in annual revenue.

Karzai, called the "Mayor of Kabul" for his lack of influence outside the palace, remains on the American payroll and maintains hope that his American protective force will continue their work uninterrupted by contract negotiations or a loss of support by the U.S. government. In May of 2005, following violent demonstrations sparked by reports of American mistreatment of Afghan prisoners, Karzai asked President Bush for more control over the twenty thousand U.S. troops in Afghanistan. Bush declined his offer. Karzai could force the issue, but since he relied on American largesse to provide the security that keeps him alive, he couldn't push too hard without endangering his own position of privilege. Karzai is wise to take his cues from the U.S. president. Karzai no doubt closely followed the downfall of Jean-Bertrand Aristide of Haiti in the spring of 2004. The Aristide coup illustrates how effectively a security detachment funded by a private contract can not only support a leader's hold on power, but also, possibly, contribute to his overthrow.

Falling Out and Falling Down

President Aristide of Haiti contracted with the Steele Foundation in San Francisco in 1998 to provide bodyguards. The business relationship was approved by the State Department, which had a vested interest in keeping Aristide alive and in power. The initial detail was about ten bodyguards but was increased to about sixty by 2000 when it became apparent that Aristide's police could not or would not put down violent insurrections that plagued the island. Aristide was paying between $6 and $9 million a year, with a weapons package hovering around a million dollars, in a country considered to be the poorest in the Western Hemisphere. There was a direct coup attempt against Aristide on December 17, 2001, by Guy Philippe, a former police commissioner from northern Haiti. Philippe returned from exile in the neighboring Dominican Republic in early 2004 to attempt Aristide's overthrow again. In late February 2004, he and sixty armed supporters took over control of Cap-Haïtien, Haiti's second largest city, from where he started taunting and threatening Aristide. By then, Aristide's detail had been trimmed down and hovered at around twenty to twenty-five men, most of them ex-military with PSD experience.

In early February, rebels began to push against the four-thousand-man, poorly trained Haitian police force. They posed little to no resistance, and Aristide ordered another twenty-five contractors from Steele to beef up his detail. One of the assumptions was that the former military supplied by Steele might be used as trainers and force multipliers for his beleaguered police force. However, the U.S. State Department denied the additional contractors permission to travel to Haiti. By that point, Aristide had been so marginalized in his own country that he no longer served the needs of the United States.

Early in the morning of February 28, 2004, members of Aristide's security detail came to him and said they were supposed to escort him to the embassy. But actually, U.S. officials had asked Steele to pull out immediately and advised that the replacement team of twenty-five contractors would not be allowed to leave the States for Haiti. Aristide later said it was "white American soldiers" who told him that he needed to leave. Hart Brown, a contractor on the detail, however, told me that Ambassador James Foley contacted Aristide at 5:00 A.M. and said that they would be holding a press conference at the U.S. embassy to announce his resignation. The American rationale was that if Aristide did not leave, there would be bloodshed with thousands killed. Aristide and his detail were driven by his military escort right by the embassy and to the airport, where he was told to get on a waiting plane. There were U.S. soldiers in uniform, including marines, and more surprisingly, his entire security detail boarded the plane as well. It was a white plane with the only notable marking being a small U.S. flag on the tail. The window shades were pulled down, and their destination was not revealed. Strangely, some of the Steele employees brought their wives and children, so they obviously had prior knowledge of the quickly unfolding events.

At 5:45 A.M., now former president Aristide flew out on a fifty-five-seat plane with nineteen employees of the Steele Foundation and twenty members of the U.S. military. There were other U.S. operators on the plane as well, and all changed out of their uniforms into civilian clothes before they landed. After a stop in what Aristide thought was Antigua (apparently it was Miami) to set up arrangements for their exile, he and his entourage were flown to Africa to be welcomed by President François Bozizé of the Central African Republic. Aristide immediately began accusing the U.S. government of kidnapping him. The U.S. government officially stated that it was "nonsense." Secretary of State Colin Powell (a former client of Steele) said, "He was not kidnapped. We did not force him on the airplane. He went on the plane willingly."

Ken Kurtz, CEO of the Steele Foundation, refused most opportunities to comment on the circumstances of Aristide's overthrow, and would usually go little further than saying that the personal safety of Aristide and his family was the only concern of Steele.

Hart Brown, a contractor on the team that escorted Aristide out of the country, had a slightly different recollection. "At the end we all knew that there might be a conflict of interest. When the State Department asked Aristide to step down, he refused and was flown to Miami. . . . It was a decision taken at the corporate level in order to keep further contracts." Aristide knew that he would never survive without his PSD, and if the U.S. government advised Steele that it would be in the best interests of their business future to pull out, Aristide had little choice but to go with them. Even considering the implications of the U.S. State Department asking Steele to pull out, the Aristide example does not seem to have been a situation of the United States backing a coup. However, it certainly exemplifies how dependent foreign leaders may feel if they know the American government could collude to withdraw security if displeased.

Part Two

The New Breed

CHAPTER 4

Confirmed Kills

"We are not merely imperfect creatures that need improvement: we are rebels that need lay down their arms."
— C. S. Lewis, *The Problem of Pain*

It's impossible to get the attention of the waitress at the Dallas Convention Center. Buzz-cut, muscular men wearing tight-fitting golf shirts pack the tiny lounge tables, creating a forest of empty beer bottles and glasses all awaiting fresh refills. Dallas is hosting the ASIS (American Society for Industrial Security) convention, and the independent contractors, or ICs, as they call themselves, have come to network. The red glow of cigars illuminates discreet discussions of potential mercenary and security work between wide-eyed amateurs and battle-hardened pros, many just back from Afghanistan or Iraq.

On the surface, ASIS is a dull security equipment and video camera convention, but it has become a social center for contractors, as well as a sprawling showcase for high-tech gizmos and for the providers of security services. It's the summer of 2004, and this is the first ASIS conference to vividly demonstrate the impact the Iraq war has had on the security industry. Gone is the old-boy networking at the now-defunct Soldier of Fortune conventions in tattered Las Vegas hotels. Since demand for security services has skyrocketed in Iraq, ex-soldiers can find plenty of aboveboard professional employment opportunities with corporations like Blackwater, Triple Canopy, the Steele Foundation, and the other private security outfits that hide among the acres of display booths. The companies come here with slick booths and displays to attract potential clients, meet friends, hand out brochures, and talk business to business. The contractors, flush with money but light on social contacts, flock to these conventions like a band of gypsies seeking like-minded tribesmen. Informal cc'ed and bcc'ed chain e-mails let the ICs know who will be at what show, and here they can talk shop, share a room, meet with potential clients, relive past gigs, and meet new people. Since it is through this vast, interconnected web of friendships that word of new contracts usually trickles down, networking these functions can minimize the inevitable periods of unemployment any independent contractor will have during his career. Although the high day rate of contractors means that hanging out at the show is costing everyone in the room at least $400 to $600 dollars a day, they don't sweat it. Professionals know that stacking too many gigs back to back leads to burnout, and then the personal life goes to hell and you can't even keep a girlfriend, let alone an apartment. In a disconnected global marketplace where contractors bounce between hot spots and hometowns, hanging here with their tribe allows many to enjoy a sense of belonging lacking even in their own homes.

In the convention center bar, an animated and loquacious young Blackwater contractor named Shannon Campbell holds court at one of the tiny round tables. As he spins his tale for me about life as a contractor, the spread of burly men surrounding Shannon expands as more stop to listen. At thirty-five, with his dark blond hair long and hanging over his forehead, Shannon looks like a dead ringer for the star of the movie *Dune*, except that he wears the T-shirt, sandals, and ball cap of a beach bum. Small-framed and comparatively short for a contractor with an almost lithe manner of movement, Shannon does not look, act, or walk military. His handle oddly enough is Cougar Bait—not because of his catlike demeanor, but because he insists that married women always target him on his home visits.

Shannon's bravado seems to mask a concern about how other contractors perceive him, since he is one of the few nonmilitary ICs working high-level security in Iraq. But if Blackwater likes to project a certain kind of image, then Shannon must be it. In the news photos of the day the CPA handed authority over to the Iraqis, Shannon can be seen out front clearing the way for Bremer and standing guard nearby as he speaks. Blackwater also thinks highly enough of Shannon to assign him to work the Blackwater booth at ASIS. He has the rapid wit of someone used to thinking on his feet, and that personality plus his superior shooting skills have made him a favorite of management. Away from the machismo of the other contractors, Shannon will admit that he is a big fan of C. S. Lewis, particularly *The Problem of Pain*. The book he carries with him is underlined, notated, and obviously read repeatedly.

Contrary to most independent contractors, who logically transition into the security industry after having careers in the military or law enforcement, Shannon just read a news article about mercenary outfits or "private military companies" like Executive Outcomes and Sandline and decided that he'd found his calling. He ran up credit card debt and worked day jobs, such as managing his father-in-law's flower shops and funeral parlor, to pay for martial arts classes and bodyguard and weapons training, until he had racked up enough experience to break into the industry. After a brief stint at Marquez Vance Marquez (MVM), a prime security contractor for the CIA, he found a home with Blackwater, where he learned that it was his mental endurance as much as his experience that would drive a successful career in his chosen field.

As he explains to me, "Contracting is not a job for higher-ups. They just work on their tan. All they do is whine. It's a mental thing. You have to put up with the rigors of working in a place like Iraq day in and day out. But really, the number one criterion for getting over is having been there. Hey, even if you are an MP [military police], I say get your shit into Blackwater."

Getting in might be easier than staying in, since Shannon tells me that even after completing training, a contractor can be knocked out of rotation. Getting out of sync with the ninety days on/thirty days off spin cycle means a contractor could make half of what he expected. "Even if you make it, your relationship with Blackwater is very shifty. . . . We bring in twenty and send home ten—trial by fire. They can't complain if they don't make it at Blackwater. Some guys can bring it on, but most of them just worry if their gear matches. They will wear the checkered scarf, or wear a Blackwater shirt, and they think they are the shit. The guys I respect are the ones that the five of them live in a small building out in the boonies. Those guys would be allowed to give anyone shit.

"The big money is in the OGA contracts. MVM hires OGA guards. They have to have SCI clearance. You could be five foot two in every direction with one eye, but as long as you have that clearance you can still work with them. And if you want to know who is OGA? They wear two IDs—DoD and embassy. Their ID is thicker because they have to open it up to show their CIA ID.

"Blackwater can be like a fucking restaurant. You've got hundreds of people coming through. They usually fall into two categories. You've got the under-thirty crowd—the whippersnappers just looking for the biggest paycheck. Then you got the over-thirty crowd—the guys with a family and kids that are looking for a company to work for. The oldest person I know working for Blackwater is Jesse at fifty-five. His claim to fame is that he has been in an unbelievable number of shootouts and survived. Just a good ole country boy. His performance is impeccable."

Shannon wants to illustrate the world of the IC in "Bangdad," and so sketches out a cartoonish map of Baghdad on a napkin. "There is the Green Zone and there is the Red Zone. The Green Zone is a well-defined area along the Tigris with three controlled entrances. The Green Zone is this arc above the 'Schlong'—a large peninsula created by a loop in the Tigris, more politely known as the 'Thumb.' The mortars come from here," he says, pointing across the river to the northwest, "to hit the military on the tip of the Schlong. OGA is right against the Tigris. They also have an awesome lounge and chow hall. You can even get Snickers bars and soft-serve ice cream. Assassin's Gate is here. Baby Assassin's Gate is just past it. A thousand-pound truck bomb went off at Baby Assassin's Gate. It shook the entire area, lifted the dust off the sidewalk. When we heard that one back at the team house, we didn't really move, just looked at each other and said, 'Sounds like a truck bomb.' The ICs live inside the

Green Zone. The most dangerous road is Route Irish—the road from the Green Zone to BIAP [Baghdad International Airport]. The road is also called IED Alley. We go everywhere. The word in the Red Zone is that we are hired killers. 'Mercenaries' they call us. Thank God for CNN!"

Shannon breaks up in laughter, which mutates into coughing. He has to stub out his cigarette and take a drink before continuing. "Some of the Iraqi chicks come up and take pictures with us. Our ID says Blackwater contractor, but we can't admit it. They think we get into fights all the time. The military sees us all jocked up. They ask stuff like, 'How many confirmed do you get every time you out?' They have no idea what we do. They think we are hired killers, too."

Clustered around the table in the haze of smoke sit a dozen or so other contractors who occasionally interject their own comments or simply nod their heads in obvious assent to whatever Shannon describes. Hart Brown is the quietest contractor among the group. A clean-cut, small-featured, articulate business grad from Arlington, Texas, Hart seems out of place while surrounded by shaven-headed, mustachioed, burly men in the blue-collar, old-boy, mostly Deep South world of the contractor. But first impressions deceive. He worked in Haiti on the Aristide security detail for the Steele Foundation before moving on to protect Bremer in Iraq for Blackwater, and he has continued with various assignments since. "I thought the Bremer detail was another high-level gig that could benefit me in the future. Five or ten years down the road, we are likely to have major investments there. I thought if I don't have experience, I wouldn't have opportunities later. I am an unusual guy to have on the operations side." *Unusual* would be the right word, considering that Hart previously worked in nonsecurity roles for the Department of Justice and World-Com, and possesses degrees in radiological health engineering, behavioral science, criminal justice, and hazards. The thoughtful intellectual obviously spends time thinking about more than just the bang-bang aspect of his career. More important, Hart has the ability to look forward, and he recognizes some of the conflicting demands of the job.

"In Iraq I am concerned about the issue of sovereignty. I had concerns about the idea of carrying a weapon under coalition control, but now it's a sovereign state. What exactly are the liabilities of carrying a gun? . . . Bremer signed a document that said contractors were exempt. I would still be more hesitant now that sovereignty has changed." Hart has also become hesitant because he has seen how the exploding demand for security in Iraq has lowered the standards of the suppliers. "If someone called me for a gig these days, I would want to know all the specifics. Business has grown so fast that the companies are not that concerned about the people that work for them." When he was working in Iraq, Hart was also concerned about having to work in concert with the State Department's Diplomatic Security Service (DSS). A great deal of animosity exists between the DSS and security contractors in Iraq, with DSS viewing contractors as overpaid cowboys and the contractors viewing DSS details as bureaucratic losers. The discord engendered by the culture clash between the DSS and contractors disrupts the group cohesion that can be key to survival in a high-risk environment. In another decision that sets him apart from other contractors, Hart decided that the combined risks of working in Iraq were simply not worth the money, so he is taking a break. Luckily for Hart, he has degrees and experience that will soften his transition back into a non-security-related field. Most of the ex-military and small-town cops who work as ICs simply don't have that luxury.

So would he take bigger money to work in Iraq? "Iraq? I can take it or leave it." Hart shrugs.

Lamont, a hulking black ex-marine who has worked in Iraq, disagrees: "Iraq is the Super Bowl. It's where the money is flowing." Lamont's only conflict is seeing his kids through the school year and making sure he gets a good enough gig so they can live comfortably. Though normal gigs typically pay between $500 and $650 a day, he was making $850 a day doing OGA security. Lamont has been seeking new opportunities that will allow him to use the security clearances he got in the Marine Corps to maximize his income potential. Although a staunch patriot with combat experience, Lamont questions why we are in Iraq—not from a legal perspective like Hart, but from the moral perspective. "In the military I was told not to question, so I didn't. But now that I am out, I want to know exactly why we are in Iraq."

His cell phone rings, interrupting the discussion. Lamont has been try-ing to put together a team to fill a short-term PSD contract in Israel. "Do you want to do Jerusalem? It only pays five-fifty," he asks after hanging up his phone.

"Five-fifty?" Shannon says with disgust.

"Sure, why not? It's money. There is also Beijing coming up."

Shannon dismisses Beijing and Jerusalem with a wave of his hand. He has had a taste of the high-risk, high-paying contracts and now doesn't want to waste his time with anything less. He plans to go back to Al Hillah, Iraq, for what he calls a "combat" PSD—a group more likely to be attacked and thrown into the middle of a conflict. "Last time I was there I got two confirmed kills. They say you are supposed to have all kinds of things go through your head when you kill someone. I just had this guy coming at me and I aimed and squeezed. Center mass. He went down. Then another guy aimed his AK from the gut at me, and I squeezed off a few more. I didn't even think about it."

The majority of contractors could be said to resemble the Lamont model—ex-military or -police who have realized that their specialized training has limited value in the civilian world, and who, in order to pro-vide well for their families, take serious risks for the healthy pay it affords. However, roughly 10 percent of those I have met consider themselves pro-fessional career contractors who do it because they enjoy strapping on armor and heavy weapons for the well-paying, high-risk, adrenaline-packed thrill ride, like Shannon. Then, of course, there are always a hand-ful of men like Hart, who enter the arena for one or two contracts and then decide the pay is not worth the risk of death or serious injury. The di-viding line seems to be the ability to replicate an average annual income of $80,000 to $150,000 in a less-hostile occupation. Some will move on to safer, equally rewarding jobs; others will be forced to work the danger zones to maintain that level of pay.

As we sit in the bar drinking and talking, a steady stream of manufac-turing reps circle around like vultures, wanting to sell the contractors new high-tech toys. They know there is no better customer than a contractor just back from a three-month, $600+/day contract in Iraq. The salesmen hover with their matching logoed polo shirts and laptops displaying mind-numbing PowerPoint presentations. Since Shannon is the Blackwater booth person, he gets to field the sales pitches and watch the PowerPoints.

One group of manufacturers breaks through the ring of contractors and pulls out a medium-sized nondescript fiberglass briefcase they claim can shut down cell phone communications for two hundred yards—an important weapon to fight against the remote detonation of improvised explosive devices (IEDs), the weapon of choice for the insurgency. Shannon is intrigued, so we walk outside for a demo.

"Watch this," the eager sales rep giggles as he pushes a red button on the briefcase handle. The signal bars on our cell phones simply vanish. "It's designed to prevent them from firing off IEDs," he feels he has to remind us. We don't remind him that he has probably shut down communications in the entire convention hall as well. Shannon takes a card and promises to pass the information up the chain of command for review.

New high-tech gadgets designed to prevent cell phone detonation of IEDs offer just one example of how the latest war is driving rapid innovation in an exploding industry. A brief chat inside with a salesman from Scaletta Moloney Armoring is more in keeping with the traditional role of security products. He pitches a $118,000, six-thousand-pound black limousine as the perfect solution for the CEO with disgruntled employees. The stretch version goes for $135,000. Either would stop a .44 Magnum bullet, an M61 round, or even a M67 mine detonated eight inches below the car, and the windows are designed to neither blow out or in with the glass heavily laminated in a thick plastic casing. Scaletta Moloney also makes a nice GMC Surburban, which has become the de facto vehicle of choice in Iraq. The former market of celebrities and CEOs who required armor-plated conveyance is chump change compared with the demand created by Iraq and the War on Terror.

It's late afternoon and the tedious displays of locks, video cameras, iris ID systems, and steel barriers have become a red, white, and blue blur. The hallmark of the post-9/11 world is that suddenly the use of everything from padlocks to guns has become not just necessary but somehow deeply patriotic. The bustle of the show vividly showcases the recent explosion in the industry; the post–Cold War enemy is "the terrorists," and everyone seems to be entering the security business. Opportunities abound for clever and aggressive upstarts, similar to the early heady days of the dot-com boom. Even the convention's keynote speaker, former New York City mayor Rudolph Giuliani, now runs a private security company with blue-chip clients. The world has apparently become a much more dangerous place to do business.

The World Market

Before 9/11, the industry had only a limited market for the services of the men who now flock to these conferences looking for IC opportunities. The war in Afghanistan opened the door to more widespread employment of independent security contractors, and then Iraq kicked that door off its hinges, stomped on it, burned it, and scattered the ashes. Iraq has been to the private security industry what the development of the first user-friendly Web browser was to the dot-com boom.

Afghanistan had been a swift and clean war with few of the troubles that would come to haunt the U.S. military in Iraq. The full force of American non-nuclear air strikes and killing technology was brought to bear on a ragtag Taliban army and their contingents of mostly Pakistani foreign fighters. Although it was initially a covert war spearheaded by the CIA, the conflict made for great TV and newsprint as the hounds of media dramatically detailed the dark-robed and medieval Taliban encounters with the high-tech American leviathan. Special Forces riding in on horseback to coordinate surgical air strikes made it look like the Magnificent Seven had taken on Darth Vader. Although the offensive quickly overthrew the Taliban and caused the dispersal of the foreign legions supported by bin Laden, it seemed too easy. The decision to go "lightly" into Afghanistan reflected elements of both strategy and necessity. Conventional forces simply could not be mobilized quickly enough and planners wanted to avoid well-learned Soviet errors in judgment, such as the massive deployment of boots on the ground. The light American bootprint on Afghan land somewhat stymied the resistance impulses of its people, just as certainly as the massive military presence in Iraq has engendered a resentment that has led to a state of seemingly permanent insecurity.

Plans for the use of "Big Army" to invade Iraq had been drawn up in the early 1990s, and throughout the decade a number of future top-ranking members of the Bush administration seemed to nurture hope that America could one day find a reason to use them. Bush's neocon advisors had long obsessed about Iraq as a critical linchpin in some kind of modern vision of American manifest destiny. The idea that America needed to exploit its global hegemony by using its military power to protect its domain of influence harked back to a 1992 Defense Planning Guidance (DPG) drafted by the then–undersecretary of defense for policy planning, Paul Wolfowitz, and rewritten by then–Secretary of Defense Dick Cheney. Wolfowitz and Cheney, along with Donald Rumsfeld and the neoconservative cabal that populated the membership rolls of the Project for the New American Century (PNAC), echoed this same theme in their 1997 statement of principles: "We need to accept responsibility for America's unique role in preserving and extending an international order friendly to our security, our prosperity, and our principles." In their January 1998 letter to President Clinton and May 1998 letter to Congressional leaders, the PNAC zeroed in on Saddam Hussein, asserting that his removal should be the number one priority in the formulation of any U.S. security strategy. Since a majority of the names that appeared on these PNAC issuances would later be seen on the payrolls of the Bush administration, it is not surprising that charges have persisted that faulty intelligence was knowingly promulgated to advance predetermined policy decisions.

The 9/11 attacks had made attacking and overthrowing the Taliban regime an obvious imperative, but shifting the public's focus toward the treachery and danger of Saddam Hussein took a skilled, and what later appeared to be intentionally misleading, marketing campaign on the part of U.S. and UK leaders. Riding off the Afghan success story and buttressed by meteoric public approval poll numbers, President Bush and his aides began by expanding the scope of the amorphous War on Terror. In his February 2002 State of the Union address, President Bush made the first indications of the war's future targets when he branded Iran, Iraq, and

North Korea the "axis of evil" and particularly singled out Saddam Hussein for a scathing description of the brutality of his regime. In the months that followed, representatives of the Pentagon, State Department, and White House worked to convince the American public and the world that Saddam Hussein possessed and was willing to use weapons of mass destruction. Direct links to bin Laden and al-Qaeda were also professed in order to weave the secular socialist dictatorship into a radical Islamist 9/11 conspiracy. By the time of the U.S. midterm elections that fall, polls showed that a majority of Americans were supporting Bush's case for war, and Congress had passed the Iraq Resolution authorizing the use of force against Saddam.

Though most of the world vehemently opposed the invasion of Iraq, the U.S. also managed to secure the support of a "Coalition of the Willing" to aid them in this questionable endeavor. Often called the "coalition of the billing," in reference to the amount of American financial assistance received by those pledging support, the coalition offered a thin veneer of multilateral spin for an otherwise U.S.-led and -financed invasion. America's closest partner, the United Kingdom, offered a significant contribution of muscle, but there was a long dropoff to the next willing coalition partner. The Bush administration never detailed exactly what the thirty publicly acknowledged and fifteen "secret" members of the coalition brought to the war effort. Those identified by the White House ranged from the still chaotic and poverty-stricken Afghanistan to the Solomon Islands, a tiny Pacific Island nation with no army, whose prime minister asked politely to be taken off the list after learning from the press of his nation's apparent willingness. Despite rhetorical comparisons to the coalition that had beaten back Iraq's invasion of Kuwait, it was clear to anyone who looked at the numbers that no such equivalent was gathering strength to return for a second round with Saddam. With about a quarter of a million Americans, 45,000 British, and a smattering of a few thousand soldiers contributed by other coalition members, the total number of troops in the theater added up to less than half of that mounted for the first Gulf War.

Critics cited the dramatic differential in troop strength as proof that the Pentagon was botching the invasion, though they would concede that the new coalition would face an emaciated shadow of the previously formidable Iraqi army. What most comparisons did not even address was that the raw troop numbers from 1991 could not really even provide an adequate benchmark against which to hold the 2003 figures, since a diminished requirement for men in uniform had resulted from how the U.S. military had been transformed over the preceding decade.

Outsourcing Support

The end of the Cold War left the United States standing alone on the world stage—the sole superpower with a massive standing military and no pressing threat to confront. This watershed event occurred against a backdrop of reform through the 1980s that had already begun to chip away at the traditional force structure of the U.S. military.

The U.S. military has relied on civilians to play support roles on an ad hoc basis ever since George Washington hired teamsters to ferry supplies and employed mercenaries to train troops during the Revolutionary period, but it wasn't until after the Vietnam War that the Department of Defense started looking for a way to formalize the partnerships. The necessary postwar reductions in force structure had left the U.S. military actively seeking a means to outsource support functions, and in December 1985, the first LOGCAP—the U.S. Army's Logistics Civil Augmentation Program—was introduced.

The LOGCAP has allowed the U.S. Army to employ predetermined corporations to provide logistics support across a broad spectrum of services such as electric supply, sanitation, shelter, maintenance, transport, food service, and construction—essentially, all the more mundane but necessary parts of fielding an army. The basic idea is that a large infrastructure company can manage an open-ended, cost-plus contract to be on call for rapid deployment in support of any U.S. operations that may arise. The LOGCAP provided a way for the army to be prepared for a rapid response to a rising crisis, without the burden of having to maintain a long-term support capability throughout a time of peace. The concept could be a force multiplier in contingency operations but was eventually viewed more importantly as a valuable way to save costs and deal with the dramatic and necessary post–Soviet era downsizing of the military. First utilized on an ad hoc basis, LOGCAP did not take its fully actualized umbrella form until after 1992 when then–secretary of defense Dick Cheney contracted Brown and Root for a $3.9-million study about how the U.S. military could fully maximize the benefits of outsourcing support functions to private corporations.

Halliburton subsidiary Kellogg, Brown and Root is the preeminent military contractor. Its corporate predecessor, Brown and Root, built 85 percent of military infrastructure during the Vietnam War. Liberal critics had derided the Texas-based company's close ties to Lyndon Johnson long before they had a modern target for scorn in Vice President Dick Cheney, Halliburton's CEO from 1995 to 2000. In 1992, Cheney tasked Brown and Root with planning and budgeting the theoretical logistical support for more than a dozen different fictional scenarios that could require the deployment of twenty thousand troops in five base camps for six months. The resulting still-classified report apparently convinced Cheney of the utility of having one megacontractor with an open-ended and overarching capability to manage logistics support, since Brown and Root soon after netted the army's first five-year umbrella LOGCAP contract. By the end of 1992, Brown and Root had a presence in Somalia working in support of the U.S. military's Operation Restore Hope. Over the next few years, Brown and Root ran support operations for the U.S. military in Rwanda, Zaire, southwest Asia, Haiti, Kuwait, and the Balkans. In 1997, Brown and Root lost the lucrative LOGCAP to DynCorp, though the renamed Kellogg, Brown and Root won it back in 2001 for the extended term of ten years.

The U.S. military's first experiment in formalized reliance on private firms for its logistics support was considered a success, even though Brown and Root garnered criticism for its apparent failure to control costs in the Balkans. Even despite the possible overbilling outlined in a Government Accountability Office (GAO) assessment of the Balkans operations, a 1997 Logistics Management Institute study determined that Brown and Root had done with $462 million and 6,766 civilian employees what would have otherwise required 8,918 troops and $638 million.

Transitioning to a greater reliance on civilian-provided services could not have happened at a more pressing time, since the military was concurrently undergoing its needed post–Cold War reduction in manpower. Between 1991 and 2001, active-duty military forces were reduced more than 30 percent to about 1.5 million soldiers, but the introduction and expansion of outsourcing for noncritical support functions allowed the Pentagon to undertake deeper cuts without seriously endangering response capabilities. As the older generation of military leaders grew to accept the utility of contractors, their use has increased dramatically across the spectrum.

Though the invasion force for Gulf War II may have been roughly half of what had been mounted to take on Saddam the first time, traveling along with them would be another army made up of American and foreign civilians who would cook their food, wash their clothes, clean their messes, and even handle shipping their dead bodies home. A decade earlier there might have been one private contractor for every fifty soldiers, but by the second Gulf War, the ratio had increased to one in ten. Only a handful of those, however, would be specifically security contractors, since the industry would not really find a lucrative market until after the number of troops allotted for the invasion proved incapable of securing the peace.

Confidence in the superiority of Western technology may have contributed to short-sightedness about the long-term prospects for the invasion and the low-tech and manpower-heavy requirements of occupation and reconstruction. American military prowess was more than capable of quickly deposing Saddam and decimating his already-crippled military, but the requirements needed for invading a country differ greatly from those for occupying one. Before the war, generals trained in military science calculated the number of troops it would take to invade and occupy Iraq, and most suggested figures in the area of half a million. In late February 2003, army chief of staff General Eric Shinseki estimated that several hundred thousand soldiers would be needed to occupy the country, and later reports put his precise figure at four hundred thousand. Shinseki had created models based on the troop presence in Kosovo and Bosnia, and extrapolated from that to come up with his recommendation for Iraq. Within forty-eight hours, deputy secretary of defense Paul Wolfowitz had castigated Shinseki, referring to his assessment as being "wildly off the mark." The Pentagon wanted to believe that the occupation would require perhaps seventy-five-thousand troops. Eventually, circumstances would prove otherwise, and as in Afghanistan but to a much greater degree, security contractors would be moved in to assist.

An Explosion of Opportunity

On March 20, 2003, over a quarter million troops began crossing the border of Kuwait, commencing the invasion of Iraq and Persian Gulf War II. Like a well-planned product rollout, the U.S. government had sold the American public the idea that the invasion of Iraq was the next necessary phase in the War on Terror. The initial invasion achieved the Bush administration's highly touted "Mission Accomplished" milestone at a rapid pace, with coalition forces barreling into Baghdad and driving the Iraqi dictator into hiding. The unprecedented media-embedding program saturated the airwaves with scenes of post-Saddam euphoria. But then the looting began.

Baghdad rapidly descended into a maelstrom as rioting mobs of desperate Iraqis stripped every conceivable item of value—down to the staplers and copper wiring—from government ministries, shops, police stations, and private residences. The chaos sparked a sense of rampant impunity as a violent criminality engulfed the capital and other parts of the country. Up until then, the army's being too far ahead of its supply chain had caused the only hiccup in the invasion. But now a critical decision had to be made: increase troop levels or manage the consequences. Considering the political costs associated with abruptly increasing troop strength soon after the invasion, not to mention the signal of weakness it would send our enemies, that option was never seriously discussed.

With the practice of outsourcing well established by 2003, it only took this explosion of instability to create the wealth of opportunity for the private industry of armed men. On April 18, less than a week after widespread looting began, DynCorp was awarded a contract—estimated to be worth over $50 million—to assess the security situation and hire one thousand contractors to begin training for the creation of a law enforcement, judicial, and penal system. The DynCorp contract offered the first postinvasion bulk commissioning of security contractors, but it really wouldn't be until the reconstruction phase got under way that opportunities began to flood the IC job market.

After the looters ran out of things to steal, a general sense of disgruntled complacency settled over much of the country. Even though many Iraqis blamed the occupiers for creating lawlessness in what had previously been a brutally secure society, most Iraqis opted to wait patiently and peacefully for their new masters to fulfill their promises of electricity, jobs, and reconstruction. Violent criminal activity certainly far surpassed what it had been in Saddam's days, but it wasn't as pervasive as during the apex of the looting phase. More ominously, however, in addition to the violence of normal criminality, signals of a more serious underlying problem for the coalition began to surface. By June, a number of targeted attacks had prompted the UN to issue a report identifying the early signs of an organized insurgency. The longer the occupation stretched on, the more the occupiers faced a violent resistance—including but not solely pro-Baathist and former regime elements, plus a small legion of foreign jihadis. President George Bush and his advisors, who chose the course of invasion and occupation, would have been well-served to incorporate into their thinking the sage observations of Colonel T. E. Lawrence, who eight decades earlier had described the region as "a tissue of small jealous principalities incapable of cohesion, and yet always ready to combine against an outside force."

What has resulted is an amalgam of anti-U.S. groups of varying size, motivations, tactics, and capabilities all jostling to kill as many coalition troops, contractors, or "collaborators" as possible. Group leaders have a seemingly endless well of anger and resentment to exploit for their motivating rhetoric and a large population of out-of-work men and disaffected youth to employ. It's not so much a classic insurgency or low-intensity conflict, but more akin to business as usual in places like Chechnya or the Gaza Strip.

It was against this backdrop of worsening violence and resistance that the reconstruction of Iraq by Western corporations was supposed to occur. In January 2003, the DoD had established the Office of Reconstruction and Humanitarian Assistance (ORHA) and appointed General Jay Garner as its director. After the initial phase of the invasion, Garner transitioned into the role of chief of the interim Iraqi administration; although, by May 2003, ORHA had been incorporated into the new Coalition Provisional Authority, and Garner was replaced by Ambassador L. Paul Bremer. The CPA and Bremer were responsible for managing the reconstruction of Iraq while working to establish an Iraqi-led and democratically elected civilian administration.

The United States chose a passive-aggressive approach of occupation by outsourcing the problem of security to the corporations and entities that wanted to do business there. Contractors would simply subcontract out for their own security and fold it into their operating costs. Contracts for construction work, electioneering, education, or even information services would all have a significant amount allotted for security, adding up to almost 50 percent of the original contract in some contracts after the situation began to spiral out of control. Operating in an active war zone—as Iraq is considered by the Pentagon and State Department, though not by the White House—requires hiring private companies who can supply everything from armored cars to concrete barriers to guns to operators trained to use those guns. And thus began the PSC boom.

Private corporations had worked in the war zones of previous conflicts, but usually far from the lines of active combat, never among such a hostile local population, and never on the scale of Iraq. The $2 billion pledged to rebuild Afghanistan would be a minuscule amount compared with the almost $20 billion for Iraq initially budgeted by Congress in October 2003. Even that initial calculation would prove insufficient, and by the summer of 2005, the projection of reconstruction costs through 2007 had risen to an estimated $55 billion, an influx of funding that has benefited the private sector in a way previously unimagined.

Adding to the already-heightened tensions of the occupation, the influx of Western corporations tasked with reconstruction contracts increased resentment toward the American presence. In a population experiencing an almost 50 percent rate of unemployment, the imported foreign workers were viewed as taking Iraqi jobs. Filipinos, Nepalese, and other labor export nations did the job of hungry Iraqis simply because some firms felt that Iraqis could not be trusted. The occupying power's intention to use Iraqi oil revenue to pay those foreigners just added to the burn.

In addition to those corporations that had come to Iraq to pursue reconstruction contracts or other independent business opportunities, an ever-expanding web of companies providing support services to the military under the overall purview of LOGCAP each required their own private security contingents. Based on the terms of its LOGCAP agreement, KBR (Kellogg, Brown and Root) enjoys protection from the army when its workforce is performing a task in the area of operations. However, to adequately provide for the entire range of military requirements, KBR subcontracts out extensively to other companies, which are each left to provide for their own security.

Some subcontractors hire local Iraqis to provide a deterrent, and some may operate under the radar without any armed protection, but the general consensus is that a contingent of gunslingers is a prerequisite for doing business in Iraq. Even KBR supplements its military guard by sometimes issuing weapons to its civilian employees. Some companies, like Zapata Engineering—which handles the gathering, transportation, and demolition of ordnance—have created their own internal security elements. However, the needs of the majority have sparked a vast market of opportunity for those who specialize in the provision of armed guards.

In a matter of months, private security in Iraq went from a fledgling cottage industry to a multibillion-dollar endeavor, with Blackwater, HART, Triple Canopy, DynCorp, ArmorGroup, Control Risks Group (CRG), Erinys, and Aegis emerging as the big players. The official Pentagon estimation of the recognized private security industry presence in Iraq by late 2003 hovered at around sixty companies with approximately twenty-five thousand employees. The vast majority of these companies did not even exist before the invasion of Iraq. Further, that number would be much higher, perhaps even double, if smaller start-ups, Iraqi security companies, and unregistered internal security divisions like Zapata's had been taken into consideration.

This large-scale and rapid transition to relying on independent contractors for security also created a contingency of armed men in Iraq working ostensibly in support of the overall U.S. mission, but as a nonmilitary entity—blurring the line between civilian and combatant. The problems were myriad: issuing IDs and weapons permits; chain-of-command ambiguity; contrary objectives; coordination of security convoys; and friendly fire incidents, not only from coalition troops firing on contractors mistaken as potential insurgents, but also between contractors and other contractors. Considering that their "uniform" resembles that of a covert paramilitary, it's not surprising that insurgency websites have crowed about striking a blow to the CIA after an attack on a convoy of contractors.

Beyond the specific operational difficulties PSCs have encountered in Iraq, the explosion of the industry has raised some other troubling issues that may require a robust public debate regarding the industry's future. There are many questions as to how a myriad of heavily armed private armies can serve the purpose of the U.S. military and foreign policy.

Academics like Peter Singer of the Brookings Institution and Deborah Avant of George Washington University have been closely tracking the developments of this growing sector since its emergence in the mid-1990s. Singer's 2003 book, *Corporate Warriors: The Rise of the Privatized Military Industry*, focuses on the emergence and shift of mercenary armies into corporate structures and the resultant problems and likely scenarios attached to outsourcing security and warfare. He is a well-known critic of the current trend in unregulated security companies but still views it as understandable. Even though the dominant view in military circles is that the privatization of support services is cost-effective, as Singer explains to me in an interview: "It's not about economic cost savings; it's about political cost savings. When things go wrong, you simply blame the company." It is

clear that beyond convenience and cost savings, relying on private contractors also makes it possible to outsource fault. Abuses are not unusual in
the military or private sector, but the consequences are quite different.
Where trigger-happy soldiers may spark an international incident and
shame a nation, a contractor would simply be fired and his employer criticized. In cases where employees or contracting companies are found
to have been involved in questionable activities, they simply lose their
contract. There is no transparency and little accountability for security
providers in Iraq. Outsourcing blame also keeps the military or government firewalled from prosecution, since contracts provide legal protection
and provide a plausible deniability that the government had officially authorized any incident of abuse.

Singer believes that an ever-increasing reliance on the private sector
also removes many of the responsibilities that would be expected from the
military and creates extensive opportunities for scenarios that could dan-
gerously compromise a mission. Guarding his words carefully for fear of
provoking a lawsuit with a carelessly phrased quote, Singer says he sees the
potential for commercial companies simply quitting midcontract or
charging usurious prices, since they make their calculations on a cost-
profit basis, rather than on a duty-honor one. His methodically researched
book cites the numerous examples of financial, moral, and legal abuses of
the contractor system—overcharging, running local scams, criminal activity, and more. According to Singer, these problems result from poor oversight of an exploding industry where even the start-ups can go from zero
to a multimillion-dollar contract in just a few weeks.

Deborah Avant, a political science professor and director of the Institute for Global and International Studies at the Elliott School of International Affairs at George Washington University, is less critical than Singer
but is still concerned that the increased employment of PSCs encourages
the growth of an industry that can provide the tools of war in exchange for
the payment of money rather than the blessing of the citizenry. In her
opinion, the major issue created by the hiring of private security companies is that the ones who hire the companies decide who gets to use force.

Avant sees the growth in the private sector as expected and normal, but she sees a dark cloud ahead. "It [the use of contractors] shifts authority from the Congress to the Executive." Where Congress would have to have a full vote on and an appropriation of funds for any military action, an aggressive executive branch could dip into a variety of sources to subsidize a small force of contractors. Avant is aware of the written and unwritten checks and balances of corporations doing business with the government, but she is concerned that private providers of security can operate well outside of the media radar, and thus without the knowledge of the U.S. taxpayers or the majority of Congress. "It erodes transparency by putting so much information in so many different areas. Troops get covered about five times more than contractors," she notes.

There is much discussion over just how far security companies will expand in services. One of the fears is that these companies could morph into offensive organizations, effectively becoming proxy armies or mercenaries. As it stands now, security contractors serve a wide variety of functions in the war zone, with the primary constraint being that they can serve only in a defensive capability. If a private security contractor were assigned the offensive duties of a regular soldier, that fine line between contractor and mercenary would be breached, and the PSC managing the contractor would have to begin identifying itself instead as a PMC—a private military company, the euphemism for a provider of mercenary services.

In Iraq today, probably their most visible and risky role comes in providing security escorts, particularly along the deadly Route Irish running to and from Baghdad International Airport (BIAP). Like Roman gladiators stepping out to do battle every day, a handful of SUVs representing a variety of companies can always be found waiting at the airport to drive their incoming passengers the short but deadly distance into Baghdad. They roll at high speeds, firing their weapons to keep other cars away, treating everything along the way as if it could be a VBIED, aka vehicleborne improvised explosive device, aka suicide car bomber. The statistics showing the frequency of attacks along the appropriately nicknamed "IED

Alley" justifies their aggressive driving manner. In addition to ensuring safe transit for everything from a carload of journalists, diplomats, or businessmen to a truckload of kitchen equipment or construction supplies, private contractors also provide static security for embassies, oil pipelines, government buildings, and other critical infrastructure. Security contractors train Iraqi soldiers and police, perform intelligence gathering, mount aerial surveillance, and handle bomb-sniffing canines. Even if they may not be technically working on behalf of the U.S. military in many of these roles, Deborah Avant says security contractors have become legitimate targets for insurgent attacks because they perform roles in support of the U.S. mission and ensure the presence of U.S.-appointed political figures and corporations.

During Blackwater's highly visible contract protecting Bremer, insurgents were reportedly offering a $30,000 bounty for the life of any one of the Blackwater bodyguards. Not only did these contractors have to operate with full knowledge of a sizable bounty on their heads, but they also knew that the man they were tasked with protecting represented the highest-value target available in the war zone. Some estimates put the price on Bremer's life as high as $45 million.

To the blossoming insurgency, Paul Bremer represented a singular symbol of unwanted Western occupation, and Blackwater had to keep this in mind when determining the level of manpower and firepower required to ensure his safety. Jay Garner initially only had a small contingent of soldiers from the Florida National Guard as protectors, but the rapidly deteriorating conditions and Bremer's insistence on moving around the country meant that he needed something significantly more substantial. Erik Prince and Blackwater were tasked to come up with a unique solution using funds from an existing DynCorp State Department contract. And so, the famous Bremer Detail—a fast-moving contingent of hired guns backed by massive firepower—was created.

DynCorp already possessed a contract to provide security for State Department needs worldwide—including guarding diplomatic installations and Afghan president Hamid Karzai—but subcontracted out the Iraq domain to Blackwater. Although the cost for Bremer's praetorian guard was never advertised, a few months after they won the job, on August 24, 2003, a separate contract for $21.3 million was awarded to Blackwater. In a good example of how new companies are formed to fill a contract in this PSC boom, a new division, Blackwater Security Consulting LLC, was registered with the North Carolina secretary of state one month later.

Blackwater's Bremer detail initially comprised thirty-six independent security contractors, a fleet of SUVs, two bomb-sniffing canine teams with handlers, four pilots, four aerial gunners, a ground crew, and three Boeing MD-530 "Little Bird" helicopters. Later, Blackwater would supplement the team with three armored Mamba trucks with swivel mounts for PKM machine guns, a Saracen armored carrier, and a CASA 212 for transport. The detail made an impressive show of force, and purposefully so, because its conduct was regulated by the State Department's rules of engagement for a personal security detail. A PSD most importantly functions as a deterrent against attack, and if hit, they are authorized to engage the assailants only until the VIP is "off the X," or evacuated away from the scene. Although many in the left-wing press call this group of armed ex-soldiers and ex-cops "mercenaries," the government agencies consider them well-armed security guards. Either way, Blackwater was essentially fielding a small private militia, and for the first time in history, Paul Bremer, a civilian contractor, protected by a small army of private security contractors, was running an occupied country.

On Rules and Resentment

Ambassador Paul Bremer, an independent contractor assuming the position of proconsul, arrived in Iraq in May 2003 with supreme authority to make sweeping changes and radical reforms to post-Saddam Iraq. A retired but seasoned diplomat, Bremer had been hired away from his position as CEO of Marsh Crisis Consulting, a company that had been formed by Marsh and McLennan Companies after nearly three hundred of their employees died in the World Trade Center.

Bremer may have been touted as a good choice for his diplomatic style, but his strong hand and seemingly unlimited power angered many Iraqis. He was widely viewed as a new dictator squandering Iraqi oil revenue on corrupt and wasteful foreigners from the same palaces where Saddam had squandered Iraqi oil revenue on his own corrupt and wasteful programs. The Coalition Provisional Authority (CPA) itself reeked of Orwellian Newspeak. The "coalition" was essentially America, the effort seemed more permanent than provisional, and the chaos in Iraq offered proof that it had no authority.

The CPA did seem to create an ancient form of mercantile company. The United States had invaded the sovereign state of Iraq, deposed its ruler, vanquished its army, and seized control of its treasury. They then installed essentially a business manager who released dicta designed to encourage commerce between coalition countries and the instantly created industry of "rebuilding Iraq." Although war-profiteering is generally frowned upon, the CPA made no effort to mask the lucrative opportunity it was trying to create for corporate interests. Economic shock therapy and all-powerful market forces were expected to quickly set Iraq on a course for success. To get started, Bremer would just need a big piggy bank—the newly minted Development Fund for Iraq—to fund all the corporations who were positioned to help with and/or earn a profit from the coalition's professed selfless act of liberation and reconstruction.

On March 20, 2003, President Bush had signed Executive Order 13290 allowing confiscation of Iraqi property in the United States and funds in American banks. On May 22, UN Resolution 1483 outlined the responsibilities of the occupying powers "to promote the welfare of the Iraqi people through the effective administration of the territory . . . ," and to that end allowed that 95 percent of the income from petroleum export sales be diverted into the new Development Fund for Iraq—a shift over from the questionable UN Oil for Food program that had been designed to prevent Saddam from looting the income for his own purposes. The first CPA regulation Bremer issued after arriving in Baghdad established the legal basis of the CPA with him as administrator, and Regulation Number Two made him the sole comptroller of the Development Fund for Iraq.

For other early official acts as head of the CPA, Bremer issued Order 1, beginning the de-Baathification of Iraqi society. This banned all Baath party members from any "positions of authority and responsibility in Iraqi society," effectively ostracizing 10 percent of the Iraqi population or between 1.5 and 2.5 million people. Order 2 disbanded the Iraqi Army and several Iraqi ministries, essentially cutting off employment or income for over four hundred thousand Iraqis. These two orders essentially created a pool of unemployed potential foot soldiers or suicide bomb fodder for the opponents of the occupation, and Order 19 and Order 14 handed them a propaganda victory they could use as a recruiting tool. Order 19 defined the legally permissible freedom of assembly and placed restrictions on the Iraqis' right to protest, and Order 14 outlined the limitations on their newfound freedom of the press. Neither of these orders were particularly unreasonable, but they did help the budding insurgency make the case that American rhetoric of freedom and democracy was little more than an elixir to lull the Iraqi people into complacency over the invasion of their country.

Further, as Bremer's numerous edicts continued with a clear slant to mercantile benefit rather than humanitarian assistance, they exacerbated the domestic paranoia that the United States had invaded the country to steal its oil and money. Even if these measures were taken with the best of intentions, to give economic shock therapy to an inarguably stagnant economy, they were not perceived as thus by the general population. Baath party assets and businesses were seized, 100 percent foreign ownership and repatriation of profits were allowed, forty-year contracts intended to ensure that any ventures created under U.S. occupation would endure, the banking system was privatized, a flat tax of 15 percent was created, excise and duties were abolished. All of these orders were issued in English with the Arabic translation lagging behind, underscoring the growing impression that the American occupier was taking control of the country for its own selfish purposes.

In the early months of Bremer's tenure as proconsul, the Iraqi people only saw marginal improvement in their economic status and way of life. As the desperate times dragged on, resentment grew, and so did the insurgency.

To add another point of tension to the already-delicate situation, the expanding reconstruction was increasing the presence of well-armed but non-military men. Their ubiquitous and highly visible security convoys drove aggressively, pushing uncooperative cars out of the way or firing shots to disable them or their drivers. No one maintains any kind of statistics on how many civilians have been injured or killed by security contractors, but anecdotal evidence from the many conversations I have had with ICs on this subject indicates that it is not an insignificant number. Even so, at the date of this writing in early 2006, no private security contractors have yet suffered legal consequences for causing any collateral damage in Iraq.

In one incident related to me by a contractor who witnessed it, the driver of a Ford F-250 "bump truck" in a security convoy drove right over the top of a small car carrying an Iraqi family while maneuvering to escape a potentially dangerous situation. In the aftermath, the car looked fairly well crushed, but the contractor has no idea if the family lived or died since the convoy fled the scene. The incident was not reported at the time, and the driver of the truck was never investigated or disciplined for the action. The contractor who witnessed the incident wanted to report it to appropriate authorities but felt he would have jeopardized his own job by doing so.

Bush had opened up the War on Terror by issuing a license to kill with his post-9/11 presidential finding authorizing targeted assassination, but it would be Bremer's Order 17 that would really unleash the security contractors in Iraq. The relevant clause of Order 17 states: "Contractors shall be immune from Iraqi legal process with respect to acts performed by them pursuant to the terms and conditions of a Contract or any subcontract thereto. Nothing in this provision shall prohibit MNF Personnel [Coalition forces] from preventing acts of serious misconduct by Contractors, or otherwise temporarily detaining any Contractors who pose a risk of injury to themselves or others, pending expeditious turnover to the appropriate authorities of the Sending State. In all such circumstances, the appropriate senior representative of the Contractor's Sending State in Iraq shall be notified." In commoner's English, this means that the Iraqi legal system would have no jurisdiction to prosecute a contractor, even for a charge as serious as murder, if the incident occurred while he was on the job.

The appropriate process is supposed to be for the contractor to be repatriated and tried for any alleged offenses in his home country. That sounds like a reasonable solution, considering the state of the Iraqi justice system, but it just doesn't actually happen in practice. Considering the impression I have gotten from contractors with extensive experience in Iraq about the frequency of accidental civilian casualties at the hands of contractors, it is amazing to me that not a single security contractor—and by that I strictly refer to the independent contractors employed in a security position by a PSC—has come under criminal investigation for any offense.

A couple of cases have set precedent for other types of contractors to be tried in their home countries for an offense committed in a war zone—such as the CACI (California Analysis Center, Inc.) and Titan translators charged after the public outcry over Abu Ghraib. David Passaro, an ex–Green Beret and independent contractor employed by the CIA as part of a paramilitary unit hunting terrorists in Afghanistan, was actually charged under terms of the Patriot Act for the death of a detainee he interrogated too harshly. Since both of these cases were brought only after controversy had erupted over the revelations about torture carried out at Abu Ghraib, it raises the question about whether the prevailing powers care about accountability only when the glare of the public spotlight is upon them.

Order 17 dissolved with the handover of Iraq, and in the ensuing time contractors have supposedly been subject to Iraqi law. For safety reasons as much as for avoidance of legal trouble, contractors do not stick around a scene after an incident. After numerous assaults mounted by insurgents disguised as official Iraqi security forces, contractors also refuse to pull over for sirens and flashing lights. So it would be up to the Iraqi police to investigate an incident, track it back to determine the individual at fault (if that would even be possible), and then appeal to the American forces for cooperation in picking up the person and turning him over to Iraqi custody—a highly unlikely scenario. If any grumbling is made over the inappropriate or overly violent behavior of any security contractor, his employers, if they judge the person to be a liability, will typically release him from his contract and send him home. He may end up out of a job, but he is unlikely to see the inside of a prison cell.

Order 17 established a virtually nonexistent standard of accountability for security contractors in Iraq that has persisted, though the specific legal grounds may have since shifted. This order not only gave non-Iraqi private security companies a "get out of jail free" card, but from what I have learned in my travels, it altered their view of the operating environment. Instead of being able to abide by local limits of force or regulation, many security contractors view Iraq as a lawless wasteland, "the sandbox," a land where one must kill or be killed. To contractors bolting out of safe blastwall-gated enclaves in armored SUVs, the local population most often appears simply as a blur of dark faces viewed through gun sights.

Allowing these armed groups to operate with impunity and very little oversight is disquieting, but it is a credit to the quality of many of the security companies and the training and discipline of their employees that there have not been any major controversies. For the most part, the vast majority of security contractors working in Iraq abide by the rules of engagement originally established by the State Department and dramatically simplified by the head of security for the Project and Contracting Office (PCO), retired British Brigadier General Anthony Hunter-Choat. The simplest and most concise summary of the security contractors' rules of engagement in Iraq is "If they shoot at you, shoot back."

That seems like such an easy rule to follow, and in the early months after the invasion—perhaps up to the entire first year—it was. However, as occupation stretched on through 2003 without providing any significant benefits to the typical Iraqi, resentment grew, the insurgency gained strength, and contractors began to recognize increasing looks of sheer hatred directed at them when they moved through civilian areas. Working in an insecure environment, and facing an ill-defined enemy that hides easily among the civilian population, that somewhat intangible but definite shift in the mood on the street can greatly influence the rapidity of the trigger finger's response. Then the Fallujah attack on Blackwater contractors changed everything.

The four contractors who died that day did not even have time to fire back. The vivid brutality of that attack put many contractors on edge and removed this naïve assumption that they were somehow immune from targeted attacks since they technically enjoy a quasicivilian status. After watching the deaths and bodily desecration of some of their colleagues played over and over again on a seemingly endless loop on TV, security contractors became much more ready to shoot if they felt threatened.

Just a few days after the incident in Fallujah, two of the most significant incidents involving contractors in the Iraq war occurred, though the reporting on these developments was overshadowed by other events throughout the country. Though the rules of engagement require that security contractors shoot only to break contact with an attacker, the formulators of those rules did not foresee that contractors providing static security at a CPA compound could come under fire for hours or days. Security contractors, surrounded, cut off from escape, and abandoned by the military, have no choice but to fight if they come up against a lengthy onslaught by hundreds of attackers. At a time when Pentagon representatives and news commentators were making the case that the Blackwater contractors should have been protected under the laws of war as civilians, since they just provided security and did not engage in combat, contractors at Al Kut and An Najaf *were* engaging in combat.

CHAPTER 5

Blackwater Bridge

"We knew even before we left Kuwait that this contract was doomed."
—T-Boy, Blackwater contractor originally
slated for the ill-fated team

I'm sitting in Las Vegas's Bellagio Hotel bar after midnight, and the room buzzes with the chatter of martini-sipping women and the boasts of gamblers flush with new winnings. Across from me sits a middle-aged man with thinning hair and a small mustache. We could be hardware salesmen or businessmen relaxing after a trade show. But he is a veteran Special Forces team leader telling me about the battle for Fallujah. "The bodies were stacking up. I had one intersection with fifteen bodies. Our team must have killed at least five hundred Iraqis that day. At least five hundred is when we stopped counting," he remembers calmly. He is due for retirement soon. He has no interest in being a contractor. The man remembers Fallujah as the single most violent encounter of his career—an offensive that focused the anger for the entire war on one town and sought payback for an attack on contractors that had triggered a violent orgy of destruction.

The battle for Fallujah began in November of 2004 as six thousand U.S. troops and two thousand Iraqis swept into the city from the north, confronting insurgents and pushing out residents. After the battle died down, Fallujah appeared a battered ghost town haunted by the reported twelve hundred fighters and six hundred civilians who died there. About seventy Americans gave their lives and two hundred suffered serious wounds in the fight to control the city. Although it can be argued that the battle for Fallujah was part of a larger plan to destroy insurgent strongholds in the Sunni Triangle, it was the brutal death and postmortem mutilation of four Blackwater contractors eight months earlier, in March of 2004, that served as the rallying cry and inspiration for the troops who fought there.

During the initial phase of operations in Iraq in the spring of 2003, troops had begun to take over Fallujah but were ordered back. For the first year of the occupation, the city remained an uncontrolled hot spot for violence and sheltered a base of operations for the spreading insurgency. Woefully unprepared for violent resistance to the occupation, the American military was strained to the limits as it dealt with manpower and supply problems.

The desperate situation created an ideal business opportunity for Blackwater. At the time, Blackwater was providing security for the CIA in Pakistan and Afghanistan, and had just set up about five dozen of their contractors on the Bremer detail. Blackwater was eager to aggressively expand their business in the most lucrative and fastest-growing market for security providers in the world. To understand the full picture of what happened to the four contractors in Fallujah, it makes the most sense to start at the top rather than the bottom, since Blackwater actually occupied a low rung on the ladder in the contract the four men were servicing.

Halliburton subsidiary Kellogg, Brown and Root (KBR) manages the lucrative $7.2-billion cost-plus LOGCAP contract to handle support functions for the U.S. military on a global basis. In the execution of the LOGCAP, KBR utilizes a massive network of contractors to manage different elements of the contract, who in turn hire contractors to manage an even narrower delegation of responsibility, who in turn may hire even more contractors to handle specific tasks—often creating layers upon layers of subcontracting.

In the Fallujah incident, Blackwater had been hired to provide security for the Kuwaiti-based Regency Hotel and Hospitality Company, which was a subcontractor of German food service company Eurest Support Services (ESS), which was itself a subcontractor of KBR in the vast mosaic of companies hired to execute the LOGCAP. Even within Blackwater, there were subcontracts to purchase equipment and hire both management and the independent contractors who would carry out the actual tasks, creating multiple layers of contracts and profits to perform the function of feeding troops.

At the time, U.S. military and State Department policy was that, although it could provide convoy protection from Kuwait, it could not provide individual or short-notice escorts to private companies, even if the corporations were working to provide vital resources to the military. Since KBR is required to provide logistics and support on a cost-plus basis, it is far more expedient and profitable to contract private security forces to protect the convoys of its suppliers. Blackwater aggressively and successfully competed for these contracts knowing that once in place, the profits could grow dramatically as the need for security became more critical.

The ESS contract picked up by Regency and Blackwater required thirty-four armed men on ninety-day contracts to guard the movement of ESS equipment and personnel. The initial security survey provided by Blackwater was not a hard bid, but rather an estimate of the $867,033.34 needed to get them going for the first month. Blackwater signed a primary contract with ESS on March 8 and a subcontract with Regency on March 12.

Although the contract with Regency was for just under $900,000, with a third paid up front, the actual costs were to be billed as the client required them. The Regency contract allotted for two "tier-one" management positions, twelve "tier-two" PSD operators, and twenty "static" or "tier-three" operators. Management positions typically paid roughly $750 a day; tier two—those operators with extensive military or police experience who would be the main providers of security—earned about $600 per day; and tier three—those with less experience who played support roles—earned approximately $450 to $500. They would all earn $150 a day for travel or standby days.

For their billing, Blackwater would mark up the base labor costs, adding on additional charges for overhead, training, equipment, housing, and so on, and pass on the bill to Regency. Regency would add its own costs incurred, if any, and mark up Blackwater's cost with its own profit and hand the bill off to ESS. Then ESS, in turn, would mark up and bill KBR, who then would mark up and bill the U.S. government based on its standard LOGCAP cost-plus arrangement. There is no direct accountability for cost or performance, since KBR considers its LOGCAP billing to be confidential and not disclosed to the taxpayer or journalists. Even the act of discussing work done for a contractor like Blackwater can result in instant fines of $250,000, something agreed to in writing by each contractor. At no point is there any incentive to reduce the layers of subcontracting, since every markup provides a profit for somebody. This particular contract had four levels of profit-making before the actual service was provided. It is conceivable that the rate charged to the U.S. taxpayer for a $600-a-day security contractor could end up being thousands. The comparable cost for an enlisted soldier of the same experience and paygrade is about $100 to $250 a day. Even if a four-star general were to provide the services, it would cost around $450 a day.

Although much is made of the high rates for contractors, their contractually stipulated twenty-four-hour, seven-days-a-week job makes $600 a day an effective $25 an hour with no benefits or guarantee of employment beyond the stipulated term of the contract. The biggest benefit for the U.S. military is that using contractors adds no long-term liability in insurance, retirement, training, benefits, or medical costs. Relying on contractors essentially provides a hard one-time cost with no commitment or liability before or after the required use date. Contractors are the ultimate use-once, throwaway soldiers—an expensive but disposable source of muscle and steel when problems occur.

Though the contracting companies have no incentive to reduce costs to the U.S. government, cutting corners in their own expenditures can maximize their profits. For example, a simple line deletion in Blackwater's subcontract with Regency, replacing armored vehicles with soft skins, could have added over a million and half dollars in profit. Blackwater's

March 8 primary contract with ESS stipulated that PSDs be comprised of six-man teams traveling in two armored cars. However, the subcontract to Regency left out the armored-car requirement, an omission that could have been key to the survival of the contractors. Prior to the Fallujah incident, John "JP" Potter, a former SEAL and Kuwait liaison officer for Blackwater, was reportedly fired for pointing out the danger of this change. While much has been made of this decision in the subsequent lawsuits by the murdered contractors' families, each man had signed an obsessively detailed contract that protected Blackwater from any liability.

Blackwater's twenty-three-page contract details how Blackwater cannot be held accountable in the event of a contractor's injury, dismemberment, or emotional distress caused by "terrorists" or even "U.S. governmental employees." The list of potential threats is impressive: being shot, permanently maimed, and/or killed by firearms or munitions, falling aircraft or helicopters, sniper fire, landmines, artillery fire, rocket-propelled grenades, truck or car bombs, earthquakes or other natural disasters, poisoning, civil uprising, terrorist activity, hand-to-hand combat, disease, plane or helicopter crash, hearing loss, eye injury or loss, inhalation or contact with biological or chemical contaminants (whether airborne or not), or injury by flying debris. The contract specifies that it is the responsibility of the contractor to get insurance. The only standard recourse Blackwater employees have is Defense Base Act (DBA) insurance, and hopefully backup assistance from the U.S. military if they get into a jam, something that would be rare and not readily available in dangerous areas.

Blackwater was taking over services previously provided by Control Risks Group (CRG), which had begun phasing out their security operations on March 18, with full pullout scheduled by the twenty-ninth of that month. The thirty-day implementation period in Blackwater's original contract would have left ESS without security from the twenty-ninth to April eighth. Since every day waiting for the contract to begin meant a loss of profits, Blackwater reduced the prep time in order to be operational by April 2. When it became clear that ESS would require a security escort to move some kitchen equipment on March 30, Blackwater management pressed harder to get their men in place. When there is a changeover in the provider of security, the incoming contractors typically do a few days of ridealongs with the departing teams, in order to develop an awareness of the terrain and potential dangers they would face. But because of the tight schedule, the Blackwater contractors were dropped in place their first day on the job and did not get the benefit of learning from the experience of CRG. Additionally, State Department standard operational procedures require at least twenty-four-hours' notice for a move, which is supposed to be used for advance prep work such as scouting the intended route, generating alternate route plans, evac instructions, and putting together a detailed briefing for the security contractors—usually in the form of a PowerPoint presentation with handouts and communications codes. What actually happened was very different. Like all preventable disasters, a series of major and minor mistakes would lead to the violent deaths of Scott Helvenston, Mike Teague, Wes Batalona, and Jerry Zovko.

The four men represented a fairly typical mix of a Blackwater contract. The oldest, forty-eight-year-old Wesley J. K. Batalona, had twenty years of experience in the army and had retired as a Ranger sergeant. A native Hawaiian, Wes was working as a security guard at the Hilton Waikoloa Village on Hawaii's big island when the Iraq war began. He reportedly wanted to start a program to help troubled youth and also needed money to help prevent the foreclosure on his ill father's home—both requiring a serious inflow of funds Batalona did not have. Having been out of the service for nearly ten years, the appeal of a return to the action likely also drew Batalona to the world of private contractors. The silver-haired and physically fit Batalona stood out from his fellow contractors in Iraq, not just because of his advanced age, but because of his proclivity for dressing in colorful Hawaiian shirts while on duty. At the time of his death, he had worked two months in Iraq with Blackwater and had put in previous time on an earlier contract with MPRI. Wes had done a thirty-day stint training the fledging Iraqi Army for MPRI in the fall of 2003, which is where he had met his partner, the youngest of the group, thirty-two-year-old Jerko Gerald "Jerry" Zovko.

A Cleveland-born Croatian-American, Zovko had joined the army in 1991 as part of the 82nd Military Police at Fort Bragg, and went on to pass qualifications to become a Ranger—but did not attend the school. Zovko was a hulk of a man, standing six foot three and weighing approximately two hundred thirty-five pounds. He had served in Croatia, and as his stint in the army was coming to an end, he decided that he wanted to transition into another career more exciting than being a sheriff's deputy or security guard. His first gig as a private security contractor began in late 1997—a straight shot into a DynCorp contract in Qatar. He learned Arabic while in the Middle East and moved on to MPRI in the fall of 2003 to train the Iraqi Army in Kirkush. He and Batalona became close friends, bonding over their difficult task of training disorganized, demoralized, and inexperienced soldiers. In November, the Iraqi recruits had gone home for Ramadan, but few returned, apparently terrified they would be killed by insurgents and unhappy with the tough training meted out by the contractors. With no troops to train, the MPRI contract evaporated. Batalona and Zovko's search for other job opportunities eventually led them to Cochise (from which they were fired) and then to Blackwater.

Their doomed team had another former Ranger, Michael R. "The Ice Man" Teague, who had been a door gunner for the elite 160th SOAR (Special Operations Aviation Regiment) out of Fort Bragg. A thirty-eight-year-old family man from Clarksville, Tennessee, Teague had spent twelve years in the army with time in Grenada, Panama, and Afghanistan. He had recently retired and decided to become a contractor after having difficulty finding any work to support his wife and son other than as a low-paid security guard. As ex-Army, Batalona, Zovko, and Teague enjoyed a tribal bond that required no translation of terminology, tactics, or acronyms.

The odd man out on the team was Scott Helvenston. Pulled from his all ex-SEAL team and ordered to fill a missing spot at the last minute, he immediately knew that the group had no cohesion. Rangers tend to stick together and view SEALs as pretty boys who don't do well out of water. Now the ex-Army had on their team a man with no combat experience but who was the ultimate poster boy for the SEALs. Steven "Scott" Helvenston, thirty-eight, was a SEAL celebrity. He had acted as a military consultant on big-budget Hollywood movies such as *Face/Off*, starring John Travolta, and *Three Ninjas*. He even had screen time as a SEAL instructor who helped whip Demi Moore into shape for Ridley Scott's 1997 *G.I. Jane*. His quest for celebrity and his good looks led him to star in Mark Burnett's reality show, *Combat Missions*, a survival game against other ex-soldiers and cops, and *Man vs. Beast*, where he raced chimps. He was recognizable to anyone who watched late-night TV as a fitness pitchman, since he had produced and aggressively hawked a series of Navy SEAL exercise videos—the main selling points being his blond hair, good looks, big smile, and perfectly chiseled California beach torso. Those Blackwater operators with a few rotations under their belt wondered why "Scotty Bod" didn't make the Bremer detail, or the "pretty boy" detail, as they called it.

By 2001, Scott was hurting financially. His acting career had stalled, and his fitness videos had not generated enough profit to pay off the advertising costs. He declared bankruptcy and had to sell his California home and take work as a campground security guard. With an annual reported income of under $15,000 and two children to support, his personal situation was bleak. Scott decided to apply to Blackwater, and despite their prohibition of hiring those with financial problems, he was accepted. Run by a former SEAL, president Gary Jackson, Blackwater's bending the rules to help an ex-SEAL is not surprising. Ex-military know that life on the outside is tough, and there is a sense of pride that Blackwater offers a second chance—a chance to get back in the action, associate with former operators, and serve your country. The fact that contractors work dangerous assignments for a financial lifeline is not discussed but does offer an evident incentive to skim the contract and sign on the dotted line. Scott Helvenston was about to find the fame he sought, in a brutal reality show, caught on tape and broadcast around the world.

Helvenston joined Blackwater in early March 2004, trained up at headquarters in Moyock, North Carolina, and deployed to Kuwait to do convoy security for the ESS contract. For Helvenston's family, their tragedy is all the more poignant because Scott wasn't even supposed to be on the run that ended with his death.

T-Boy, a thirty-seven-year-old former marine from California, had been slotted for a position on the doomed four-man team, but missed it because of a delayed flight into Kuwait. "By the time I made it to the hotel, 'Team November One' had already left and drove to Baghdad. Scott Helvenston took my place from another team because of my absence and was killed two days later. A few guys were very upset at me for a while after that. They didn't understand what had happened to my flight. They just knew one of their close friends that had replaced me on the team had been killed."

Mental replays of the contractors' brutal deaths, perhaps tinged by some survivor's guilt, have haunted T-Boy. "A few of the guys I worked with didn't think I was stable enough to be here and tried to get me fired. No one really knows how they will take death until it happens. But here I am, more than a year later, still in Iraq and doing what I think is right."

Scott's instructor in Moyock had been Justin "Shrek" McQuown, a former marine who was promoted from instructor and assigned to run the ESS contract as project manager from Kuwait. Scott and Justin had butted heads during training, and that animosity persisted in Kuwait. When T-Boy did a no-show at the airport, "Shrek" chose Scott to fill in the open slot on the November One team. While Scott was having dinner late in the evening of the twenty-eighth, Shrek told him to pack his stuff and be prepared to head up to Baghdad at 5:00 A.M. At first Scott begged off, saying he wasn't feeling well. Though another contractor offered to take Scott's place, Shrek came into Scott's room later that night and began berating him, calling him a coward, confiscating his weapon, and screaming that he was fired. It was enough of a confrontation that Scott fired off an e-mail to Blackwater headquarters describing the situation and asking them to intercede. He had received no response by the next morning and so packed his stuff and headed to Baghdad.

November One's job for ESS was to accompany a truck convoy carrying kitchen equipment from Taji to Camp Ridgeway. Acting as security escort, they were to watch for anything unusual, deter any attacks, and, if engaged, deliver enough "lead on target" until they and the convoy could escape. Their weapons were standard M4s and Glock pistols, gear they were accustomed to in the military and knew how to use. However, they weren't familiar with the terrain and didn't know where and who the enemy was—that knowledge could only come with time and experience. The November One team was a typical security contractor detail—experienced men with enough skills between them to get out of most jams—but they hadn't all worked together before and lacked group cohesion. Additionally, they were handicapped by a deliberate shortage of manpower. Although they had the capability to send out full six-man teams, and Blackwater's contracts with ESS and each individual contractor required convoys to be accompanied by six-man teams, the manager in Baghdad, Tom Powell, decided to send out only four men that day.

Of all the questionable choices made by Blackwater management, T-Boy has been most confounded and troubled by the decision to send out only four men in the convoy. "The four-man issue is still a mystery to me as of today. Each team was made up of a six-man detail. Lessening their team by two was a decision that Tom Powell made. This was actually the first of two times this happened that I know of. My team was the second time. That morning, March 31 of 2004, my team was tasked with a mission to drive to the Jordanian border to pick up one or more VIPs and transport them to Baghdad. . . . Myself and another operator were held back by Tom while our team was sent out to complete this mission. We were told we would be assisting Tom with a movement somewhere, and he needed a few guys to help. I believe the other two guys from the other team were to assist as well. We never did, though. . . . We all know how crazy that would sound today if someone suggested such a trip under those conditions."

Minimum standards for a security convoy dictate that an escort vehicle should have a driver, a passenger gunner, and a tail gunner to keep traffic back and respond with heavy fire to any pursuits. Rolling with just two men per vehicle meant that the driver would not only have to drive, but also watch his nine o'clock to twelve o'clock, as well as the rear sector. Even if the driver had a keen eye and quick reflexes, his gun would not be at the ready, but typically slung across his lap with his pistol rotated up to the top of his leg in the thigh holster. The passenger would have to watch the entire front right around to the back but could not respond to a threat outside of his field of fire from his front window. That left most of the vehicle open to rear ambush, hit and run, and continuous fire if the contractors had to speed away. Having another car with only two people did not double the effective force but could provide a getaway car or could double back to provide support fire if one vehicle came under attack.

Also contrary to Blackwater's contract with ESS, and each individual operator's written agreement with Blackwater, as previously mentioned, November One did not have armored vehicles. There are pros and cons to running hard skins or soft skins. Typically, a soft skin allows the team to shoot from open windows and rear tailgates if attacked. Awareness is heightened in a soft skin, since there is more access and sound coming from outside. A hard skin requires the doors to be cracked, since the windows are usually sealed and soundproofed by heavy glass. Blackwater drove hastily modified Pajeros with a steel plate crudely welded into the back to provide some protection for a well gunner, which did November One no good since the contractors chose to ride in the front seats.

Blackwater reportedly wanted to prove to ESS that they could rise to the challenge of such a tight schedule, and it seems management was under intense pressure to get men on the job. Soon after he had arrived for the ESS contract, T-Boy sensed that too many compromises were being made to get the convoys up and running ahead of schedule. "We knew even before we left Kuwait that this contract was doomed. The lack of resources and equipment were the most talked about issues. Some guys had more experience than others, but the general consensus was that this was going to be a really fucked-up contract. . . . Knowing what I know now, I will never operate under those conditions again. We didn't have the proper leadership or equipment to accomplish it. We were moving at warp speed and most of us had never been in a situation like this. The training was too short at that time. We deployed with semiautomatic weapons and NO machine guns, as required by contract. We were given soft skin vehicles and not hardened vehicles as per the contract. There was not enough cohesion amongst the guys to just drop into a hostile area like this and get the job done that quickly. It seemed like the only thing anyone was concerned about was the timetable, and we all know what that means—

dollars. It was rush, rush, rush from the beginning. We never had a real chance at success."

For their first security escort for ESS, which was scheduled to run days before the Blackwater contract was even scheduled to take effect, Powell was essentially sending out a token force that would barely be able to defend itself, let alone the large red trucks they were hired to protect. Essentially providing a security force in name but not in effectiveness, Powell's decision sent undermanned and underprotected teams into not just "a" danger spot but "the" danger spot, since the area around Fallujah was then a well-known base for anti-American insurgents.

In the spring of 2004, after a year of American presence, the violence in Iraq seemed to be evolving into near chaos, with kidnappings and armed attacks mounting. Residents of the Sunni Triangle in particular expressed a growing sense of anger as it appeared that the United States could not stem the tide of violence, but actually seemed to be exacerbating the insurgency by issuing "orders" that crystallized a view that Iraqis were living under American occupation. The perception of America as oppressor increasingly began to replace the idea of America as liberator.

Fallujah, along with Ramadi and other cities in the Sunni Triangle, were the strongholds of a rapidly expanding Sunni insurgency. Kidnapping gangs, insurgents, and former Baathists were using Fallujah as an operating base. In early March, the marines had taken over positions on the outskirts of the city from the 82nd Airborne, but their policy was to not venture into the urban combat zone that was the center of Fallujah. Instead, they decided to get tough on the growing insurgency by shutting down main roads and doing reconnaissance in force. On March 29, in an event cited by local leaders as the precipitating event that led to the violent orgy of bloody celebration after the contractors' murders, American soldiers opened fire on a crowd of protesters. Residents of Fallujah had come out to protest the U.S. military's occupation of a school building, but the soldiers said some among the crowd carried weapons. Seventeen locals died in the incident.

Fallujans had noticed that in addition to the military presence, groups of military-looking Westerners dressed as civilians were shuttling around the region working in support of the U.S. occupation. They could be easily identified by their sunglasses, short hair, safari-style clothing and, of course, their weapons. They shuttled between military bases and hotels in Iraq in tan pickups and white SUVs and had adopted an abrasive "guns up" attitude to keep plenty of distance between ordinary Iraqis and convoys. The word on the street was that these were CIA and their mercenaries. The Fallujans had no interest in the fine distinctions between real military OGA and civilian military contractors; they were all the enemy.

On March 29, the November One team stayed at a run-down hotel in Baghdad used by Blackwater as their Iraq headquarters. The next day, they were to drive to Taji, north of Baghdad, to meet up with three empty ESS trucks and escort them to Camp Ridgeway, west of Baghdad and Fallujah, in order to pick up some kitchen equipment. T-Boy thinks the men knew they had not been thoroughly prepared for the drive: "I know that Wes and Jerry didn't want to do this mission. I had heard that they protested this mission. This, I believe, was the day or evening before to Tom, but of course they went on and did as they were told."

Batalona and Zovko had worked the area, but Helvenston and Teague had never been there before. The four men didn't seem to be sure of how the move was set up, and one Blackwater source says that the night before the move, the men asked the staff at the hotel for directions. Much public controversy has surrounded reports that the contractors had headed into unfamiliar and extremely dangerous terrain without even the benefit of maps to guide them. While T-Boy knows that the men were not issued maps by Blackwater management, he finds it highly unlikely that the men would have commenced their drive without tracking down a map from another source.

"It was reported that they didn't have any maps of that area. I'm not sure how true this is—that is, if they had maps in the vehicle with them from another source. I know Blackwater didn't issue them any maps because we were told they didn't have any of that area. This was untrue, of course, and I personally found several maps of Fallujah the day of the incident—but before we knew it was happening—amongst many other maps of the entire region of Iraq. I was tasked with sorting maps that morning, and knowing that we had been told that there were no maps of Fallujah, I was surprised to find them." T-Boy didn't really think about the maps again until he read about the various charges made by the families.

November One had made it to Taji for their rendezvous with the ESS trucks but had become lost as they tried to find their way down to Camp Ridgeway. According to the lawsuit brought against Blackwater by the families, the convoy stopped at Camp Fallujah, a military base five miles east of Fallujah, to spend the night, though other unconfirmed accounts have them checking in to a hotel. What is known with certainty is that they set out on the morning of the thirty-first heading west on the road that would take them directly through the heart of hostile Fallujah. Batalona and Zovko took point in the blue Mitsubishi Pajero, while Helvenston and Teague brought up the rear of the five-vehicle convoy in a red Pajero. If they had been aware of the extreme level of threat they faced in central Fallujah, they may have chosen to take a couple more hours of drive time to do the normal indirect loop around the city. However, they either did not know of the dangers, or believed they could handle it.

Whenever possible, convoys try to bypass heavily populated areas, especially dangerous ones like Fallujah, since buildings lining city streets offer perfect cover for snipers, and it is far too easy to block off escape routes for an ambush. According to one theory, the convoy intended to link up with an American-trained Iraqi Civil Defense Corps (ICDC) team on the eastern entrance to town, which would guide them through the city center, providing more firepower if anything happened. However, this would have required coordination the evening before, and there is no evidence that the marines at Camp Fallujah, or the Blackwater contractors themselves, had made this contact. A confidential internal investigation conducted by Blackwater after the attack suggested that the contractors left Camp Fallujah driving along Highway 10 until they came in sight of the ugly eastern industrial end of Fallujah, where they ran into an ICDC checkpoint at about 9:00 A.M. According to a senior Blackwater executive, a phone call from the contractors back to headquarters and eyewitness accounts support this theory.

Two trucks loaded with tan uniformed ICDC apparently offered to guide them to their destination and headed on a detour through the heavy traffic of Fallajuh. According to an Iraqi policeman who had been working the main intersection into town that morning, the men stopped and asked him for directions, which suggests they may have been concerned about the motives of the men in uniform they were following. They pushed on into the city and got about three hundred yards past the intersection when they were stopped by the traffic for about ten minutes. At about 9:30 A.M., traffic started moving again, and the convoy of three red Mercedes-Benz trucks, two Blackwater Pajeros, and two Iraqi civil defense trucks continued on at a slow pace. Batalona and Zovko took lead directly behind the Iraqi trucks, followed by the three ESS trucks, with Teague and Helvenston bringing up the rear.

About a mile and a half into Fallujah, as they crawled along Highway 10 through town, the lead Iraqi vehicle suddenly stopped. In a car-to-car chain reaction, the entire convoy ground to a halt. Immediately, a small group of young men carrying AK-47s and wearing *kefiyas* to cover their faces emerged from the nearby shops and began firing at the contractors from behind. At that close range, the 7.62 bullets punched through the glass and thin steel and into the bodies of the contractors in the rear vehicle. Helvenston and Teague never even had time to react.

Terrified by the gunfire, the drivers of two of the ESS trucks pulled around the lead Pajero and the Iraqi police trucks and sped away. Zovko and Batalona heard the shooting and immediately started to pull a U-turn into the other lane to provide backup. A wall of insurgent gunfire riddled them with bullets before they could even get in position to respond. Hit multiple times at close range, the car accelerated, rear-ended a white Toyota at high speed, and came to a stop almost wedged under the bumper. The two men had been shot through the head and lower extremities. A Iraqi cameraman began filming as soon as the ambush had achieved its objective, creating a permanent record of one of the most publicly gruesome displays of the Iraq war, parts of which would seem to play for days on a seemingly permanent loop in news broadcasts around the world.

As the jolting handheld video opens on the scene of carnage, Zovko can be seen in the passenger seat, mouth agape, head back, and dead. Batalona is slumping lifelessly forward into his friend's lap, his white and red Hawaiian-print shirt stained even more red by his own blood. A chorus of triumphant shouting and tributes of *"Allahu Akbar"* run in the background, as the insurgents somewhat tentatively begin to strip weapons from the contractors' still-warm bodies. The cameraman films a carefully staged display of DoD identity cards as "proof" that the mujahideen had just killed "CIA agents."

As the shooting and shouting could be heard for many blocks, and word of the attack spread quickly through the streets of Fallujah, locals begin to swarm the scene and set the vehicles on fire. Chanting, dancing, and yelling, the crowd continues to grow, all celebrating the glorious victory against the great American invader. As the gasoline finally burns out, the mob tugs at the charred bodies, pulling them from the still-smoldering shells of the Pajeros. Men with shovels hack at the blackened bodies, children stomp them with the soles of their sandals, one man continually kicks at the head of one until it severs from the burnt body, and another ties a burnt leg to a rock and throws it up to snag a power line. The crowd plays to the camera, shouting anti-American slogans and praises to the mujahideen, as they dance on top of the destroyed vehicles.

Someone ties two of the bodies to the bumper of a car and begins to drag them down the main thoroughfare, named Sheik Ahmed Yassin Street in honor of the Hamas spiritual leader assassinated by the Israelis. The route takes them right past the police station, though the officers do not appear much interested in getting in the way of the raging mob. One cameraman interviews the police as the bodies are being desecrated, and an officer makes it clear that they don't think the incident is any of their business. They obviously recognize the swift and brutal penalty for assisting Americans.

The car dragging the bodies stops as it reaches the Euphrates River, where the crowd then hoists up the contractors' remains to dangle from the joists of the bridge. Someone posts a sign on the bridge reading that Fallujah is the graveyard for Americans. For hours, the bodies dangle in a macabre spectacle as an everyday flow of traffic passes over the bridge.

The insurgents quickly put together a video of the event and posted it on the Internet. In claiming responsibility, they edited together film of captured documents and the dead bodies and provided a testimonial from one of the insurgents. He appears in front of a black backdrop, his lower face covered with a black scarf, with only his steely black eyes visible as he intones in Arabic the insurgents' version of events. The man begins with a typical Koranic tribute:

"Thanks to Allah and praise to the messenger who is Mohammed. We do not kill them, they kill themselves. If you do not do it, Allah will do it for you.

"On the morning of Wednesday March 31st, after prayer, a mujahideen spy arrived with information. He told our commander that a group of CIA will pass through Fallujah on the main road to Habbaniya [the town to the west of Fallujah] because they have a special meeting. The commander ordered for us to be ready to kill these people. After we had prepared our weapons and ourselves we left at 6 A.M. We scouted the main street from the bridge to Habbaniya. We did that three times.

"After that our commander selected the intersection for attack. He chose this intersection because it was busy with traffic so they could not escape. Our commander then identified all of our positions. Myself, the commander, and one mujahideen stayed at the position together.

"Later on, I went to the teahouse to have my tea. I sat and drank my tea. It was 9:15 A.M. After I finished my tea, my commander and his assistant arrived and sat with us. As final instructions from the commander, we were told to verify the vehicle, since they would be in civilian cars. They would not have bodyguards with them and they would wear civilian clothes—this is all to avoid being captured by the mujahideen, because every American that passes through Fallujah will be killed.

"I talked to the commander's assistant, who told me we would need to scout the street again at 11 A.M. to see if they were still coming. We then checked once more with our spies to verify they were still coming. They told us they would be there in one or two hours. We were told originally 10 A.M., but when we checked it was 8 A.M. to noon. They actually arrived at 9:45 A.M. The owner of the coffee shop saw them and said, 'Why are those people in our land? They will be killed by the mujahideen!'

"Then the commander ordered all of us to take our positions because the time had arrived. We were told to move the cars into position. We should be ready to use our weapons and to capture the people. We started and everybody moved to their positions. The commander decided to attack the last car and capture the first one. We attacked the last car and the first car tried to escape by turning around. They could not escape and we captured them. We then killed the people in the first car. Thanks to Allah we were victorious and we captured the weapons and supplies.

"The commander then told us to leave some of the weapons behind. Our families in Fallujah went and set fire to the cars. We then withdrew in the way our commander told us to and we waited for news.

"Our family in Fallujah came and told us Allah had given us victory. They told us they burned everything in the cars. You saw the results in the news. Allah has given a great victory to the people of Fallujah. Allah gave us the victory and gave the victory to the mujahideen.

"We will continue to fight the jihad."

The marines at Camp Fallujah learned of the attack from Fox News. Hours later, the marines still did not dare enter Fallujah, but instead contacted the Iraqi police to cut down the bodies from the bridge. The Iraqi police also hesitated to get near the scene, so it was ten hours later before the marines and the Iraqi police went together to retrieve the bodies so they could be shipped to Dover Air Force Base for autopsies. Though rumors circulated that the men had been pulled from the SUVs and burned alive, the autopsies proved conclusively that they had been killed first by the barrage of bullets. Another rumor circulated, charging that two of the bodies had been chopped up and fed to dogs, but that, too, proved false.

After video snippets of the violent deaths and celebratory desecration hit the news, Americans could have believed any depths of depravity by the crazed Fallujans. To the Iraqis involved, this had been a traditional lynching and a great victory against the infidel invader. To Americans, it represented a grave offense against any standards of human decency—in wartime or otherwise—and looked like a new cast of players reenacting the 1993 Somali tragedy. One has to wonder if the Fallujans performed for the cameras with the Blackhawk Down episode in mind, since that incident has been lauded on insurgent and Islamist websites as proof that, as bin Laden phrases it, "the United States is a paper tiger." After video of dead Army Rangers being dragged through the streets of Mogadishu hit the evening news, a public outcry of shock and revulsion had pushed Clinton to call for the withdrawal of all American troops from Somalia. The Fallujans may have thought they could achieve the same with a very public display of the same brutality. There is little proof that the event was anything other than a murderous lynch mob taking out frustration on what they thought were CIA paramilitaries, but the visual connection to Somalia was clear to an American public squeamish at the sight of death.

By Wednesday evening, riveted and horrified, unable to watch but unable to look away, the American public was transfixed by edited clips of the jubilant aftermath of the contractors' deaths as they played over and over on the cable and network channels. After the initial shock of the footage wore off, the media moved on to its typical phase two—the self-obsessed introspective debate about whether they were broadcasting scenes too gruesome for public consumption, giving too much coverage to the story, or lending aid and comfort to the enemy by showing video that had been filmed for the primary purpose of propaganda. Whatever the conclusion of these debates, two things became clear: The footage made for good ratings, and the viewing public was demanding more information. People wanted to know what function armed civilians were serving in the Iraqi theater of war. Though the U.S. government had been relying on independent contractors for some time, the issue seemed a new one to the American public. They demanded to know why men described as "civilian" contractors would be escorting trucks through a hostile war zone without the protection of the military.

So ingrained in the American psyche are the tenets of the 1949 Geneva Conventions that accidental deaths of civilians in war are abhorred, and intentional murder of civilians is condemned absolutely. But these contractors appeared to occupy a shady zone between civilian and military.

While not active members of the military per se, they were armed and ready to shoot if necessary, were providing critical support for the U.S. military's core mission, and their paychecks—once the multiple levels of subcontracting is stripped away—were ultimately financed by the Pentagon. Even though those facts tilt the assessment essentially in a military, though nontraditional, direction, some analysts continued to argue that the contractors were essentially playing a civilian role because they were not engaging in combat operations. However, if Teague, Batalona, Helvenston, and Zovko had been given even a moment to respond to incoming fire, they would have been deeply engaged in combat.

As the very public lynching of the contractors forced a heated debate over issues surrounding the military's reliance on independent contractors, four families were very privately grieving the death of husbands, fathers, or sons, and the men's fellow contractors were mourning the loss of their friends and colleagues. T-Boy was told to gather up the murdered contractors' possessions to ship home. "It was me alone that had to go into their room after they died and pack all of their personal belongings. I cried for the first thirty minutes in their room before I could even get started. Just seeing letters and pictures from their families took its toll on me. Mike and Jerry's muscle magazines and Wes's Hawaiian shirts. I was a mess that day for sure."

Blackwater had sent company representatives to inform the families of their loved ones' deaths, and returned their personal effects, but that was the extent of their legal responsibility to the families. The contractors' next of kin would receive $64,000 paid out by the Defense Base Act insurance, and a belated letter of condolence from Paul Bremer. The surviving family members chose to channel their suffering into a lawsuit and publicity campaign that highlighted the men's deaths as a direct result of the rush to get the ESS contract in place and Blackwater's alleged thirst for profit.

In January of 2005, the families of Mike Teague, Wesley Batalona, Scott Helvenston, and Jerry Zovko filed suit against Blackwater in North Carolina courts. The lawsuit also specifically names Tom Powell and Justin "Shrek" McQuown, and charges that decisions made by these two individuals and, by consequence of liability, Blackwater Security, constitute a gross negligence that led to the deaths of the four men. As the lawsuit states, "Blackwater, Justin McQuown, and Tom Powell intentionally, deliberately and with reckless disregard for their health and safety, sent Helvenston, Teague, Zovko and Batalona, and each of them, into the very high-risk area of Fallujah without the required six (6) man team, without a minimum of two (2) armored vehicles, without a rear-runner, without heavy automatic machine guns, without 24 hours notice prior to the security mission, without having conducted a Risk Assessment to determine the threat level of the mission, without the opportunity to review the travel routes, gather intelligence regarding the mission, perform a pre-trip inspection of the route, determine the proper logistics or even review a map of the area, and without permitting them to test and sight the weapons they were actually given."

The lawsuit alleges that all these requirements were stated in the men's contracts and that Blackwater's misrepresentation of the actual conditions under which the men would be expected to work constitutes fraud. Further, they claimed that "when the Defendants sent Helvenston, Teague, Zovko and Batalona out on this security mission in this condition, without the proper protections, tools and information, they knew that they were sending them into the center of Fallujah with very little chance that they would come out alive. . . . As a proximate result of the Defendants' intentional conduct, willful and wanton conduct, and/or negligence, as alleged herein above, Helvenston, Teague, Zovko and Batalona, and each of them, were killed March 31, 2004."

Blackwater moved to have the case heard in U.S. District Court, arguing that the Defense Base Act grants the federal government sole authority in deciding matters related to the death or injury of contractors working in support of U.S. military operations. Blackwater then attempted to have the case dismissed from federal court, arguing that the Defense Base Act provided comprehensive coverage for the men's deaths and that each contractor had signed a release accepting that dangerous working conditions could result in his untimely demise. In an interim victory for the families, the federal court ruled against the dismissal request, and in August 2005 sent the case back to North Carolina state courts. At the time of this writing, no decision has yet been rendered in the case. Erik Prince, owner of Blackwater, cannot settle because it would forever change the precedent for civilian contractor deaths. Blackwater as of fall 2006 has nine lawsuits against it.

The lawsuit sets no dollar amount for damages, leaving that instead to the discretion of the jury, but the families assert that the case is not about the money. As Danica Zovko said in an interview with Raleigh-Durham's *News and Observer,* "I don't intend to receive a penny of that blood money. . . . I am doing this so they do not mistreat others like they did my son and the other men." The insured are collecting regular payments under the DBA.

Blackwater worked diligently to get its operational procedures in line immediately after the attack in Fallujah, but death was still to stalk the ESS contract. On June 2, a Blackwater Suburban was driving at high speeds along a highway near Basra when it hit a pothole created by a mortar. The heavy weight of the vehicle threw it out of control, and the truck flipped and began to tumble, ejecting one of the contractors, who died of his injuries. One of the men who survived that accident would die just three days later, along with three other contractors, when they suffered an ambush on the road to Baghdad International Airport. In all, nine men had died out of thirty slots on the ESS contract, which would equal an extraordinary mortality rate even if it had been from a combat unit in Iraq. None of the other deaths on the ESS contract, however, would provoke the kind of public, political, and military response as those of Helvenston, Teague, Batalona, and Zovko.

The day after the four contractors' deaths, Paul Bremer issued a statement: "Their deaths will not go unpunished." Brigadier General Mark Kimmitt, deputy director of coalition operations, also threatened, "It will be at a time and a place of our choosing. We will hunt down the criminals. We will kill them or we will capture them, and we will pacify Fallujah." While the four men may have "only" been contractors, the fighting men on the ground in Iraq obviously viewed it as a loss of four of their own, and the graphic and inhumane desecration of the bodies seemed to deserve severe punishment. A brutal vengeance would be meted out, and the soldiers were just waiting for the signal to go.

Media pressure and moral outrage galvanized the president, and a horrified public demanded swift action. The marine commander, Lieutenant General James T. Conway, urged caution and said the military should resist calls for revenge. Fallujah was not only the most dangerous city in Iraq, but it also had the potential to become another Stalingrad or Grozny—a bloody urban battleground. Lieutenant General Ricardo Sanchez overruled Conway, and five days after the murders, U.S. marines rolled into Fallujah. Seven dead and a hundred wounded marines later, Operation Vigilant Resolve ground to a halt after less than a week of fighting. The marines had temporarily pacified Fallujah and transferred control to the Fallujah Brigades, an extemporaneous militia cobbled together from a thousand former Iraqi soldiers based in Fallujah. The Fallujah Brigades, rather than keeping the city free of insurgent activities, ended up either assisting them or joining them. All the equipment and weaponry that the U.S. military handed out to the Fallujah Brigades ended up in the hands of the insurgency, and members of the security force were implicated in attacks and kidnappings. Then in November, the hammer dropped. Operation Phantom Fury coordinated the full force of U.S. weaponry and manpower, leaving Fallujah a destroyed city. In Arab countries, stories about the heroic defense and ultimate sacrifice of insurgents in Fallujah vaulted the industrial city into legend. Even in Mogadishu, Somalia, gunmen wear T-shirts that simply read FALLUJAH.

On March 31, 2005, the first anniversary of attack, the marines then in control of the area around Fallujah invited Blackwater to a memorial service for their fallen comrades. Mike Rush, Blackwater's director of operations, and a small group of contractors went to Camp Bahariah, east of Fallujah, where the commanding officer provided a complete briefing on how the marines had taken over the city. Everyone present agreed that the Fallujans deserved it after what they had done en masse to the four contractors. Then, even though Fallujah was considered neutralized, a company of marines set out in advance to secure the area around what they had renamed Blackwater Bridge. The Blackwater convoy rolled into the city, passing rows of abandoned-looking houses still marked with *X*s and *O*s to signify a good-guy or bad-guy residence. They all piled out at Blackwater Bridge for a brief, solemn ceremony above the swirling murky waters of the Euphrates.

Mike Rush made a short speech on behalf of Erik Prince and thanked the marines for what they had done to Fallujah. The Mamba team took pictures, handed out Blackwater T-shirts, and talked to the marines about confirmed kills and the urban combat in the battle of Fallujah. The marine commanding officer told Blackwater that his men were still chomping at the bit to "get it on"—their near-destruction of Fallujah having apparently not sated their appetite for the complete decimation of the city.

T-Boy says he loves the marines for what they did to Fallujah, and evinces pride that he once served as one. But even the most rigidly professional soldiers are not automatons, and the furrow crossing T-Boy's brow and the tremor straining his voice testify to a difficult struggle in controlling his emotions when he recalls the day of the memorial. "I was the last one to reach the bridge after we had pulled up. I was feeling very sluggish and emotional. . . . As I walked up to that fucking green bridge, I couldn't control my tears anymore. I had not cried like that since the day I packed their belongings. There I was in full combat gear and helmet crying like a baby. I spent several minutes just looking at it—looking up at the spot where my fellow Blackwater operators had once hung mutilated. It was very emotional for me. I was very angry, too. I wanted so bad to run out into that town and start killing people with no remorse. I didn't care who I killed; I wanted some payback of my own. There was no doubt in my mind that some of those people that day were in fact a thousand meters away down the street. A lot of the news coverage showed the vehicles being looted and bodies being mutilated by local townspeople—some were teenagers and others old men. I was very angry at the thought that some of these people were just a stone's throw away."

T-Boy shelves the anger when on the job, but it's obvious the incident has left him with a deeply wounded psyche. When I first met him while riding along with the Mamba team on the airport run, I thought his moments of solitary "zoning," as his teammates called it, was just his way of maintaining focus for the dangerous drive ahead. As I got to know him better, it seemed to me that his solitude represented the torture of inner demons more than anything else. In addition to the weight in his heart, T-Boy carries with him a memento of his four dead compatriots—one he anointed on the beams of Blackwater Bridge the day of the memorial. "I had brought an American flag that I had taken from their room. I couldn't tell you which guy it belonged to, but as far as I was concerned, it belonged to all of them and was a part of me, too. I took that small American flag out of my pocket and rubbed it on the bridge a few times, and I thought to myself how glad I was for the payback that the marines had inflicted on Fallujah."

Recalling the punishment exacted on Fallujah seems to steel T-Boy's nerve, and the vulnerable and tortured young man visually transforms into a venerable and imposing ex-marine. "I still have that flag today, and I have carried it on every mission since."

CHAPTER 6

Under Siege

"Yea, though I walk through the valley of the shadow of death,
I fear no evil, for thou art with me."
—Psalm 23

I'm plowing through the air in a Blackwater Little Bird, and the earth below looks like the undulating blur of a sepia-toned kaleidoscope. My feet are braced on the side skids as I sit out the open doorway of the helicopter, wishing that the harness securing me to the floor of the bird had come in a full-body variety. Peering down, I see what looks like an ancient city under siege, replete with towers and crenellated fortifications. The modern world begins where a murky brown haze envelops the square-edged squat buildings that make up the rest of Baghdad.

As we're dropping elevation for a better look at the city, massive monuments built by Saddam materialize out of the miasma, towering above the brown maze of featureless houses and shops. While the air feels cool and the sky peaceful at a thousand feet, descending for a low run drives us straight into a settlement of twenty-first-century urban warfare. The occupiers have transformed the ostentatious architecture of Saddam into an ugly utilitarian patchwork labyrinth of sandbagged houses, white trailers, T-walls, dirt berms, tanks, SUVs, and military vehicles. Flying over a residential area, the landscape of rooftops evinces a more pedestrian life amid

143

the war zone. As my eyes flick over the roofs and streets, patterns emerge. I can instantly see traffic jams, military movements, and isolated individuals walking through fields and alleys. The pilots don't run below a hundred feet just for the good view it gives them of the ground, but for safety reasons—moving at a low trajectory shortens the amount of time an insurgent could have to aim and fire an RPG at them. They also fly erratically back and forth, just in case someone gets off a shot at them. "We don't get hit much but we do run into wildlife," Steve, the pilot, tells me. Steve has painted white outlines of cartoonish bird figures near the window—one for each they have hit. Silver duct tape also covers three gashes from shrapnel.

At a calculated point, the two pilots arc the helicopter upward from the tan landscape into the blue sky, crushing me against the polished aluminum floor. Curving over, all I see is sky and sun and then feel the weightlessness. I mumble a few words of expletive-laced prayerlike gibberish and contemplate puking.

The Little Bird then turns in a steep accelerating dive down toward the turbid mess of the Tigris. I brace myself and consider the sad fate of having my last breath drawn from that liquid putrescence, but the expert pilots make a smooth last-minute adjustment, and when I open my eyes, we are sailing up the river a few feet above the artery of brown swirling goo. The pilot's flat compressed voice comes over the headset, telling me to keep an eye on the water, since this is where they usually get to see pale bloated dead bodies floating down the muddy channel. It must have been a slow night in Baghdad—no corpses today. In the flat, clipped intonation of a surreal tour-guide spiel, the pilot points to one side to indicate from where the mortars that regularly rock the Green Zone are fired, then to the other side so I can see the site of yesterday's suicide bombing. The helo flicks up into another nauseating arc, and we head at high speed along the main road into the Green Zone.

We sweep over the main parade grounds, flanked by the triumphal Hands of Victory—massive hands modeled on Saddam's holding two swords to form an arch and cast from the melted guns of Iraqis who died in the Iran-Iraq war. The Blackwater pilots are renowned for flying under the swords instead of over, but for my sake they restrain themselves. After another gut-wrenching lurch upward, we cross over the dividing line into the world outside the Green Zone. As we head toward Gate 12, the helos swoop close enough to the rooftops that I can see the look of terror that spreads across a man's face as he looks up from doing his laundry to see a chopper bearing down on him. One more twisting ascent tests the tenacity of my stomach; then we float down back inside the massive blast walls that line the palace. Landing as softly as walking in slippers, the ride comes to an end. I welcome the firm feel of mortar-blasted concrete.

The Blackwater Aviation pilots live at the airfield next to the palace in the Green Zone. The landing zone is a large empty paved lot bordered by high blast walls. It sits right next to the main palace area—a favorite target of mortar attacks. With the splatterlike impact damage or spawl marks from mortar hits etched into the surrounding concrete, the area resembles a grotesque modern sculpture garden.

Inside the hangar, which houses three of the teardrop-shaped helicopters, country-western music blasts from the boombox. Two Little Birds glisten with fresh black and gray paint, while mechanics tinker on the third, which has been gutted for service. The Hughes 500 Little Bird (now made by Boeing as the MD-550) first flew in 1960, and the tiny helicopter quickly set a list of records that included fastest speed, fastest climb rate, and highest sustained altitude. They are quick and mobile—the sports car of helicopters. The back would normally seat two passengers, but Blackwater has modified the platform for two snipers/gunners, who use heavy drum-fed squad automatic weapons, or SAWs, which hang from the top of the door frame. These helicopters have no doors, so the gunners sit in the open door frame, held in by restraints and locking their feet on the skids. Special Ops use Little Birds to insert Delta operators via plank, cable, or fast rope. Blackwater uses them to do reconnaissance and to provide backup and surgical firepower for their contractors.

One of five divisions of Blackwater, Blackwater Aviation not only provides air support with the Little Birds, but also transportation and logistics in Iraq and Afghanistan using the twin-engine CASA 212 aircraft. Black-water Little Bird pilots provided air cover for both the Bremer and Ne-groponte details, and now mostly provide backup for convoy runs by the Mamba team. Whenever Mamba gets in a jam, the Little Birds appear like guardian angels, swooping in like an aerial cavalry to fly just a few feet above the convoy—making an impressive show of force to deter attackers and lay down fire if required by circumstance.

Flying would probably be the wrong word to describe what they do, since these former 160th Airborne pilots are the lowest, fastest, most ag-gressive pilots in Iraq. "They get on us about flying low and erratic, saying we are going to crash," Steve explains, "but around here that's the safest way to fly. The lower you are, the less time they have to spot you and the more cover that is provided by the buildings, trees, and overhead. We go out and run the routes, and if we see something that is out of place or wasn't there before, we mark them and see if they have changed. Or if they look like IEDs, we shoot 'em up."

Walking back to their air-conditioned trailer, we pass a crudely lettered sign: CAMP ASSMONKEY—FUCK YOU WE ALREADY HAVE ENOUGH FRIENDS. The term "Ass Monkey" came about when the Blackwater Bremer detail gave it as a radio call sign to the hotshot pilots providing air support, re-ferring to the amount of time they spent sitting on their butts waiting to scramble. Steve thought of the sign. "When we first got here, everybody had a camp with a name on it, so we figured we needed a sign, too," he tells me with his dry Texas humor.

The long wall inside the trailer displays a large satellite map of Bagh-dad and a collection of binders and smaller maps. The pilots spend their time either in the air, sleeping, or sitting in this simple ten-by-thirty struc-ture waiting to scramble. The bitter smell of cooked coffee and pungent helo exhaust fill the confined space. The pilots, conditioned to be cautious about operational security, sit across from me and just stare at first. Only when silence doesn't work do they answer in clipped tones. The gunners spit Skoal and say nothing. They are visibly uncomfortable.

Steve shows me where a bullet went in through the sole of his tan desert boots and then out the top. He was shot in the foot a few days ago while flying at his usual hundred-foot-high altitude over Baghdad. Steve has the accent, lean looks, and squint of a Texan and wears a bandana covering his shaved head. He uses his finger to trace the bullet's trajectory through his ankle. The other pilots just shake their head. One says, "He's just showing off." They all laugh.

Steve took the bullet in the foot during an ordinary run on an ordinary day. Amazingly, during the most dangerous runs of his time in Iraq—as he ferried supplies and wounded to and from a battle in Najaf—he escaped completely unscathed.

The argument about security contractors being civilians because they do not engage in combat became completely moot within a week of the March 31 incident in Fallujah, after Moqtada al-Sadr's Mahdi militia attacked a Blackwater-guarded CPA compound in Najaf. The U.S. military did not send in any backup, so the contractors had no choice but to fight an intense four-hour battle against the insurgents themselves. As the CPA compound ran low on ammunition, Steve flew from Baghdad with a resupply for his buddies, picking up a wounded soldier to medevac him out to a hospital. For his efforts, he received a pointed reprimand. I ask Steve if the reason he got in trouble for the mission was because they are technically supposed to be civilian pilots not involved in combat. Dan, another pilot who had remained silent up until now, interrupts to say, "We are Americans first, contractors second."

An Najaf

In the postinvasion jostling for political leadership of the Iraqi Shia community, one radical firebrand quickly rose to prominence. Thirty-year-old Moqtada al-Sadr had the lineage of respected religious leadership. Both his father and grandfather had risen to positions of great eminence amongst the Iraqi Shiites. His grandfather had served as prime minister, and Sadr's father had gained the respect of a martyr after Saddam had him assassinated in 1999. Sadr did not possess the reputation, education, or support his father and grandfather had enjoyed, but as defaced photos of Saddam were torn down and replaced by Sadr's father, it became apparent that Moqtada was using the power vacuum to his advantage. He worked to gain support by playing upon historical precedent, religious fervor, decades of persecution by Sunni elements, and an inarguable right of the Shia to gain governing authority in Iraq by sheer virtue of their majority.

Attempts to marginalize Sadr proved unsuccessful, since his radical anti-American message appealed to a community that felt it was suffering under the rule of foreign imperialist aggressors. Moqtada and his black-shirted Mahdi Army began to push back against the foreign occupiers, adding prestige and notoriety to a man who had not previously been accepted as a sage, religious expert, or political leader. In order to advance his position of authority, Sadr organized large rallies, made firebrand speeches, and began a campaign of assassination to remove more moderate rivals.

In an attempt to bring Sadr to bear, a secret warrant was issued for his arrest, and Iraqi and coalition forces started rounding up a select list of his associates, charging them with complicity in the April 2003 assassination of Abdul Majid al-Khoei, a rival cleric. To counter his enemies, Moqtada al-Sadr had been working hard to whip his followers into a frenzy.

The spring of 2004 saw large, angry protests raging across the southern cities and the Shia slums of Baghdad, and violent attacks by Sadr's Mahdi Army and its allies were on a dramatic upsurge. Sadr had impeccable timing, since Sunni resistance was also building in the Sunni Triangle. On March 28, Bremer had ordered the closure of Sadr's newspaper, *al-Hawzah*, charging the publication with incitement of violence. On April 3, one of Sadr's top aides had been arrested for involvement in al-Khoei's assassination. While these two moves had the intent of weakening Sadr, they actually increased his prestige by making clear that the Americans were closing in on him in an effort to shut him down. Sadr capitalized on his own persecution, and thousands of Shiites poured out into the streets of their communities to rally in his support.

Protests had become such a commonplace occurrence that the angry Iraqis gathering outside Camp Golf in Najaf on the morning of April 4 garnered little attention at first. Photos of the protest show a few hundred people gathered outside the gates. Flags in a variety of colors, representing different Shia tribes, fly over the crowd. While the majority of the protesters appear to be tribal representatives, a handful of figures hovering in the background dressed in the black attire of Sadr's Mahdi Army suggest an ominous influence.

At the time, Camp Golf housed an Iraqi police station, a contingency of Spanish and El Salvadoran troops, a handful of American military police, and the CPA's Najaf headquarters. CPA headquarters in the main capitals were fortified and guarded by private security contractors who worked under loose rules of engagement written by Anthony Hunter-Choat—a retired British general and former mercenary in the French Foreign Legion. Despite the rules of engagement allowing contractors to shoot back if attacked, there was no further formal legal guidelines on what contractors should or should not do in combat situations.

Blackwater Security had the contract to protect the CPA operations in Najaf and had eight contractors, mostly former SEALs, stationed there to guard the headquarters. Not even a week had passed since they had seen the violent ambush of their colleagues in Fallujah, so when shots rang out from the crowd of protesters outside the gate, the Blackwater contractors were ready to, as one phrased it, "get it on."

Twenty-five-year-old marine corporal Lonnie Young, a defense messaging system administrator, had passed the protesters when he had arrived at the compound that morning. He had come to Camp Golf with another marine and a handful of civilian contractors tasked with upgrading the base's communications equipment. What should have been an easy half-day assignment for the communication specialist turned into a harried afternoon of heavy fighting.

Young recounted to the *Virginian-Pilot* that he remembers it being shortly before noon when he heard the sound of incoming AK-47 gunfire. While the occasional smattering of an AK burst is not unusual anywhere in Iraq, hearing a volley of return fire usually meant something serious. Young pulled on his gear and helmet, grabbed an M249 SAW, and headed upstairs to the roof of the CPA headquarters, where he joined the Blackwater contractors already positioned and returning fire. Young settled in behind the cement wall where he watched in horror as armed men outside the gates unloaded from trucks and took aim at the building. His military training made him shout out, "With your permission, sir, I have acquired a target." But there were no other soldiers on the roof, and Young yelled his request over and over until one of the Blackwater contractors shouted back to commence firing. So at this point, not only had the contractors been pushed by circumstance into engaging in combat, but they had also de facto assumed a command position over a U.S. marine. Eventually, a handful of U.S. military police and another marine would make it up to the roof to join the fight.

While the roof of the CPA headquarters offered a prime high-ground position for shooting down on those gathering on the ground outside the gates, a nearby multistory hospital, a high-rise apartment building, and other recently half-assembled construction made the entire compound vulnerable to snipers. For what seemed like hours, the men put controlled bursts into the crowd below while Blackwater snipers targeted gunmen shooting from windows a few hundred yards away. Estimates of how many insurgents were attacking the compound vary, though most have reported numbers in the hundreds. Years hunting around his small town in Kentucky had given Young the ability to acquire a target, fire, and aquire and fire again, and he did this over and over as bearded men in long robes kept charging toward the front gate. At one point, a couple of American Apaches circled overhead but didn't lay down any fire and left without landing in the compound.

Then a young captain let out a scream and yelled for a medic. They had no medic on the roof, so Corporal Young rushed over to see what he could do. Young removed the captain's gear and carefully cut away his clothing to expose wounds in the arm and back. Bullets pinged into a tin air duct and ricocheted off the cinderblocks above their heads as Young applied compresses from his first-aid kit. Young yelled for the contractors to lay down cover fire and helped walk the bleeding man down the four flights of stairs to the ground floor, where an impromptu emergency room was established.

The marine corporal loaded up on magazines and carried roughly one hundred fifty pounds of Blackwater's ammo up four stories to the roof.

Jamie Smith at the Afghan/Pakistan Border   Afghan "campaigns" in the hunt for bin Laden

The Paramilitaries

Erik Prince at Shkin   The view from a typical Pashtun compound
in Gardez

An Afghan proxy soldier's view of Pakistan

The CIA forward operating base at Shkin

The Mercenaries

Executive Outcome pilots in Sierra Leone
with Mi-24 Hind gunship

Kamajor fighter with magical
script and amulets

Cobuss Claassens with Executive Outcome's 32
Battalion vets in Sierra Leone

"Blood diamonds" fueled
war in Angola and Sierra

Sandline head Tim Spicer escorted to court in Papua New

The DynCorp Karzai protective detail at work in the palace in Kabul

Shannon Campbell on the Bremer detail in Iraq

The Praetorian Guard

Gardez, Afghanistan, where CIA contractors and Afghan proxy armies hunted for members of al-Qaeda and its leader Osama bin Laden

Craige Maxim (fourth from left) on the first Karzai detail (Karzai is sixth from left)

Billy Waugh, the oldest CIA paramilitary

Keith "Jack" Idema in Tora Bora

The Contractors

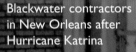

Blackwater contractors in New Orleans after Hurricane Katrina

Besieged Blackwater contractors and U.S. soldiers under fire in Najaf

The deadly mortar attack on the Gurkha camp from the Blackwater compound

Griz and Tool relax between runs

Blackwater Little Birds resupply ammunition to
contractors on a roof in Najaf

The Iraqi view of a PSD

The trunk monkey and the Hillah team's
hate truck

Iiyagi

The Blackwater Mamba team

The Coup

President Obiang of Equatorial Guinea discussing the coup

Simon Mann in Harare
© Getty Images

The view from the Hotel Bahia in Malabo, where Frederick Forsyth wrote his classic novel of a mercenary coup, *The Dogs of War*

The *Roslyn Joy*, part of Triple Options' transport fleet in the 2004 coup, in Bata Harbor

Niek du Toit in 2002 and 2006

The Antonov leased by Niek

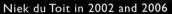

Young had time to resupply the Blackwater contractors, but no time to return to the fight himself. Blackwater's Arabic linguist was hit in the face—
blood sprayed over the floor from a quarter-sized hole in his jaw. Young
reached in with his finger and fished around in the gore until he found the
man's carotid artery and pinched it hard to close it. With his free hand, he
dragged the translator by his vest toward the stairwell. Then an incoming
bullet smacked into Young, knocking him to the floor. A bullet had
smashed into his left shoulder, coming to rest an inch from his spine. A
piece of shrapnel had also lodged in his left eye, partially blinding him.
Under fire and too amped up on adrenaline to pause for the searing pain in
his back, Young grabbed the linguist again and dragged him behind the
air-conditioning duct. He put his fingers back into the hole in his jaw and
pinched again to stop the bleeding, and a Blackwater medic applied a hasty
compress. Young then picked up the linguist and carried him down the
four flights for further emergency treatment before returning to the roof
to continue the fight. Dripping with sweat and blood, Young kept hammering away. He didn't realize that he had been shot until someone yelled
at him to get off the roof and get some medical attention. Once down
below, he faded and almost passed out.

When they heard the sound of helicopters outside, the medic told
Young he needed to catch a ride to the Baghdad hospital. Young stumbled
outside to see three helicopters with rotors buzzing, but they were black,
not green. Under fire and running low on ammo, Blackwater had called
upon its own helicopters after the U.S. military had failed to respond to
requests for backup. The three Blackwater Little Birds had flown in from
Baghdad with reinforcements and a fresh supply of ammunition, and
picked up the wounded to fly them out for medical attention.

With a new stock of ammo, the contractors continued to lay down fire
and beat back the insurgents. Two Spanish soldiers in full combat gear sat
joking behind the thick concrete wall. The Spanish contingent was supposed to be functioning in a strictly peacekeeping role and had been ordered not to return fire. They just sat and watched the action without
taking part. Lionel, Blackwater's armored car rep from Texas Armor, was
pressed into service as a spotter for Cread, a skilled shot with a sniper rifle.

Cread saw an insurgent sniper shooting from a window in the hospital building near the compound and carefully tried to pick him off. Every time he shot, Lionel winced and looked for the puff of dust as the bullet hit around the window. "A little to the left." BOOM! Wince. "A little to the right." Boom! Wince. "More." Boom! Wince.

While varying accounts by witnesses portray a compound under heavy attack, the incoming fire was not heavy enough to prevent the contractors from filming their own videos and taking pictures during the battle. Most of the video captures a steady stream of outgoing fire, with an occasional burst of incoming. One video has Blackwater IC "Mookie Spicoli" yelling, "Jesus Christ, it's like a fucking turkey shoot!"—suggesting a plethora of slow-moving easy targets and a contractor methodically picking them off.

A Blackwater contractor remembers that Sunday: "When Blackwater was hit in Najaf, in April, it wasn't a big secret. They even taped it. Clive was taping, Cread had the other camera. The military was out there, but they weren't prepared. The Blackwater guys were getting it on. Even the sales rep for the armored cars was running up and down the stairs carrying ammo. We were shooting M4s, and there was a marine on a SAW. The bad guys got hung up in the hospital. They just picked them off one by one until the Apaches showed up. The Apaches never fired a shot. They just hovered. We found out later they had orders not to engage. About twenty or thirty bad guys got into the compound. It was close."

The U.S. military apparently had larger worries than what was going on in Najaf that day. In an apparent uprising in defense of Moqtada al-Sadr, armed attacks had popped up all over the country. Fighting had also commenced in Fallujah. When the Apaches flew over assessing the situation, they must have determined that the tiny force inside the compound could handle the resistance they faced. A Navy helicopter did come by in the early evening to lay down some fire, but the heaviest of the battle had ceased by then.

"They fought all day and all night. When you read the press reports, it sounds like the military was there and Blackwater just happened to be there, but it was a Blackwater PSD in the shit—even the civilians pitched in. There were eight people defending that compound. . . . eight," the contractor emphasized.

"The army wouldn't help," Steve, the Little Bird pilot, remembers, "so we got busy." Steve had been back at the Blackwater Aviation headquarters in Baghdad when the call came in reporting that his fellow contractors were under siege in Najaf and that one marine had been wounded. The contractors started loading up three Little Birds with supplies, and Steve went to see a marine commanding officer he knew to ask permission to medevac a wounded marine back to the Baghdad hospital. Even though the CO had assented, Steve's actions still got him in trouble with the State Department. "The boy lived, but there were some folks who weren't happy and told me that they would make sure I wouldn't get paid. I told them to go right ahead and take it out of my paycheck," he says angrily. Steve was supposed to be a civilian pilot flying support for the Bremer security detail, but when his comrades needed help, he felt he had no choice but respond—even if it meant bending the rules.

Top commander in Iraq Lieutenant General Ricardo Sanchez, and his spokeman, Brigadier General Mark Kimmitt, arrived the next day to survey the aftermath of the battle and to speak in heroic terms about the fighters who had held off the insurgents. Kimmitt stated to the press, "I know on a rooftop yesterday in An Najaf, with a small group of American soldiers and coalition soldiers, Spanish soldiers and Salvadoran soldiers who had just been through about three and a half hours of combat—I looked in their eyes, there was no crisis. They knew what they were here for. They'd lost three wounded. We were sitting there among the bullet shells, the bullet casings, and frankly, the blood of their comrades, and they were absolutely confident."

They made no mention that Blackwater contractors carried the majority of the fighting and that Blackwater Aviation had provided the only supporting resupply and medevac flights. The military seemed to fear what was happening—Blackwater Security versus the Mahdi Army while the U.S. military stood by watching—essentially an American mercenary militia battling an Iraqi mercenary militia. While the rules of engagement allowed contractors to fire in defense of their lives, the formulators of those rules had not anticipated contractors being dropped into a situation where they would have to engage in hours of combat without outside support. The other outcome that became very clear was that ex-soldiers given a license to kill may choose not to cut and run as they are trained and paid to do, but eagerly and repeatedly fire into the crowds that surround them.

The next day, however, two more groups of contractors would come under fire in the town of Al Kut and would fight an intense and losing battle until they could secure their withdrawal.

Al Kut

Located about a hundred miles south of Baghdad right on the Tigris River, Al Kut is a mostly Shia city, and its roughly three hundred thousand inhabitants make it comparable in size to Fallujah. Al Kut had been taken over by the marines in April 2003, and early attempts by the clergy to take control of the city's security were gently defused. The Shia of Al Kut had no love for Saddam—particularly since he had brutally cracked down on them following the Shia uprising after the first Gulf War—but they also bristled under the rule of American occupiers, though armed attacks were infrequent. When marines handed the town over to a small peacekeeping force of Poles and Ukrainian troops in the fall of 2003, it was heralded as a model for pacification in other cities across Iraq.

The CPA had set up their headquarters on the banks of the Tigris across from the city in a compound that included an appropriated hotel and a number of other buildings. Paul Bremer had established a Regional Governance Project, which included an intelligence-gathering component, and the U.S. Agency for International Development (USAID) had contracted North Carolina–based RTI (Research Triangle Development, Inc.) to help develop a system of governance for the region. The governate coordinator (GC), Marc Etherington, was to interface with local leaders and be point man on local reconstruction efforts on behalf of Paul Bremer. A handful of Ukrainian and Polish troops stayed at the compound, but most lived on a military base about a half hour away.

KBR had a contingent tasked with construction and fortification of the compound and had hired a British company, Control Risks Group (CRG), to provide for their personal security. On March 15, 2004, Triple Canopy took control of the overall security of the CPA compound. They hired sixty-nine Iraqi guards from the surrounding area and stocked in weapons, ammunition, and communications equipment. Despite the rosy projections by CPA headquarters, things were not going well in Al Kut. Posters had gone up around town charging the RTI operation with being a Zionist and CIA-backed organization. Local leaders had asked the RTI and CPA component, along with the Ukrainian soldiers, to withdraw their people from the area.

Few local residents had jobs, even fewer had money, and the CPA was the most glaring example of American occupation. A not-insignificant percentage of the Shia community was growing impatient with the American presence, and leaders like Moqtada al-Sadr had successfully amplified their anger and frustration. Well-organized and motivated protesters gathering outside the CPA gates became a common sight. They carried flags of allegiance to Moqtada al-Sadr and followed young men with bullhorns in anti-American chants. The Iraqis, especially the Shia, had taken up protesting almost as a national sport. They were usually peaceful, if vocal, and most were ignored.

On April 5, the demonstration was a little different. After a number of Sadr-inspired armed attacks, such as at Najaf the day prior, Paul Bremer had declared Sadr an outlaw and warned that his recent spate of uprisings would not be tolerated. CPA authorities also finally made public the secret arrest warrant an Iraqi judge had issued for Sadr in August 2003, giving further provocation for pro-Sadr protesters to turn to violence. Iraqi employees of RTI had called early in the morning to warn that the day's demonstrations would be far more serious than before and that an attack could be launched that night. The group of protesters that had numbered a couple hundred a few days before had grown to over a thousand, and AK-47s and RPG launchers could be seen bobbing up and down above the crowd. Inside the city, Mahdi Army militiamen and other angry young Iraqi men were gathering. A mob had blocked the bridge spanning the

Tigris leading into the city from near the CPA compound, and the GC requested the Ukrainians secure the location. Etherington soon learned that the militia had also seized the local government offices, television station, and traffic control points. Reports were coming in that the local police were quitting in droves, with some of them just changing out of their uniforms to join the militia—all ominous developments.

When John Turner, the head of the Triple Canopy security detail, heard these reports, he put the compound on high alert. Turner soon learned that he had other problems—many of his locally hired guards had not shown up for work that morning, and others had since abandoned their posts. Some had left with their radios and weapons. His security force decimated, Turner sent out a call for reinforcements from Hillah. KBR sent home all their local workers, except three translators, and instructed other employees to prepare for a siege. Water and ammunition were broken out of boxes and stacked in places of last resort. They packed the SUVs for evacuation and filled "bug out" bags with a two-day supply of food and water. The staff was told to put on armor and helmets, if they had them, and everyone received instructions that in a worst-case scenario they should retreat to the hotel—the most secured structure in the compound. The four KBR and eight RTI employees, four CRG and six Triple Canopy security contractors, six CPA staff members, four Polish and thirty-five Ukrainian soldiers hunkered down and waited for an onslaught to begin.

When word reached Paul Bremer that one of his CPA offices was on high alert, he warned that whoever was sending the urgent appeals should tone down the wording on their communications. The GC echoed that concern and characterized the event to his boss as just a small clash with a group of fifty or so teenagers.

But as the sun climbed in the sky, bad news continued to pour in. The Mahdi Army had given notice at the Ukrainian military base that all coalition forces and representatives should pull out within twenty-four hours or face attack. Local intel sources reported that insurgents were preparing a red Opel and a white Opel as car bombs for demolition against the CPA compound. At one point, a car made a run at the front gate to test their response, then turned around and did it again. On the other side of the river, men were assembling near the police station with RPGs pointed at the compound. This infuriated the security teams because they had told the GC, Marc Etherington, many times that the compound needed high concrete barriers, or T-walls, to protect the river side from enemy fire. The British diplomat in charge of the compound, however, had not recognized the security threat and thought the ugly concrete walls would block the view of the river.

At 2:30 P.M., Bremer's office once again demanded that KBR stop mentioning the CPA in their e-mails. Baffled that the Americans snuggled safely in the Palace in the Green Zone would respond to their requests for help with instructions to stop exaggerating the situation, those hunkered down in the compound began to feel abandoned.

Just after 3:00 P.M., Triple Canopy's John Turner assembled the staff for a tersely worded briefing. Things were not looking good in the city of Al Kut. The police had surrendered control of the town to approximately three hundred members of the Mahdi Army, who had looted their weapons and equipment. The nearest contingent of coalition forces—the Ukrainian and Polish peacekeepers—were refusing to leave their base, and it didn't look like they could expect any support from the Americans.

The small group of civilian and security contractors and the remaining Polish and Ukrainian soldiers were completely cut off from escape. The KBR employees were now turned into soldiers as Triple Canopy distributed weapons and ammo. Although Turner explained that the arms were strictly for self-defense, they had in effect been drafted into defending the U.S. base. The decision was made to move into the hotel, since the perimeter was impossible to defend.

As the sun began to fade, they started generators to light the compound. Everyone was in lockdown mode—eating MREs (meals ready to eat) in the hotel, guns loaded, just waiting for the first shot. Then it began. A large blast just after ten o'clock rocked the compound, startling everyone. Then nothing. Ears straining. Eyes scanning. Just a wake-up call.

As the night progressed, the KBR team members took turns on watch, but the hours of darkness passed without incident.

After a sleepless and stressful night, April 6 began with a handful of Iraqi Triple Canopy guards and seventeen local KBR and RTI employees showing up at the gate for work. They knew why the staff was wearing armor and helmets, but they went about their work maintaining the compound and equipment until they were dismissed before 10:00 A.M. Around midmorning, fifteen Iraqis sent in as reinforcements from Triple Canopy's Hillah operation arrived. As former Free Iraqi Forces vets, they were expected to stand up better than the locals who had run away. Around 11:00 A.M., those in the compound began to hear the sound of gunfire coming from across the river—Ukrainian reinforcements had finally come off their base to try and take the bridge back from the militia. The fighting built in size and swelled with the large booms of RPG fire. The insurgents had aimed a few RPGs at the CPA compound, but they were poorly aimed and fell short.

Across the river from the CPA compound, a house used by HART security was in the unfortunate position of being right on the front line of positions set up by the Mahdi Army. In the house, South African Gray Branfield, an experienced ex-member of the Rhodesian and South African police, briefed a four-man HART security team that had just arrived from Amarah. Gray recounted four RPG rounds fired at the CPA between noon and 12:30, along with sporadic gunfire that seemed to be aimed at the CPA from a location behind their house. Just after 12:30, another RPG went off and the team discovered that two doors down to the right, the education building was being used as a base to mount the attacks, along with the roof of the building directly behind them, and an intersection to their left.

Gray called the Ukrainian military base to see if they could provide some help in getting his men out and to safety. The Ukrainians told Gray to call the nearby CPA and then hung up on him. Gray then phoned the CPA headquarters in Baghdad and received the response that they would take his report under advisement but could offer no immediate assistance. So Gray Branfield and his HART team settled in for their front-row seat watching the Mahdi attack on the CPA compound.

The Mahdi Army was trying to push across the bridge toward the compound, but the small detachment of Ukrainians held them back. Vehicles and buildings began to burn, sending up fat black columns of smoke. The Ukrainians had called for air support, and jets streaked over the city trying to locate targets but could find nothing to engage without risking collateral damage. Around 1:00 P.M., the CPA compound took its first direct RPG hit on the west side of the compound, and small-arms fire erupted on the east side. Inside the embattled garrison, Ukrainian soldiers and Triple Canopy contractors raced to elevated positions in the compound's towers to defend the perimeter. Triple Canopy security chief John Turner moved to the roof of the hotel to view the situation and direct fire. A heated battle ensued.

Across the river, the HART team found itself caught in a triangle of bullets and mortars fired back and forth between the insurgents and the CPA. Gray Branfield started negotiating with members of the militia to try to gain safe passage for his men to evacuate. The militia assured Gray that they only intended to target the CPA and offered to provide an escort out of town for the HART group. Gray went upstairs to consult his men and discuss their options. They could lock down and sit out the fighting, relying on the militia's guarantee that they were not targets; they could take the militia's offer of safe escort out of the area; or they could wait for coalition forces to extract them. The contractors didn't know if the offer of safe passage was genuine or a trick to get them out into the open. Since they could see about fifty militia members in the street around the house, they were suspicious. In a joint decision, and weighing the unknowns of an angry mob and a diffident Ukrainian response, the HART team decided to sit it out.

When Gray went downstairs to tell the assembled crowd that they planned to stay, the other team members readied their weapons to set up protective cover. Angered by their foiled ruse to bring the contractors outside, the militia members began shouting at Gray. Then there was the unmistakable clack of an AK being taken off safety, and two shots rang out, then a long burst of gunfire with bullets splintering the parapets on the rooftop and cracking into the open door.

Gray stormed back inside the house and tried to slam the door as an

Iraqi ran toward him with a pointed weapon. One of the HART contractors fired a shot, and the Iraqi went down. The team member called out asking if Gray was okay and heard back, "I'm not good." Two contractors ran to help him but quickly realized he was almost beyond help. Though still alive and conscious, he had obviously suffered a full blast on auto from an AK at close range and was bleeding profusely from multiple wounds in his torso and shattered knee. Their first thought was to get away from the unsecured doorway and drag Gray up the vertical steel ladder to the roof, but before they could, one of the militia members tossed a grenade inside the house. The men dove behind a steel water tank to shield themselves from the blast. Grenade shrapnel ripped out whatever life had been left in Gray's body, and the other contractors reluctantly left his corpse to retreat to the relative security of the rooftop.

Bullets ricocheted off the house as more militia began to arrive and moved to surround the building. After a brief pause in the gunfire, four local Iraqi HART employees, who the contractors suspected had joined the militia, showed up at the house and begged the men to leave. The men looked at the four of them and the crowd outside and shook their heads. "No."

Across the river, the CPA compound was still under heavy attack. RPG rounds were exploding with increasing tempo, mortars slammed home, and bullets whined and ricocheted off the structures By 3:00 P.M., they were surrounded, with attacks coming at them from all four sides as what was estimated to be a few hundred Iraqis poured fire into the compound. An air-raid siren sounded throughout the compound, and word spread quickly that reinforcements were coming by air. Fighter jets thundered over the city, but again dropped no ordnance.

Ammunition was beginning to run low in the towers, and the civilians shuttled boxes of ammo and reloaded magazines as fast as they could. One civilian was pressed into service as a spotter for a contractor in the northwest tower. An RPG hit the concrete T-wall directly below them, and bullets kicked into the sandbags and wall of the tower. Another RPG exploded against the wall before the shooter went down with a well-aimed shot from a contractor. With the towers under increasingly heavy and accurate fire, Turner ordered everyone to retreat into the hotel. An e-mail arrived from headquarters at 3:53: "Please know we are doing all we can from this end. The MND [Multi-National Division] is working with some fast movers [jets] and they do have some identified targets and collateral damage is not a concern. Be prepared and keep your head down."

Nothing. The jets patrolled the air, pushing the insurgents into positions of cover, but refused to drop their load. By 4:30 the contractors were exhausted and running out of water. The civilians offered to replace the contractors manning the firing line.

At 5:47, both the KBR office and the Triple Canopy house were hit, and more mortar rounds began landing closer and closer to the hotel. The staff moved to the inside hallways to avoid the intense and increasingly accurate hits.

At about 6:00 P.M., just as it seemed they were about to be overrun by the insurgents, an odd silence settled over the compound, making for a surreal pause in what had been a long day of nonstop violence. John Turner received word by phone that the Ukrainian general had arranged for a ceasefire until nine the next morning and that he was scheduled to meet leaders of the Mahdi Army at 7:30 P.M. Shortly afterward, however, bullets began to fly between Ukrainian soldiers, Triple Canopy contractors, and the militia on the northern edge of the CPA compound. An intense firefight lasted roughly five minutes before the compound fell silent again.

Two Apache helicopters showed up to hover over the area for a few hours. The besieged men took advantage of the lull in fighting to resupply ammunition to the defensive positions. They broke MREs out of their heavy brown wrappers and swallowed bites of food in between loading magazines. The Ukrainian soldiers were poorly equipped in general and certainly weren't prepared to fight at night. The KBR contractors supplied them with flashlights, radios, and other equipment, and Triple Canopy gave them fresh ammo after their stock ran low.

At 8:00 P.M., the group was informed that General Ostrovsky of the

Ukrainian contingent would not negotiate with the militia but that the ceasefire remained in effect. One hour later, however, they heard more incoming RPGs and mortars from across the river, lasting about fifteen minutes. Then John Turner received word that a Special Forces ODA team was readying for insertion and would come help defend the compound. A helicopter extraction plan was supposedly also in the works. The optimism for salvation would last a few hours, until new word came to inform them that the Ukrainian general had scratched the plans because he deemed it too dangerous to land a helicopter in the compound.

Meanwhile, in the besieged HART house, the cat-and-mouse battle continued as the militia fired up at the rooftop. In the midafternoon, a HART team member had called the CPA and the Ukrainian military base, informing them of Gray's death and their retreat under attack to confinement on the roof of their building. He had requested immediate evacuation. The HART team had prepared the roof for a helicopter extraction, but by early evening it appeared obvious one would not be coming. Taking regular small-arms fire and an occasional RPG, the HART men were surrounded and abandoned. The militia sent a negotiator up to a neighboring rooftop and urged the men to come out. The Mahdi militia said it wanted to take the men to their headquarters, where another group would escort them out of the city. It sounded like another trick, or hostage trap, so the HART team tried to buy time, hoping that the Ukrainians or Americans would finally send in a team to extract them. They went through the motions of negotiation until well after midnight, when it became clear that the ruse could be continued no longer. The men broke off their talks with the militia members, and were within minutes under attack by more small-arms fire and a couple of grenades tossed up on the roof. The vicious attack lasted only briefly, until the militia redirected its weapons toward the more attractive target across the river.

The Mahdi militia were put on the defensive after AC-130 gunships started circling, coordinating with those inside the compound to target insurgent positions. Many of the Triple Canopy contractors had been trained in their previous military career to do close air support, and a chain of communications was developed to relay the targeting information provided by the contractors to the aircraft prowling the sky above. The AC-130 circled at a constant altitude, providing a stable platform for 105-mm manually loaded cannons, 20-mm chain guns, and 40-mm grenade launchers, selecting targets with their powerful FLIR (forward looking infrared) spotlights, which identify humans heat sources and even warm engines as bright white glowing objects on the targeting screen.

The military requested that every gun in the compound open up to draw the insurgent fire for targeting purposes—an old trick to flush out the enemy. Cheered on by having the big guns for support, the civilians headed to the roof of the hotel, until the GC, Marc Etherington, ordered everyone to respect the nonexistent ceasefire. Disappointed, they stood down. But their shooting to draw enemy fire was apparently unnecessary, since a few minutes later the insurgents unleashed everything they had with devastating effect. The hotel rocked with multiple hits. Tracers and muzzle flashes quickly revealed enemy positions across the river. The gunship operators kept up a steady radio chatter with the Triple Canopy contractors, since the barrage of fire had allowed them to locate multiple enemy positions. They paused for permission to engage, but the Ukrainian general refused to allow the gunship to open fire, reasoning that the enemy positions were on top of schools, houses, and civilian structures. Despite the order, the AC-130 took out locations across the street from the compound and at least one mortar position. At 1:45 A.M., two Apache helicopters showed up, replacing the gunship and providing rotating air cover. Their presence alone successfully suppressed the heavy fire against the compound.

Turner had realized by then that the insurgents had been listening on the radios stolen from the compound by the fleeing Iraqi guards. He assembled the exhausted group to relate the good news in person—the Ukrainian command had put together ten armored troop carriers with air cover, and just before dawn they would break through the city to rescue the men inside the compound. A sense of jubilation overcame the exhaustion, and the men set to work planning for their evacuation. At 4:35 A.M, the group gathered together with their go bags, weapons, and critical equipment, waiting impatiently for the sound of helicopters and diesel engines. They soon learned that General Ostrovsky had canceled the extraction plan as too risky and likely for failure. John Turner and the CPA-based Ukrainian commander began immediately creating their own plan using the available resources in the compound. They had a collection of armored and soft-skin SUVs belonging to the security companies and could coordinate for air cover with the hovering Apaches. They had to hurry to make a self-imposed 6:00 A.M. launch date, since after morning prayers the Mahdi Army would begin setting up their mortars and readying for a new day's offensive—something the compound probably couldn't endure for another day, considering how low their supplies had run.

When the men in the HART house heard that the CPA was pulling out, they decided to trust two of their employees who offered to help them make a break for it. They put on local headscarves and made their way to the roof of an adjacent building, climbing down in the darkness to a silver Pajero SUV. They drove slowly out of town in the direction of al Amarah as the sun rose into the sky.

By 6:00 A.M., vehicles were loaded and Apaches circled above the CPA compound. KBR staff piled into the CRG armored vehicles, but there was some shuffling to see who got the favored seats in the armored vehicles and who would ride out in the soft skins and large military trucks. The CPA pulled rank. By 6:15, the convoy was ready to go and lined up on the road leading out of the compound. The Ukrainians bookended the convoy in their BTR-60 Russian-made armored troop carriers, with the security companies' armored cars driving in the next layer, while the one soft skin and the rest of the military vehicles rode in the middle of the convoy. The entire group was just waiting for the GC to get off the phone.

Marc Etherington, the CPA's governate coordinator, was still talking to General Ostrovsky, begging him to reverse his order and send in reinforcements. It was apparent he did not want to abandon his post. He ordered a CRG car to block the convoy's departure route, but the security contractors refused to obey his orders. A near revolt broke out as the group of men began shouting at the GC to get the hell in the car. Finally, an army captain of the force protection team told the GC he would be left behind if he didn't get in one of the trucks. Etherington relented, and at 6:20 the convoy left out the back gate. Not a shot was fired as they drove through town. At 7:40, the convoy pulled into the MND base at Al Kut airfield. Pulling themselves out of the vehicles—tired, dirty, and worn—the KBR and RTI employees handed their weapons back to the Triple Canopy contractors and became civilians again. The United States had abandoned a CPA regional headquarters, but its inhabitants were safe. Shortly afterward, the Ukrainian Army turned control of the town over to Sadr's militia, though U.S. forces would take it back from the Mahdi militia a couple of days later.

Later, the recriminations would fly. The Ukrainians insisted that their 1,650 men—the fourth-largest non-American contingent behind the Poles, the Italians, and the Brits—were there as peacekeepers, not combat troops, and thus were limited in their capability to respond effectively to heavy attack. Others members of the besieged teams would be more blunt. One described the Ukrainians as "cowards," explaining, "They had all the resources and support to extract us and didn't." The CPA would blame KBR for not having delivered items like sandbags and SCUD bunkers, and for not having adequate communications. Etherington would come under scathing criticism for risking the lives of the civilian and security contractors, and RTI would reduce its commitment of employees to Iraq after the violence of Al Kut. For the third time that spring the contractors were the target and the thin red line. Although the incidents in An Najaf and Al Kut were downplayed by Bremer and never fully reported in the media, it was clear that Blackwater and other private teams were a far better and more willing partner than many in the war in Iraq. When under fire, the coalition of the billing had stood their ground while the coalition of the willing stood by and watched.

CHAPTER 7

The Dog Track and the Swamp

"We thought this was something that was scaleable."
— ONE OF THE FOUNDERS OF TRIPLE CANOPY

The Southland Dog Track lies just on the outskirts of West Memphis, Arkansas, set amidst a crowd of low-budget motels and twenty-four-hour diners. Traveling southward from Triple Canopy's Chicago headquarters on Amtrak's overnight City of New Orleans, I have come down to watch a few days of their training and selection process. The sixty men vying for spots on one of Triple Canopy's contracts will bunk at the Ramada down the street but will split most of their waking hours showing off their driving ability at the dog track or their shooting skills at a private shooting range. The hardscrabble surroundings of the training enterprise offer a concrete example of the contrast between the big-money lifestyle of private security firm owners and the low-budget existence of those who make their contracts and business pay off.

Triple Canopy is one of the newest and most aggressive players to appear on the private security scene. The name refers to the multiple layers of greenery that protect the floor of the rain forest and draws a metaphor for the multiple layers of security Triple Canopy applies to keep their clients safe. The company was founded in September of 2003 by a group of friends and investors. The core group consists of two army buddies from Special Forces, Matt Mann and Tom Katis, and John Peters, an investment banker. Iggy Balderas, former command sergeant major for Delta, makes the fourth for the current board of directors. Within their first year of operations, the company had grown from the original core group to a business supporting over eight hundred employees, and had generated over $100 million in revenue.

Triple Canopy likes to promote their corporate culture as derived from Delta, in comparison to Blackwater's SEAL legacy and HART's SAS ethos. Promoting a Delta-based image implies a secretive and management-oriented method of doing business, compared to Blackwater's boisterous and aggressive persona, while HART likes to maintain the lowest profile possible.

Like many start-ups in the exploding private security industry, Mann, Katis, and Peters started with little and scrambled to flesh out the corporate structure and hire and train operators after they had won their first bid. Matt Mann recalls how aggressively they worked to get that initial contract and the major financial risks they all assumed in order to pursue the opportunity. When a contract came up for bid to protect the governates in Iraq, Mann said, "The only catch is that to bid, you had to go over and do a security survey of the sites." Of the four companies that were asked to bid on the $300-million blanket protection contract over six months, MVM and ArmorGroup never showed up, so Blackwater and Triple Canopy directly competed to win the contract. Matt Mann and former Navy SEAL Hal Poff "ran around the country in the back of a BMW with a towel around our heads," but Blackwater only showed up to survey half the sites, opening it up for the nascent Triple Canopy to win the rest.

According to Matt Mann, "We won seventeen out of thirty-three [contracts]. The first six months was $80 million. The renewal was in the forty to sixty million range. We ended up lining up fifty million in credit from Wells Fargo and spending nine million in capital. To get in place, before we received one dollar, we would have to spend eight million. We had already spent a couple of million before we even had a contract. We were paying eight percent for our money, the penalty for being a new company. And it was a fixed-price bid so the government didn't guarantee us a profit."

Their investment has paid off, since Triple Canopy is now one of the biggest American providers of private security services, referred to as one of the "Big 3," along with Blackwater and DynCorp. In early 2006, the "Big 3" won a shared $1-billion contract to provide American embassy security worldwide.

By the time of this writing, Triple Canopy had made the big jump from their original Chicago offices to a suite near the locus of power in Herndon, Virginia, outside of Washington, DC. They've also dramatically upgraded their training facilities, but when I visited them in mid-2004, they were still living in the spartan existence of a fledgling start-up. Spending a week with the men of Triple Canopy training in West Memphis, Arkansas, I got to know the blood and flesh on which the Triple Canopy empire has been built.

During the fighting in Afghanistan and very early in the Iraq war, private security contractors were drawn from the most qualified and experienced operators, but that pool of potential recruits has been depleted by the demands of the security problem in Iraq, and now the applicants span a wider spectrum. Triple Canopy gets in an initial pool of roughly eleven hundred résumés a month, of which about one hundred fifty have any real credentials. About 15 to 20 percent come straight from military service, and the rest come from private companies, though they may still have a military background. The men in this class come from a variety of backgrounds and range from the experienced and cool to the intimidated and desperate. They have passed the initial résumé review and background check by personnel, and now have to prove that they can do the job. The ages range from midtwenties to early fifties. None of them are being paid while they go through the training, but Triple Canopy buys them a ticket to Memphis and pays for their accommodations.

By the time I arrive, the aspiring contractors have checked into the Ramada, two to a room. The hotel also houses a gaggle of senior citizen tourists, who watch and whisper about the men as if they're some variety of exotic species. The men sport what looks like all brand-new out-of-the-box 5.11 brand khakis and contractor gear—a fashion interpretation of OGA gear for plainclothes missions. Right now in West Memphis they belong to an ill-defined warrior class, but back home they are mostly average middle-aged men getting slightly paunchy and shaving their heads to hide the bald spot. They have wives, families, mortgages, car payments. Most possess a high school diploma and a decade or two of experience developing skill sets that have few applications in the civilian world. More than once in my time with them I will hear the common Special Forces joke that after twenty years in the service, an SF operator will have only a topaz ring, a Harley, an ex-wife, and can apply for a job as a Wal-Mart greeter.

A big, blond, and jovial Midwesterner named Jim Troutman—nickname Moose—heads the Triple Canopy training program. Jim holds court in a spartan suite on the second floor, though he tells me that his instructors stay at the nearby Holiday Inn because they don't like the bedbugs here. An ex-army and former Delta operator, his health and demeanor make him appear at least a decade younger than the "pushing fifty" he gives me for his age.

He was in the military for twenty-two years and six months before he was shown the door. He phrases it, "You do your twenty years and phhhhht," as he mimics the trash being thrown out. "I was in Beirut, El Salvador, Zaire—forty-six countries."

Since then he hasn't really retired. "I worked mostly in security—a year and a half in Bosnia, a year and a half in Kosovo. The Philippines. Afghanistan. After 9/11, I trained air marshals."

Jim has been successful in his professional life, but as he advises me, "You can't hold a personal life together in this line of work. . . . I am not married anymore. In this work, you can't even keep a girlfriend." He shows me a picture of his latest flame—a very young and attractive Hispanic-looking woman. Since I spend so much time away from home, he offers me a tip he has picked up on how to manage personal relationships over long distances: "Go on FTD.com and set up everyone's anniversaries and birthdays in advance."

The ever-smiling and bespectacled Jim exudes pride about the quality of his makeshift training program, bragging that all his instructors have PSD and military training, and some have had recent combat experience in Iraq. He tells me the locals around West Memphis call his students the "Iraqi Killers" and claims that "crime has dropped dramatically in this town since we moved in." He doesn't believe that you need the affluence of Blackwater's seven thousand acres and a bunch of bells and whistles to train and select. "It's all about the quality of instructors and training," he assures me. "We invest about twenty grand in these guys before we hire them. We don't want their planes crashing, so we even stagger their flights."

Corporate usually sends down about sixty men for a class, but Jim expects almost a third will be sent home without an offer of employment. Over the five-day course, they will cover State Department and higher protection detail skills and make sure the men can work cohesively on ever-changing teams. The men learn first aid, how to use a GPS (Global Positioning System), security fundamentals, advance work (checking out a location), and driving. The weapons training will start with the Glock 9-mm pistol using individual movement, and then advance to moving and shooting in large groups using the M4 rifle. As Triple Canopy gets up to speed, they will integrate heavier weapons like the Mark 19 grenade launcher, .50 cal machine gun, and more sophisticated group driving and shooting techniques.

Cecil, a sixtysomething ex–Special Forces who helps out with training, takes me to check out their driving course at the dog track—a dilapidated facility that can barely fill a dozen seats for the races. Luxuries for the mostly comatose dog race fans consist of plastic seats, cheap hot dogs, and watery beer. The muzzled greyhounds walk at a glacial pace to the starting booth. A starting bell sounds as a mechanical pink "rabbit"—actually just a bit of worn-out fluff—sets off on a circuit around the track with the dogs trying desperately to keep up. Somehow it seems it is a fitting allegory for the men who have come here to chase their dream to be contractors. From the bored looks of the few spectators, it seems that the shelter from the afternoon sun provides more of an attraction than the dogs.

Outside on the empty side of the track, the trainees are driving a circuit of drills. The track looks like a circus of orange cones, smoking tires, and weaving rented GMC Suburbans. Although a trained eye or ear can quickly sort out a marine from a cop from a Green Beret, the idea is to judge them solely on their skills and teamwork. If hired to do personal protection, they will have to work well within a team and be able to react to changing situations regardless of their past training.

On the side of the track, Cecil explains the system: "We use the big Suburban so they can get used to a big vehicle being moved. . . . They do swerve tests, reverse outs, and other exercises using orange cones." The drills are designed to simulate a convoy coming under attack. Instead of grenades, the instructors throw fluorescent yellow tennis balls in front of the trucks. The students slam on the brakes, coordinate reverses, and re-form the convoy for escape. In Iraq they might drive anything from a small import to an armored sport utility vehicle, but in West Memphis, they rely mostly on GMC Suburbans and Chevy Sedans from National Car Rental. They buy full insurance on each one, and Cecil tells me National doesn't seem to mind when they're returned a little bruised. "Or at least they never complain. We returned one that was rolled many times. I can't remember the story we invented, but they just looked at it and at us and smiled."

The students vary widely in their driving skills. Many hesitate to lay on the power, while others lose control. One smashes into another car in yet another incident that will have to be explained to the rental company. A palpable tension hangs over these seemingly mundane exercises. Some panic and turn left when the instructor yells "Right." Others make excuses, some curse. The instructors don't get angry, but just calmly suggest improvements and provide critiques to get the trainees up to Triple Canopy requirements. "We drive aggressively but try to strike a balance between being conspicuous and being a bullet magnet," Cecil tells me.

In his time as a trainer for Triple Canopy, Cecil has learned one important lesson: "Cops know how to drive; soldiers know how to shoot."

Tap, Rack, Bang

After a short drive past cotton fields and across weathered plank bridges, we arrive at a shooting range that makes the dog track look upscale. I see a sign with the Triple Canopy logo draped across the worn fence as we pull into the parking lot. The local shooting range complex Triple Canopy has hired for training looks about as permanent as the sand dunes on which it is built. A couple of trailers bolted together act as the main office. Inside, photos, plaques, and rows and rows of dusty hats from police, military and other units who have trained here cover the walls. There is even a signed photo of George and Laura Bush. The range has portable classrooms, storage containers, and a rambling collection of ranges and dilapidated "kill houses" constructed of railroad ties. Kill houses are crude mock-ups of building layouts that will be used to teach lessons in clearing rooms and close-quarter battle techniques using live fire.

The temperature is about eighty degrees and humid—a hazy day with few clouds. When we arrive, the teams are already practicing moving and shooting in teams. Today they are training with live ammunition in their M4s—the shortened version of the standard-issue M16. Most are conversant with the standard military rifle.

The ranges look low key. Old railroad ties pounded into sand berms soak up bullets, and makeshift shade structures with large, wide tables provide a space for loading and cleaning weapons. The instructor, Dave, a young athletic man wearing Oakley sunglasses and a white Under Armor shirt, lays out the program for me.

"This drill is an immediate action drill. They are trained to break contact because they are bodyguards, not infantry. The secondary purpose is proper utilization of cover. The tertiary point is using buddy teams. . . . I am just trying to get them to communicate. Most of the people are fairly good shooters, but they have to work as a team. We get guys that have a lot of tactical background. You also get a wide variety of shooting skills. Some infantry guys have never shot a Glock. Some cops haven't shot a long gun. Just their ability to handle stress is a key element of success here.

"We're looking for a guy who can be led, who can listen, who doesn't come with ears shut, and who can shoot. A guy who doesn't play well with others is not going to do well. In this type of environment, about sixty or seventy percent of the people are leaders. If they are a leader that can't follow, they don't make it here. You can really read a guy just by watching. The eyes will tell a lot. You can stop a guy in the middle of an exercise and ask him what he is doing. If he gives that big deer-in-the-headlights stare, chances are his brain is a big dry-erase board with nothing on it. I tell them, 'If you don't know what you are doing, don't do it faster.' There is no suppressive fire for contractors. They have to account for every round."

He excuses himself to address the class of a dozen students carrying M4 assault rifles. They are pretending they have come under attack and are working on extraction techniques. The men split off into two-man teams and practice a "scoot and shoot," where one lays down covering fire as the other retreats, and then they switch so the other can reload and move back while the other fires at the cardboard assailants. "Okay, let's remember to communicate. Plain, unbroken, American English," Dave yells.

Although the instructors love plain American English, they yell out commands through a small megaphone in their own special language: "Download your primaries. Leave your pistol hot. We go dry first and then we go live. Suck up the shade. Drink water. Get your sling on. Observe your weapon." The instructor uses an air horn to pause the drill. Sometimes it's to communicate a better technique, like shooting around a corner; sometimes it's to point out that they would have all been killed in a real-life scenario.

In one instance, a gun jams—a stovepipe in gunnery lingo—and the student, Miller, stops to unjam it. Dave, the instructor, stops the lesson and shows him the correct way to eject the bullet casing from the M4 without endangering his teammates. "All right, you get a stovepipe. Remember . . . slap." He flips a switch on the side. "Pull." He pulls back the bolt with two fingers. "Observe." He peers into the barrel to make sure the bullet has been ejected. "Okay, then, release and tap." Dave calls the method "SPORT."

A hand shoots up. "We never use that acronym," says a beefy blond-bearded student. "In the Navy we use 'tap, rack, bang.'"

"Whatever tribe you are from, just follow the procedure," replies Dave.

That evening, the instructors get together back at the Ramada for a closed session to decide who has survived the day. Each day they meet for distillations of the day's performances and a culling of the class. Of the nine instructors and staff in the room, four will go over the driving and five evaluate the shooting. Jim explains, "We started at forty-six. Two dog handlers have dropped. Right now we are at thirty-eight. Not bad, but there are more to go. Last class we dropped nine in one day. Now we are looking at dropping some for weapons safety."

The instructors lock the door to the coincidentally named Delta Room, close the curtains, and break out the beer and chips. The tan manila folders on the conference table contain the men's full personnel files and a full-page black and white photo of each person. Even though it contains the men's personal information, they refer to the candidates by number while discussing each individual performance. One instructor pulls a file, calls out a number, and looks around for agreement. "A little nervous but performs well as a team player?"

The rest nod while sipping their Miller Lite.

"Forty-two, thirty-eight, thirty-five, forty-five, and thirty-one are not looking good."

As the instructors go through the class roster, it becomes apparent that their focus is on the 20 percent who may or may not make it. Although most of the washouts got booted early on, a few candidates still run hot and cold—retained because they initially displayed skills but progressively show more incompetence or questionable decision making.

One of the instructors reads from his hand-written notes and expands: "Sixteen came up early on the radar after we changed his title to NUG [for knuckle dragger]. He is an 'excuse-er.' I told him until he sees targets, the weapon stays on safe. The dumb-ass award goes to the guy who puts his weapon on fire. His critical thinking consists of dog turd."

Another instructor compares his notes. "Sixteen is a cork in the river.

He has no cognitive ability. When they ran, he ran. When they stopped, he stopped. And, oh yeah, Mike had to take him aside to talk to him about his urination. He was pissing on the range." The instructors laugh.

Another instructor adds, "By the way, sixteen on the end of his last run didn't give a 'last man' call out. He let three run by his barrel. It has been sixteen, sixteen, sixteen all day," referring to the number he had been admonishing.

After evaluating everyone's shooting performance, the discussion turns to driving class. "We can count all the good drivers on one hand. They picked up the two-car motorcade pretty quick. We are evaluating about two or three drops. We are discussing four. We had a little fender-bender today between the lead and the follow. The scenario was this—we pulled out of the circle, the lead comes up and blocks up and the limo swerved. Someone hit a bumper." The instructor pauses. "We have insurance on this?" The rest nod. "Okay, I don't have a problem with that. Decision to drop?" The chorus nods again silently. "Okay, we can get 'em home in time for church."

They've worked their way through the stack of personnel files and go back to review their discussion. They have decided to drop three applicants just one day short of the final exercise. One other, Don Stout, an ex-cop, they deem to be "too immature," but they decide to retain him, though they agree he will need an "ass whipping" to correct his "cockiness and lack of focus on the task." An ass whipping is a term to describe a serious talk about how close he came to being dropped. The instructors pack up their empty bottles and corn-chip bags and head back to their rooms at the Holiday Inn.

At dinner the students discuss their career expectations. They're nearing the end of the training class, and if they make it through the final cut, they figure they will make it to graduation. Strangely enough, the candidates seem to have a limited understanding of what will happen if they are hired. Angel, a former Special Forces and current Triple Canopy employee, is eating with them and answering questions.

Don Stout, the small-town cop from Mississippi, opens up. "This job means more than you know. I just got married eight months ago. I've never had to provide for anyone before. I've got a lot riding on this." Don has trouble coming to grips with the 90/30 cycle of rotations, but Angel explains it clearly: "You get ninety days in-country, then thirty on leave, and then another ninety if you get back on a detail." They all know they will make between $500 and $700 a day. Don does the math and calculates that it adds up to $18,500 a month, and at best $162,000 a year. There may be a $30-a-day per diem, one suggests. His fellow trainees chide him about his need to continually ask questions, but Don appears oblivious to their criticism. His next topic of concern is about what there will be for his wife if he gets killed. Angel explains that he will get Defense Bases Act (DBA) coverage that only pays out $65,000 if he is killed but that many contractors get supplemental insurance if they can afford it. Don pipes up with one last comment on his possible demise: "For my funeral, I want them to play the Black Watch on bagpipes." The rest roll their eyes.

The Cut

Saturday begins with a downpour. The sun has not yet risen when the men begin trickling down to the breakfast area. They sit together in clusters, trying to make a decent meal of the motel's tiny buffet-sized muffins, cereal, and junk food. By 7:00 A.M. they have gathered outside the classroom, standing around the closed door in a huddle that emanates the smell of soap and drugstore aftershave. An instructor opens the door and beckons Poor, a bald SWAT team leader from Orange County, California, to come inside the motel meeting room. Minutes later, Poor reappears to read from a list of candidates. "The following will go in for counseling, the rest will wait in their rooms until called."

As Poor calls out the numbers, each of those asked to stay behind react as if punched. When he hears his number, Don Stout winces and drops his head. All the bravado of yesterday has vanished. When the rest of the group heads off to begin another day of training, they leave behind four very nervous and dejected men.

First, the instructors call in Summer, an SF retiree in his early thirties. The other men all look at Summer, shake their heads, and wish him luck.

As the door closes, a tangible, almost theatrical, tension settles over the remaining three as they wait to find what their future holds. When the classroom door opens, the men meet Summer's eyes with hopeful, imploring looks. Summer makes a cutting motion across his neck. The rest know for sure they are out. Stout starts chain-smoking Marlboro Reds.

The ritual repeats itself as the next two go in looking nervous and come out looking depressed. Only Stout remains. He can't stand the pressure. He turns to me and a torrent of almost panicked words seem to just fall out of his mouth: "I have to provide for my family. How can I provide for my family? There is not much in the Smokey Mountains." He pauses for a moment, clenching his jaw to fight back the tears. "I am a Medal of Valor recipient. My mother was dying of cancer, so I turned down Blackwater, turned down a couple of offers. I need this job. You know how much I spent on this gear and getting here?" It is all crashing down. He stops blabbering, appearing to become resigned to his fate. "I have never met a better bunch of guys. It's poetry to watch them work. I have seen some Feds do this, but they don't match what these guys do."

As he shuffles through the doorway, Stout carries himself with the air of a defeated man. When he comes out ten minutes later, he looks like a man transformed. They've granted him a reprieve; he only got a warning about his performance level and pointers on how he needs to improve. "Man, that was an ass puckerer," he tells me. "First thing I said when I sat down was, 'Permission to release bowels, sir.'" He chuckles at his good fortune, but then he snaps back into his recalcitrant mode. "If you saw *Deliverance*, that's where I am from. . . . There is nothing else out there for me."

Afterward, Jim Troutman comes out and tells me that two of the men have been asked not to come back, but the third (Summer) was told he could reapply in one year. "He needs seasoning. I think he will do fine when he comes back." Jim feels for the men, particularly since they made it through all but the final day of the course. "Some of them cry. Some of them get angry. It can be tough, but you also know the guys over there, and you don't want to send them over because they might end up killing someone." Of the two dozen men they have scrubbed, the final cull is the toughest. He explains, "They passed the black and white part of the course, but here we deal with the intangible." He feels bad for most of the guys but recalls one particularly memorable candidate he was glad to let go. "We had a guy just like David Koresh. He had knee pads on, a bushy beard, long hair—a real wild man. He was pissed when we let him go. We don't want happy triggers. You want numbers, but you don't want a guy to turn a Mark 19 [grenade launcher] on a crowd."

The washouts have a couple of hours to pack before Cecil drives them to the Memphis airport. I bump into Miller, an olive-skinned and slightly overweight ex-Ranger, on the upper walkway of the motel shortly after he has been told to pack his stuff. He tells me, "It's the first time I have done the duffel bag drag and I wasn't happy." He admits that he has not been performing well and invites me into his dim room to discuss things out of range of the other students' stares. He begins by admitting that he accepts the instructors' critiques. "What I could do at twenty-six is not what I can do at thirty-six."

Still, it burns that a small-town ex-cop made the cut over him. "I jumped into Panama in eighty-nine," he says as a way of protest. "The other guy they dumped is SF. They left in two cops!" Miller's incredulity exemplifies the IC world's unspoken pecking order, shaped by shooting skills and combat experience. Retired cops fall at the bottom of the food chain, followed by army reserves, FBI, regular marines, Army Rangers, Marine Forward Recon, all the way up to Vanilla SF, DEVGRU (SEAL Team 6), and finally Delta Force. Each of these has a different language, culture, affiliation, and loyalty, so they nearly always break into like-minded groups and view the other tribes as somehow suspicious. Miller just doesn't think that makes much sense to hire ex-cops if they're supposed to end up in a place like Iraq. He feels himself getting angry and changes his tone. "Even though they binned me, the instructors are top-notch. I thought that with these guys I would have a better chance of staying alive."

Miller has relaxed enough to really start talking, and within minutes he pours out his story. "My legitimate business is a moving company. My hobby is big-wave surfing. My other hobby is skydiving. I was also a professional freestyle fighting teacher. I am thirty-six and won't even be boxing and wrestling for much longer. Even though I have a furniture moving business, I do some gigs part-time, mostly in the private sector. Mostly bodyguard work. I would just reenlist, but I am too old. I have two kids, an ex-wife, and a mortgage. We are older now. We have more responsibilities. The first time I went downrange in Panama, I was making fourteen hundred dollars a month. When you are older, you are stupid if you don't make money with your skills.

"When nine-eleven happened, I was pissed. I wanted to go downrange. So I went this route. My money from my first rotation was going to be for my daughter. I want to get in a custody battle for one of my daughters. Unlike some of the other guys here, I know the realities of what this work pays. Let's say you make sixty grand for your first rotation, you are only going to bring home forty. If you did three rotations, you might make one-twenty a year. My wife is making ninety, and she is not getting shot at.

"I had one bad day because I brought sixteen years of muscle memory of shooting my way, and two days the way they want. It's not that they are wrong and I am right. One day I froze on the range, not because of a stovepipe—I froze thinking, if I don't get this, I won't have money for my custody battle.

"The common denominator here is that we are all veterans. We want to be involved, but we can't just be Private Snuffy and make no money. One of the kids who got binned today was a Ranger. He just got out of the army as a spec four, so he thinks this is a shit ton of money.

"When I was a Ranger, I was very proud. I felt like I was doing something with my life. There is no pride in what I do now. I might make seven grand in a day moving boxes. I am around all these corporate types. A CFO making a quarter million looks down on me and, dude, he is not entitled to carry my jock. You need to be around people you respect. In five hundred years they are not going to give a fuck about my wife's oil company, but Iraq will matter. We want to do something worthwhile with the time we have left."

Feel Good Jammie Jammie

Those trainees not flying home today will be sitting in a classroom to learn the finer points of working a personal security detail. For their final exercise, the class members will be put in teams and given as close to a real-life mission as possible. The exercise will revolve around protecting a "principal," or client, while transporting them to and from a predesignated site. The scenario will create a staged violent incident, and the trainers will evaluate how the men react. No one ever has immunity from being dropped, but the instructors feel confident at this point that all students will do well, and the graduation diplomas have already been printed and personally signed.

The instructor starts the class with a briefing on the basics of the PSD and the peculiar vocabulary of the work: "You have a principal or client. When we are out of the car, we are walking the diamond, one in front, one in back, and two on each side. Some people call him the VIP. He rides in the limo, which can be a truck or a car. There is a lead car and an advance vehicle. There can be a bump truck—a heavy vehicle that moves in around and beside the VIP to push him off the X, or point of contact. There is also a CAT team, counterassault team. This is the firepower in the rear. CAT team members are double-A personality types. They are looking for a fight. In our experience over there, the Iraqis—Sunni or Shia—will not stay and fight. The guys that come over the border will fight. They are like us. The idea is to engage the enemy long enough for the principal to get away. Once that is done, we break contact.

"The CAT vehicle has a load plan for crew served weapons, extra ammo, jack, medical kit, litter . . ." He uses a dry-erase board and queries the class on what else should go in the CAT vehicle. Hands pop up. "Grenades?" asks one student. "Smoke," offers another. The list fills out: night-vision or other optics, countersniper gear, gas masks and chem equipment, breaching tools, tow strap, hi-lift jack. The instructor makes a separate list for the gear carried by the rear car in the convoy: "Water, chow, comms, GPS, batteries, spare run flats, armor, and helmets." The students dutifully take notes on how to pack.

For Sunday's run, they will use car models as code names. For example, if the operation has been compromised, "Corvette" will be announced over the radio. Codes are important, even on scrambled transmissions, since locals can overhear radio conversations and signal attackers.

Before the course ends for the day, the instructor restates one last time that they actually get paid to run away, that their job is not to engage the enemy but to get them off the X. The students will find out the next day how good they are at "running away."

Sunday arrives. The rain has dissipated and the sun is rising on a beautiful morning as we drive out to the range. Dave, the shooting instructor, speaking in his own special language, says that he set up extra targets on the range for the trainees so they can get some "feel good jammie jammie." He also mentions that the range will be empty today. "All the zipperheads [cops] won't be on the range when we pay a thousand a day."

The students crowd into the small portable classroom while Dave goes over the rules of the range. He holds up a target. "The brown side of a silhouette is a shoot target." He flips it over. "A white side is a no shoot." They will be using live ammunition and will be graded on their performance. The students don't know if more will be dropped in a final elimination before graduation. I wonder if that ambiguity drives their obvious tension more than the exercise that awaits them.

Outside the men collect their weapons. They are going hot.

The instructors have real-world experience, and they do their best to replicate actual conditions. With a little imagination, West Memphis has become a city in Iraq. The range echoes with the dry mechanical clacks of M4s and Glocks being checked and loading. The students do radio checks using plug-in earphones and wrist mikes. The men sit in their vehicles at a sideways slant so they can shoot out the window. They hold their doors mostly closed so they can throw them open at a moment's notice. Although they worked on thoroughly planning their drop last night, they know some unknown contingency awaits them.

The first exercise simulates a meeting between a local mayor and his group of irate citizens. The principal is a State Department official sent to meet the mayor. The advance man goes in to survey the situation. He jots

down some quick notes and radios back with details on the number of
people present and the locations of entries and exits. The lead person
seems nervous and tramples over an area described by the advance person
as a precious flowerbed when they're escorting the principal into the
meeting. Suddenly, before the meeting begins, the instructors fan out and
fire blanks into the ground around the meeting area to simulate an assassination attempt. The agent in charge (AIC) covers the principal and pushes
him into the Suburban while the others provide covering fire and shoot
into the brown targets. The team does well but is mildly lectured about
the importance of being sociable and not antagonizing the locals by stepping on their flowers.

The last scenario played out on the ramshackle range is more complicated. The team has to walk their principal to a meeting over a hundred
yards of soft sand from where the cars must be parked. The rooms and
entry are confusing, and this time they will have to protect two principals.
There are also groups of men hidden inside the rooms. Some are hostile,
but others are simply designated as rabble. A few wrap T-shirts around
their heads as turbans. The shooting begins once the PSD is inside the
meeting room, and the crowd begins chanting and yelling at the men. The
situation becomes confused as one of the two principals dives under a table
in mock terror. Distracted by the surging mob, the PSD shoots their way
out of the house only to discover they have left one principal behind. The
instructors urge the mock group of angry men to take the remaining principal hostage and taunt the men. The team fights their way back to put their
one principal in the car, losing a few members of their team as casualties,
who then must be dragged, complete with armor and weapons, through
the heavy sand. Exhausted and panting, the remaining team members
must fight their way back into a far more dangerous and hostile situation.
As they work their way slowly back to the house, the team is "gunned
down" and the instructor decides that the principal would have already
been killed. Now with most of the team killed or wounded and one of
their principals dead, it has become a heroic but pointless attempt.

The instructor calls them over and asks the team what they think.
"That we fucked up?" answers one, dryly. "Shades of Fallujah," says an-

other. The instructor gives them his own assessment: "You guys did a good job getting in, but when it became complex . . . you didn't assign a second AIC—usually the shift leader—to watch the second principal."

Don follows up with a point that elicits a groan. "Now we have to notify his next of kin that he has been killed. We are going to be up all night writing after action reports."

Despite the screwup, none of them are bumped off the graduation roster. The instructor just gives them one fundamentally important thing to remember from the experience of the third exercise: "The lesson is everyone you take in, you bring out."

Terrorist Training

A bleak industrial panorama intermingles with the flat yellow grass marshlands of the East Coast on the drive south on I-95 from Washington, DC. Near Williamsburg, we whiz by the exit for Camp Peary, "the Farm" of CIA training fame. Around the mouth of the Potomac, Norfolk Naval Base, the nerve center of the American naval machine, rises out of the landscape in a tangle of towering gray cargo cranes, massive ships, and sprawling storage yards. The East Coast Navy SEAL teams call the nearby Little Creek Naval Base home.

I'm heading down to the Blackwater training facility with Walter Purdy, an ex-marine and former security staffer for the presidential helicopter, to help him teach a week-long training program he runs called Mirror Image. Purdy's literature describes the course as "an intensive, one-week classroom and field training program designed to realistically simulate terrorist recruiting and training techniques, and operational tactics." About sixty Special Forces, Secret Service, marines, FBI agents, independent contractors, and other hand-picked attendees will spend the next week learning to think and act like terrorists so they can better understand and anticipate their tactics. Purdy has invited me to participate, working under the assumption that I've learned something from my years of traveling and living with rebel terrorist and paramilitary groups. Though the course is operated under the purview of the Terrorism Research Center,

Purdy has worked out a deal with Erik Prince so he can take advantage of Blackwater's spacious and well-equipped training compound.

Although Prince has had Navy experience on a non-covert SEAL team, Blackwater's image is culturally rooted in black-ops SEAL Team 6, or DEVGRU, the elite antiterrorism group and navy equivalent of the U.S. Army's Combat Applications Group, better known as Delta. Given the secretive nature of much of their work, and their almost paranoid suspicion of the media, few outsiders earn the privilege of visiting the Blackwater training complex.

It's a three-hour haul from downtown DC, and the back of our rented Ford Expedition is loaded with Glock weapons, ammunition, Simunition, coolers, and protective gear. Crossing the border into North Carolina, the two-lane highway begins passing through a collection of low-slung and haphazardly arranged industrial buildings, churches advertising bingo or a fish fry, and small modular homes set back on neatly manicured lawns. We've been warned that the local cop relishes trapping visitors with the audacity to speed through his jurisdiction, welcoming them to Moyock with a friendly $128 ticket.

Blackwater is the biggest employer around here, with at least two hundred fifty men and women working in the steel target factory and on the ranges. If they have a full slate of classes going on to train security contractors for a Blackwater gig, that number might grow to five hundred. That does not include the contractors or employees working in Afghanistan, Iraq, or other areas. Before 9/11, the bears probably outnumbered the employees on Erik's seven thousand acres of swampland.

The streams that flow through the swamps of Camden and Currituck counties, which run dark from tannins leached from decaying vegetable matter, inspired the name "Blackwater." The land is flat, pine-covered, and swampy in areas, green rolling fields in others. The large black bears, which gave the company its bear-print logo, can be seen at dawn and dusk, lurking at the edge of the bogs as they forage for berries.

We almost miss the turnoff onto the narrow, potholed Puddin Ridge Road, which dead-ends just a short way down at the gate and the empty guard shack that secures Blackwater from the outside world. Walter punches in the simple four-digit security code, and the gates slowly swing open to allow us entry. Driving into the compound, we pass an ocean of what look like junked cars with grease-stick numbers on the windows. Blackwater's driving range, designed with State Department standards in mind, looks like a racetrack and sounds like a movie set. The contractors use it to learn how to dodge improvised explosive devices and escape attackers, and to practice high-speed close-protection moves. The "Boy's Own" adventure scenario is reinforced by the hulks of old airplanes used for practicing hijacker assaults and by the gray steel ship's superstructure used for teams to practice ship boarding and clearing. The late-afternoon sunlight makes the coarse crushed stone of the shooting range glitter with the brass of spent bullet casings. No one keeps count of how much ammo is shot here, but many recruits and trainees will shoot more rounds in a week than they have in their entire military or police career. Large yellow earthmovers kick up clouds of soft brown dust as they carve out space for more shooting ranges. A 6,000-foot airstrip and a modern headquarters building are two plans in the works for the future. Erik always has plans upon plans for expansion to keep the Blackwater facility state-of-the-art.

If not for the sound of gunfire, the log arch with the bear-paw logo we drive under would remind me of a Boy Scout summer camp. We seem to have entered the kingdom of bang, since the constant sound of gunfire—automatic, single or short burst, small caliber, machine gun, or high-powered—provides a pervasive and inescapable soundtrack to our drive. Even at seven thousand acres, the sound follows us all four miles to Blackwater headquarters in the center of the compound. The headquarters for one of the fastest-growing and aggressive security companies look incongruously picturesque, since the offices inhabit a cabinlike building set on the edge of a large lake and surrounded by dense greenery. A nearby rudimentary building provides a bunkhouse for the students.

Shortly after we arrive, everyone gathers for an introductory briefing. I meet the other instructors—a British cop who worked undercover in Northern Ireland, a marine who survived the Beirut embassy bombing, and a gaggle of other experts with a variety of special skills from explosives to the terrorist mind-set. We meet the students—men and women who work in the rapidly growing antiterrorism business. From the round of introductions, I get the impression that most of the major players in the War on Terror have representation here, since I meet security contractors, Homeland Security, army special operations, police, marines, admitted intel folks, and a sizable contingent who don't name their employer. Some of them have come on the government's dollar, some have self-funded the experience. Since this is an advanced course, all have a background and experience related to counterterrorism, whether from behind a desk in a stateside bureaucracy or on the ground in the Middle East. Any independent security contractors accepted to this course have already gone through the low-level induction and would take Mirror Image to boost their professional skills and standing. The students are excited that there will be shooting, so the course won't be all PowerPoint hell. After a few sodas and conversation, it's off to get a good sleep before tomorrow's long day.

Other than a few quiet moments at dawn and at dusk, the sounds of weapons being fired and explosions detonated continue to harass the peace of the countryside day and night. The crickets, birds, and other noisemakers of the forest have long since fled the squealing of tires interspersed with loud BOOMS and the constant howling of high-powered sniper rounds. Summer camp for mercenaries, I joke as the muffled cacophony lulls me to sleep the first night.

The first day out is a predawn roust for the instructors. We have to get the students out of the sack and into their first exercise. The men roll out in shorts and T-shirts. Everyone is issued *kefyias*, the style of checked headscarf usually worn by Palestinians. Walter buys them in bulk from a Jewish guy in Brooklyn. Everyone gets a copy of the Koran as well. The entire class is divided up into teams of about ten each, with each one representing a different terrorist group. Because of my time spent with the rebels in Grozny, I make my team "Chechens."

The predawn warm-up begins with an exercise where each team must silently slip each member through a section of a rope spiderweb without touching the rope or making a noise, simulating the Palestinian-style tactic of penetrating a perimeter. One man is stationed to listen for any sound. The "Chechens" take their shoes off to make less noise. The other teams don't want to get their feet wet and dirty. Bad move. They end up spending a lot more time repeating the exercise over and over again. Then, after a quick British Army–style jog, where the students have to high-step and occasionally slap their knees or feet at the appropriate time in the sing-song cadence Walter sings, we head off to morning prayers. Most students who attend the course have a limited understanding of the Islamic religion and culture, so day one starts out with a lecture on the subject and a rough show-and-tell on how to pray.

After morning prayers, the class showers and heads to breakfast. The buffet serves the basic building blocks of a generic brand Egg McMuffin—questionable and rubbery yellow disks, greasy patties, biscuits—as well as cereal, yogurt, and mini muffins. The sign says ONLY ONE TIME THROUGH THE LINE, though few ever have the desire or the stomach to challenge the rule.

The course is broken up into morning instruction and afternoon field exercises, so after breakfast we head over to the classrooms. The architecture of the teaching facilities looks like industrial metal meets spartan shed, and a growing neighborhood of portable outbuildings and range structures looks like it has recently expanded from the nucleus. The classroom walls are decorated with posters of guns, and a lonely lineup of naked life-sized pink rubber punching torsos stands at attention like a phantom army.

Outside, the constant din of gunfire has driven the bomb-sniffing Belgian Malinois and German shepherds of Blackwater Canine into a frenzy. We can hear the "pop ting, pop ting, pop ting" of a good shooter making hits on the white-painted steel silhouettes on the range outside the classroom, and the loud boom and crack of another range off in the distance where operators practice their .50 cal sniper skills. The metal sheds of the classrooms and target manufacturing plant add an eerie whine to the high-powered shots. Although the racket makes the students hungry to get on to the ranges and start shooting, we have to start the PowerPoints and videos. Luckily, the classroom material deals with such boring and erudite subjects as how to build a bomb. We discuss the tactics used in successful bomb attacks and the philosophy of different terrorist groups—all delivered from the terrorist's point of view. On the breaks between being cooped up in the classroom and squeezed into tiny student chairs, the students go outside and do the sniff test. They bond over cigarettes and Skoal, feeling each other out and bestowing nicknames when they decide someone is okay with them. While Mike, John, and Janet may go outside for a break, Abu Asian, Angry Dwarf, and Soccer Mom return. The group bond has begun to develop.

My classroom presentation isn't until later in the week, so I decide to wander over to check out the main Blackwater headquarters. As I push through the glass doors, the blare of a TV permanently set to Fox News greets me. The room gives me the immediate impression of a gun store or taxidermy showcase, since it houses a stuffed black bear shot on the property, a mounted deer head, a bobcat perched on the drapery rod above the curtains, and a fox positioned in an eternally unrequited scene in which his mouth has been frozen midsnap just inches from a stuffed partridge.

Most contractors cross the threshold of headquarters just to visit the gift shop, which sells an overwhelming array of bad-ass gear that can easily clean out a week's worth of a contractor's salary. In the shop, anyone can get geared up, and the well-heeled civvy can buy most of the gear needed to look like an IC. Erik has his own Blackwater clothing line modeled on what the fashionable contractor wears to work, but Royal Robbins 5.11 shirts and pants in tan are the most ubiquitous choice. The latest Suunto "hockey puck" watch adds good accessory to the outfit. Tactical gear in a green and tan made by BlackHawk (not affiliated with Blackwater); adventure hiking shoes; web utility vests; Camelback hydration units; "go" bags; day packs; and plenty of gun gear like sights, holsters, and carrying cases can wreak havoc on credit cards. And, of course, the most important part of a contractor's outfit—the sunglasses. A single pair of Wiley X, Oakley, Maui Jim, and other top-end shades can set an operator back over three hundred dollars. However, the right sunglasses are a must-have, since contractors say you can tell exactly what an operator is about by his shades. Maui Jims are for Frogs or SEALs, old-school wraparound Oakleys for Delta, Wiley X for SF, cool-guy Oakleys for marines. Experienced contractors consider knockoffs, or even Ray-Bans, the sign of an amateur.

If a visitor plunked down between $800 and $2,500 in the store, he could walk out almost looking like the real thing.

Back inside the classroom, the students are chafing at being kept inside for so long. We break for a dull cafeteria lunch, and then the afternoon exercises begin. In addition to shooting at targets, students will be shooting at each other. They will use Simunition, a plastic-tipped bullet casing with a reduced charge and filled with bright-colored gooey soap. Though nonlethal, the bullets can make painful and ugly red welts or blood blisters on close impact, so everyone puts on protective gear.

In a standard PSD training class, the students would play the role of protecting the VIP while instructors would act as the terrorists or insurgents. In this course, however, since the students are working to learn the thought process of the terrorists, the roles are reversed. The instructors will play the bodyguards, and the students, trying to subsume the motivations, goals, and tactics of a terrorist, will try to identify the weaknesses in security and mount an attack. For our first field exercise, we have to ambush a VIP scheduled to drive down an L-shaped road. We are supposed to wait until the VIP car turns the L corner and cut them off in front and box them in from behind with our pickup trucks. We have to be prepared for resistance from a driver, two security guards, and the high-value target inside. They are all to be "killed."

I pull my students into a group huddle to discuss how the real Chechens would plan such an operation. Everyone gets jihadi nicknames, which shift around so the "spies" in our midst can never really identify us. I try to instill in them the audacious and energetic mind-set of a motivated guerrilla fighting against a large killing machine. I tell them we have to attack, attack, and attack, taking full advantage of our most powerful weapon—our complete willingness to die.

Though we have been given guidelines on where to hide and how to carry out the operation, real terrorists would never be constrained by such expectations. The most successful terrorist or insurgent attacks always achieve an element of surprise. In Iraq, the insurgents have consistently altered their tactics once it becomes clear that coalition forces have grown to expect and anticipate a certain type of strike. For example, early in the insurgency, suicide bombers would attack security convoys with a speed-ing approach coming up from behind. After the PSDs became more at-tuned to watching their rear quadrant, the cars began to slow down in front of the convoys before detonating. When the PSDs adjusted to that tactic, the bombers developed a method of darting across the median from the opposing lane of traffic. As proposed, the exercise might teach my stu-dents how to ambush a car, but it doesn't communicate any deeper lessons about terrorist thinking or tactics. So applying guerrilla thinking, I propose an unconventional plan.

One great advantage terrorists or insurgents have over conventional forces is that members of the military have had the rules of conduct and warfare drilled so deeply into their heads that it subconsciously shapes their expectations. Insurgents and terrorists will exploit that lack of imag-ination, often using their enemies' restricted rules of engagement or cul-tural presuppositions against them. This can most prominently be seen in certain terrorist or insurgent groups' lack of restraint with regard to civil-ian targets. Another common ploy, though less frequently cited in the media, is the insurgents' adoption of disguises to get their potential vic-tims to let down their guard. Security contractors in Iraq have told me that many of them refuse to stop for the Iraqi police or military under any cir-cumstances, since there have been so many incidents of insurgents using stolen uniforms or of infiltrators exploiting their official position to create the conditions for an attack. Most law-abiding Westerners have the idea that one must pull over for the police deeply ingrained in their thinking, and the insurgents have exploited this conditioned response to great ef-fect. With this in mind, I remind one of my students, a Secret Service agent, about the undercover car with sirens and lights he had earlier men-tioned he drove down from DC.

When our turn comes up, my students hide themselves on either side of the road, ready to shoot in case any of our victims tries to escape. I strip off all my protective gear so I don't look so conspicuous, and keep the un-dercover car idling as I sit in wait for the SUV with the VIP in it. When they pass me, heading to the ambush spot, I pull out from behind and begin following. Just before they enter the kill zone, I flip on the siren and flashing lights. Even though the driver knows he is in the middle of a scenario, he dutifully pulls over and stops. When I walk up to the car and motion for them to roll down their windows, they obediently comply. Then pulling out my gun, I "shoot" each occupant at point-blank range. I jump back in the car and speed away as the security guards stumble out and start firing back at me. When the "dead" guards both pause to simultaneously reload, I reverse back at high speed and shoot everyone dead again. Though we may not have done it in the conventional way, we achieve the objective of killing everyone. My Chechens understand the point of the lesson I was trying to teach them, but are still pissed that they didn't even get to fire a shot.

For the next few days, we settle into a routine. When I wake up in the morning, the former British cop is usually doing one-handed push-ups in the dark. After the students roll out of bed, they do the rope spiderweb test, jog, have morning prayers, and then after breakfast head to the classroom for instruction. One day we watch a film about suicide bomb victims that illustrates the brutal realities of dealing with people who operate outside the laws of war. The students learn how to pick locks and about the explosive mechanisms of cell-phone-detonated bombs and other varieties of IEDs. The instructors with firsthand experience lecture on how the IRA blew up buildings, and how Hezbollah blew up the marine barracks in Lebanon. I lecture on how the motivation and mind-set of different terrorist factions influence their tactics. Field exercises simulating different scenarios of attack consume every afternoon, and as the week progresses, I can see the students adjusting their thinking to adopt a more unconventional approach to the operations.

The last day of the course involves an assault on the "village," an attempt to kill a VIP, and a truck bomb to blow up the building he is in. My students have learned by now that thinking outside the box and using the enemies' own cultural rules and assumptions against them achieves the most dramatic success, so I tell them I will keep out of it and let them prepare and execute the entire operation. They impress me with a plan that involves multiple assaults, including giving a gun to a visiting news crew to shoot the VIP.

The targets will be expecting the attackers to approach via one of the roads that leads into the village, so the Chechens sneak in from behind the berm of a live firing range and attack from behind, something that freaks out the lead instructor, but gives my team's attack the perfect element of surprise. When the VIP's bodyguards try to hustle him into the SUV for escape, the news crew's cameraman pulls out the gun we smuggled to him and shoots the principal dead. While everyone is distracted by the unconventional methods and chaotic results my Chechens have unleashed, one of them drives straight into the village on the main road and "detonates" his car bomb next to the target building, "killing" himself and everyone nearby. My team has learned their lesson well. Hopefully, they'll now be able to think like terrorists so they won't be killed by one.

CHAPTER 8

Running the Gauntlet

"'Twas the night before Christmas in Baghdad, Iraq
All the Mamba Crewmen were tucked in their rack
The defenses were set in impeccable form
And I had just settled down to surf Internet porn
When out in the street I heard such a clatter
It wasn't a mortar so what was the matter?
In full kit I ran out and what should appear
It was Rudolf, he was wounded, he was one fucked up reindeer.
He said Santa's sleigh had been hit by a Strela
The old man burned in and was captured by al Qaeda. . . ."
—EXCERPT FROM CHRISTMAS E-MAIL FROM THE MAMBA TEAM HOUSE

The Blackwater team house sits off the main road inside the Green Zone, through a field of smoldering trash piles and dead dogs. The pungent smell of rotting carcasses and the smoke from melting plastic burns my nostrils. In a rudimentary form of security gate system, an armored blue truck blocks the turnoff toward the house. An Iraqi relaxing in a white plastic lawn chair gives us barely a glance before jumping into the truck to move it out of our way. The Triple Canopy contractors who have driven me from the airport talk shit about Blackwater's apparent lack of security, bemoaning the Iraqi's failure to even ask for IDs. I just view it as being polite. Who else would three bulky Americans in a black BMW 7 series be, other than fellow contractors?

Most of the closely set houses lining the street look abandoned, though security firms or squatters have overtaken many. We pull up in front of the open gate of a walled compound. Two massive untrimmed date palms decorate the small front yard of Blackwater's two-story nondescript dust-coated cinderblock box of a house. Even with squalid, trash-filled sur-roundings, real estate prices in Baghdad could match that of Paris, London, or New York, and this slightly dilapidated structure costs Black-water $80,000 a year, a virtual steal since now nothing is available for less than $12,000 to $15,000 a month. Sandbags cover the windows; ammuni-tion boxes, coolers, and broken lawn chairs litter the yard; and the thrum-ming of an uncovered diesel generator provides the background pulse of the scene.

Inside, the Chileans are watching a Spanish satellite channel on the big-screen TV, while the Americans sit perched with large laptops, look-ing up briefly at my entrance before getting back to e-mails and Web surf-ing. Posted on the wall above them reads a sign warning, NO PORN, in a show of perhaps unintended irony. Men weighted down with tan utility rigs walk bowlegged in and out of the kitchen door where three smiling Iraqi women are frying indeterminate meat patties. I have arrived at what will be my home for the next month, since I've come to Baghdad to hang out with the Blackwater team and to ride along on their daily airport runs. I will be here through most of November and early December 2004, a time period that will coincidentally turn out to be the month with the highest rate of attacks on the airport road. The director of operations, Mike Rush, has been assigned to babysit me, but Mike seems to be out. No one seems to take particular notice of my presence, so I decide to take a look around on my own.

The house smells of cooked coffee, frozen hamburger patties, and sautéed onions. Past the front door is the kitchen, where most of the men will eat standing up and the coffeepot is always on brew. I note that it looks like the flies swarm as furiously inside the house as outside. The washing machine hums as it churns the sand out of tan clothes, and pyramids of glistening blue bottles of water stock all the available shelf space. Down the hall in the briefing room, a giant map of Baghdad with dozens of marker points indicating locations of recent attacks covers one wall.

I peek inside the office marked with a sign reading KEEP DOOR CLOSED where a barrel-chested man with a salt-and-pepper goatee is sitting at a desk talking on the phone. "Yeah, we will send in air assets. . . ." Looking up and noticing my presence, he growls, "Whoever you are, get the hell out of my office and close the door."

"That was Guy Gravino, former Special Forces reserve team sergeant on a mar ops team," a contractor explains as I turn back to the hallway. Guy is former Special Forces but current C1 commander of the Mamba team. The Mamba team was initially created as a heavy, gunned-up rapid-response team for the Bremer detail but now runs contractors and VIPs to and from the Green Zone to BIAP.

I'm advised that I can stow my backpack in one of the bedrooms, so I head for the stairs. On the second floor, stacks of M4 rifle cases, ammo boxes, and sandbags line the hallway. Postings on the wall outline defense perimeters and evac plans. Each bedroom sleeps three to six in a random mixture of bunk beds, foldout cots, and simple wooden-framed singles. The only common theme to the décor is that nothing looks permanent. Each man has a locker and his shaving kit, and collections of CDs, books, and mememtos. It's clear from the lack of clutter and the perfect stacks and right angles of things that the military discipline of keeping personal space impeccably clean does not wear off. Even so, I have the odd feeling that I have moved in to a frat house filled with heavy weaponry.

The roof has a deck covered with heavy netting where I will end up spending many late evenings drinking, smoking, and talking with the guys over the next month. What looks like new exercise equipment sits abandoned and coated in a thick layer of dust. Some of the apparatus looks homemade, like coffee tins filled with concrete, but some is the latest in high tech. Regular mortar and sniper attacks in the area make the open roof vulnerable, so most of the men work out at a gym in Saddam's old palace.

The roof offers a bleak view of the surrounding city—an endless panorama of featureless tan structures stretching into the distance on all sides. Just beyond the house, tanks and other tracked vehicles roar and clatter up a road that looks boxed in like a canyon with its high concrete T-walls. Concertina wire decorates the back side of the T-walls, supposedly to keep the Iraqis from getting close to the road. Blackhawk and Apache helicopters rumble low across the sky, adding a mechanical soundtrack to this vision of a war zone.

Heading back downstairs, I go into the TV room to get to know my new temporary housemates. Looking around at the guys hanging out in the TV room leaves no doubt that this is a type of tribal gathering. These men appear connected through their style of dress, manner of speaking, attitudes, and culture. Sharp-edged swirling tattoos, shaved heads, bulging biceps, and short beards or goatees comprise the common "look" they wear. Their inside jokes, reliance on acronyms, and use of nicknames makes them seem to even have their own particular way of communicating. Contractors each earn a radio call sign nickname, which often changes if the contractor does something new that deserves to be enshrined in permanence for future ribbing purposes. They can't pick their own names but have to live with whatever the others may have chosen for them. For example, Shrek and Miyagi are named after film characters they resemble, while 86 and Cougar have done something to earn their titles.

Barry, or "Baz," an ex-SAS Kiwi, and Rick, aka "Baghdaddy," a blond-haired American former police chief, run the house along with the gruff Guy Gravino. Miyagi leads the team I'll be riding along with on the daily Mamba runs. He explains to me that I'll meet "nothing but type A guys here." In the peculiar parlance of the team, he says they are all "shit hot."

Although most people would assume that guns are the primary obsession of any contractor in Iraq, it is actually the laptop. Contractors can buy generic laptops cheaply at the PX in Camp Victory near the airport, and the computers provide a lifeline to their home, family, and news from outside the sandbox.

Inquiring about the NO PORN sign posted on the wall brings a round of laughter from the room, and the group finally starts to relax and feel comfortable with my presence as they delve into a lengthy discussion about the best XXX sites on the Web. They all seem to enjoy Bangerbus.com. One suggests I would like GBS—Gang Bang Squad—but another disagrees and they argue. The conversation descends into bickering, and I hear other suggestions for MILF Hunter or Mike's Apartment before we return to more serious topics.

I learn in my first conversation with the Blackwater team that, for them, living in Iraq means boredom, fear, and the type of deep friendship born of shared extreme experience. Most of all, however, Iraq means money. Every time the clock ticks past midnight it means another day, another mission, and another $500 to $600 in the bank. Many of those with wives and children seek contractor gigs in Iraq because their specialized skill set qualifies them for little more than low-wage security work in the States, and the money they are able to send home somewhat tempers the pain of separation. For some without a wife and kids waiting at home, the extra income does little to assuage the loneliness of feeling disconnected from their home community. T-Boy has made some unconventional friends to keep him company during his stay in Baghdad, and they carry on in the screeching chorus that underlies our entire conversation.

Just outside the door and under the stairs, T-Boy keeps a large cage housing two budgies, small colorful and speckled birds. T-Boy shows me their nest and explains that they lost one baby, and he is hoping their last egg hatches. Most of the house can't comprehend why the former marine loves the little things so much. They can't get past the damned shrieking. During my month in the house, I will come to enjoy the incongruous portrait of this muscular, shaven-headed man, dressed head to toe in black with a variety of aggressively macho T-shirts and festooned with skull tattoos, who spends time quietly cooing and talking to these delicate little birds after hard runs to the airport.

Blackwater VP and head of security Mike Rush arrives, to the relief of the team charged with keeping a "reporter" occupied. Tall, quiet, focused, and intense, Rush gives the immediate impression of being a man with too much to do. He has no shortage of problems to manage, considering that he not only handles operations for such a rapidly expanding company as Blackwater, but also must do so amid the chaos of Iraq. His only chance to unwind comes at night, up on the roof.

That night is cold and clear on the roof of the team house. Two big bottles of Crown Royal, a bottle of Jack Daniel's, and a case of Belgium-made Corona appear. Baz brings out a black Pelican case that holds his best expensive cigars—Macanudos, Monte Cristos, and a selection of various special-edition Cubans, all shipped in from a cigar business he has on the side. The team gathers around and starts the joking and ribbing. The sound of our laughter echoes off the square ugly buildings around us, while the generator hums quietly below.

Then we hear a small boom followed by a massive ba-DOOM! It sounds like a car bomb, somewhere in the direction of the palace a few hundred yards away. The men cock their ears, listening for more. It's apparently unusual that they haven't heard the spinning, whooshing sound of mortars all evening. Four Gurkha contractors were killed in a mortar attack yesterday, Mike tells me, pointing off to one side of the roof. They lived in tents about a hundred yards away and were attacked while they slept. Four dead makes for a particularly bad day in their world, since Mike recalls that during one of the statistically worst periods there were 3.24 contractors killed every week. The sound of a loud hailer and sirens emanates from a nearby military checkpoint, but the drinking, smoking, talking, and laughing resumes, unfazed by the sounds of war floating up through the darkness.

Despite driving daily on what is arguably the most dangerous road in the world, the contractors say the job is boring. The car bombs, road closures, snipers, IEDs, and endless morning briefings have grown routine. Some days, incoming intel about a possible attack causes a delay. Sometimes Route Irish closes while the army cleans up yet another massive explosion. Occasionally the Little Birds will ferry the VIPs to the airport, leaving the contractors at the team house to putter around doing maintenance or cleaning, but on most days the Mamba team has to gear up and psych up for the drive themselves. I have a hard time imagining how a four-mile, high-intensity, hard-rolling run through the gauntlet could ever become boring, but my new friends tell me I will learn differently soon enough. Around midnight, the trash bag clinks with the sound of empty Corona and Crown Royal bottles as the contractors drift off to catch a few hours of sleep before the sun rises.

The next morning the routine begins. The Mr. Coffee hums on constant perc as contractors dump each freshly brewed pot into their large mugs or flasks. Iraqi gals arrive to fry up a greasy breakfast of potatoes, eggs, and some type of ground and compressed meat patties. The smart contractors settle down in front of their own recently purchased personal laptops with wireless connections, while the others have to compete for the two house computers. With their mugs of coffee nearby, and amid a din of raucous banter, the contractors settle into the overstuffed chairs of the TV room for a long morning session of instant messaging, Hotmailing, and Yahooing across time zones. For those who don't have girlfriends or wives, bills need to be paid or online finances need to be otherwise managed, since the general crap of life continues regardless of the circumstances of their job. Griz opens an e-mail to discover that his wife has painted the walls of his house brown. "What the fuck!" he complains loudly, calling over the rest of the team to look at the photos. As the others huddle around his computer, expressing their sympathy for his wife's bad taste, Griz continues to grumble, "It's too dark. Fuck! Fuck . . ."

The team mechanic, Tool, so named for obvious reasons, has already gone outside to start his work for the day. Tool inspects the Mambas to make sure they're all running smoothly, particularly checking for water in the diesel fuel tanks since they have had some problems recently. Tool takes extreme care with his routine once-over, since it could be disastrous to have one of the Mambas come to a sputtering stop at mile two on Route Irish.

At 9:30 we have the first daily morning meeting. Guy Gravino calls everyone into the briefing room to discuss administrative and housekeeping issues. Oil filters needing to be bought, the new crop of contractors arriving soon, and other mundanities of the team house are the current topics under discussion. The house meeting lasts maybe fifteen minutes, and the guys return to another hour of e-mailing, and Web surfing before reconvening for the 11:00 daily security briefing.

Critter collects and analyzes all the intel relating to the particular day's operation, and Miyagi puts it together in a PowerPoint presentation for the briefing. A chart showing the latest statistical trend indicates that attacks along Route Irish are on the rise. In the past forty-eight hours, there have been sixteen violent incidents on the road to BIAP. The number of attacks has gotten so great that they've stopped bothering with the routine repetition of the daily incident reports and just talk about the overall count and any new major developments in tactics.

The last attack Blackwater had to fend off a couple of weeks ago involved over two dozen Iraqis with PKMs and bounding assault tactics. Most attacks come in the form of sniper hits or short bursts of small-arms fire as a convoy passes, but the most high-impact destruction comes in the form of IEDs, or VBIEDs—the new military lingo used to describe a suicidal insurgent piloting an explosives-laden car directly into a security convoy. It's increasingly a game of cat and mouse, the insurgents consistently changing their tactics to adapt to new defenses the military or the contractors develop. We learn in that morning's briefing that the latest suicide bombers have attacked by heading straight across the median from the opposing lane, since convoys have learned to watch for and disable any cars slowing down in front or speeding up from behind. The problem is that many average Iraqis will also cross the median if their side of the road is blocked.

Critter has picked up a nugget of intel from the military this morning that they have received reports of a possible suicide attack in the works for later today. Miyagi flashes up a PowerPoint screen listing the make, the model, and the license plate number so the contractors can commit the info to memory. As usual, the insurgents have chosen for targeted destruction a small, older, Japanese auto resembling countless other cars the Mamba team will pass today. The insurgents typically steal older Asian imports for their attacks, assumably because they blend in so well with other traffic. The irony of their strategy is that since cheap older imports would otherwise not seem to be a lucrative catch for a car thief, a stolen one can trigger an alert to be on the lookout for a specific VBIED. Unfortunately, though having license plate details sounds helpful for police purposes, contractors don't have time to verify numbers if a car is speeding toward them for possible detonation.

If they do come under attack, Blackwater has a policy of using overwhelming firepower to break contact, as do most security teams operating in Iraq. The team can strike back in response to an onslaught, forcing the attackers to seek cover long enough for the convoy to begin a safe retreat from the scene. Or if one of the vehicles is disabled, the contractors can either commandeer a passing car to escape, flee on foot, or hunker down in a defensible position to wait for an additional counterassault team to arrive with more firepower.

As we finish the briefing and head outside to gear up and load up, I'm impressed by the show of force the Mamba team represents and come to understand why in most incidents the attackers strike and hightail it away. On most occasions, the Blackwater team makes the airport run in a convoy led by a Mamba, followed by a flat-bed unarmored "bongo" truck carrying luggage or supplies, and another Mamba that would transport any civilian passengers, with a third Mamba bringing up the rear. The white three-quarter-inch steel-armored Mambas are anti-mine troop transports converted into heavily armed battle wagons. Altogether they carry a total of four mounted PKM heavy machine guns, with the last truck in the convoy sporting two. One of the gunners shows me how in a pinch he could pull the PKM from its pintles and fire from the hip, blowing through an entire belt of bullets in a few seconds. Each PKM is fully loaded and has a box nearby holding an extra belt of ammo, making them prepared to unleash somewhere between sixteen hundred and two thousand rounds of 7.62-mm bullets if provoked. Gecko usually also brings along a rocket launcher for good measure, and today he tucks it behind the front seat of one of the Mambas. Some of the crew also sling HK MP5 submachine guns over their shoulders, though the Chileans say they prefer AK-47s with double-taped magazines.

In addition to those manning the PKM heavy machine guns, each

Mamba convoy also typically carries at least three well-armed contractors, who are stationed either in a front passenger, back passenger, back window, or side hatch position. Each position has an assigned sector to cover. Miyagi tells me that each contractor usually carries an M4 rifle loaded with two thirty-round magazines double-taped together for ease in ejecting, flipping around, and reloading if necessary. Eight slots in the multi-pocketed Rhodesian rigs they wear hold additional magazines, making each man stocked with a cache of three hundred rounds of 5.6-mm ammo. Everyone also carries a loaded Glock strapped to their legs and a couple of spare mags of pistol ammo, though one reminds me that I'd be in serious trouble if they ever got down to using their Glocks. Since tossing a fragmentation grenade would be the most effective way to break contact if ambushed by a large number of insurgents—as the Blackwater team was a few weeks ago—the crew usually tries to keep a couple around for backup. The grenades and rockets are technically outside the bounds of weapons allowed to contractors, but since the insurgents don't tend to play by any rules of restraint, the marines try to keep the Blackwater teams fully stocked with whatever they may require to keep safe. Even without the grenades, rockets, or pistol rounds, the typical Blackwater Mamba security convoy could within moments unleash upward of seven thousand bullets against an attacker.

I don't intend to carry a gun, but the contractors insist. They convince me that if I'm riding with them, the enemy would not stop to differentiate between writer and contractor. Additionally, they say that if the convoy really gets in the shit, my backup ammo could be useful. In other words, they want me to be the "bullet bitch," so in case we get into a shootout, they can pull supplies from my dead body. Reluctantly, I pick up an M4 and pull the charging handle to the rear, locking the bolt open. I inspect the chamber to make sure it's empty, then slap in a magazine and release the bolt catch. Making sure the weapon is on safe, I set it aside and begin loading up my Rhodesian rig with spare M4 and Glock mags.

Under my kit I'll be wearing black cargo pants and a T-shirt, which is not so far from the typical contractor's "uniform." They're mostly dressed in tan Royal Robbins 5.11 pants or jeans, with tan BlackHawk webbing gear, and a small triangular chest plate with their blood types written or sewn on patches. A few of them wear Blackwater hats or patches—most famously Griz has the company logo tattooed on his bulging bicep—but beyond these small details, there is no way to discern their employer. With all the gear, however, they look far from civilian.

The heavy Kevlar and ceramic plate armor glides smoothly over my head and straps tightly around my chest with wide Velcro straps. It fits securely, like a turtle shell, and I feel protected even though I know the insurgents have adapted to the use of body armor by aiming shots for the head or femoral artery. I can feel my chest thump against the inside of the hard plates as I pull on my loaded Rhodesian rig on top. Next comes a Kevlar helmet strapped on with chinstrap, plus gloves and knee pads. Even with the knee pads and helmet, the Mamba team wears the look well, and they pose for my camera looking like "shit hot" badasses. Convinced I look more idiotic than manly in all the gear—like a writer playing dress-up— I clamber up into the lead Mamba and take position with my cameras and handheld computer. I'll keep the M4 nearby just in case but will hopefully spend all my time taking only deadly accurate photos and notes.

Word comes in that the U.S. military has closed the BIAP road again because of another car bomb—this time on an armored military convoy. We will have to reroute through crowded city streets in order to make it out to the airport to pick up an incoming crop of contractors. The traffic makes the path through the city more difficult, and potentially more dangerous, but the contractors are accustomed to having to make this kind of last-minute change of plans.

The diesel engines of the convoy rumble to life like a stable of tubercular steeds. Looking like a train of ungainly elephants, the Mambas jerk forward, gears whining, with wheels churning up dust as they slowly roll down the wide main road. We head for "Brooklyn Bridge," an exit from the Green Zone that heads into the city through Baghdad University's campus. After a brief pause and wave to the jarheads and Gurkhas manning the gate, we leave the Green Zone and "go red." The mood changes instantly. No more joking. Individuality dissolves into team, creating an interconnected web of intensity. Each man has his job—driver, front gunner, rear gunner. Each man has his sector to watch—front, rear, side. The typically easygoing, open expressions of the contractors transform into masks of focused concentration.

If we had taken Route Irish, the speed of the open road would have made the convoy a more difficult shot for sniper or small-arms fire, but being a slow-moving target ups that risk exponentially. For this run, the contractors will expend more concentration watching for suspicious figures to appear from behind every tree or open window, rather than keeping track of every older Japanese import on the road. Although heavy traffic makes progress slower on the city streets, it also adds a layer of protection from car bombs, since an attacker would have to weave his way through the phalanx to get close enough to detonate.

Most drivers know to keep a safe distance away from the convoy, but as one seems to drop behind the pack ahead of us, I hear an abrupt burst of gunfire and smell the acrid scent of cordite as T-Boy lets off a warning shot from his PKM. A voice crackles through the radio, warning us the traffic will get bad ahead. The Mambas groan and whine through the gear changes as we slow down, speed up, slow down, speed up. Finally, we stop moving entirely.

Word comes across the radio that Big Army has shut down the road. An operation? A car bomb? "We don't know. We don't talk to Big Army; we just do what they tell us to do," Gecko grumbles.

Although cars are kept back in the front and rear, Iraqis driving in the opposing lane of traffic start creeping past us. Some stare up at us with bored expressions, some with an unmistakable look of intense hatred. One mimes an explosion with his hands and mouths the word "boom" before giving a sinister smile and pulling away. Young kids gather in clusters around lampposts and glare in our direction. Another man is walking quickly through an alley toward us, holding something beneath his dark suit jacket. We have become a glaringly obvious target trapped in a sea of shimmering heat and idling cars. We are completely exposed on all sides and critically vulnerable to hostile action at a moment when the surrounding traffic would block us from any easy exit. I begin to have one of those rare moments of self-reflection when I question why I've chosen my particular profession. We console ourselves by reminding each other how difficult it is to maneuver a bomb-laden car in heavy traffic, but the unspoken thing everyone also remembers is how it only takes a few minutes for insurgents to gather a group together for a quick ambush if they see a prime target stopped in an exposed position. I will recall this precise moment a few weeks later when I read that an Edinburgh Risk team suffered a "shark attack"—security lingo for a hit-and-run assault—while waiting for the U.S. military to clear the same road, less than two hundred yards away from where we got stuck.

All guns have been up with safeties off since we left the Green Zone, but the contractors now assume defensive positions with fingers nearer the trigger and eyes concentrating on their optical scopes. Doing my best to act as an extra pair of eyes on the situation, I watch out my window and scan the compressed panorama of traffic, curious onlookers, square rooftops, and satellite dishes. With the vulnerability of our position, the contractors have an unquantifiable profusion of possible threats to monitor in their assigned sector. The radio chatter between the cars grows louder and more frequent—the voices beginning to show strain.

"What the fuck is going on up there?!"

"Dunno. Big Army has it shut down."

"Let's get the fuck out of here!"

"No, wait until we see if it clears up."

The debate goes back and forth for a few minutes until Miyagi, the team leader, makes the final call. He coolly announces that the Little Birds will just have to pick up the new contractors at the airport today.

The team jumps out of the Mambas and starts walking the fenders. They walk along tapping on car windows with their guns, easily convincing the drivers that it would be in their interests to make room for the Mambas to turn around. A couple of guys walk out into the opposing lane of traffic to halt the oncoming cars, and the gun-bristling convoy reverses, turns sideways, and crawls over the concrete median to head back in the other direction.

When we get back inside the Green Zone, the safeties go back on and the team starts recounting to each other the possible attackers they may or may not have seen circling around us during those last few hairy moments stuck in traffic. As we unload, a few grumble about the hassle of the trip, but most don't bother. In the next month I spend with the Blackwater Mamba team, I will learn that today's run was more typical than not. Sometimes a car bomb closes the road. Other days, a wide variety of problems can crop up to abort a run. I would roughly estimate from my limited sample that only three out of four scheduled Mamba runs actually make it to the airport and back without encountering some kind of non-attack-related hitch. Most employees would relish a day off from their duties, but the airport runs actually break up the monotony of the team house. A few contractors grumble about boredom as they stream off to find something to occupy the rest of their afternoon.

That night, the team gets back together for another evening of drinking and smoking on the roof. This time the Green Zone stays relatively quiet. Helicopters thunder in the distance, and sirens are of course pervasive, but the din never really rises above a level you might expect in New York City.

Miyagi and I are sitting off to one side, so I scoot over closer and start asking him way too many questions about his life. At fortysomething, Miyagi is probably one of the shortest, quietest, and most mild-mannered of the entire crew. Over the coming month I will come to view him as impressively impossible to rattle, probably a result of growing up in Echo Park, a rough, gang-infested neighborhood of Los Angeles.

Miyagi worked patrol and undercover in the tough Central and Ramparts divisions on the LAPD for seventeen years. With his wife bringing in a second income, the couple managed to buy a nice little home in Simi Valley, an hour and a half commute from his beat. After seventeen years, however, Miyagi's take-home pay was barely $1,400 biweekly, so he quit the police force to seek more lucrative security work for FedEx. When his ex-sergeant called and told him to write down the phone number of Dyn-Corp, Miyagi did as he was told. "I remember in the late nineties, mostly the brass would leave for one or two years to do peacekeeping missions for DynCorp. You were a private contractor, so there was a loophole—Dyn-

Corp paid you from an out-of-country account so you didn't get a W-2. Tax-free. You can make a hundred thousand dollars tax-free."

So Miyagi ended up signing on with DynCorp in early 2003. "Back then, East Timor was 105K, Bosnia was around 90K, and Kosovo was 89K. I worked in Kosovo for a year. I had applied for Blackwater in November of 2003 and by mid-January they sent me a letter offering me six hundred dollars a day. They were looking for already-trained people to do the Bremer detail. A dozen guys had left DynCorp in December of '03 and sent us an e-mail in Kosovo saying this was the real deal.

"The class I was in was the standard ten-day training. Our class was condensed to six days, but we got paid for ten. They said it was some kind of advanced course and we all had some knowledge. Within the first forty-eight hours, they sent ten guys home. There were forty-seven in the beginning and thirty-seven at the end. One guy couldn't do one pull-up, now he's working with the State Department. By the middle of the week, they were giving assignments out, and our class was split up into those guys who had top-secret clearance, and the other guys. Everybody wanted to be on the Bremer detail. The joke was that if you didn't make it, you weren't pretty enough."

None of these guys up on the roof must have been "pretty" enough, since they all ended up running Route Irish instead of watching over Bremer. Baz would be the closest thing to a "pretty boy," considering his status as the Mamba team's only reality celeb. A few years ago, Baz starred in a *Survivor*-type show shot in Fiji for a Kiwi audience. The other guys like to rib him about it, but obviously with a simmering jealousy. It comes out that night that Baz became notorious during the show's broadcast not only for running off into the jungle to "survive" by himself, but for spending most of his time off-camera screwing the show's supermodel host.

It's getting late and a couple of the guys have already gone to bed when Baz moves his chair over to my side and begins telling me the rest of his story. He talks at great length about his two sets of identical twins—fourteen-year-old boys and twelve-year-old girls. He loves talking about them, and his eyes sparkle as he reels off a list of their accomplishments.

He also confides happily that he has decided to marry his longtime girl-friend the next time he goes home. She has stood by him, lived with her worry, and tolerated his unconventional lifestyle and extended absences for a long time.

Back when he was in the New Zealand SAS, Baz worked in East Timor, hunting down a group of rebels who had cut off the ears of a kidnapped aid worker. When he got out of the service, he did bodyguard stuff, mostly for celebrities and the Sultan of Brunei. After outlining the basics of his life and career, Baz leans in close. I notice a marked change in the atmosphere between us and sense that a collective weight of painful memories has fallen across Baz's mind. In a strained voice, he tells me, "My dad was so hard on me. He was a jockey—a tiny man who didn't stand this high." Baz holds up his hand about four feet off the ground and continues. "I could never please him. He had a car accident that left him crippled and in a wheelchair. God, he was tough. I was working for the Sultan of Brunei's family and had to fly with him, so when I found out my dad was ill, I couldn't get back in time. I caught the next flight home, but he died on my way over. I went to take care of his things, and there was all my stuff from the SAS—all my press clippings. He had saved everything I did." Baz pauses and looks away for a moment, only the glowing red tip of his cigar visible in the darkness. When he looks back, he asks a pained question for which I have no answer: "Why didn't that fucker tell me?"

Although the rooftop gatherings are an important part of the routine, the contractors are restrained in their drinking. Mike asks me if I want to go with him the next day for a wade through the bureaucracy of the palace. The conversation reminds Mike to apologize, since the State Department had recently reversed on its permission for me to ride along with Blackwa-ter's State Department PSD in Hillah. "Frank, the RSO [Regional Secu-rity Officer], is on our ass. He said I took a picture of a State Department guy and said he was a mercenary." He shrugs and shakes his head, obvi-ously confused by the charge. As punishment, it's obviously a no-go for the writer who just wants to hang out, but I am surprised to learn that they have even barred Mike from Hillah. It appears that he is fighting the war on two fronts—the government and the insurgents.

The next day, I head out with Mike to try to get a simple ID badge that would allow us access to bases and government facilities. The DoD has changed the style of their ID again, so Mike needs to get a replacement for his old one. Considering that he holds top-secret security clearance and directs operations for one of the biggest security contractors in Iraq—the one that kept Bremer alive and protected State Department installations—one would think the replacement would be issued automatically. Mike already put in a request for a new pass when he was in the States but hasn't heard anything about it since. He suspects the "20-Minute Rule"—referring to the need to check every twenty minutes to see which new rule is in effect—has somehow voided his first request. Even though he has allotted all day to roam the palace halls if necessary, he does not sound very optimistic about his prospects for getting the pass issued, and even less so for the one I am supposed to get for myself. Mike wants to try working personal contacts and lower-level functionaries first and tells me we will only go to the head of security as an absolute last resort. The two of them don't like each other, and Mike suspects the guy wouldn't help him get a pass even if he was able.

While most of the walled community of the Green Zone has assumed a decidedly functional and commercial American persona, the over-the-top ostentation of the U.S. government's main center of operations, "the Palace," retains some sort of unrepentant Iraqi character of gaudy splendor. Inside, a great labyrinth of large vaulted rooms with high arched entryways and decorated ceilings unfolds with each step farther into the building. In one particularly grandiose hall, the military has constructed a vast grid of office cubicles out of plywood—a fascinating architectural decision that has transformed a set from *1001 Arabian Nights* into a corporate chicken coop. The vision reminds me of the ancient Greek credo that lofty architecture inspires lofty thoughts.

We walk down a long row of soldiers, airmen, and bureaucrats sending e-mails and shuffling papers before we find the allotted three-foot-wide plywood workspace of a contact Mike heard has helped others get the new pass. The toothy air force officer is pleasant but unhelpful. He explains that the military's ninety-day rotations mean "your first thirty days is figuring things out and cleaning up the mess left behind. Then you have a month of decent work. Then by the third month you realize that anything you start is not going to finish, so you just leave it in a pile for the next guy that replaces you." The officer has three weeks left in Baghdad and is ready to check out.

The back channel has failed, so we head off to seek a particular State Department underling. We find him in a cluttered office behind a flimsy door, working on a plywood desk with a locked rack of M16s behind him. He seems to approach his job and life with little real enthusiasm and blandly offers to give Mike a lower-security pass, even though most of Mike's work is with high-level people on secure facilities. He suggests that the only alternative is to go over his head to see his boss—the grumpy security chief Mike mentioned earlier. Begrudgingly, Mike agrees.

Frank is an older silver-haired man wearing jeans and a Glock on his hip. He shuffles through the papers on his desk and tells us he is rushing to tie up loose ends since his rotation ends this week. "It's been a rough few days," he says with the condescending exhaustion of someone with too many important things to do. He informs Mike of the sixteen-attacks-in-forty-eight-hours statistic everyone has been citing this week, as if Mike would not be privy to such info.

While Frank talks about how busy and important he is, my attention is caught by his secretary brusquely informing a dark-haired American woman, "You want thirteen passes? I can't issue thirteen passes. You already have nine. Why do you want more?" The aggravated young woman hisses over the end of the question, "Due to the sensitivity of our mission, I can't discuss this." She has told the secretary that she needs the additional passes for Iraqi linguists staying at the Al Rashid Hotel—a way station used by American intelligence. The wink and nod is apparently insufficient to sway the secretary, and the woman demands to see her superior. Frank retreats to a small room for private discussion with the woman, but emerges very quickly to ask his cranky secretary to issue the remaining passes. He then turns to Mike and apologizes for not being able to help him, saying, "There is nothing I can do." It is apparently easier to get passes for Iraqis than for Mike.

Back at the Blackwater team house, Guy Gravino tells me that Mike should have taken me by to meet Lawrence "Not Larry" Peter while we were in the palace. Peter used to coordinate the security companies under the CPA, but when the CPA folded, he hit up the companies for the funding to keep him afloat as a private entity. As director of the Baghdad-based Private Security Company Association of Iraq (PSCAI), he works to come up with standardized methods and better communications for the contractors working in Iraq. Peter had originally been very resistant to my requests for a meeting, so a little face time with a Blackwater representative present may have eased things over a bit. I get the impression from Guy that Peter may be a little high-strung, but realize when I meet with him a few days later that "high-strung" does not quite capture his style.

Lawrence Peter is a short man with a lisp who wants everyone to know that he was SEAL Team 6, though other DEVGRU members who know Peter stress that he was an intel analyst and not an operator. When going to meet him, I wander past cramped offices holding clusters of gray-haired, paunchy, middle-aged civilians doing hunt-and-peck typing before finding the PSCAI "headquarters" buried deep inside the palace. Inside the tiny white box sits Lawrence Peter with two other middle-aged men.

Peter does not want to meet with me. He immediately tells me so himself. He says he is only talking to me because the security companies told him he should. After a few minutes of lecturing, I get the idea that he doesn't like journalists. I'm not really surprised that the dominant decoration in his workspace is a WWII-era poster that reads HOW ABOUT A NICE CUP OF SHUT THE FUCK UP?

Peter's last PR coup was inviting in a journalist, Tish Durkin, who insisted she was working on an in-depth and balanced piece about contractors and the industry. Peter introduced her to the major players, but she ended up zeroing in on a flamboyant and atypical contractor. What resulted was probably the single most damaging in-depth industry-related piece ever written. The *Rolling Stone* article "Heavy Metal Mercenary" profiles "Wolf" Weiz, a self-described rock star, born-again Christian, and ex-marine whom Durkin portrays as a muscle-building, steroid-popping, trigger-happy freelancer. Wolf was later killed by an insurgent's bullet, but not before his persona became embedded in the public imagination. *The Rolling Stone* article helped crystallize the image of contractors as blood-thirsty, gun-loving Jesus freaks hyped up on heavy metal music and 'roid raging on innocent Iraqis.

So it's understandable that Lawrence Peter thinks that I, as a visiting writer, might be the latest version of the anti-Christ. I try to emphasize the distinction between a journalist and a writer, but in his mind I am unmistakably "one of them." I give up trying to convince him and try to start the interview, getting his permission first to tape the conversation.

The first thing he wants to tell me: "I represent upwards of twenty-five companies and we do it all on a handshake. Some contribute around ten thousand dollars, others pay what they can." Though only twenty-five companies finance his job, Peter says there could be anywhere between sixty to a hundred companies operating in the country. Though the companies are all supposed to register with the Interior Ministry, the government doesn't share the exact number with Peter, and there is no comprehensively accurate public count.

Despite my genuine interest in listening to Peter, he seems edgy and combative, and eager to keep blaming me for all the bad press the industry has gotten. At every opportunity, he reminds me where the media has gotten it wrong. We're interrupted by a coworker stopping by, and I have to suppress a laugh when the two middle-aged men do a somewhat effeminate knuckle bump as a good-bye.

Peter returns to his computer and pulls up a PowerPoint presentation, warning me not to cite any of the company names in it. Glancing down, he notices my iPod digital recorder that has been sitting on his desk throughout the conversation. "ARE YOU TAPING ME?!" he yelps, sounding panicked. I remind him of our earlier conversation in which I asked him if it was okay, but he staunchly refuses to continue unless I put it away. I tell him it's a good practice to check notes against a recording to ensure accuracy and that if he disagreed with any quotes, I would let him check it against the transcript.

Still not entirely comfortable with the idea, he at least settles down enough to continue. "We are breaking a lot of paradigms. We are outsourcing defensive operations not needing done by the military. You don't need them moving people around. You don't need them guarding the movement of supplies. . . . We are strictly involved in the defense of personnel, facilities, and logistical movements. We don't think we need soldiers to protect people. Let the soldiers kill people, render violence to our enemies.

"No company operating in Iraq has been hired for offensive operations. I read that they are conducting the war—that's bullshit." Peter is getting himself worked up about the media again, so I ask for some hard numbers on how many contractors operate in Iraq.

He takes me through his own semiofficial estimates. He figures there are three to five thousand Americans working security, seven to ten thousand expats like South Africans or Brits, fifteen to twenty thousand TCNs (third-country nationals)—men from countries like Fiji, Nepal, the Philippines, and El Salvador—and twenty-five to thirty thousand Iraqi HCNs (host-country nationals). He admits that he bases his figures on anecdotal information, since the Iraqi Ministry of Interior will not give him those statistics, either, if they even exist. The thought gets him defensive again. "People think this is a clean-functioning country. Even Iraqi ministers use Hotmail and Yahoo accounts! People think that we sprinkle pixie dust and everything works!" My sitting calmly listening to him riles him up even more before he can manage to grit his teeth and return to the PowerPoint.

The next screen shows statistics about the typical security contractor. In Peter's estimation, the average security contractor working in Iraq is in his early forties and is a disciplined operator with more than twenty years in the military, including multiple overseas tours. He stresses that "just because a man gives up his uniform, does not means he gives up his professional ethics."

He covers up the next slide on his computer monitor with a piece of white paper and asks me for my real opinion on contractors. I tell him that the Americans seem to be mainly nice people, mostly ex-marines or small-town cops with a smattering of senior special operations people. He stares at me with incredulity and asks with an exasperated tone, "No, tell me what you really think." I repeat myself. Angrily, he lifts up the paper to reveal "Overpaid, Out of Control Cowboys."

"Look, we are not talking about angels dancing on the head of a pin! You tell me if you have ever seen this phrase before!" he demands in rapid-fire speech as he leans forward and stares intensely into my eyes. I say no quietly, provoking a torrent of vitriol. "I expect YOU to give ME INFORMATION IF I AM GOING TO GIVE YOU INFORMATION!" I begin to silently ponder the tiny Mr. Peter's grip on reality. Luckily, a U.S. soldier comes in to discuss badge colors and something that sounds like the "MNF-ITAV sash policy procedure."

The mundane bureaucratic exchange seems to have a calming effect on Peter, and we return to a more reasonable discussion of the public perception of contractors. Peter blames the media for not understanding the industry and for taking a few isolated examples and portraying them as being representative. "Who are the bad guys? Are they brought in maliciously? Are there unethical lawyers, priests, journalists? Or are all of them perfect?" Peter's mood has turned to one of divine absolution, seeking pardon for the sins of a few with the sacrifices of many.

"Contractors are doing it with limited weapons, struggling against overwhelming odds. I welcome Peter Singer [Brookings Institution fellow, author of *Corporate Warriors*] to come over and spend a month here. The pundits like to chuck javelins in here. We have regulation! CPA Order 17 covers the status of civilians here, and CPA Memo 17 says there is a code of law here!"

It is obvious as I leave Peter's cubicle that he doesn't get out of the Green Zone or mix with the average contractor much. If he did, he wouldn't be under the false impression that Memo 17—the CPA document that made contractors immune from Iraqi prosecution—ever significantly restrained their behavior.

One morning I wake up to find the combined mental energy of ten men trying to figure out how to jury-rig their satellite hookup to broadcast on the briefing room's computer projector. It's Thanksgiving in the States today and they want to watch football on the big screen. A cooler of steaks is scheduled to arrive on a transport flight from Amman, and the Mamba team doesn't want to be late, since their only alternative for Thanksgiving dinner would be processed turkey product and questionable gruel dished out at the KBR chow hall in the main palace.

We head for the airport, and the talk of steak takes away from the constant drudgery of watching for signals of an attack. It turns out to be a fairly uneventful run on Route Irish. As we pull in to the airport, however, we notice that a car that drove in the airport gates after us has pulled up a safe distance behind on the Arrivals level. An Iraqi man gets out of the car and starts shouting at us in Arabic. He waves what we assume to be an airport badge in the air and makes an attempt to appear less menacing by smiling through his anger as he approaches, trying to speak in broken English. He looks irate, and slightly comical, but not dangerous.

One of the contractors recognizes his car and says, "Hey, he was following too close, so I lit him up." Since the Iraqi has authorized clearance to work at the airport, where he encounters Americans on a daily basis, he apparently did not understand why he should have to stay back from the convoy. When the warning shot zippered across the road in front of him, the man was actually pulling up closer to the rear Mamba to show the airport badge dangling from his rearview mirror—an innocent mistake that could have easily cost him his life.

Though it may sound like an example of a private security contractor wantonly endangering yet another Iraqi civilian, the standard rules of engagement did actually work as they should have in this instance. In a situation such as this, when a security convoy notices a car coming too close, State Department guidelines dictate that a contractor is first to give a shout and hand signal. If they keep coming, they get a warning shot across the road in front of them. If they continue, a shot is aimed at the engine or tires of the car. If the contractor has to fire again, they get a lethal burst of bullets to stop them dead. Depending on the speed of the car, it could be a matter of only a few seconds between the hand signal and a bullet to the head.

This Thanksgiving we would be thankful for the successful warning

shot, but not for a delicious steak dinner. After all that hassle, it turned out
the steaks somehow never made it, and we had to make the deadly run
home without our precious cargo.

Some of the contractors, too dejected by the delayed steaks to think
about eating, head to the gym to unwind after the run. The others, hungry
enough for the bad cafeteria food provided by Kellogg, Brown and Root,
head to the KBR chow hall in the main palace. The Iraqi women who cook
breakfast and lunch must be home by curfew, so the guys have to take care
of themselves for dinner. The army and contractors would probably live in
squalor and nearly starve if they didn't have other contractors taking care
of mundane tasks like cooking, laundry, and cleaning the toilets.

Baz, Guy, Rick, and I jump into one of the tiny armored Nissans to
make our way to the cafeteria. At night, the Green Zone takes on an over-
whelmingly eerie feel. Thick dust turns headlights into solid beams, and
the growl of tanks and trucks seems always just on the edge of where the
light falters. The ever-present guttural rumbling of heavy machinery is
haunting, though it is impossible to actually see the military vehicles unless they turn on their blazing spotlights. We drive past the traffic circles
and pull into a massive parking lot filled with an ocean of SUVs. It takes a
quick wave of ID to get past the ever-smiling Global Security–contracted
Gurkhas. Guy waves to the rows of filthy dusty vehicles and tells me that
the insurgents have learned to identify Americans because their cars are
never washed. "Iraqis don't drive dirty cars," Guy says.

Along the broken sidewalk and concertina wire, a steady stream of soldiers and military contractors intermingles with an army of helmeted and
armored aging civilian contractors dragging their briefcases. These days,
civilian contractors must wear armor and helmets inside the Green Zone
because of the mortar attacks. They are not issued guns. Even so, watching them slog slump-shouldered through the dark, I think of how they are
Baghdad's tired mercenary army of Samsonite-bearing bureaucrats.

Just outside the palace entrance, contractors and bureaucrats stand
around and smoke just as they would outside any other office building
where smoking is banned. The Green Zone seems, in effect, a miniatur-
ized quasi-America with U.S. rules imposed on a secured island in the

midst of chaos. Or perhaps more accurately, the exaggerated architecture of Saddam suggests an Iraq pavilion at EPCOT, if Disney would duplicate the background soundtrack of mortar fire and bomb blasts.

The surreal effect continues once inside the palace. A massive central hall with an impressively high arching ceiling dominates the entryway, designed by Saddam to intimidate by invoking the type of scale and drama found at the Vatican and other famous public buildings. Down below on the marble floors, lines of drably uniformed soldiers, young volunteers, and paunchy bureaucrats line up for a cafeteria-style dinner. Signing in on the contractor clipboard means the meal will be billed back to Blackwater at $27 per person. A row of smiling Filipinos, all workers subcontracted to KBR, serve the lukewarm food. Much of the food is flown in from the States, with all the familiar brands and logos found half a world away. The Green Zone even has an American telephone area code.

The main chow hall brings together a spectacular gathering of khakis and bad haircuts. Long-haired civilians, young Republicans, contractors with T-shirts and sunglasses, Americans of every shape and size have all come to Iraq for their own reasons—some out of patriotism or a sense of duty. Most civilians, if not all, have come because they can make more money working in Iraq than they ever could back home.

In the crowded field of cheap banquet furniture, we find a big round table left over from Saddam's days. Guy waves at other contractors wearing armor plates and carrying weapons along with their food trays. Those in civilian dress stand out. A young man of about twenty-five with long hair, sunglasses, and a loud shirt—an out-of-place hip dude with a big camera—comes over to join us at our table. He is one of many Republican congressional aides recruited and sent over to work for the CPA. He starts chattering immediately and gives an introductory self-description: "I was a congressional aide in Miami making up numbers to get money. I signed on for this and came over for a job that didn't exist. I have done all kinds of jobs I know nothing about. Now I am doing accounting. I hate accounting. I hate numbers."

He calls himself a New Yorker, which catches the attention of a Blackwater contractor, a former cop from New York, who says, "Hey, stop telling people you're from New York. Just tell them you're from wherever you live. You make New Yorkers look bad." The contractor with the Brooklyn accent then apologizes and explains his crankiness by telling of the difficulties he has had repatriating the bodies of dead Blackwater contractors. The experience has made him sick of the bureaucracy in the Green Zone. "We're trying to send an American citizen home with his brother on the same flight, and they're making us jump through hoops. When a government employee dies, he is a 'special agent'; when one of us dies, we're 'security guards.'"

There are no "heroes" in the private security world, just dead employees adding to a company's tragic attrition statistic. Mike says that Blackwater tries to take care of its own, but that can make for a delicate balance since each contractor does sign on fully aware of the risks and without any promise of postmortem benefits other than basic DBA insurance. Perhaps this offers the coldest and clearest sign that the business end of warfare requires a mercenary attitude. Private security has no ideology, no homeland, no flag. There is no God and country. There is only the paycheck. If a contractor dies in the defense of his paycheck, his employer sends his family a final one, often calculated to the hour of his death, along with a cardboard box containing his personal effects. Beyond that, neither the contractor's employer nor the U.S. government has any legal responsibility to the surviving family members.

A contractor's death does not dictate any formality other than repatriation of the remains and the filing of forms for insurance purposes, though Mike Rush personally flew to Hawaii to inform Wes Batalona's wife of his death. "We think of these people as our family, and we do what we can."

Dinner wraps up on a fairly somber note and we head home. At the final U.S. military checkpoint before the house, a massive spotlight blasting into our SUV turns the dirty windshield into a glow of brilliant white. We are supposed to wait until waved forward, but it's impossible to see the marine at the gate. "You would think they would buy these guys flashlights," Guy says.

He rolls down the window as we pull up, taking time to talk to the soldiers manning the checkpoint as he shows his ID on his arm band. "How you guys doing tonight?"

The young marine asks, "You guys Blackwater?" with a sense of awe palpable in his voice.

"Everything all right?" Guy asks again in his best cool-guy voice.

The soldier hunches his shoulders against the cold, his breath making small white clouds. "Fine, sir."

In the cold night, the marines guarding the gate appear just scared, tired, pimply kids. The contractors of Blackwater are the war's rock stars to them, and one asks, "Hey, can we come by your compound and get a hat?"

Guy answers, "No problem."

As we drive off, Guy says, "Those guys are the front line. I always take the time to ask them how they're doing. When there are suicide attacks, they go against this gate."

Despite the considerable drawbacks of the job, American military contractors are the top of the food chain in the war on Iraq, though they'd never admit it. They get the most pay, and even though insurgents may target them during their daily routine, they don't have to go down dark alleys, kick in doors, or spend a whole year away from their family. One of the scared, tired, pimply faced marines guarding the gate that night will be shot in the neck and killed by a sniper tomorrow. Others will go home in a few months to broken marriages, high debt, and nothing in the bank. The contractors know they can change jobs, change their minds, or just go home at any time. Unlike the marines shivering at Gate 12 and counting the minutes until daylight, the experienced know war is too ugly and dangerous to fight for too cheap. As Rick tells me on the drive home, "some people are making a thousand dollars a day; some make two-fifty doing static. Everybody is making money here, except the soldiers fighting the war." In addition to their day rate, Blackwater contractors also get to cash checks for $650 a week, just to have a little spending money in-country. Gecko recently purchased a $1,300 MP5 submachine gun. T-Boy bought a used BMW 7 series for $5,000. Some have never had this much money.

But considering our earlier death-related discussion, the possible trade-off just doesn't seem worth it to me. I soon realize, however, that each contractor I meet uses his own personally unique calculus to weigh the risks and rewards of the job.

The next morning is so cold that the generator has to be jump-started. After fixing the problem, Rick, the logistics manager, stays outside for his first Newport menthol of the day, and I join him for what has become our routine early morning chat. As he takes a drag off the cigarette, Rick absentmindedly rubs the large scar on his neck that marks where he had his lymph nodes removed after a cancer diagnosis a few years back. I half-ass suggest that he might one day think about quitting smoking, which spurs the response: "Hey, you want to hear a sad story?" Rick apparently did stop smoking for a while after his brush with cancer, but started again when he couldn't handle the stress of estrangement from his daughter. He tells me, "I gave her anything she wanted, but then I had to put my foot down. I said, 'No more money; you're on your own.' She said she hates me. I started smoking again." The rift obviously weighs heavily on him, but he doesn't think there is any way to resolve it yet. I ask him if he is worried about getting cancer again. Rick shakes his head and says, "We all have to die sometime." Rick usually volunteers to drive the slow and unarmored bongo truck.

Later that afternoon, I'm sitting in the TV room writing when I hear a roar of truck engines that fades into the unmistakable guitar riffs of AC/DC. I walk outside to see a thick cloud of dust floating over the compound walls from streetside. The Blackwater Hillah team has arrived.

They've pulled up outside the Blackwater compound in their convoy of three armored GMC Suburbans and a soft-skin, "trash-armored" hate truck. In official nomenclature, the "hate truck" is the counterassault team, or CAT, since it hangs back so it can rush into an ambush in progress to engage attackers long enough for the VIP to escape. Inside, rusty steel plates have been fitted to the doors, making for a cheap but effective armor. The team keeps the Suburbans immaculate for VIP transport, but it looks like they have swathed the hard welded steel plates of the hate truck in silver duct tape, and road dust coats both the outside and the interior. The well gunner rides with the rear gate open, which sucks dirt into the back end, covering everything with a fine brown powder. The "trunk monkey," a lanky, blond ex-SEAL, wants to give me a tour of his position to show off his toys. In the back, he rides in a homemade steel box with a selection of weapons hanging from the ceiling: a pump-action shotgun "for up close," and a SAW machine gun for "serious shit." Unlike the air-conditioned civility of the armored Suburbans, the hate truck exudes, well, hate—from the four-inch white plastic skull mounted on the dashboard to the raw, rusty metal edges of the homemade armor to the pounding rock music that blasts from the mutilated vehicle.

The Hillah-based Blackwater contractors dismount their mechanical steeds and literally strut around the yard, stretching their legs after the long run from Hillah. They're dirty and tired, and have some time to waste before they have to pick up an incoming crew from the airport. Even though they have time to relax for a while, the Hillah team doesn't switch off. They don't even really come into the house, preferring to stand around and keep watch, not straying too far from their war wagons. The Hillah team and the Mamba team are going to roll out to the airport together in one long convoy, though the plan doesn't sit well with the Hillah guys. "We gotta roll with the Mambas? We are going to get shot to shit!" one bearded man jokes, displaying a kind of interteam suspicion common throughout the security industry.

The Mamba team is mostly marines; the Hillah team is predominately SEALs. Even though they all do the same thing for the same company, each team within Blackwater represents its own tribe. Sometimes teams are fully stocked with either retired SEALs, marines, or SF, making the group identity even stronger. The only guys who don't seem to trash-talk the others are the ex-cops. They just don't have the necessary ego and swagger. Team cohesiveness is so strong, one may hesitate to trust or rely on anyone outside their own tight circle, always suspecting that another team's methods are somehow less safe than their own.

I start snapping pictures outside as they get ready to leave. Before he poses with the group, the tail gunner rips off a piece of black tape to hide his eyes. "Hey, don't they add those later?" one asks jokingly. Another shouts out his suggested caption for the portrait: "Mercenaries in Iraq." A short, burly ex-marine fully decked out in heavy gear and walking bow-legged like a cowboy lets out a stream of brown tobacco juice as he stops to tell me, "I got twenty years in the Marine Corps. I don't know what else I could do. Hell, I don't know what else I am good for!" The contractors load up the convoy, check gear and communications, and disappear in a rolling cloud of dust and a blast of Metallica.

A few hours later, on their way home from the airport, the Hillah team will be ambushed by a group of trucks that materialize out of nowhere and begin hammering the Suburbans with PKM heavy-machine-gun fire. The insurgents don't seem to notice the hate truck, with its blaring music and skullhead talisman, bearing down on them at high speed from behind. The blond tail gunner pulls his SAW and continuously drills holes into the trucks, killing one attacker and forcing the others to break contact and flee. As the insurgents speed off in disarray, the amped team has a split second to decide whether or not to pursue and keep firing, but they choose to get off the X instead. The blond tail gunner will angrily tell me later that he wishes he could have finished the job, particularly since the insurgents returned to the attack site later to booby-trap the body of the man he had killed. The trap ends up killing two marines who come by to inspect the site and roll over the body.

Leaving Iraq

A few days later, I head out with the Mamba team on an airport run from which I won't return. My month is up. I'm going home. On my last ride down Route Irish, all the blackened, gravel-filled craters and burnt car hulks along the way look familiar. It has become much easier to distinguish the suspicious from the mundane. I say my good-byes to the team in the shade of the airport Arrivals lobby, and they all wish me well. I have enjoyed being the Mamba team's bullet bitch, late-night confessor, and chronicler. Some of the guys will rotate out in a month, and despite the intensity of violence, I think Miyagi and his no-nonsense coplike view of the job will keep them safe.

With one last wave, I head inside to meet the crew of the Blackwater CASA 212, a small private plane that ferries contractors in and out of Iraq. Unlike the Royal Jordanian flight that uses a pressurized Fokker twin engine jet, the CASA is a long, noisy, cold ride over a featureless tan desert.

Preflight procedures at BIAP comically replicate the diligence of the Transportation Security Administration in the United States. Young Iraqi women search carefully through our baggage but miss anything tucked away. At the gate, an older American with a bad comb-over pats us all down in a needlessly touchy body search—particularly needless when a flight crew member admits to Mr. Comb-Over that he is wearing a loaded 9-mm Glock. He gets searched anyway, and they hilariously put his gun through the X-ray machine before returning it. Noncrew members are not allowed to carry any weapons onto a flight, and one of our team has a folding knife seized. The security guard hands it to our pilot, who just hands it back to the contractor. The outgoing contractors wear looks of disgust as they go through the charade. We are all well aware that only days before someone managed to sneak an entire Mercedes loaded with explosives aboard a DHL plane. Wearing a loaded gun or carrying a pocket knife seems minor, particularly since we'll be traveling on a private Blackwater flight.

As we walk across the tarmac and out to the plane, one of the guards yells at us to walk between the yellow barrier tape. It makes no sense, but then again, it is BIAP.

Once we're on board the plane, the Blackwater crew breaks open a large aluminum box and hands out loaded M4 weapons to each passenger. If this plane gets shot down and anyone survives, they won't go without a fight. To make sure we can escape a crash, the pilot lowers the rear hydraulic ramp. The CASA doesn't just take off; it leaps into the air and heads straight up—the much more violent reverse of the corkscrew spin the Royal Jordanian flight does when it lands. Only the ground is visible through the open rear door. Once the CASA has rocketed up to a safe cruising altitude above the range of surface-to-air missiles, the weapons are put back on safety and locked up again. What may seem like a bit of overly paranoid precaution will prove to be an appropriate security measure three months later when insurgents shoot down one of Blackwater's helos and drag the injured pilot out to shoot him at point-blank range.

After we land in Jordan that night, a single bullet found in one of the contractors' luggage causes us onerous delay in Jordanian customs. Although Jordan has shipped thousands of tons of light and heavy weapons to Iraq, they don't want any returning. The Blackwater fixer is a former officer in the Jordanian secret police who works out the problem with customs and gets us out of there in a little over an hour.

A generic Amman hotel houses the incoming and outgoing Blackwater contractors, and Justin "Shrek" McQuown is there to greet us when we arrive. Though it is the first nightspot the outgoing contractors have seen in at least three months, and the last one the incoming will see for three more, a grim atmosphere hangs over Players Sports Bar on the eighth floor. The outgoing sit silently thinking of the thousands of mundane things that need to be taken care of when they get home. The inbound reflect on the risks and rewards of being thrust in between the insurgency and the U.S. occupation. With early flights to catch, bags to pack, and phone calls to make, the contractors clear out of the bar early.

As I sink into bed, I think about the dozens of runs back and forth along Route Irish. Throughout my month in Iraq, Blackwater PSD teams had come and gone, new ICs rotated in and others rotated out. Car bombs, snipers, blocked roads, suspicious packages in the median, and the high-speed drive to and from the airport all turned into a day at the office. The morning briefings, once ominous and frightening, became routine as Miyagi reminded us at the beginning and the end: "New Day, New Mission." Every successful run the Mamba team made reduced the odds that the men would not make it home safely to their families. T-Boy told me before I left that I must be a lucky charm, since none of the Mambas had been hit or any of the close-knit team killed or injured while I was riding along. I didn't know that in a few weeks the Mamba team would be blown up by an IED, killing one and seriously injuring two, including Miyagi. For now, I was out.

Part Three

Of Rogues and Tycoons

CHAPTER 9

An Army of One

"I want to kill every fucking Afghan I can."
—"Jack" in The Hunt for bin Laden

*"The only thing that that Jack should be allowed to attack
and kill is his bar tab."*
—Owner of the Mustafa Hotel in Kabul

On September 10, 2001, Jonathan Keith Idema was living the less-than-idyllic existence of an ex-soldier and convicted felon in Fayetteville, North Carolina. The next day, as he watched thousands of Americans murdered on the command of a turbaned and bearded Arab hiding in a South Asian cave, Idema discovered a new sense of purpose. He was going to kill bin Laden, along with any other suspected terrorists he could find. He informed friends and family immediately that he'd be packing his bags and heading to Afghanistan as soon as he could find a way. For Idema, President Bush's demand in a nationally televised address a few days later for bin Laden to be brought in "dead or alive" was the directive he sought to buttress his already-simmering ambitions. The post-9/11 world opened a Pandora's box of prospects for adventurers, conmen, and opportunists, and created the perfect environment for a man like Idema to satisfy the most dominant aspects of his character: his fervid patriotism and need for action and admiration. The multimillion-dollar bounty on bin Laden's head also stimulated his ambition. He soon began planning his first trip into Afghanistan—the beginning of a dark odyssey that would ultimately see him arrested in Kabul for operating an illegal prison and torturing its prisoners.

Idema's transformation from a down-on-his-luck ex-soldier and felon to the "superpatriot" he now calls himself began on September 12, 2001, when he managed to arrange an appearance on Fox affiliate KTTV, billing himself as a counterterrorism expert. In this capacity, he suggested to viewers that three Canadian aircraft may have also been hijacked the day before. While the idea seems preposterous, Idema offered it with the same characteristic bluster that would enable him to operate so successfully in the many roles he would assume over the next three years. From his first appearance as an expert on September 12 until his arrest in July of 2004, Idema would come to be known as many things—documentary producer, humanitarian, CIA contractor, DoD contractor, Special Forces member, Northern Alliance advisor, tour guide, Pentagon official, media consultant, freelance prison operator, torturer-interrogator, and bin Laden bounty hunter. Some roles were real, some imagined, but few were questioned or investigated until overwhelming pressure from Idema's victims spurred authorities to arrest him and his tiny band of mercenaries. Idema's exploits were no more than a sideshow to the real action in Afghanistan, and Jack himself was no more than a bit player with no real role in the legitimate private security industry. However, what Idema did manage to accomplish in Afghanistan speaks to a hidden danger created by the increasing profusion of armed civilians in a theater of war.

The many layers of deception in which his life is shrouded makes it difficult to fully dissect the enigma of Jonathan Keith Idema, and the wildly incorrect and compulsively dishonest tales he has fed to the press suggest that an interview with him would be more for entertainment than illumination. But through my conversations with many associates and others who've known Idema, a very disturbing portrait has emerged of how easily an ordinary, if deeply flawed, individual can take advantage of the shadowy modus operandi of covert operators and the recent explosion in the U.S. government's use of private contractors. Idema has proven that an ambitious civilian upstart with certain key skills can soldier on independently of any government oversight, command, external financial support, or approval.

After 9/11, spurred by anger and his deep sense of patriotism, Idema felt certain he could hunt down bin Laden if given the opportunity, but he had to find a way into Afghanistan first. For his first trip into the war zone, he managed to create an opportunity for himself working on a National Geographic–financed documentary that was supposed to chronicle the work of two humanitarian organizations. While that sounds like an innocuous and even valiant endeavor, in reality Idema ended up scamming two well-meaning NGOs and attempting to make a documentary of his own dramatized heroism.

A small man with a tiny frame, bad eyesight, and black-dyed, thinning hair, Idema has a dominating persona and a talent for charm, when he chooses. Although he only stands five foot nine, he makes a lasting impression on the people who meet him. Edward Artis, director of one of the scammed NGOs, holds Idema in about as much regard as many others who have crossed the man's path: "If his hod is full of shit and falls on him, that's okay with me."

Artis, a former army airborne soldier from the 82nd, has specialized in frontline humanitarian work since the early 1970s, including many trips to Afghanistan. His tiny NGO, Knightsbridge International, keeps things simple and moves fast. Though he already had a filmmaker following him to South Asia, ever mindful of the donation-generating benefit of publicity, Artis agreed to allow another film crew from National Geographic television to join his caravan when a friend referred Idema.

"The Nat Geo thing happened through Idema. I admit, I fucked up. In October of 2001, Jim Morris, who is a fellow Knight of Malta, a former Special Forces major, and writes for *Soldier of Fortune*, contacted me. Then Idema approached me via e-mail after being introduced by Morris. The way I figured it back then, Idema was a guy just out of prison, looking to do something honest. . . . He said he was producing a documentary for National Geographic with producer Gary Scurka and former CBS cameraman Ed Caraballo."

Despite Artis's first impression, Jonathan Keith Idema did not view himself as a felon trying to go straight. He had reinvented himself as "Jack," a crime-fighting, bad-guy-punching, ex–Green Beret using his amazing skills and secret connections to save the world from evil. In reality, Idema was broke and involved in multiple frivolous and self-enriching lawsuits, including suing Dreamworks for allegedly stealing his life story and even suing a company for repossessing his Jeep when he missed payments. A cursory investigation into Idema's background would have found arrest records for receiving stolen property, disorderly conduct, resisting arrest, being a fugitive from justice, two counts of assault by pointing a firearm, discharging a firearm into a dwelling, communicating threats and assault on a female, and federal convictions on one count of conspiracy and fifty-five counts of wire fraud. Idema had never been to Afghanistan or been seriously involved in humanitarian work but saw an opportunity to use the lens of a documentarian's camera to record for posterity all the heroic deeds he intended to commit, or at least to dramatize.

The Nat Geo documentary wasn't the first time Idema had tried to cast himself in the role of hero. In May 1995, Jim Morris had sent a film pitch to Steven Spielberg entitled *Loose Cannon: The Keith Idema Story*, described as a "treatment based on Idema's exploits but replete with fictionalized accounts," a pattern Idema followed faithfully even in real life. This film treatment became the basis for a 2000 lawsuit brought by Idema and Morris against Steven Spielberg, Dreamworks, George Clooney, and others involved in the 1997 nuclear smuggling film *The Peacemaker*. They sued for $150 million, but the case was dismissed and Idema was later ordered to reimburse Dreamworks's legal fees of $273,000.

As sketched out in *Loose Cannon*, Idema claims that while he was in Lithuania training police in the early 1990s, he learned about an extensive network of black-market smuggling in nuclear materials from the former Soviet Union. Upon his return to the United States, Idema reported this information to the Pentagon and the FBI, but when pressed to turn over his contacts for this information, he refused. When Idema was later arrested on more than fifty counts of wire fraud, he contended that the FBI was unfairly punishing him for not turning over his sources. He says this conspiracy was behind his prosecution, conviction, and stint in federal prison, not his actions in falsifying credit lines to purchase, but not pay for, supplies for his failing mail-order business. Abuse by conspiracy, hatred of the FBI, alleged theft of property, and total denial of any wrongdoing had been common themes in Idema's life for years before he capped off his life's performance in Afghanistan.

During his trial, Idema ignored his court-appointed attorney and acted as his own lawyer. He constantly made claims of conspiracy and belittled the evidence, as well as the judge and prosecutor. The judge presiding over the case took umbrage at Keith's claims, excuses, and behavior. Magistrate Wallace Dixon told Idema, "In my assessment, you are a bully who apparently likes to talk, to hear his own tongue wagging." Later, Dixon continued, "I think you are sick. I don't know of any other way to say it. I think you have a mental illness." Judge Terrence Boyle's opinion of Idema was equally harsh: "All of the things you purport about what a wonderful patriot you are and what a singled-out person you are is pure fantasy." Idema's response was typical: "I'm going to sue the FBI," he said. "They know I'm going to go on TV. They know I'm going to go to Congress. They know I'm not going to give up until I prove my innocence." On April 11, 1995, thirty-eight-year-old Keith Idema was sentenced to four years in prison and fined $250,000.

Defeated and chastised in the courts and penal system, Idema did turn to the media to fight his battle. Jim Morris, a longtime friend and cocomplainant in the Dreamworks lawsuit, supported Idema's tale of persecution and reported on the case of the Lithuanian nukes for *Soldier of Fortune* in April and May of 1995. It didn't take long for CBS to send one of their top investigative journalists, Gary Scurka, to interview Idema in prison. The October 1995 *60 Minutes* segment on Lithuanian nuclear smuggling ended up winning awards for investigative journalism, but those assembling the broadcast felt uncomfortable about the quality of one of their sources and completely excluded the interview with the bug-eyed federal prisoner from the segment.

Idema reconnected with Scurka after being released from jail in 1997, and the two started a production company together called Point Blank News. Idema pushed for their first project to be *Any Lesser Man: The Keith Idema Story*, but despite Scurka's belief in Idema's story, networks and financial backers did not share their enthusiasm. Of the $1 million they needed to start production, they managed to raise only about a quarter, and ended up shelving the project.

Mr. Potato Head

After September 11, when Idema heard about Ed Artis's planned trip into Afghanistan, it must have sounded like an opportunity for the reformulation of *Any Lesser Man*. Though the documentary pitch ostensibly focused on the work of Ed Artis, Idema envisioned a starring role for himself as another ex-soldier turned humanitarian braving danger to lessen the suffering of poor Afghans. As war against the Taliban loomed, and the American public thirsted for any information on their newly discovered enemy, media organizations scrambled to fill programming hours with anything related to Afghanistan. In this environment, it seemed of little consequence that Idema had no humanitarian, military, business, or any other connection to Afghanistan. The pitch to National Geographic, called "Operation Pathfinder," portrayed "Keith" as a leader of a team of ex–Green Berets who would come to the rescue of "Sir Edward Artis," a Vietnam vet and "one of the world's most renowned humanitarians." The pitch describes Keith as a man who did time for a crime he did not commit and now wants to "get back into the action."

Idema first contacted Ed Artis as Artis was waiting in Tajikistan for passage into Afghanistan with filmmaker Adrian Belic, who was shooting a documentary, *Beyond the Call*. Even in that first conversation, Artis remembers Idema as being less than forthcoming about the focus of the documentary. Artis recalls: "We're in the convoy getting ready to go over and I get this call on my sat phone from Idema. We filmed that call. I got pictures of him telling me about Nat Geo. 'Gary Scurka of Nat Geo wants to come in and do a doco on you.' 'What's the pitch?' I asked. 'I've been in the biz. Let me see the outline.' Idema says, 'We will get the outline to you before we come over.' Idema told me, 'Gary Scurka doesn't want to give it to you by e-mail. We will bring it with us,' he says. I say fine. The idea was they'd do a documentary on Knightsbridge International's efforts to help the people of Afghanistan. You know, ex-military guys doing humanitarian work while bombs fall around them kinda stuff. Coverage is good, but with me it's mission first. It's not about me."

Artis didn't want to delay his mission into Afghanistan and quickly became impatient with how long it was taking his new documentarian tagalongs to get moving. "I told Idema to come via Tajikistan and to get a visa. I told him, 'Look I am not waiting for you. We're going to a fucking war zone, buckwheat.'" Although NGOs were being blocked from entry at that time, Artis and Belic went in on October 14 under the guise of journalists and actually did some radio reports to justify their visas.

At the end of October 2001, Idema and Scurka finally made the trip, joined by retired Special Forces Lieutenant Colonel Greg Long, a humanitarian from Partners International Foundation, the other NGO whose work was supposed to be featured in the Nat Geo documentary. As Artis recalls, the group encountered problems before their trip really began. "They fly into Russia and then Uzbekistan without a visa. I TOLD them to get a visa. I figure they are with NGOs, they know how to get a visa. The Uzbeks arrested all three of them for three days in the VIP lounge." On November 2, 2001, Idema managed to convince a young desk officer at the embassy that he was a DoD contractor. It may have been an understandable error, since Idema had the embassy verify his citizenship through the head of Partners International Foundation, who also happens to be an active-duty colonel at SOCOM, or Special Operations Command, from where many covert operations are managed.

Artis continues, "Colonel Bob Morris says he received a phone call from somebody at the embassy, and as an active-duty colonel and someone that wants to retire a pay grade higher than private, he was asked to verify that they are U.S. citizens. That's it. He probably didn't know what kinda tales Idema was spinning at the other end. He was asked to confirm that they were U.S. citizens and they got the letter. How they got a letter saying Scurka, Idema, and Greg Long were DoD contractors, I will never know."

Colonel Bob Morris does his humanitarian work on the side of his regular full-time as active military. It is not difficult to imagine Idema giving embassy officials a little wink and nod as he asks them to get him out of this detention problem by verifying his citizenship through Colonel Bob Morris at SOCOM. Ordinary verifications usually go through the State Department. An e-mail from the U.S. embassy confirmed that a low-level military attaché thought he was doing Bob Morris a favor.

"My guess is that Idema has a fake ID from the U.S. military saying that he is a major. That got him in-country. Then one lie became another once he had that embassy letter."

Even later, after Artis had recognized Idema's aversion to truth and tried to alert others, he felt many of his warnings went unheeded. Artis blames that initial letter with giving Idema all the "top cover" he needed to pass himself off as an undercover contractor. "I tried to warn people about him. I warned the Afghans about him, but now I know why they didn't do anything. . . . That letter gave him the ability to trump my warnings. Every time I said he did this or that to the Afghans, they ignored me."

Artis remembers certain early warning bells. "Idema had sent e-mails from Tashkent telling me he was bringing an interpreter—a female who spoke Russian. I sent back: 'Stop! DO NOT bring a Russian-speaking woman into an Afghan camp.' Turns out Idema had picked her up that night and she was his whore. And he invited her to Afghanistan.

"He also didn't have a cameraman, which is another odd thing for a film crew to show up with plenty of gear but no cameraman. It was obvious to me that Scurka couldn't work a camera, and Idema couldn't, either. They had those new cameras that aren't Beta cameras, but give a professional quality image. At that point, I hadn't met them and I had my doubts, but I figured I have dealt with nuts on location. That's why they make gaffer tape." He laughs.

"Idema and Scurka hire a guy named Neil Barrett as a cameraman—a long-haired good guy, but Idema made him cut his hair off to get the job. Idema wanted him to look more military."

Artis had begun to feel slightly uneasy because of some of his interactions with Idema, but it wasn't until after they had met in person, on Idema's first night in Afghanistan, that Artis's antenna really went up. They had all been invited to share dinner with some of the high-ranking local commanders at Khowjaboddin, the Northern Alliance forward operating base. As Artis recalls, "They pass out the meal. Scurka reaches in with a piece of naan bread like you're supposed to, and Idema yells, 'Don't touch that fucking food! It's unclean. Don't touch the food!' He throws an MRE at Barrett and at Scurka. 'You will eat MREs, and do not drink their tea.'

"That was just the first night. That was when I kinda felt I'd fucked up. I realized that Idema, not Scurka, was the leader of this group." Agitated and suspicious, Artis decided to put down some ground rules for the filming of their documentary. "I tell him, 'Look, you follow me and shoot it. You don't get a retake. He called me a motherfucker. 'You like to give orders,' I said, 'you get the fuck out of here right now.'

"The next morning I went to see Jim Maceda of NBC to get my morning coffee and daily update. . . . Jim asks me, 'Who is your new friend?' I said, 'My new friend is Keith Idema.' Idema says, 'My name is Jack. And don't tell anyone who I am with.' By then, [Idema] was wearing his dark vest and the shades."

Artis had been under the initial impression that he would be working with Scurka and that Idema would just be there for security. He had not even been informed that the documentary would also feature another NGO. "[Idema] brings out this EKG worth about six to ten thousand. That's when this guy Greg Long, who said he was with another NGO named Partners International said, 'Let's go up and deliver the EKG.' Then Idema pushed Greg Long aside for the photo op. I was confused and pissed."

As the tension continued to build, Idema's lust for the media spotlight soon proved reason enough for Artis to blow up at him. "Idema started doing interviews about the desiccant packages poisoning the Afghans.

They'd put these small desiccant packages in with the yellow plastic humanitarian meals, and the Afghans were supposedly eating them and getting sick. Somehow now Idema is a medical and military expert on something other people had brought to the military and media's attention.

"I took Idema aside—and Neil Barrett filmed this—I put my bony finger in his face and said, 'I don't know what your agenda is, but I don't want you at any of our sites. You're out of my fucking life.' To make it perfectly clear, I told Idema, 'Cease and fucking desist,' and then Gary Scurka tries to defend him. I tell him, 'If Idema is needed to make a documentary, then you can take all the tape you shot so far and shove it up your ass.' Scurka was allowed to stay when we did our distribution because he was still following us and doing a piece about us." Artis thought he had solved his problem, since from that point forward Idema was not allowed anywhere near him while they were shooting, but that was before the artillery attack incident.

On November 11, Veterans Day, after a long day of distributing humanitarian supplies, Artis was heading back to base camp after dark amid a backdrop of not-so-distant artillery fire when he heard an urgent voice crackling over his cheap walkie-talkie: "Ed Artis. Are you there? An American has been wounded. They want you down at the helipad."

Artis hustled down to the site, where he first saw freelance journalist Kevin Sites, shooting film, and Idema, "walking around like a caged animal and talking to someone on the sat phone saying he needs a Blackhawk."

Idema ignored Artis the first time the humanitarian asked who was wounded. "And I ask him again, 'Who is wounded?' Idema says, 'Scurka.' They're sitting up in the back of the king cab pickup truck and Scurka is talking to his wife on another sat phone."

Artis went up to examine a wound that had torn through the flesh of Scurka's knee, abdomen, groin, and leg. Scurka and the other journalists had been standing out in the open when a brief barrage of Taliban artillery had erupted. They had tried to take cover behind a Northern Alliance tank, unaware that the tank was the actual target of the attack. The shrapnel of an exploding artillery shell had hit Scurka.

"The situation is that there is a lieutenant colonel Special Forces medic there. I am a combat medic. Greg Long takes a look at the wound. I ask him is it serious enough to order a evac? The answer is no."

Trying to put the brakes on Idema's overreaction, Artis went back to where he was still pacing around yelling into the sat phone about needing a Blackhawk.

"I ask him who he is talking to. Idema tells the guy on the phone that he's talking to some aid worker here. I grab the phone out of his hands and ask, 'Who am I talking to?' It's a major at the embassy in Tashkent. I tell him 'Major, I was a combat medic in Vietnam. I have not seen anyone wounded bad enough here to send in a helicopter. If you want to check out who I am . . .' I give him a number of a congressional aide at Dana Rohrabacher's office. I tell him that there is no need to risk lives or to cause an international incident. Then I take the antenna off Idema's phone, hand it back to him, and let him have it."

Artis says he yelled at Idema, " 'If you fuck with me again, I will have you arrested or shot. We are going to take Gary up to the hospital.' And Idema just deflates. Idema is panic-stricken. I said, 'Get the fuck out of here. We'll do the rest of the filming that you can see in the documentary.' "

Journalist Kevin Sites also remembers the event as being one in which Artis's action was appropriate, and Idema was grandstanding for effect. Three men on the scene, including Artis, had advanced medical training; Idema did not. However, Scurka later credited Idema with finding an exit wound on the ride to the hospital that had escaped the first treatment.

Artis and others are of the opinion that Idema knew perfectly well the value of the filmed scene. The "daring rescue" would be a part of his documentary, portraying him as the hero who saved the day. Artis had his suspicions confirmed when he finally read the script outline for Idema and Scurka's documentary proposal.

"Right up to the day before we got on the helicopter to leave, I still believed the film piece was on us. They never did give me the script. The last day before I left, I went through Scurka's backpack. I am up early. Idema and Scurka are out on the tennis court interviewing each other. There was a folder in there that they were always looking at while I was busy doing good-guy shit. It's a letter with a big gold seal from National Geographic signed by Tim Kelley saying, 'To whom it may concern, Gary Scurka is filming a documentary on a UN-sponsored mission to Afghanistan and is working with Keith Idema. Mr. Idema has enough money to support his mission . . .' or words to that effect. Then there is a five-page script. A shot list of them coming in, matching up with us, and the NGO fucks up, and then Keith Idema steps in and saves the day. We were set up.

"Later on, Gary calls me and he says he wants me to sign a release. I tell him, 'You're not allowed to use my image, my voice, until I see the script. If there is one image or one mention even in the credits of Idema, you cannot use my name.' That's why you don't see him in that doco." National Geographic had been duped, having unwittingly paid for and supported "Jack's" entry into the War on Terror.

"Jack" had been once again cut out of his reality show, and far from starring in his epic of humanitarian relief and derring-do on the battlefield, he found himself unemployed in South Asia. Widely renowned for his resourceful, if morally compromised, opportunism, Idema kept himself busy after parting ways with Artis, selling himself as an "expert" to members of the media and granting numerous interviews. Journalists also recall Idema selling premium-priced transit into Afghanistan on one of Northern Alliance commander Massoud Khalili's battered Mi-17 helicopters.

Most of the media privately ridiculed Idema as a wannabe hero and strange war tourist. According to Artis, the journalists in Khowjaboddin referred to the tiny, bug-eyed, gun-toting aid worker-slash-mercenary-slash-terrorism-expert-slash-huckster as "Mr. Potato Head" for the number of slightly different disguises he could adopt. Although Idema seemed to be friendly with the leadership of the Northern Alliance, nobody could quite figure out who Jack was. Artis had at least figured out who Idema wasn't, and started contacting Northern Alliance and American officials to warn them of Idema's duplicity.

In mid-November, Haroon Amin, the spokesman for the Northern Alliance, wrote a letter to Artis stating that Idema wasn't working for them. A couple of weeks later, Idema told a reporter from the *Fayetteville Observer* via a sat phone that he was "working with the Northern Alliance." If

Idema had managed to convince the Northern Alliance he was a covert operator, they would have denied that he was working for them, or Idema could have just directly approached the local commander, Massoud Khalili, to set up the lucrative journalist transport endeavor without the knowledge of the higher-ups. The one thing that can be deduced with certainty is that a real security contractor in South Asia at that time would have had a more pressing assignment that didn't involve profiteering off journalists, and a covert operator would not have been so actively seeking the media spotlight.

While Jack hustled to make a living in the war, Artis contacted Billy Waugh to do a little more research into Idema's claims. As Billy recalled, "Ed Artis wrote me and said Jack Idema has put the word out that he is working for the CIA. Ed asked me, 'Is that true?' I didn't know who Jack Idema was. . . . I told him he wasn't working with us because I knew everybody on the ground. We only had about eighty guys involved in our operations. Idema wasn't one of them."

As the war progressed, Jack moved south to Jalalabad, where he continued his war profiteering by charging journalists money to attend press conferences and offering $800 battlefield tours to people like Jon Lee Anderson of *The New Yorker*. Well-funded reporters, desperate and under pressure from editor desks back home for exclusive stories about the war, became Jack's greatest benefactors in Afghanistan. A media circus of epic proportions descended on the tattered Spin Ghar Hotel in Jalalabad during the battle of Tora Bora. Since Idema could often be seen storming in and out of hotels followed by his small group of armed Tajiks, journalists assumed that Jack and his band of mercenaries were busy hunting bin Laden. At that time, Army Special Forces, Navy SEALs, and the CIA were actually doing just that, working a badly disguised covert operation, flitting in and out of hotels, military bases, and commanders' camps in dusty SUVs. All had orders to stay away from the media and, if needed, to use their Afghan proxies to threaten, rough up, or arrest journalists who got too close. By contrast, Idema would put on his prescription sunglasses, throw a checked Afghan *desmal* scarf around his neck, wear U.S.-looking but Afghan-made tan combat attire, and with a pistol strapped to his thigh and an AK in his hands, hold court with hundreds of newly arrived and gullible journalists. He perfected the knowing but enigmatic nod of the head when responding to difficult questions and would baffle them with bullshit use of SF terminology and angry outbursts against unpatriotic sentiments. Idema became a seasoned purveyor of exciting tales. He had become the media's favorite oracle, with few insiders willing to call him out. Journalists who did their homework quickly figured out that Jack's tales didn't always square with reality, but others were taken in by his charm and swagger, assiduously recording his every word.

Relishing the attention, he often possessed a keen talent for becoming whatever the media wanted him to be. But he could also be wildly erratic. He once fired his gun toward Tod Robberson of the *Dallas Morning News*, but warmly congratulated Linda Vester of Fox for scoring an interview with "a Special Forces guy." His new nickname among the growingly skeptical media was "Jack Shit," a sum-up of what he actually delivered for the money he charged. He told journalists and whoever would listen an ever-changing series of tales, billing himself alternately as a "Northern Alliance advisor" or the ever-elusive "expert," even very briefly snagging a paid position with Fox as a news consultant. Even Idema's supposed Northern Alliance clients weren't immune from Jack's predatory need for cash. Jack told CIA-backed warlord Hazrat Ali that he needed to brief an important delegation of Pentagon officials at the Spin Ghar Hotel. The "officials" turned out to be reporters Idema had charged $100 to attend an "exclusive" briefing by Hazrat Ali.

Although he managed to make money here and there from the media, he didn't score big until January 2002, when he sold seven hours of purported al-Qaeda training tapes to top-bidder CBS News. Although in his auction to the media, Idema's William Morris agent suggested bids in excess of $150,000, CBS reportedly paid somewhere between $30,000 and $60,000 for the first rights to air the tapes. Secondary sales to other networks like BBC, ABC, NBC, and others increased Jack's income. CNN was a notable dissenter; they'd done their research on Idema and didn't even bother responding. In mid-January, CBS featured him on *60 Minutes II* and the *CBS Evening News* with Dan Rather. According to Ed Artis, "he made his first big media hit when he convinced CBS to buy his bogus al-Qaeda tapes." Artis points out that the tapes were shot on archaic 8-mm Hi-8 videocassettes—the same format as the cheap camera Idema brought in with him when he met Artis. "First he claimed he captured them; then he claimed he bought them; then he said that they were given to him, and even that they were shot by a Japanese cameraman."

Jack's self-imposed tour of duty came to a screeching halt in June 2002 when his mother's death forced him to return home to upstate New York. Not long after his mother's funeral, Idema headed down to Fayetteville, North Carolina, for the Special Forces 50th Anniversary celebration.

Idema has said that he wanted to join the Special Forces ever since he saw John Wayne's movie, based on Robin Moore's book *The Green Berets*. Idema's father was a battle-tested World War II–era marine and Idema's short stint in the army played a huge role in his sense of self-identity, though Keith's record speaks to a spotty background and capability. On the surface, his army record shows that Idema was released after three years of service in February 24, 1978, with an honorable discharge. However, a March 18, 1977, evaluation report describes Idema's performance as "marginally average," citing lack of attention to detail, failure to follow instructions, and inability to accept constructive criticism as just some of his failings as a soldier. Another report by Captain John D. Carlson says Idema "is without a doubt the most unmotivated, unprofessional, immature enlisted man I have ever known."

Despite these scathing reviews, Idema used his military training and skills to start an antiterrorist training school in Red Hook, New York, called ConTerr. The business did not survive long, but he did manage to get a photograph of Ronald Reagan's son visiting the school. Still capitalizing on his military background, Idema's next career move was to start running Special Forces trade shows, which offered the latest in relevant military equipment and a place for military types to network. At one of these shows, he first met Robin Moore, the author who had first sparked his interest in the Green Berets.

According to Moore, the two later reconnected at the Special Forces anniversary celebration during the summer of 2002, where Moore told

Idema of his current writing project—a book about the Special Forces in Afghanistan. Idema quickly convinced Moore that the book could benefit greatly from his knowledge and recent experience in the country. Thus began an unfortunate collaboration that resulted in the book *The Hunt for bin Laden*.

Because of *The Green Berets*, Robin Moore had plenty of credibility with the military, so when the war kicked off, Moore used his contacts to get access to do a new book on Special Forces in Afghanistan. The problem was that Moore was in his late seventies and afflicted with Parkinson's. Unlike his first book, where he went through basic training and spent time in combat on the ground in Vietnam, the elderly Moore contented himself with doing interviews with Special Forces teams as they exfilled from Afghanistan to K2 air base in Uzbekistan. As one of the men of ODA 595 pictured on the back of the book remembers, "Moore would often fall asleep during interviews or forget to turn his tape recorder on."

Much of the work was done by Chris Thompson, who helped Moore gather and edit the interviews and put *The Hunt for bin Laden* together. It was understood that the book needed something to pull the disjointed chapters on each team together. Jack Idema suggested that he'd be the perfect central character—a mysterious ex–Special Forces operator turned contractor who enters Afghanistan to wage a one-man war on terror. Moore and Thompson thought the idea of Idema just going over as a private citizen added an exciting touch.

Jack was smart enough to cut a back deal with Moore's agent and actually got a percentage of the profits in exchange for writing large parts of the book. In the acknowledgments to the book, Moore gives great credit to Chris Thompson, a former soldier whose father was in Special Forces, but Idema's contribution is elliptically referenced to an "anonymous Green Beret." Intended to be about U.S. Army Special Forces, the book turned into a showcase for a man named "Jack," even featuring a bandana-wearing Idema on the cover, strolling with an AK-47, a pistol on his hip, and flanked by two Afghan cohorts. "Jack" is listed in the index as a "Special Forces operative."

I am actually featured in *The Hunt for bin Laden* and can speak from my

own experience in saying that much information is wrong, poorly researched, and written from afar so that minor details are confused or
transposed. The Special Forces team I traveled with is pictured on the
back cover. Though they never met or talked to Idema, and despite the
fact that almost all team members had carefully detailed their actions to
Moore at K2, the first chapter puts forth an account of the team's infil into
Afghanistan that the men tell me has been entirely fabricated. Contrary to
the book's reporting, there was no gunfire, no drama. They landed at
night, were welcomed by an advance CIA team that included Mike Spann,
and set to work unpacking their gear.

Idema makes the fatal mistake of including the real names of the team
and inventing actions that never occurred. An air force controller named
Matt sustains much of the action in the first chapter, though the real Matt
didn't actually fly in until days after the rest of the group. The book has
Matt screaming, "We're about to be fucking overrun. . . . I need ordnance
quick." B-52 pilots are quoted as uttering the cheesy cliché "Bombs away."
Low-key SF operators are reputed to have said, "Holy shit, un-fucking-
believable," while watching "bodies of maybe a hundred Taliban and AQ
troops drawn from the ground upward, arms and legs kicking for a frac-
tion of a second, before disappearing into a pink haze without a trace of
solid matter left of their bodies or clothing." While the story of the team's
infil may be the tallest tale in the book, elements of B movie–inspired fiction permeate the work.

One of the soldiers Idema creatively described as singing the "Ballad of
Green Berets," after a battle figures "the more crap they write about us,
the more our OPSEC [Operational Security] is protected." His wife, however, is furious about the decision to expose the real full names as well as
photos and ranks of the soldiers. She feels any terrorist with a little computer acumen could find the home address of any of the cited soldiers to
attack their families while their husbands are away on long deployments.

At the end of the fictional nonfiction book, "Jack" waxes poetic, drunk
on vodka and pomegranate juice, wearing two Makarov pistols, and spout-
ing badly mangled lines from movies. "God, I hate it when a war ends,"
the character mimics Colonel Kilgore from *Apocalypse Now*. With "his

teary eyes glassed over from the booze," Jack ponders the imponderable. "Throughout the war it seemed Jack was everywhere. . . . But was Jack one person, or several?" Perhaps therein lies the key to "Jack's" mental illness and his destructive view of the truth and loyalty.

To make the situation worse, an appendix to the book's early runs listed six charities that purportedly assist Special Forces members, their children, or the people of Afghanistan. Only a sharp eye would catch that one of the cited charities, the U.S. Counter-Terrorist Group, also garnered photo credits for images used in the book, including one of Jack riding a horse. It is none other than ConTerr. The U.S. Postal Service has been tipped off that another address, purportedly for a charity to assist Special Forces soldiers, led to a post office box and a bank account controlled by Idema.

Upon the book's release, it began climbing the bestseller lists, initially delighting Moore. But he then began receiving dozens of e-mails from Special Forces members and families of members who had been there. Moore confessed to the betrayed soldiers that he'd had to "sex it up" and said he'd submitted changes that were never incorporated. The teams wrote off the duplicity to Moore's failing mental condition, since they had no idea about the involvement of the unknown man pictured on the book's cover. In the end, the man who had created the legend of the Green Berets had, because of Idema, destroyed four decades of trust between himself and the Special Forces community. Moore watched, heartbroken, as Amazon and his own personal Web page filled with angry postings denouncing *The Hunt for bin Laden* as fiction and a disgrace.

Ed Artis was one of those who posted his views about Idema on Moore's website, actually provoking Jack into filing a lawsuit against him. "I am being sued for ruining his reputation," said Artis. "Fuck him. He can sue a dead man." (Artis suffered a mild heart attack in 2004 while on a humanitarian trip to the Philippines.) A judge dismissed the case in late 2005.

Billy Waugh also managed to provoke Idema's ire, though Waugh's background in the Special Forces has inclined Idema to hold back on the lawyers thus far. "Idema said I bad-mouthed him," said Waugh. "I said I didn't bad-mouth him; I told the truth. He was not in the CIA, and he didn't do any of that shit he said he did in Robin Moore's book." Idema started a verbal and written pissing match with Billy (with cc's to Jim Morris, Bob Morris, and Bob Brown, the publisher of *Soldier of Fortune* magazine). On March 17, 2003, Idema told Billy via a threatening e-mail, "Everyone who thinks they ought to jump on this bandwagon of hate and bullshit better buckle up because we're going to court and let's see who wins this fucking round, and billy boy, I got no problem suing your ass too if you want to keep passing on this bullshit." Billy remembers the war of intimidation escalating beyond the simple possibility of a lawsuit. "Idema calls me up and threatens me. So I say, 'Bring your shit, man, cuz I got about six guns and a few Claymores set up around my house.' Then he calls me back fifteen minutes later and says, 'I am not going to do anything because I know you have a great reputation.' Which I do. If he thinks he's going to buffalo me, he's mistaken."

Idema didn't sue Green Beret legends Billy Waugh or Robin Moore, but in March 2004, just before returning to Afghanistan, he did file suit against Chris Thompson, Thompson's parents, and Robin Moore's girlfriend, in addition to Fox News, Colonel Bob Morris, Ed Artis, and other perceived enemies. Jack, it appears, was desperately trying to protect his newly created image as a one-man army hunting bin Laden.

Lawyers, Guns, and Money

In April of 2004, allegedly bolstered by funds from Moore's book, forty-eight-year-old Idema returned to Afghanistan, this time with a crew on his payroll that included filmmaker and CBS veteran Ed Caraballo, and Brent Bennett, an ex-soldier and former waiter at Ruby Tuesday in Fayetteville. Once on the ground, Idema rented a house and car and hired a few Afghans for local support. He called the mercenary group "Task Force Saber 7," a play on Task Force Dagger, the official name for the original Special Forces campaign in Afghanistan. They wore U.S.-style uniforms, American flag patches, and often carried weapons, leading many locals to believe that they were a covert unit of contractors working for the CIA or U.S. military intelligence. From his large house in Kabul, Idema and his new crew began filming what could have been a bizarre reality show. Idema had a keen eye for mimicry and had created what could easily be confused for a CIA paramilitary operation complete with its local safehouse, hired Afghan "campaigns," and tight-lipped aggressive posture toward inquiries, though when it suited his purpose he incongruously sought media exposure for his exploits. Networks were paying good money for any action story on terrorism in Afghanistan, and Idema seemed intent on taking advantage of the demand.

Idema soon claimed he'd uncovered a plot to load taxicabs with explosives and attack U.S. and Afghan targets. Three times he convinced gullible foreign peacekeeping troops to provide backup on raids, which Jack led with maximum high-impact drama and bellicose bravado as Caraballo's camera rolled. When he thought he had hit the jackpot, Idema offered the videos of his captured "terrorists" for sale for a quarter of a million dollars, but the networks had started to suspect Idema's veracity and didn't buy.

Task Force Saber 7 also plied local sources for information and went about "arresting," or effectively abducting, Afghans Idema deemed to be al-Qaeda or Taliban. The detainees were held, interrogated, and abused in Idema's Kabul house of horrors. On May 3, Jack and his gang even turned an Afghan over to U.S. custody, photographing the exchange at Bagram for posterity. Jack described the battered Afghan as an HVT, a high-value target, but the U.S. military released the detainee without charges two months later. Idema's most famous prisoner was not one well known for terrorist ties, but for his position as a prominent Pashtun and Afghan Supreme Court judge.

Idema didn't know it, but his rash of threats, lawsuits, and betrayals had created a rapidly growing cabal of former friends who were bound and determined to shut him down. He no longer had to be unjustifiably paranoid about a conspiracy out to get him, since he had forced the situation. A private investigator he'd screwed out of 15 percent from the proceeds of a successful lawsuit, a humanitarian he'd conned, an author he'd destroyed, an army officer who'd been used; the list goes on: all developed a covert network to share documents and information designed to expose

Idema's true nature. Several U.S. government agencies, the military, and the media were also investigating Jack's activities, though he was unaware of the gathering storm.

Jack also had no idea that he had a mole inside his organization. A man in Afghanistan working as an engineer had met Idema and been taken in by his charisma and "Action Jack" persona. After some time hanging out with him, however, the man started to recognize Idema's pathology and started funneling out pictures of Jack brutalizing Afghans to a number of people. The mole didn't really need to circulate the photos secretly, since Jack himself was sending out photos and video of his "operations" in an attempt to get the media to pay for his one-man show. Still no one wanted to arrest or even stop Jack. Media outlets were asked to bid on Jack's new, and this time admittedly self-made, terror tapes, complete with action scenes of him kicking in doors and rousting Afghans. The media watched in horror but said nothing.

Jack had become his own private army, with his own independent contractors assisting him in his brutal for-profit task. Caraballo acted as filmmaker for the action scenes, and then manned the camera to faithfully document the interrogations. Was this journalism, entertainment, or documentation of evidence? Idema's high profile and sheer audacity led most to believe that Jack really must be doing something important and secretive with high-level approval. The CIA and DIA (Defense Intelligence Agency) already seemed to be using ill-defined relationships with ex-military turned independent contractors in Afghanistan, so Idema's operation fit into the pattern.

Jack cultivated this impression and may have actually been attempting to jockey himself into an officially sanctioned position. While no available evidence suggests that Idema had achieved this, calls he made to the office of Lieutenant General Jerry Boykin, the Deputy Undersecretary of Defense for Intelligence and Warfighting Support, indicate he was trying.

Boykin has a reputation for lending a sympathetic ear to ex–Green Berets with a patriotic cause. Idema began a series of interfaces with Boykin's office, and their like-minded goal of rooting out terrorists made the exchanges positive. Junior and midlevel bureaucrats encouraged Jack to develop hard intel, and Jack promised them in effusive e-mails that he was on the verge of a major bust. Not surprisingly, Jack had Caraballo film his telephone calls to Boykin's office. During one call, a man named Jorge Shim answers the phone and confirms that he has passed on information to Boykin and says they'll get back to him. While intriguing, and offered up by Idema as evidence of his ties to the U.S. military, the exchange really only offers proof that Idema had spoken to Boykin's office. As Ed Artis likes to explain, "There is a fiber of truth in everything Idema does, and then he goes and weaves an entire carpet." Every branch of the U.S. military has officially denied any connection with Idema, and a call to the Pentagon's press office will evoke an immediate and forceful: "There is no—repeat no—connection of any kind with Idema." As standard practice, the Pentagon would, of course, deny any connection with a covert operator, particularly one who had sparked a scandal of such gargantuan proportions. In the case of Idema, however, they were actually telling the truth. Since Idema was so keen to film his every move, particularly those that made it appear he was more important or connected than he really was, he would have had more damning evidence of a connection if he'd actually been operating with official approval. If Boykin had ever returned his call, Caraballo would have most certainly had the camera rolling. Further, that Idema was recording and attempting to sell film of his operations makes it even more impossible to imagine he was really running a sanctioned program.

The irony is that if a real U.S. contractor had cultivated such a close relationship with the media and was attempting to profit from footage of supposed covert operations, the military would have likely managed to shut down his operation faster than they did Idema's. While he clearly didn't have U.S. government funding or formal approval, the fact that Idema ran his makeshift jail at a static address in Kabul for months suggests that those U.S. officials who'd become aware of Task Force Saber 7's activities initially may have tacitly assented to allowing them to continue unhindered. With bin Laden on the loose, and former al-Qaeda and Taliban roaming the streets of Kabul, a completely deniable freelance operation run by a like-minded ex-military guy could have been an asset to the U.S. government's goals in Afghanistan, if Idema had ever been able to produce any verifiable results. However, no marked achievements and a building controversy about the excessive tactics of Task Force Saber 7 meant Idema and friends wouldn't enjoy their freedom of operation for long.

As soon as a real covert operator, Billy Waugh, heard about what Idema had been doing in Afghanistan, he started to sound the alert. "I told General Brown at SOCOM that Idema is beating people up and running a POW camp. . . . They put bulletins all over the place saying do not talk to the son of a bitch. In Bagram, Tashkent, and all over. The CIA put it out, too. Before he was nailed, believe me, I made sure the word was out. But one thing you can do is simply tell people like Boykin that you're doing sanctioned operations. That's pretty clever." Even Afghan minister Yunus Qanuni admitted Idema had duped him into thinking he represented the U.S. government.

On May 15, 2004, two and a half years after Ed Artis had alerted Afghan and American officials to the presence of an armed and dangerous con man roving through Afghanistan, U.S. authorities in Kabul started circulating a poster for Idema with an "arrest on sight" order. Still, it took until July fifth for Jack and his crew to be picked up in a raid by Afghan police on his Kabul house.

As expected, Idema insisted he was doing supersecret work with direct approval from the top. Jack produced his evidence of calls to General Boykin's office, but Boykin was not about to say he endorsed Jack's activities. Idema also insisted he had records of phone calls to Rumsfeld's office and other groups. These turned out to be correct, but again they proved to be one-sided inquiries from Idema.

After a very brief—and by all accounts, farcical—trial, the Afghan government convicted Idema, Bennett, and Caraballo of running an illegal prison and of torturing Afghan citizens. Idema and Bennett were sentenced to ten years each, and Caraballo got eight, though their sentences were later reduced to five years for Idema, three for Bennett, and two for Caraballo.

Despite incarceration in Afghanistan's most notorious prison, Task

Force Saber 7 enjoys the poshest setup available. Idema allegedly bribed the commander of Policharki Prison, a Tajik under General Fahim, to allow him to have couches, carpets, Internet access, and a sat phone. Caraballo was released in the spring of 2006, pardoned by Karzai for the Afghan New Year. While serving out his five-year sentence, Idema continues to publish a website and do interviews with those he considers friendly, all the while protesting his innocence and damning the conspiracy that keeps him from fighting his own war on terror.

Those who had met Idema in Afghanistan assumed there was something more important, someone more powerful behind the tough-guy façade. Those who know Idema well write him off as low-grade con artist who ends up revealing himself in his desperate hunger for publicity and money. The Afghan/American owner of the Mustafa Hotel in Kabul where Jack held court takes a more humorous approach: "The only thing that that Jack should be allowed to attack and kill is his bar tab." Others have been financially, emotionally, and professionally damaged by Idema's serial litigation, slander, and hyperaggressive campaigns to threaten or discredit former friends.

That such a transparent criminal could so easily label himself a contractor to act out his own covert paramilitary fantasy is a warning about the growing ubiquity of independent contractors. Bill Hagler, a private investigator and former associate of Idema's, blames Idema's long run in Afghanistan on the vague world of covert operations. "A world where the military can neither confirm or deny covert operators. That's fertile ground for con artists like Idema."

CHAPTER 10

The Very Model of a Modern Major Mercenary

The bitter chill of a winter night has settled over London as Michael Grunberg picks me up in his brand-new twelve-cylinder Bentley. As we glide silently through the darkened city, streetlights bend and flow along the glossy black hood. The interior smells of expensive leather and is lit by the dull glow of the backlit dials. Michael Grunberg not only has a mews house in an upscale borough of London, but also elegant homes in Guernsey and Paris. The son of a garment manufacturer, Michael has done well for himself—not just in his official profession as an accountant, but also as a careful proponent of the export and sale of military services. Although not a military man himself, Michael has played a pivotal role in creating and promoting the idea of privatized warfare over the past decade. Although his clients Tony Buckingham and Simon Mann originally formulated the vision for a modern corporatized version of mercenary action, Grunberg can take credit for the detailed structuring of ironclad contracts and constant behind-the-scenes media promotion of the concept.

As we glide by statues of statesmen, warriors, and mementos of wars fought in far-off lands, Grunberg outlines the history and genesis of Executive Outcomes and Sandline, the two original attempts in the 1990s to create a corporate structure for the sale of overtly mercenary and private military services. Understanding the rise and fall of these earliest examples of the private military company, and the motivations and ambitions of the key players behind the two ventures, opens a window into the more foreboding possibilities of an unregulated and unchecked industry dedicated to the sale or rental of armed men. It's an examination of how purveyors of organized violence perfected and honed while serving for God and country can be effectively privatized and exploited for corporate or other interests. I tell Grunberg that I am particularly interested in the role played by Timothy Spicer, former president of Sandline, since he has emerged from the mercenary scandals of the 1990s with only shadings of taint on his image and has since gone on to become wildly successful by reinventing himself as a respectable security provider.

Britain is the perfect place to understand the mercenary and the complicated and delicate subsets of privatized warfare. London is littered with reminders of warfare's capacity to reshape the world and the resultant commercial benefit that arises from controlling a vast colonial empire. Here, pursuit of aggressive commerce, national policy, and international soldiering helped drive the British Empire's world dominance. The Victorian view of proxy warfare led to the training of foreign nationals to fight wars from Afghanistan to Borneo, the seconding of former colonials like Gurkhas into Her Majesty's army, and the renting of British officers to advise foreign rulers in Oman. Warfighting skills and tools are considered necessary and vital exports in the United Kingdom. The military culture of England is woven from exported might, noble failures, exotic punitive expeditions, faraway massacres, and famous victories. From Abyssinia to Mesopotamia to Sarawak to America, the military culture of England is second to none in complexity, color, and history.

Legendary British privateers and adventurers, such as Sir Walter Raleigh and Rajah James Brooke, created the image of swashbuckling government-blessed privateers—businessmen whose personal fortunes rose and fell by fulfilling the needs of the current monarch but who were always subservient to the Crown's guiding hand. The word "mercenary" has more often been used by those whom they conquered, usually in the pejorative, since men who fight for money instead of just for a cause are often considered to be morally guided by a narrow self-interest. Today, "mercenary" is a term that is connected directly with the word "criminal" by the UN and many governments, even though those same governments often actively employ mercenaries and support proxy armies in clandestine operations.

European mercenaries and third-world proxy armies have continued to be tools of foreign policy in Latin America, Africa, and the Middle East. Some of the more famous Cold War soldiers of fortune have been Bob Denard, Rolf Steiner, "Black Jack" Schramme, and "Mad" Mike Hoare, all of whom came from former military backgrounds and were hired by intelligence services or foreign rulers to train and lead forces in "dirty wars." Mike Hoare fought in the Congo in the early 1960s, and then narrowly escaped a botched coup in the Seychelles. Steiner fought in Biafra in the late 1960s but was later imprisoned and tortured in the Sudan after helping the southern rebels. From 1978 to 1988, Denard was the de facto leader of the Comoros after he had overthrown the previous government in a coup. He now finds himself on trial in Paris for attempting to return for yet another coup attempt on the Comoros in 1995.

The men behind Executive Outcomes and Sandline may not have been mercenaries in the traditional sense, but key individuals did seek to exploit business opportunities that would require killing people in combat operations, regardless of any lip service paid to "training programs," "advisory roles," and "stability operations." Unlike most military men who might consider warfare an emotionally scarring and destructive activity, chartered

accountant Michael Grunberg views it clinically, as a business—the lucrative application of low-cost basic ingredients like South African soldiers,
Eastern European weapons, and Western military management in a tight
turnkey package. It's a business endeavor that has served Michael well,
considering the luxuries he enjoys. Of the other major players in these
early experiments with the formalized private military company, Simon
Mann now sits in a Zimbabwe jail for a failed "regime change" in the tiny
oil-rich nation of Equatorial Guinea; Tony Buckingham manages his rapidly rising oil revenues, much of it earned from ventures in hostile environments; and Timothy Spicer heads Aegis Defence Services Ltd., the
main provider of security in the maelstrom that is Iraq. Though each may
have taken divergent career paths in the new millennium, all came from
the Executive Outcomes/Sandline petri dish or "private military company" world of the 1990s.

In the early 1990s, Tony Buckingham founded the Heritage Group, a
company dedicated to oil and resource exploration. Tony describes himself on his Heritage Oil website as a "self-employed businessman with a
wide array of international business interests, particularly in Africa."
Buckingham began his involvement in the oil industry as a North Sea
diver and subsequently became a concessions negotiator acting for several
companies, including Ranger Oil Limited and Premier Oil plc. Throughout the nineties, Tony worked to negotiate deals in Oman, Uganda,
Namibia, Angola, and even Iraq—transforming himself into a wealthy oil-
man. Simon Mann and Tony were jet-setting friends; they drove a 1964
Aston Martin DB4 at a car rally together, sailed Tony's yacht, and talked
about the money that could be made in the developing world. Tony and
Simon, unlike many other investors, viewed the provision of security as
just a stepping-stone to financial wealth from exploitable resources such as
diamonds, oil, and precious minerals.

In 1992, Simon Mann's contacts in Angola had helped land a shallow
water offshore oil concession called Block 4, which he brought to Tony to
exploit. Buckingham negotiated a joint venture between his Heritage
Group and the Calgary-based Ranger Oil called Ranger Oil West Africa
Ltd. (ROWAL). Ranger invested $2 million to have Heritage build oil

platforms and agreed that Tony's company would earn 10 percent of the ultimate proceeds to be generated by the venture.

By 1993, Tony Buckingham and his ROWAL operation had encountered a major glitch in their plan. Jonas Savimbi's UNITA rebels had seized the oil port of Soyo, including some expensive controlling equipment needed to operate the floating drill rig called the *North Sea Pioneer*. Without the controlling equipment, the *North Sea Pioneer* could be nothing more than an expensive and worthless piece of hulking metal sitting off Angola's coast. Tony was paying around $20,000 a day to lease the rig and the pumping equipment, and every day of lost operations cost Buckingham big money in the lease and lost income potential.

Tony and the Angolan government attempted to negotiate with UNITA, but since oil revenue would have enriched the dos Santos government, the rebels weren't interested. Desperate, Tony contacted Richard Bethell (Lord Westbury), who was at that time heading up a security company called DSL. Tony asked Bethell if he could arrange the sabotage of the rig for an insurance claim. Bethell refused and told Tony, "A deep water rig sunk in a shallow silt-filled harbor wouldn't fool even the laziest insurance inspector." Tony then urged dos Santos to have his troops liberate the harbor, but it was clear that the ragtag Angolan army did not have the capability for such an operation. Mann had gotten his friend Tony Buckingham involved in Angola, so after the fighting trapped Tony's investment, it fell on Simon to help redeem the situation. Mann introduced Tony to his friend Eeben Barlow.

Afrikaner Eeben Barlow had founded Executive Outcomes in Pretoria in 1989. Barlow had formerly worked for the Civil Cooperation Bureau (CCB; an intelligence arm of the South African apartheid government) and was former assistant commander of 32 "Buffalo" Battalion—called "Buffalo" because most (about 70 percent) of the troops in 32 Battalion were black, though the officers were white Afrikaners. The 32 Battalion specialized in conducting unconventional bush wars and during the apartheid era would run long-range counterinsurgent operations to track terrorists and communist rebels back to their bases across the borders in Angola and Namibia. The CCB was essentially a dirty-tricks bureau that assassinated foes in other countries, created disinformation, and propped up the apartheid government. Having been a covert operator for South African intelligence, Barlow knew well the dark world of warfare, assassination, psyops, denial, and cover organizations. He also knew that in Africa, a few well-trained armed men with weapons could provide a valuable service to businessmen and rulers. The intent of his new business could be easily gleaned from his choice of company logo: a knight chessboard piece derivative of Paladin's "Have Gun, Will Travel" calling card.

Some of Barlow's initial clients were ranchers plagued by poachers and other small local security contracts—including training programs for the South African Defence Force—though he always had feelers out for more interesting projects. Barlow put together a brochure that offered complete training in sabotage, behind-the-lines operations, and weapons—in essence what he and his cohorts had done in the military. When Simon Mann contacted Barlow on behalf of a friend with a little problem in Angola, Barlow was prepared to respond with a mercenary solution.

The opportunity for Executive Outcomes to fight for dos Santos against UNITA provides proof that mercenaries value money above morals, since Barlow and his former 32 Battalion soldiers, who had spent their careers fighting with UNITA against dos Santos and his Movimento Popular de Libertaçao, or Popular Movement for the Liberation of Angola (MPLA), would now be fighting for their former left-wing enemy against their formerly U.S.-backed ally.

Simon and Tony approached the state oil company Sonangol for cooperation—or, more precisely, funding—for a plan to free up Tony's drilling equipment and get the oil revenue flowing back into government coffers. When Tony Buckingham was asked what it would cost to liberate Soyo, he suggested off the top of his head that it would take $10 million. The Angolan director simply asked for their banking information. One insider present at the discussions recalls that after the meeting, those involved had this sense of "Holy shit! We are on!" The promise of big money kicked the men into action, and, "The next thing you know Simon is sitting in the backseat of a Angolan MiG fighter doing the recce for the operation."

At first, the plan was supposedly only for EO to provide training, equipment, and support for the Angolan army to liberate the oil port, but their obvious shortcomings as a fighting force led to EO moving in to be the sharp end of the spear for the operation. Using only a few dozen EO hires—mostly black Angolan and Namibian expat veterans of South Africa's 32 Buffalo Battalion—Lafras Luitingh led the Executive Outcomes mercenaries in by ship. Helicopters were used, plus two battalions of Angolan troops as support, as the offensive pushed back UNITA and recaptured the port and Tony's equipment. Three South African mercenaries died in the battle for Soyo, many were wounded, and EO soon extracted the rest once they had successfully completed their mission. With the port under guard of Angolan soldiers, a fresh offensive by UNITA again wrested control away from the government a few months later.

Impressed by the success of the initial EO operation, dos Santos realized he would need their assistance again to reverse UNITA's recent progress and to enact a more long-term solution. Dos Santos sent his personal jet to pick up Tony in London and fly him to Angola to discuss a long-term training contract for the Angolan army. The two ended up negotiating a deal that satisfied Angola's need for a robust and effective security force and Executive Outcomes's requirement for providing them at a profit. The rebels controlled the diamond areas, and one of the key objectives would be to deny Savimbi that income. It was not too difficult to figure out who would be first in line to help exploit and develop the liberated areas.

Recognizing the future possibilities for a corporate army prepared and capable of providing security in unstable environments, the new business associates registered a UK-based EO to work the Angola contract as a joint operation with the South African EO. Though the public documents filed for the creation of the new EO list only Eeben Barlow and his wife, Sue, as the owners, all accounts indicate that Mann and Buckingham were the real forces behind the creation of the new entity. With offices in South Africa and the UK and a lucrative contact opportunity in Angola, Executive Outcomes only required a stable of clients to transform itself into a fully developed, multimillion-dollar, multinational business entity. The recruiting commenced immediately, but not before Simon Mann contacted his old friend in the Scots Guard, Tim Spicer, to offer him an executive position with the new company. Since he was still active military and hoping for a promotion, Spicer declined the invitation on the grounds he was up for a long-awaited command position.

While Mann and his EO cabal may have envisioned themselves as the vanguard of an entirely new industry, they had to achieve success with their first big operation before declaring the new golden age of the modern mercenary. Their first hurdle would take the form of training a ragtag government force of ill-equipped, ill-disciplined, inexperienced, and somewhat indifferent Angolan soldiers. Though the initial contract dictated that EO was only supposed to train and equip the Angolan army, it again became quickly obvious that that alone would never make them an efficient fighting force. Mann and Buckingham renegotiated the contract to support their mercenaries' moving into full combat operations, jacking the price up to $100 million for one year, which eventually expanded to $300 million for three years.

As is the case with current ex-military becoming independent contractors, the new EO hires could expect a significant pay bump over what they had earned earlier in their careers. Frontline grunts, primarily black Angolan, Namibian, and South African 32 Battalion veterans, were paid $2,000 a month, and Ukrainian and other foreign pilots could earn upward of $10,000 in U.S. dollars. The average pay for a white officer was around $4,000, which could be five to ten times what they had been paid in the South African army. It was not a piecemeal white mercenary army in the mold of Bob Denard or Mike Hoare, but rather a privatized reconstruction of the classic counterterrorism structure of white Afrikaners leading and fighting side by side with Angolan and Namibian tribesmen. As a result of South Africa's program of decommissioning the 32 Battalion, the recruitment drive for EO's mercenary army would require only a couple of phone calls.

Since many fighters of the 32 Buffalo Battalion had engaged in combat against the nations of their birth throughout the seventies and eighties, these veterans had found themselves essentially refugees with no homeland to which they could return without fear of persecution after the SADF (South African Defence Force) no longer required their services. As part of the transition from apartheid to majority rule, the South African government agreed to grant citizenship to all foreigners who had fought in the 32 Battalion and to provide somewhere for them and their families to live. In an audacious demonstration of the ANC's (African National Congress) lack of appreciation for the black soldiers' defense of the apartheid regime, the new government resettled the veterans to a former SADF military base, which had been abandoned because of the health threat lurking in the air, water, and soil of the surrounded asbestos mining town. Pomfret occupies a barren land on the edge of the Kalahari Desert, about a hundred miles from the nearest town. With no arable soil for farming and no industry for employment, the ex-soldiers settled into a desperate existence devoid of any opportunity, facing a bleak future of poverty and hunger. Fighting someone else's war was often the only way to feed a family, and the number of eager takers always exceeded demand.

For the EO operation, the ex-soldiers could obviously endanger their lives, though that would be a calculated risk, since African bush wars tend to start with a brief intense firefight until one side decides they are over-powered and retreats to fight another day. Greater fears would be the risk of contracting a prolonged or debilitating injury, or the worst—capture. While some mercenaries or African rebel leaders may have at one time in their long history of fighting heard the two words "Geneva Convention," rebel groups and mercenary armies don't tend to think of themselves as bound by the tenets of an agreement designed to dictate laws of war be-tween nation-state signatories. Despite the dangers, the men of Pomfret needed to provide for their families, and EO was able to field its small army of a few hundred men in short order.

EO's air support, unconventional tactics, and use of advanced weap-onry such as fuel-air explosives dramatically tilted the balance of the con-flict. The EO fighters and the Angolan army aggressively pushed UNITA out of all key diamond-producing regions, restarting the flow of money into government coffers. The rapid offensive drove UNITA to the negoti-ating table, and in November of 1994 the two warring groups signed the Lusaka Protocol, effectively ending the three-decades-old war.

Though UNITA had specifically added a demand to the peace agreement that EO leave the country, it took the Clinton administration's threatening to block UN aid to Angola for dos Santos to actually break off the relationship, leading EO to withdraw in January 1996 before the term of their contract had ended. It wasn't so much that Clinton wanted to force dos Santos to honor his commitments under the Lusaka Protocol, but more that he wanted Angola to replace EO with the politically correct version of a private military company: Military Professional Resources Inc. (MPRI), a collection of American generals and contractors who train foreign armies with the blessing of U.S. policy. The idea of mercenaries propping up a corrupt oil-rich dictatorship was apparently not a palatable arrangement. The United States preferred to provide their own private military company to train troops to prop up an oil-rich dictatorship for the much more reasonable fee of $2 million a year.

Even though the lucrative Angola gig had drawn to an abrupt close, Mann and Buckingham had no reason to worry about future prospects. EO had succeeded spectacularly in proving the utility of their professional fighting force in resolving Angola's long-simmering conflict, and in doing so had introduced a new working model for modern mercenary warfare. A new paradigm had been set whereby corporate sponsors could pay for the provision of security if granted the assurance of a certain return on their investment. The leader of a nation and the president of an oil company could enjoy a symbiotic relationship in that they both would benefit from the uninterrupted flow of oil. Politics, human rights, democracy, and all other warm and fuzzy considerations commonly enjoyed, expected, and revered in Western nations were little more than secondary concerns in the pursuit of wealth through natural-resource exploitation. EO had stripped away the moral pretense of war and made it a profitable business.

Buckingham, Mann, Luitingh, and Barlow represented the central core of Executive Outcomes in the early days, but as the venture expanded, Barlow's participation petered off and the nucleus grew to include business advisor Michael Grunberg. A former Stoy Howard accountant, Grunberg had greatly impressed Mann when he assisted in restructuring a financial deal for dos Santos while on vacation in Angola with Simon. As the cousin of Mann's then-future wife, Grunberg had more than just professional reasons to loyally manage Mann's most sensitive undertakings. Grunberg cleaned up the sloppy financial end of the business and created ironclad contracts—taking great pains to protect his clients from any potential legal liability. Grunberg also began to handle the ever-expanding stable of business ventures developed by Mann and Buckingham with their Angola money. At one time, at least eighteen different businesses listed Grunberg's Plaza 107 office in Chelsea as their mailing address. New companies developed under the EO umbrella ranged from air charter companies and tourism ventures to software security products, one of Mann's particular areas of expertise. While software security and tourism sound like rather innocuous endeavors, most of the new businesses—such as the charter airplane service Ibis Air—were designed to serve a dual purpose for their parent company. While Ibis publicly operated as a standard civilian business enterprise running flights for nonmercenary clients, having an air charter business in the family would enable EO to economically arrange for air transport without having to worry as much about the operational security of their more sensitive undertakings. What stunned the normally hush-hush world of contractors was the audacity of EO to actually have a public website that offered a full menu of military services, showcasing images of tanks, jet aircraft, and combat operations in a manner that made selling violence as innocuous as pest removal or extermination.

As a legitimate corporate entity with a recent dramatic influx in revenue, EO behaved like most aggressive and ambitious upstarts trying to expand their operations and publicize their successes. They embedded journalists like Al Venter and Jim Hooper. They did interviews that spun off articles with headlines like "An Army of One's Own." The marketing offensive apparently achieved some degree of success. When the Angola operation wound down, EO already had another contract lined up and flew one hundred twenty-five of its mercenaries directly from Angola to a tiny country in West Africa in their well-worn Boeing 727. On board was a group of white South Africans and black Ovambo tribesmen who were only told their destination just before landing. The mercenaries had come to save Sierra Leone.

Sierra Leone is a tiny West African country known more for its status as a refuge and repatriation center for former British slaves than for its mostly unexploited wealth of diamonds and minerals. Backed by the notoriously rapacious Charles Taylor, rebel leader Foday Sankoh entered Sierra Leone with about a hundred Liberian mercenaries in March of 1991, and began a four-year brutal bloodletting in their slow push toward the capital. By April of 1995, with Sankoh's forces battling on the outskirts of Freetown, it appeared the festering war teetered on the cusp of a final, bloody resolution.

The leader of Sierra Leone was Captain Valentine Strasser, who had come to power in 1992 at the age of twenty-five after a group of military officers knocked on the president's mansion to demand their back pay. The president had fled and the officers decided to install Strasser in a de facto coup.

In early 1995, after Sankoh's Revolutionary United Front (RUF) forces had scored some major successes against the Sierra Leone military, Strasser contracted renowned American mercenary Bob MacKenzie to command a group of four thousand Gurkha soldiers hired from a Channel Island company named Gurkha Security Group (GSG). Within two months, RUF forces had killed MacKenzie and a number of the Gurkhas in ambush and GSG pulled out their remaining troops. The rebels were approaching the outskirts of the capital.

Strasser then turned to Executive Outcomes, which was just coming off its successful operation in Angola. According to a source close to the contract negotiations, not only was EO eager and capable of undertaking the assignment, but they had also figured out a way Strasser could charge the security costs to International Monetary Fund (IMF) payouts. The contract initially was for one year but eventually added up to $35 million for 21 months.

In May of 1995, pilot Neil Steyl flew one hundred twenty-five EO men directly from Angola to Freetown in a white 727, and within days the mercenaries began military action against the rebels. After nine days of aggressive contact, the rebels had retreated from the outskirts of the capital and the EO fighters had pushed them back into the jungle. The RUF could not withstand the Hind gunships manned by expert pilots and the mortar skills and aggressive counterambushing tactics practiced by the experienced mercenaries. Within a matter of weeks, EO troops had pushed to reclaim a broad swath of territory; the diamond fields were secured and the mines locked down. This time there was no need to pretend that it was a training or a support mission. The men of EO had simply "sorted out" the opposing mercenaries of the RUF.

Following popular protests, Strasser consented to hold the first democratic elections in thirty years, which brought Ahmed Tejan Kabbah to power in March 1996. As part of his peace negotiations with the RUF, Kabbah agreed to cancel the contract with EO. Grunberg would bill $35.2 million but would only receive $15.7 million before leaving due to non-payment of their contract in January of 1997. A number of mercenaries stayed as contractors under the corporate name of LifeGuard, one of EO's security start-ups, to guard critical diamond and mineral mines. With EO gone, another coup quickly replaced Kabbah in May of 1997. The new military junta allied itself with the RUF and chaos reigned again. This time EO did not come to the rescue.

Even though they had difficulty extracting payment for the second operation, the men had generated an extraordinary personal income. After the successes in Angola and Sierra Leone, EO had come to a natural end. According to Grunberg, "Eeben took ten million and walked away. They all did very well. Simon pocketed $60 million and Tony banked $90 million." Grunberg doesn't mention his own take, but considering the multiple houses, multiple cars, and other obvious trappings of wealth he enjoys, it must have been significant. Further, the direct revenue generated by the operations does not include the potential proceeds from future mineral exploitation.

Although EO fought their way across Angola to push back the rebels and secure diamond mines, Grunberg claims there it was only a coincidental link between mercenaries and diamonds. "The goal was to push the rebels out and recapture the towns. Were there diamond areas there and were they secured? Of course. But you go for the towns because that's where the civilian population is, not the mines." Grunberg's interesting logic sounds convenient and would have a more solid resonance had the

principals in Executive Outcomes simply walked away from both countries. Michael is correct in that once Savimbi's UNITA lost the diamond
areas, he quickly lost the ability to pay his army and himself. But, Buckingham's Branch Energy (a company he bought from Eeben Barlow in
1995) negotiated and was awarded two diamond exploration concessions
in Angola in 1996. Branch Energy then folded their Angola and Sierra
Leone properties into DiamondWorks, a public company that was traded
on the Vancouver Stock Exchange in which Tim Spicer and Simon Mann
also had significant stock options.

It is fair to say that there was no direct quid pro quo between the provision of mercenaries and the granting of mineral concessions; after all,
natural resources need significant development and management. However, having the same people involved in businesses in both areas raises
some troubling issues. Cobuss Claassens, a former EO contractor who
fought in Sierra Leone, finds it hard to believe that the thirst for valuable
resources was not a driving force underlying the company's business
model. After a hard fight to liberate the Kono diamond fields in Sierra
Leone, he remembers Tony Buckingham arriving in midsummer 1995.
"There he was sitting on the hood of the Land Rover wearing a forage cap
and drinking a beer at ten o'clock in the morning, while all these geolo-
gists he had brought in were showing him chunks of laterite to show how
rich the diamond field was." After seeing that, the connection between the
acquisition of precious resources and the use of privatized warfare were
cemented in Claassens's mind. Further, a 1995 classified British Defence
Intelligence Staff report concluded, "It appears that the company and its
associates are able to barter their services for a large share in the employing nation's natural resources and commodities."

Mann and Buckingham had done well for the countries of Angola and
Sierra Leone, and had generated a significant profit from EO. Unfortunately for them the "Have Gun, Will Travel" image of the company had
triggered soon to be crippling antimercenary legislation in South Africa,
making future potential clients nervous. Their solution was to go upmar-
ket, create a new company with high-profile, first-world leadership, which
would then simply subcontract the heavy lifting to the South Africans who

had made up EO. Once again, Simon Mann contacted his old friend Lieutenant Colonel Tim Spicer.

Sandline

In the time since Mann had first asked Tim Spicer to join Executive Outcomes, Spicer had retired from the military and moved on to a lackluster career in the financial world. In their initial meetings, Mann sold Spicer on his new vision to have a new "private military company," or PMC, designed to add a more palatable layer of Western executive management to outsource the more mercenary concept of EO.

Spicer admitted to me that maybe he was a little naïve about setting up the new iteration of Executive Outcomes. "I was only eleven months out of the military. I had no benefit of hindsight. . . . It was a risk, but I had been offered a job in the security industry." Simon offered Spicer about twice what he had made in the army, plus arranged for a loan so Spicer could buy a new Aston Martin. Spicer took the job and set about laying the groundwork for the new company. "I went to visit EO in Sierra Leone. The new company was to be a separate organization. We were going to set it up, and it was going to be onshore. There was a discussion of the moral aspect. Anyone who has talked about Sandline agreed it had to be legitimate." Although the official version is that Buckingham, Mann, and Spicer first conceived of Sandline during lunch at Chelsea's La Famiglia restaurant in October 1996, inside sources indicate that Tim Spicer had actually begun negotiations on what would come to be Sandline's first contract as early as May 1996, almost seven months earlier.

In the spring of 1996, Richard Bethell (Lord Westbury) and his company DSL had been working in Papua New Guinea (PNG) but had not been terribly impressed with the government's willingness or ability to make payments on their mining security contract. The government had been in a financial crisis since 1989 when secessionist-minded locals on the island of Bougainville (the Bougainville Revolutionary Army, or BRA), irate over the flow of money and resources going away from the local community to enrich the central government, shut down the massive Panguna copper mine. Mishandling of the dispute led to nearly a decade of civil war. Since Panguna had generated nearly half of PNG's hard currency when fully operational, control of the mine was a key strategic objective. When the government asked about DSL's ability to solve this problem, Richard simply passed the inquiry on to his friend Simon Mann. Tim Spicer's first task as head of Sandline was to bring in this bit of business.

Almost immediately, Spicer began communicating with the cash-strapped government of Papua New Guinea about their security problems. Considering the output of the Panguna mine when it was operational, the right negotiations could generate a flow of income that would dwarf any deals Tony had made in Angola or Sierra Leone. The autonomy demands of the island residents and the underlying problem that had led to the shutdown and sabotage of the mine were never a consideration.

During the early discussions with PNG, Spicer used the stationery of Plaza 107, Grunberg's real estate management/business advisory company. Only after it became clear that PNG had the potential to turn into a major contract did they begin to reconsider how this opportunity could best be exploited. Spicer and Mann went to a designer down the hall from Grunberg's office and slapped together a business card and stationery using the name Sandline. The logo they designed for Sandline was essentially little more than two scribbles, almost perfectly symbolizing how quickly companies can be put together to meet a lucrative opportunity.

Though evidence indicates that work on what would eventually become a Sandline operation had begun long before the October 1996 lunch cited by Spicer in his autobiography, that does not mean that the La Famiglia restaurant meeting was of no importance. The first appearance of the term "private military company" in the media a few weeks after the lunch suggests that the conversation may have revolved around a public relations strategy to recast the role of mercenary in what would become one of the most significant developments in hundreds of years of privatized warfighting. EO had tried to develop a new, corporatized model for soldiers-for-hire, but the apartheid-era taint and fear of unrestrained private armies remained. Part of the solution was to rebrand the concept by using EO's Rolodex from behind Sandline's superficial sheen of respectable leadership. The bigger initiative required an aggressive public relations strategy that would alter public perception of the entire concept of mercenaries. While much of the shift may look like mere semantics, the deliberate change in language usage either represents a significant theoretical development, or intentional spin.

The principals involved began working to rebrand a politically correct band of soldiers-for-hire as a "private military company," and the word "mercenary" was to be replaced with "contractor." It was to be the new enlightened age of the mercenary. The Sandline sales pitch always privately included the two EO success stories, though Grunberg would work to maintain the public perception of a firewall between Sandline and EO. In a demonstration of their quest for legitimacy and business expansion, in November 1996, EO hired retired U.S. Special Forces Colonel Bernie McCabe as director of Sandline's American office. With a highly respected career as a Delta commander in his past, McCabe could use his contacts and position of authority to generate new business from American clients for Sandline. Before Sandline could start cultivating the Americans for business, however, the men would have to prove themselves.

Spicer's careful cultivation of a possible opportunity in PNG finally paid off in December 1996, when he was given $250,000 to do a security survey on how to quell the rebellion and allow PNG to reopen the mine. He came back to the government with a $36-million estimate for logistics, weapons and manpower, a sum that PNG did not possess.

On January 6, 1997, Spicer met with Prime Minister Julius Chan to convince him that a speedy and covert action to retake Panguna would result in positive results in the upcoming elections. Although there was no budget item for the mercenary operation, called "Operation Oyster," Michael Grunberg showed Chan how cutting a series of smaller checks would let him escape the need for a parliamentary vote. Much of the money came from cutbacks in current budgets, and half of the amount was to be paid up front. The contract's stated purpose was to "train the State's Special Forces Unit [SFU] in tactical skills specific to the objective; gather intelligence to support effective deployment and operations; conduct offensive operations in Bougainville in conjunction with PNG Defence

Forces to render the BRA military ineffective and repossess the Panguna mine; and provide follow-up operational support, to be further specified and agreed between the parties and is subject to separate service provision levels and fee negotiation." Tim Spicer signed the contract, along with South African EO member Nick van den Bergh as "consultant." The players behind EO and the company called Sandline were fused contractually and conceptually, though still publicly separated.

Concurrently, negotiations began for Tony Buckingham to purchase depressed shares of the now shuttered but soon-to-be-liberated Panguna mine. Buckingham faxed a letter to PNG's minister of defense about how he currently held $200 million worth of investments, specifically mentioning Sierra Leone and Angola, and stating that "all of the investment has been into the extraction of mineral resources (oil, copper, diamonds, gold) and all have involved high risk security/military situations." Once again, the parallel tracks of mineral resources and mercenaries were being laid in another country. Without Sandline, there would be no prospect of a reopened mine, and without Tony's direct offer of investment and potential continued provision of security, there would be no payoff.

On February 7, Nick van den Bergh and the first South African mercenaries arrived to begin the training and operational phase, and soon the entire contingent of forty-four had arrived. On Feburary 19, the PNG government mentioned to the Australian government that they had paid for a training program from what was essentially Executive Outcomes. The news was leaked to the Australian press. An uproar began, and the Australian government—which considers PNG within their sphere of influence—pressured the PNG government to get rid of the mercenaries.

The PNG military, which was shocked to find that the cash-strapped government had planned to pay foreign mercenaries $36 million for a three-month operation, began to plot against Chan's leadership. The head of the PNGDF (PNG Defence Forces), Jerry Singarok, decided to round up the Sandline and EO contractors and deport them. At the same time, their leader Tim Spicer would be arrested and jailed. On March 16, they sprang into action. The mercenaries who were already billeted on a military base were quickly put on a plane and flown out of the country. Tim

Spicer was lured to a meeting and then roughly forced into detention. Singarok demanded that Chan and his defense and deputy prime minister resign because they had taken kickbacks. Chan responded by firing Singarok, but to defuse the situation, Singarok resigned. As a result, Singarok's soldiers poured into the streets in his support as the situation rolled toward total meltdown. The Sandline operation had accidentally pushed the country to the brink of a military coup.

Despite the government's crackdown to control the fallout of the scandal, massive outcry by citizens still pushed for Chan and his government to step down. The governor general of PNG even took out a newspaper ad accusing the government of corruption. The Australian government threatened to cut off all aid, and finally, on March 25, Chan resigned. Without even firing a shot, Sandline had in effect deposed the government it had been hired to protect.

Spicer was quickly released from jail after Michael Grunberg arrived with a large satchel of money and the UK government got involved. PNG dropped the cursory charges of possessing a pistol and 30 bullets, and Spicer quickly exited the country before his fortunes reversed again. After conducting an investigation, Papua New Guinea's chief ombudsman, Simon Pentanu, described the hiring of Sandline as a "criminal act" and a decision by leaders who were "quite mad."

Despite the dramatic failure of the endeavor, Spicer still defends his Project Oyster as simply misunderstood. He claims PNG was not a planned mercenary operation, but rather a legitimate support and training gig in which the PNG Defence Forces were supposed to do the fighting, and Sandline would provide the skills and resources to guarantee success. Even though they had not completed the operation, Sandline pursued legal recourse to get their full payment. By May of 1999, Sandline's lawyer, Richard Slowe, and his firm, JS Berwin, had negotiated a settlement with PNG that was paid off in increments.

Tim Spicer was not slowed down by his failure in PNG and quickly moved on to another project, one that would ultimately turn out to cause an even bigger scandal and nearly bring down the British government in its wake.

Rakesh Saxena, a fiftysomething fugitive financier of Indian origins and Thai nationality, had a problem with the government of Sierra Leone. The former prime minister, Ahmed Tejan Kabbah, had promised Saxena generous mineral concessions but had been deposed before the rights could be exploited. Saxena thought he had an easy solution: depose the upstart coup-installed government of Johnny Paul Koroma and restore the democratically elected Kabbah to power so he could exercise his mining options. Saxena had become aware of Sandline's activities through the PNG scandal and thought they might be an outfit that could help. He contacted Spicer and contracted him at $70,000 to formulate a plan on how to accomplish his objective.

From the beginning, it was clear that this would be an interesting project. When Tim Spicer arrived in Vancouver, B.C., for his first meeting, he was briefly detained and questioned by the Canadian police about the purpose of his visit. When Spicer arrived at Saxena's oceanfront apartment, he couldn't help but notice Saxena was surrounded by Serbian bodyguards, who each reportedly earned $10,000 a week. It appeared that Saxena was under court-mandated but self-financed house arrest.

Although Saxena was not technically a criminal, he had been arrested at a business meeting in a luxury off-season ski resort in Whistler, Canada, on July 7, 1996. Freed on $2-million bail, he was fighting extradition for embezzling money from a Thai bank. He complained that many of his assets were frozen, making him that much more eager to get his hands on Sierra Leone's mineral resources. Despite his hardship, Saxena committed to pay $10 million to the Kabbah government in exile, which Kabbah would then use to pay Sandline to restore him to power. Saxena could only scrounge up $1.5 million immediately, but Spicer decided that was sufficient to get the plan under way.

Conveniently, Executive Outcomes still had some men inside Sierra Leone, who had rolled into the country in 1995 and stayed behind to guard the Bambuna dam and the rutile mine after the coup. These mercenaries turned security contractors were to provide intelligence-gathering, training, and support to roughly four thousand of Kabbah's supporters, primarily local Kamajors, a militia primarily drawn from the Mende tribe under Chief Hinga Norman. Sandline had a Russian-made helicopter that would ferry troops into Freetown, as well as bring back casualties, do evacuations, and deliver humanitarian supplies. Sandline also arranged for the air shipment of over thirty tons of weapons to the proxy army of Kamajors.

At that time, UN Resolution 1132 was in effect, which laid out the arms embargo against all sides of the conflict in Sierra Leone. Further, the conservative government in the UK had publicly adopted a new "ethical" foreign policy, which wasn't supposed to include undertaking or approving of things like weapons shipment to a rebel group in Sierra Leone. Not one to give up in the face of complications, Spicer thought he could work his way around the embargo. His men on the ground would liaise with the Nigerian troops who were in-country as part of ECOMOG, the UN-mandated peacekeeping force. The argument would be made that since the weapons were to be delivered to Nigerian soldiers working under a UN mandate, the arms embargo had not been broken. Spicer had discussions with the British foreign office, and he felt he had the tacit approval of the UK government for the plan, and so proceeded.

The plan fell apart when the Nigerians unilaterally decided to roll into Freetown and scare out the rebels in March of 1998. The incident led to the exposure of the arms embargo violation by a British company, and an international "Arms to Africa" scandal erupted. The UK government denied knowing anything about the arms shipment, though Spicer and Grunberg embarrassed the government by steadfastly maintaining that the Foreign Office had been fully briefed. Soon photos surfaced of the Sandline helicopter being serviced by the British military in Sierra Leone, fueling the speculation that it had been an officially sanctioned operation. The British government played its part of diligent enforcer of the rules by calling for an investigation and raiding Sandline's offices and the homes of its top managers. In the end, Tim Spicer and Sandline would be proven right and Peter Penfold, the British high commissioner, would apologize for having not realized that the arms embargo extended to cover weapons shipments to the supporters of Kabbah's democratically elected government-in-exile. This illustrates how in the morally gray area of coups and countercoups, the same incident can be simultaneously viewed by different people as either an example of a resource-hungry criminal hiring mercenaries to overthrow a government in clear violation of international law, or a British company assisting the restoration of a democratically elected government. Sometimes it can be both simultaneously.

The leader of the Kamajors, Sam Hinga Norman, would be later tried for war crimes in his own country, and Saxena still fights his deportation to face trial in Thailand for stealing $73.5 million. Today, Spicer is sanguine in his recollections of how his company's project in Sierra Leone had become the "Arms to Africa" scandal and their undertaking in PNG had become the "Sandline Affair." He admits only that "Sandline stuttered forward into evolution. The growth of Sandline took everyone by surprise." But he stands by his mantra that "it had to be for a legitimate purpose. It had to be lawful. The purpose was to do something properly and make money at it." He is also candid about its failures: "Because it was ahead of its time in concept, [Sandline] had a number of operating difficulties and perception problems."

Others inside Sandline blamed Spicer directly for the screwups. "A large gap between planning and execution" is how one principal describes it. In that general sense, Spicer's problems seemed to last long after the demise of Sandline, and in the ensuing years he rolled through starting up a series of security-related companies—CRM, Sandline Consultancy, Trident, Trident III, Trident Maritime—each of which achieved something between a limited degree of success and total failure. Even so, Spicer forged ahead.

Now in his fifties, Spicer heads one of the industry's most profitable purveyors of security services, Aegis Defence Services. A company he started in late 2002 with little more than a handful of backers and a dubious track record, Aegis sparked a dramatic comeback for Spicer when in March 2004 the company was awarded the most lucrative security contract of the Iraq war. The Pentagon hired Spicer's company at $293 million for a three-year cost-plus contract that will eventually add up to almost half a billion dollars in revenue for Aegis. For 2005, Aegis declared revenue of £62 million, or around $130 million, and the Pentagon extended the contract for an additional year. Now Spicer's start-up is a direct industry competitor to the older generation of British security firms like ArmorGroup, HART, and others, which have all privately expressed shock that Spicer could convince the U.S. government of his qualifications, despite the facts of his past exploits.

Aegis now occupies more than eight thousand square feet of a drab modern office building on Victoria Street in London, in a space that looks more like it should be home to an investment or accounting firm. I sense that the office has the feel of a short-term rental as I make my way down the long hallway to Tim's office. Dash, his black French bulldog, greets me at the door and sniffs me until satisfied I'm no threat to his master and finally retires back to his bed in the corner. Spicer is dressed in standard business attire. His famously boyish long hair has been replaced with a tight business cut, though his baggy eyes and downward glower remain fully in effect.

Before the conversation begins, I have to agree to a list of ground rules his lawyers have had typed up for me: no personal stuff, no answers to suppositions or comments on third-party discussions, and no straying off Spicer's role as leader at Aegis and the financial success of his company. They have arranged the chairs so Tim sits at his desk directly in front of me, with his former Sandline attorney and now Aegis director, Richard Slowe, off to my nine o'clock, and Spicer's biggest investor, Jeffrey Day, staring at the back of my head. Every time Tim starts to stray off message or act pugnacious, his two corporate minders interrupt with polished truisms to keep the conversation on track.

Spicer doesn't trust the press and has good reason not to since they have lambasted, insulted, insinuated, extrapolated, and libeled him ever since he appeared on their radar as the head of Sandline International. The media has had no lack of sources willing to talk dirt about Spicer, since, as one of his ex-associates phrases it, "his career path is littered with the wreckage of friendships past." Some of what appears in print is invented and most of it mean-spirited, but Spicer made himself a target by continually climbing back into the ring and proclaiming himself the oracle of the neo-mercenary, the tip of the privatized security spear, the vanguard for a new force in world affairs. In his new mantle at Aegis, Spicer seeks to reinvent himself as the sage of privatized security.

Spicer shows a bit of his former style by saying, "My view is the people who this company deals with are not concerned with rather florid stories. Those who matter know what happened. It's irritating. . . . It's like mosquitoes." He dismisses his critics with a shrug of his shoulders and a derisive tone. "What we are interested in is being judged on our performance."

Sensing the old Spicer reemerging, Richard and Jeffrey jump in to steer him back on track, as Jeffrey interjects, "That is the dilemma of this industry—how transparent it is, how transparent it should be. We should be as transparent as a private corporation should be. We have armed people who operate in dangerous places. There is an obligation. This is the whole mélange of transparency, regulation, and wish to get sorted out. I am and have always been a fan of regulation."

Spicer has intelligently approached the idea of ex-soldiers providing value to armed forces (both foreign and domestic) and has very publicly made the case for separating intervention, peacekeeping, and security operations from traditional military capability. His new position as a leader of a multimillion-dollar private security company with first-world clients has led him to recant some of his earlier enthusiasm for mercenary operations. Years of touting armed intervention in foreign lands must now be tempered with politically correct statements and adjustments.

Not surprisingly, with a lucrative U.S. Pentagon contract under his belt and money pouring in, Spicer no longer advocates the use of mercenaries: "My view is there is a distinction. 'Mercenary' and 'private military company' are not the same. There are very distinct differences. Essentially a mercenary is there as an individual. The private military company has led to people using the pejorative distinction. Most private security companies will not consider mercenary work. My view has always been that there is plenty of legitimate work to be done." He continues to insist that Sandline, despite being the spit and polished front man for the armed paladins of Executive Outcomes, was not a mercenary organization. "The crux is, are you working legally or illegally? Overthrowing a government, whether you like it or not, is illegal." I refrain from pressing him on the point of how Sandline managed to deftly violate an international arms embargo to ship weapons in to a group that intended to overthrow a government, or how the Sandline affair in Papua New Guinea, led to riots and the abrupt downfall of Prime Minister Julius Chan.

Instead, I ask him if winning the Iraq contract shows that his "mercenary" experience with Sandline has paid off. Now magically sensitive to the term, Spicer immediately challenges me with my interpretation of what a mercenary is. He insists again, as his minders bob their heads in support, that he never did anything illegal and points to the long history of the British government providing "loan service officers" or being seconded to fufill foreign contracts in places like Oman.

Before 9/11, Spicer's string of corporate iterations were mostly small ventures trying to chase contracts in maritime security, since at that time the biggest demand came for antipiracy programs. After 9/11, Spicer recognized the major opening for the private security industry to step in and shore up governmental efforts in the War on Terror. Aegis began in 2002, and in its first full year of operations generated £554,000, or about a million dollars in revenue. Tim admits that at the beginning he had to work hard to overcome the huge baggage train from Sandline. "After the Sierra Leone business, which we came out of completely clean, there was a feeling of bruising. We could have done without that." He defends his controversial history with Sandline and presents Aegis as being unrelated by saying, "We work hard to keep that separation. There is enough time and space and proven track record between the two issues. Our view is we have had to counter a lot of very negative, nonsensical rubbish. Our line is to counter it when we choose to."

Around the time Aegis won the Iraq contract, a new EO/Sandline-style controversy arose, dragging Spicer into the center of yet another mercenary scandal. Spicer barely managed to avoid implication in a plot to overthrow the government of Equatorial Guinea. The direct involvement of his former colleagues like Simon Mann made some Spicer-watchers suspicious. When the British government got word of an impending coup, they called Spicer into a meeting in order to find out further details and to issue implicit instructions to warn off his friend Simon Mann.

The first time Spicer had an important meeting with the Foreign Office regarding his involvement in foreign intrigue, neither side kept notes, which led to the post–Arms to Africa confusion as each side called the other's veracity into doubt. The second time, both sides would be careful to keep a detailed record of the conversation. Spicer recalls the event: "We thought we were being asked to talk about some business. I had absolutely no idea, no contact with Simon [Mann] for six months." Spicer even claims he had to crack an atlas to make sure he knew the exact location of the tiny African republic, since he had been informed in advance that Equatorial Guinea would be the subject of the meeting. This assertion actually creates significant doubt about Spicer's entire claim that he had no foreknowledge of the coup, since it is inconceivable that someone who had been working for years to develop opportunities in Africa and the developing world was unfamiliar with the geographic coordinates of one of the world's fastest-growing and least-secure economies. Further, Richard Bethell (Lord Westbury) says that he had a lunch with Spicer in mid-2002 where Bethell mentioned he would be bidding on some maritime security work down in Equatorial Guinea. Spicer called Bethell a short time afterward to tell him that he was also thinking about pursuing some maritime security contracts in EG and asked if Richard would mind the competition. It is unclear why Spicer would have needed an atlas to refresh his memory about the country's location.

According to Spicer's account, as soon as the meeting started, "they asked did we know anything about a coup in Equatorial Guinea. We were surprised to be asked that question." Spicer apologized that he didn't have any information for them and was told in response that the UK government had information indicating that former members of Sandline and Executive Outcomes were involved in planning a coup to take down the Equatoguinean government.

When, a matter of weeks later, Simon Mann was arrested in Zimbabwe picking up a weapons cache to take into Equatorial Guinea, the British government initially tried to claim it had no foreknowledge of any coup attempt. Again, the truth would ultimately surface, and minutes of the meeting with Spicer would be released. Despite the involvement of a number of his former cohorts, and persistent rumors that he had been informed through his relationship with Mann, Spicer insists: "We had nothing to do with the coup. We have never been down there." Once again Spicer would be vindicated, even though both times the Foreign Office has had to "clarify" its initial recollection.

After the Arms to Africa scandal, the former senator Jesse Helms had Spicer's passport flagged and required a personal interview before he could enter the United States. Reportedly, Spicer was once chained to a chair while American officials sorted out his purpose in the country. It was only after the intervention of high-powered friends of friends that Spicer's black flag as an arms dealer was lifted. In their rush to field hired guns in Iraq, the Pentagon and State Department found it convenient to turn a blind eye to the more questionable aspects of Spicer's past.

Even with Spicer's "colorful" business history and long list of professional and personal enemies sharpening their knives, the former head of Sandline leads a charmed life. No one, not even Spicer, has been able to adequately explain how his fledgling company won the largest single-security contract ever awarded in Iraq.

As Spicer explained it to me during the interview, he found the RFP (request for proposal) while surfing the Internet looking for work opportunities in Iraq. However, multiple sources with intimate knowledge of Aegis's bid have alleged to me that PMO (Project Management Office) security chief Brigadier General Anthony Hunter-Choat and Brigadier General James Ellery helped formulate the specifications for the RFP with Aegis in mind. Some security insiders claim that Spicer had a personal relationship with the two brigadiers from their days as contemporaries in the British military, but others are of the opinion that the awarding of the Aegis contract arose from a wish to have more British companies profiting off the reconstruction. Not surprisingly, Spicer vehemently denies all insinuations and charges, and claims, "it is a standard U.S. tender issued by the northern region. They wrote the spec."

The one RFP specification that Spicer's Aegis did not match would seem to be the most important qualification: experience. Spicer admits he had no previous experience in Iraq, even though the RFP asks for proof of similar jobs within a recent timeframe, but dismisses that as a problem: "The weighting on each part is different. They put more emphasis on the other parts." So if Spicer's company had an idea for response that exactly fit the expectations of the RFP, instead of actual experience, those evaluating the proposal would have ranked him ahead of DynCorp, Olive, CRG, and other companies also bidding on the job that already had extensive operations in Iraq.

If Spicer didn't have advance notice, or at least inside assurances that Aegis would be selected for the job, I am curious why he had advertised job openings for ex-military Arabic-speaking radio operators a full month before the contract was awarded. Spicer machine-guns me with a stream of responses: "We had put in place some anticipatory measures. If we get the call, how are going to do it. That increased in tempo. We were getting more and more queries. Foolish to put in place things related to winning. We were sort of prepared. We have an action list ready for implementation." Spicer continues to reel off reasons: "We put out feelers to the people who recruit. We knew before it was made public. Because we were very keen to get things in place."

It is understandable that Aegis would want to simplify the public understanding of how they won their singular contract. But the story of Aegis's ascent becomes far more convoluted and questionable when talking to insiders who were in Baghdad while the decision process to award the contract was taking place. A former State Department official who was working in Baghdad at the time surprised me with the bluntness of his view: "Spicer should never have gotten that contract. He got that contract because of Hunter-Choat."

The awarding of the Aegis contract shocked even Baghdad-based Coalition security insiders, and intense discussions developed revolving around how the vast differential in experience between Aegis and the bidders could have possibly led to Spicer's company being the one selected as most qualified to take on such a massive responsibility. To the State Department official, it was obvious how it happened. "I tipped a few back with [Hunter-Choat] and I think I know him well," he continues talking about the decision process that took place in Baghdad. "You put Hunter-

Choat in a room with four other junior [military] people and he can steer the decision. He wrote the specs, he knew Spicer, and he should have recused himself from that process. It was just Hunter-Choat, Steve Barton, an air force guy, and three other junior guys going over those proposals."

Pressing him for a direct connection between Hunter-Choat's alleged influence and the awarding of the contract, I ask if he has any proof of his claim: "No, it's more of a negative proof." He laughs at my naïveté. "We just assumed he would end up working for Aegis when he left here. We had a saying there like those Las Vegas commercials: 'What happens in Baghdad, stays in Baghdad.'"

There is no proof that Hunter-Choat went on to significantly profit from Aegis's new business, but his associate at the PCO, Brigadier General James Ellery, did. Ellery had been in charge of managing security for the reconstruction of the power industry, and was most likely not present at the meetings where the decision to award the Aegis contract was taken. However, a former employee of the PMO who worked with Ellery on a day-to-day basis has said that Ellery did advise Spicer throughout the bidding process. Very soon after completing his official assignment in Iraq, Ellery returned to set up Aegis's Baghdad office. He began encountering problems almost immediately. The State Department official said that he had caught Ellery lying about certain benchmarks of progress. According to the official, coalition officials warned Ellery on a few occasions, but after he ignored a specific request by the U.S. embassy regional security officer (RSO) to not travel, the State Department reportedly used that as the reason to demand that Ellery be fired. Ellery did leave Baghdad, but instead of firing him, Spicer promoted him to the board of directors. When I ask my State Department source if Ellery's almost immediate return as the Aegis project manager should have raised questions of impropriety, he thinks about it for a second and says, "You know, I never really thought about that."

So Ellery got a promotion, even though he had been essentially expelled from Baghdad and the operation he set up was criticized on many levels. Since they began with no existing apparatus on the ground in Iraq, it should have been expected that they would encounter significant problems as a result of their sudden requirement for over six hundred trained armed men, a fleet of vehicles, a dozen intelligence centers, and much more. To be fair, one insider sets the scene: "The insurgency was cooking; there was not an armored car to be found; getting weapons was equally difficult. On a daily operational level it was a clusterfuck. They didn't even have an office. . . . Aegis was essentially building an airplane in flight."

Even though there was intense pressure on Aegis to get their operation up and running, a lack of manpower available in Baghdad to manage oversight had made it difficult to keep track of their progress. "People were coming and going, things were hectic, contract managers handled an average of sixty to seventy contracts each. . . . The Aegis contract was handled by a fifty-two-year-old woman who wouldn't know which end of a gun was which. The PCO had no security officials managing that contract."

Despite the failure of official oversight, it became widely known that Aegis was having serious problems getting up to speed, and the State Department started to investigate. One visit made Aegis's problems obvious. "They were not prepared when I came and walked down there. . . . They had nothing. They didn't have people. They didn't have standards. . . . Aegis people didn't have skills, tactics, or even vetting. They [Aegis] would take people out to the range and have them fire a few shots with no judging. [Aegis] started hiring Iraqis and giving them guns and giving them passes to enter the Green Zone. That gave us a heart attack." He laughs. "We were doing everything we could to keep armed Iraqis out and he was inviting them in." As a result, the RSO triggered an audit.

According to Spicer's version of events, the Office of the Inspector General for Iraq Reconstruction, as a matter of course, would audit contractors beginning from the biggest and working their way down the food chain. "Aegis deployed on the fifth or sixth of June and was audited in October." Spicer partially attributes the negative report they received after the audit to the rapidity with which Aegis was trying to get their operations up and running in Iraq. "Two people came in with a statement of work and said they wanted weapons training records. In that mad kerfuffle, they were not complete. Show me an army that has complete records."

Spicer's claim that the main problem was just with recordkeeping contradicts the recollection of the State Department official and the Inspector General's report. The audit report released in early 2005 indicated that Aegis had not thoroughly vetted or even trained a significant portion of their personnel. The audit also confirmed publicly what many detractors were saying privately—that Aegis was cutting corners to get people in the field, doing things like showing up with taxis and Iraqi guards instead of armored cars and Tier One operators. One competitor jokes that based on the professionalism he has seen in Aegis contractors, Spicer must have "cleaned out the jails" to ramp up as quickly as he had.

Dissension inside the company had grown so extreme that an ex-employee set up a website to air grievances of drunkenness, incompetence, and Aegis's negligent and remote management. Spicer's most recent controversy first arose when a video posted on that employee website surfaced, showing unidentified contractors—though presumably employed by Aegis—in a security convoy shooting at Iraqi civilians. It's not unusual for a PSD to shoot at cars that come too close to a security convoy, but the Aegis-hired South African contractor in the controversial video did not appear to be going through the mandated warning steps before spraying nearing cars with bullets. The Elvis soundtrack didn't add any sense of propriety to the actions, either.

"The video came out and you know you can put anything together. This was not good," says Spicer. Although Spicer does not officially claim ownership, he is careful not to disown it. "We needed to establish what are the specific incidents. We want to find out what is going on, and we want to do it as objectively as possible."

Spicer assures me that "there will be a public explanation, in due course. [Aegis' internal] board of inquiry consists of a senior lawyer and recorder of the crown court, a retired deputy chief constable who had also been a police advisor in Iraq, and a former special air service warrant officer who had recently left the army. They conducted a frame-by-frame analysis: Was it Aegis? What were the circumstances? What systems and procedures should be implemented? They spent a week or ten days in Iraq formulating and writing a hundred-page report with a hundred-page

annex." Tim seems so proud of the way he has managed his latest controversy that I grow to expect he is building my anticipation to reveal that the
results of the inquiry completely absolve him or his company of any
wrongdoing. So I find it curious when he concludes discussion of the subject with an abrupt "You will never see that report because we are contracted with the U.S. It is confidential to the client. The report may never
be released." On June 10, 2006, the Pentagon Criminal Investigative Division ruled that "no one will be charged with a crime." No report will be
released.

It's obvious that that line of inquiry has closed, which brings me again
to a confrontation with the lack of accountability, shielded by a complete
lack of transparency, for security contractors working in Iraq. According
to most of the security contractors I have spoken to about working in Iraq,
the vast majority of incidents involving contractors and civilians go unre-
ported and unexposed. When news of the "Aegis PSD" video first broke
publicly, it seemed for an instant that the public controversy could force a
reckoning with these issues. However, Spicer may have learned a little PR
savvy since the fallout of Sandline and quickly issued statements that the
company would undertake an immediate and complete investigation. Despite the lip service he pays to regulation and accountability, it appears that
Spicer would be the last one to push the Pentagon toward reforming the
system. He owns nearly 40 percent of a company that just grossed over
$120 million (75 percent from his Iraq contracts) and has a private army of
nine hundred men on the ground in Iraq. With his U.S. contract up to just
under half a billion dollars and extended for another year, he doesn't need
anything to upset his current position.

The future of Aegis may be rosy if their UN contracts and other business continue to grow. However, it seems their single biggest contract—
set to expire in May 2007—may be in jeopardy. According to the former
State Department official: "They [DoD] are looking to dump Aegis as fast
as they can." Spicer has created enemies and, reportedly, he's started to
look like a potential liability to those who hold the purse strings. At the
end of the day "he is an unsavory character. He [Spicer] is a snake. We

have a joke around here when we talk about that contract—'Didn't any-body Google him?' "

The former State Department official takes it further, summing up his view of the recent boom in the private security industry: "Contractors at the end of the day are mercenaries. They are self-interested. They work for money. You can dress up a pig but they are still a pig. . . . Spicer at the end of the day is a snake."

Despite his early love affair with the controversial idea of PMCs providing offensive fighting capabilities, Tim Spicer has achieved an extraordinary degree of success as a legitimate purveyor of freelance armed men. Spicer could be said to have proceeded down the "respectable" route with Aegis Defence, while his former partner Simon Mann reverted to the more traditional mercenary route. However, to hear Spicer and other industry leaders talk about the future, it's difficult to not wonder if these post-9/11 iterations are attempts to find the sweet spot—the balance between naked aggression and passive peacekeeping—the neo-mercenary, if you will.

We could discuss Spicer's self-chosen role as spokesman for regulation and accountability forever, particularly as it pertains to his own company's handling of the Aegis video controversy. But Spicer takes obvious pleasure in being able to say that he has conducted a thorough investigation, while concluding that, alas, it will never be publicly released. There's a bit of the old "fuck you" look in Spicer's eyes as he looks at his watch to let me know my time has run out.

It is oddly comforting to see Spicer back in his old form. Perhaps proof that there is an unbendable trajectory to some people. It is hard to decide if his success is a result of changing standards in how governments view contractors or whether Spicer has finally abandoned the path that Simon Mann set him on. This time, if he keeps his head down and keeps his legal and financial wingmen at the ready, he might make it through to the end of the Iraq gold rush a kinder, gentler, and wealthier Spicer.

CHAPTER 11

The Lord and the Prince

"I can launch a thousand armed and trained men."
— Erik Prince, owner of Blackwater and Greystone

"Yeah . . . Janjaweed-Be-Gone."
— Director of business development for Blackwater

"We want to to be a PMC," Gary Jackson, the president of Blackwater, tells me enthusiastically, indicating that one of the fastest-growing American private security companies has ambitions that go far beyond the functions it performs under current U.S. government contracts. The controversial history of Executive Outcomes and its morphed genesis in Sandline has put the term "private military corporation" into disrepute, creating connotations of foreign mercenaries wresting mineral wealth from the control of local insurgency groups. That doesn't stop Gary from becoming enamored with the possibility of future business expansion opportunities for Blackwater.

I've come to the Blackwater training facility and headquarters in Moycock, North Carolina, to meet with Gary Jackson and his manager of business development, Jerome McCauley, in order to learn more about the past development and future plans of Blackwater. An energetic man in his early forties, barrel-chested and gray-goateed, Gary Jackson has the kind of presence that seems to fill a room and create a draft behind him as he walks. He describes himself as a former SEAL instructor and proud member of Alcoholics Anonymous. Jerry McCauley is a lanky man and another former SEAL, and as quiet and reseved as Gary is animated and effusive.

After Gary's surprising admission about Blackwater's ambition, the M word comes to mind—not *military*, but *mercenary*. I remind Gary that if he presented his enthusiastic offer of a fully armed mercenary army-for-hire to the media, they might react with horror. Gary has somehow forgotten the negativity in the public perception of private soldiers fielding massive firepower for a paycheck, which is surprising given that Blackwater has become a member of the International Peace Operations Association (IPOA). The IPOA organizes lectures, conferences, and other media engagements in an attempt to create awareness and garner support for the practice of using private military companies to bolster and/or supplant UN peacekeeping efforts—a remote but not unrealistic possibility.

To evaluate the viability of such a practice, we discuss the best-known private mercenary operations, agreeing that Angola in 1994 and Sierra Leone in 1995 both achieved their objectives, but that Sierra Leone in 1998 and Bougainville in 1997 were unmitigated disasters. Gary dismisses the idea that there might be anything ethically or philosophically questionable about standardizing the practice of guns-for-hire, and instead focuses on how Tim Spicer's management of the last two incidents led to their failure. He points out that an unfettered army in the field can change history by removing tyrants, establishing security, and propping up emerging democracies.

"We can field a full army or operational group at battalion level anywhere in the world. We can provide air assets, logistics, and everything needed to bring stability and security to a region. . . . We will have the complete capability to replace the military in some operations."

Gary brings up Darfur as Blackwater's most recent pitch for business. Colin Powell called what was going on in Sudan genocide, but with the bulk of U.S. forces tied down in Iraq, the United States doesn't have the manpower to field soldiers to do anything about it. "The UN takes forever and we are ready to go. We would first send in a hundred guys to set things up," Gary machine-guns me with enthusiasm, "then send in men and equipment." He points to a picture recently taken in Iraq of three Boeing Little Birds hovering behind a row of four armored vehicles; in front, a dozen men pose with weapons, wearing armor and extra magazines.

"We are turning a CASA 212 into a gunship that would cruise around at thirty-eight degrees"—he mimics the angle with his palm—"and when we find the bad guys, we would lay into them." Jerry smiles and drolly interjects, "Yeah, Janjaweed-be-gone!" They both erupt into hearty laughter at the joke.

Janjaweed is the camel-mounted militia that has been on a killing, raping, and village-burning rampage in Darfur. Given the snail's pace of response by the international community as the Janjaweed have steadily chipped away at the population of southwestern Sudan, few could argue against a private company making a humanitarian intervention an easier, faster, and more cost-effective option for the Western powers. However, regardless of the benign intentions proffered in this incipient stage, empowering an industry willing and able to mount a military offensive for profit could be considered a big step in a potentially dangerous trend. Since, according to Gary, about 15 percent of Blackwater's current business comes in the form of "black ops" for the CIA, it is not difficult to imagine a return to the pre–Church/Pike method of doing business abroad. With the lack of transparency, a check written to a private corporation for an "urgent and compelling need" could cover just about anything. The reality is that most of their secret work is simply static and personnel security.

"We are going to field a brigade-sized peacekeeping force. You can quote me on that," Gary asserts with confidence.

The idea of fielding a private army should not be shocking to the United States, since privately sponsored militias helped mount the American Revolution. What is controversial is the idea that a private corporation can put together a paramilitary force and field it for a profit. However disconcerting the trend toward the privatization of the use of force may be, Gary and Jerry make clear that they view their current roles to be a mere extension of their obligations as SEALs and Americans. To be fair, Jackson does not suggest that Blackwater would field an army on behalf of any client or cause. Gary leaves out some key modifiers in his bombast and sales hype. He forgets to add "in the service of the U.S. government," because as a former SEAL surrounded by other ex-military and -police, it is assumed that it goes without saying. I have no doubt that no matter what may come in the way of future opportunities for Blackwater, Gary and Jerry will never execute a contract in contravention with what the American leadership views as key to U.S. security and economic interests. But given the history of an unrestrained and aggressive CIA in the days before Church-Pike and Congressional oversight, acting on the orders of American leaders could be just as scandalously problematic. Here in the swamps of North Carolina, Gary Jackson insists quite correctly that a private army can be used for good.

Few people have the resources to recruit, train, and field an army, but the owner of Blackwater, Erik Prince, does. Prince works to communicate this message as he travels the halls of Capitol Hill, Langley, the Pentagon, and the State Department.

The New Industrialists

The President's Sport Bar at the Renaissance Hotel in Washington, DC, is an odd place for a meeting between a lord and a prince. Lord Westbury, one of the founders of HART security; his head of operations, George Simm; and Erik Prince have arranged a meeting to talk shop in the nation's capital. Westbury, Simm, and I arrive early and settle into an empty corner of the pub for the privacy it affords our conversation.

In his midfifties, Lord Westbury, or Richard Nicholas Bethell as he was known before he inherited his father's title, is one of the seminal figures in the privatized security industry and one of the early major proponents of its expansion. A laid-back gentleman and former SAS officer, Richard wears tiger-striped reading glasses and dresses the part of a wealthy Englishman in crisp custom shirts and a dark blue wool overcoat. Often to be seen with an expensive cigar nestled between his fingers, he wears his flowing, silvery white hair down past his shoulders and expresses himself in an upper-crust accent with the incongruous attitude of a puckish eighteen-year-old.

George Simm is Richard's operations man, the wound-tight, go-to guy who makes it all happen—a position for which he is well qualified after his long career managing operations for the SAS. George is crisp, outspoken, and no nonsense, and looks like he could be a small-town cop. He speaks with pride of his upbringing as a coal miner's son and professes an unabashed admiration for Lord Westbury, someone he describes simply as "a legend." He credits Lord Westbury with formulating the strategy that brought the IRA to the negotiating table, though he'll offer no further details. George and Richard are like opposite parts of the British military spectrum—Richard, an officer and lord; George, a well-read, intensely intelligent working-class man.

The sixth Lord Westbury has set up a number of security companies and is now the driving force behind HART. HART's president, Olle Sundberg, is a sagacious Swede with experience running an ad agency and a shipping company. Richard is their star "door knocker," using his celebrity in the British military community to drum up support and business for HART.

In the UK, the modern era of private security businesses began soon after World War II when the founder of the Special Air Service, Scotsman Sir David Stirling, founded Kilo Alpha Services (KAS), a clearinghouse for ex-SAS to continue providing expertise and security services to industry and foreign potentates. Many UK companies, such as Olive, Kroll, Pilgrims, and AKE, still provide the low-key service of ex-SAS operators. For the former SAS, "invisibility" remains their key modus operandi.

Tapping the glowing ember of his Romeo y Julieta cigar into the pub ashtray, Lord Wesbury tells me, "The best are the Hereford boys," or SAS. "The SAS . . . can deploy in ones if need be. Told to keep their eye on so and so or this group, salute, and they are off." Former SAS are multiskilled and flexible in their approach to complex problems, "the result of sixty-four years of combat in low intensity and counterterrorist ops." The other main source for British military contractors, the Special

Boat Squadron (SBS), are Royal Marines at heart. Westbury considers them square pegged into a round hole when they try to work as security contractors on the ground. Woefully underequipped for modern scenarios and "not to be allowed out without an adult," he says, "their success stories could be written on the back of a hamster's testicle."

After retiring from the SAS, Richard Bethell joined Defence Systems Limited (DSL) in 1991, a company started by Alastair Morrison, former 22 SAS number two and Scots Guard officer. Although the founder of the SAS, David Stirling, had created his tiny consultancy in London, there had never been a proper corporate structure overlaid on the concept of providing expert military skills until DSL. British Petroleum (BP) did business in places where their operations and employees were rich targets for insurgent, criminal, and guerilla groups, and the nations they worked in had either limited resources or insufficient security. At BP's behest, DSL simply provided the ability to hire, train, and maintain an independent armed force to deter attacks. The potential of lost income for a pumping rig or pipeline made the costs of security insignificant.

Although DSL could be pointed out as the first modern private security company, the model was very similar to the use of "levees" or local soldiers under foreign officers to guard the colonial assets overseas. DSL would become a model for other companies that realized insurgents could more easily achieve their objectives by attacking undefended corporations and their assets, as opposed to military outposts. Some accused Bethell of being a mercenary because he trained local guards to defend BP's oil rigs in-country against rebel attacks, but Bethell and Morrison both made it clear they provided training only and were never involved in the actual operations.

In 1997, Bethell and Morrison sold their ownership in DSL (which then was grossing over £50 million a year) to a body armor manufacturer in Jacksonville, Florida, called Armor Holdings for £26 million pounds. Armor Holdings would go on to become ArmorGroup and provide armed forces in Iraq and around the world. Both DSL founders went on to start new security companies.

In July 1999, Bethell started HART and a sister company named

Global Marine Security Systems Company (GMSSCO), which specialized in maritime security. One of HART's more innovative early projects was working for the president of Somalia. Fees derived from fishing are the lifeblood of the struggling Somalian government, and HART used their personal relationship with the president of Somalia to present a program to prevent piracy of their fishing grounds.

George explains, "Our first big job was Somalia. Our underlying mission was to license fishing ships to provide income to the government. Their main catch is tuna—a valuable catch. Blue fin tuna is the Rolls-Royce of fish. You can get twenty thousand dollars for one tuna. So we did the math. There is your hard cost and then there is overall revenue sharing from impounds and fines, but you have to be careful to balance things. You get too tough and the fishing goes away. Too little and the fish go away. We were authorized to impound the ships. Properly done, the concept we rolled out in Somalia would be a multimillion-dollar concept." He shrugs his shoulders.

"Our main thrust was to regulate the industry and make sure it was managed properly. You have to be careful how you define a pirate. We sit on the horn and then we see them "hoovering" their resources. We detained a Spanish boat that was fishing illegally. It goes back hundreds of years. The Spanish complained that we were English pirates. It was a fun job. Then the civil war broke out, and it fell apart."

Other similar ventures by former soldiers have always collapsed due to the inherent corruption in local governments. In Sierra Leone, an identical concept launched by a former Executive Outcomes mercenary failed simply because the fishing companies found it cheaper to bribe the governing official, thereby eliminating the cost of a license or the threat of a fine.

HART's initial role in Iraq was to provide security for media. George explains, "When this war started, I was guarding the BBC. There is a security group inside the BBC called the Chryon Group."

As instability began to rock Iraq, HART soon picked up a contract to guard an electrical power line. "We had a crazy period; we grew from fifty to seventy people to one hundred seventy in one month. A lot of people coming and going. We look for ex-military, but we prefer to hire someone we know. It's word of mouth. HART is based close to Ianapa (Cyprus), so we know the ins and outs of an offshore business." George also knows that a contractor who works offshore makes more money than an American who pays U.S. taxes.

The British boom in private security companies has not only benefited from Iraq, but has created an odd U.S./UK synthesis to take advantage of the global War on Terror. Bethell's worldy SAS experiences from Afghanistan to the Falklands to Oman to Northern Ireland to Iraq combined with George Simm's equally experience-rich background as former regimental sergeant major for 22 SAS would serve HART's interests well in exotic locations. George's background in the SAS has taught him that the excessive use of money or violence accomplishes little. He explains how the minimum application of force must be combined with good human intelligence. "We have a peculiar way of doing business. What drives us on any given day is the threat and the perception of threat. We only use the minimum amount of force required. Don't you think if you drive around all day pointing guns at people and shooting at them it will come back to you?"

Though they work in the same industry, there is a vast difference between the operating styles of American and British security companies. A Blackwater PSD tries to ensure safety by rolling aggressively with a prominent and imposing display of force, while the traditional British style has contractors relying more on natives and trying harder to blend in and be discreet, hoping to pass unnoticed below the radar of those who might want to attack them. This philosophy mandates that HART work with Iraqis recruited by a local sheik—the real source of power and influence in the region they were tasked to protect. Of course, this knowledge of who is in charge doesn't always match the occupying army's opinions. American military intelligence investigated the sheik for possible collaboration with the insurgents, but then the sheik ended up being assassinated by the insurgents for collaborating with the Americans. After a long history ruling a sometimes-unruly empire, the British have learned to excel in making distinctions in the fine shadings of gray found in complicated insurgencies. Foreigners, usually Brits, South Africans, or Americans, command HART PSDs, supported by local Iraqi hires. "We had twenty-five hundred Iraqis working for us making ten dollars a day. It always has a positive effect. It bumps up their economy, but it also has a negative effect. Those that don't get hired get pissed," George tells me. The teams use hired or bought local cars, keep their weapons below the windows, and move with the least amount of disturbance. "It's something we learned in Northern Ireland," George says, "and it's no different in Iraq."

HART's use of Iraqis gives them a better understanding of the situation but has a dangerous downside, since it is not uncommon for Big Army to attack one of these low-key security convoys. In one incident, an American military convoy shot at a HART convoy, killing a young Iraqi interpreter on her first day on the job. After the American convoy fled, another American rapid-reaction force showed up and attacked the HART team again. HART may risk targeting by the Americans, but the insurgents don't tend to take notice of their low-key convoys, leaving HART with a statistically lower casualty rate than most of the large Western-owned security companies operating in Iraq.

Erik Prince bounds in to the meeting late. Looking very youthful for his midthirties, he wears a conservatively cut suit, an American flag lapel pin, and a severe haircut more appropriate for a Navy officer than a wealthy industrialist. As mentioned previously, Erik is the sole owner of Blackwater, and the word on the street is that his company now does $800 million a year. Critics say that at best he might gross $600 million, and there is speculation that many of his operations don't make a profit due to his insistence on fixed-price contracts. Erik is on a high today since Blackwater has just picked up a multimillion-dollar contract to support the drug eradication program in Afghanistan and has replaced Triple Canopy in all of the State Department's contracts in northern Iraq. The contrast between the sage and circumspect Lord Westbury and the ebullient and effusive Erik Prince is fascinating and representative of the cultural difference in their respective approaches to the work they do.

A former Navy officer, a SEAL from Holland, Michigan, Erik Prince is a rare breed of moneyed heir who joined the military solely to perform a service for his country. Erik's father, Edgar Prince, had started the family business in 1965 with a little die-cast shop called Prince Machine Corps. After being in business a few years, the business exploded, and Prince Automotive began to develop other types of car parts and invest some of their sizable profits in developments like shopping malls, ultimately expanding their assets into a billion-dollar-plus enterprise. With his new wealth, Edgar set up the Prince Group to manage a growing financial empire of real estate, factories, and other investments.

Devout Calvinists, Edgar and his wife actively participated in community affairs and contributed to furthering the interests of conservative Christianity. Erik began a career of public service early on, after his father got him an internship at the Family Research Council, a family-values lobby group that received generous funding from his father. In 1992, he spent six months interning for President George H. W. Bush, but then switched loyalties to work for Pat Buchanan's election bid.

Erik first attended the heavily Libertarian, privately funded Hillsdale College before transferring to the U.S. Naval Academy. He tendered his resignation before graduating, though not before he met his future wife, Joan. After leaving the Academy, he joined the Navy, earning a commission as a lieutenant. Prince did one four-year tour with SEAL Team 8 (based out of Little Creek, Virginia) before his life changed dramatically.

In 1995, Edgar Prince suffered a massive heart attack and died. The twenty-seven-year-old Erik's family values and work ethic compelled him to take over the day-to-day operations of the Prince Group. To add to his hardship, Erik's wife was also diagnosed with cancer that year. Erik left the SEALs to attend to his new responsibilities. The decision was made to sell the family's automotive business to S. C. Johnson Controls for 1.35 billion dollars, making Erik's family one of America's wealthiest. Outside of business, Prince had converted to Roman Catholicism and remained active in religious, human rights, and political causes like Christian Solidarity International, the Institute of World Politics, and the Republican Party.

In mid-1997, Erik broke ground on the six thousand acres in Moyock, North Carolina, that would become today's Blackwater. Erik's original business idea was simply to create a shooting range to service the needs of the surrounding special operations community. He also began Blackwater Target Systems, manufacturer of an innovative system of weighted metal targets that would bounce back up after every hit. September 11 and the rush to get into Afghanistan spawned Blackwater Security. After the war in Iraq made private security his most lucrative venture, Erik began to spin off more supporting divisions such as Blackwater Airships, Blackwater Canine, and an aviation division based in Melbourne, Florida, including Blackwater Aviation, Presidential Airways (a formerly defunct airline), and STI. Prince has even designed an entire line of uniforms and gear for his contractors, effectively creating his own brown paramilitary uniform for his own army. Hundreds of men in Iraq have the Blackwater bear paw and gun sight logo displayed on their chest, covering their heart.

Erik aggressively works to develop new technology and particularly loves airplanes, even flying his own Maule Caravan to commute back and forth from Tysons Corner in Northern Virginia to the Blackwater site in North Carolina. Blackwater's latest aviation innovation is a CASA 212 gunship modified with two A12 guns. It can spit out forty-two hundred 50-caliber bullets per minute, which can travel thirty-four hundred feet per second. Seventy bullets per second creates a steady stream of red tracer fire that with depleted uranium shells can easily turn armored vehicles into Swiss cheese.

Erik tells us that he has also been investing in the development of a new personnel carrier for Blackwater based on the South African Caspir, a high-speed armored vehicle. The Blackwater Grizzly will use a bigger turbocharged diesel engine and have the suspension created and built by Dennis Anderson, a legend in the monster-truck business. When Erik describes his armored monster truck, homemade gunship, and other toys, he looks like an excited twelve-year-old at Christmas. "We are having a South African armored vehicle modified by the guy that made Gravedigger. [Anderson] is doing the suspension and he is just down the road from us," he explains with unrestrained excitement. Since Anderson usually designs his fifteen-hundred hp monster trucks solely to crush rows of cars and fly through the air with impunity, combining that with armed men seems like an odd creation out of a bad eighties action show like *The A-Team*.

Among his many multimillion-dollar contracts, Erik provides a maritime operations force that monitors smuggling and terrorism in the oil area for the Azeri government, has contracts with the CIA in Afghanistan and Pakistan, and protects State Department operations in Iraq, Israel, and Haiti. His company has quickly come from nowhere to have the same brand awareness of older and larger corporations like DynCorp, KBR, Kroll, ArmorGroup, and Control Risks Group. He has injected an intense political, military, and some say ideological focus that sets him apart from direct competitors like MVM, Triple Canopy, USIS, and other well-known providers of ex-soldiers with guns. The weekly newsletter put out by Blackwater contains stories of possible global threats, right-wing analyses, supportive articles about the War on Terror, and a concluding section written by a chaplain. In the War on Terror, Blackwater stands somewhere slightly to the right of the Bush administration. Erik's wealth, personal connections, influence, and devotion to the cause makes Blackwater the one to watch.

Prince maintains an office in Virginia to keep himself close to the purse strings of government contracting opportunities and has just come from Capitol Hill. His business requires a careful mix of visits all around Washington, and he regularly pushes his PowerPoint past Republican congressmen, the State Department, Pentagon brass, and the CIA. One of Erik's friends told me Erik's real ambition—he wants Blackwater to be the fifth column of the U.S. military.

Erik has just come back from his latest pitch to the U.S. government on how to go after Iraqi terror cells. Prince believes targeting the foot soldiers of the insurgency to be a dangerous waste of time, money, and effort. "I want to launch a plan to go after the bomb makers," he says excitedly. "Instead of just going after the insurgents, follow the technology, go after the real centers of the organizations." He briefly lays out his plan to develop an independent intelligence network to target the bomb makers, and then abruptly launches into other ideas like speeding up the formation of an effective Iraqi military by inserting his own men among the Iraqis in training and in combat.

Hyperanimated and energetically gung ho about the benefits of privatization, Erik bursts with ideas and is always selling "better, faster, and more effective." All the ideas he pitches to the U.S. government come with a fixed price and no-risk guarantee, and are dovetailed to the Bush administration's efforts to privatize everything from Social Security to running the war in Iraq. Prince can't help doing missionary work, even on pragmatic and seasoned vets like Richard and George. Erik explains how he is bringing efficiency to the battlefield: "We replaced 183 men with twenty in one of the CIA installations," he says proudly. "The army needs that many support troops and men to provide the same effective force that we did with twenty."

Erik, George, and Richard don't take criticism of the industry by academics and the media very seriously. "We have been trying to get Peter Singer [of the Brookings Institution and author of *Corporate Warriors*] over to Iraq for months. He won't go," says Erik. When asked what he thinks about Singer's constant criticism of the unregulated use of private security contractors, he thinks for a moment and says with a chuckle, "Let's just say that Peter Singer has very soft hands."

HART's biggest frustration doesn't stem from the theoretical criticism of the regulation of their industry, or obstacles encountered in hiring out their services in the war-torn areas of Africa. George expresses vehement incredulity that the U.S. government could hand out multimillion-dollar contracts to controversial start-ups like Aegis, headed by self-proclaimed mercenary Tim Spicer, and demonstrably incompetent groups like Custer Battles, which has been under investigation for a variety of misdeeds.

He tries to sum up the almost unthinkable concept of Tim Spicer landing an almost half-a-billion-dollar contract. "I call it 'the Cult of Tim.'" It's enough to make George apoplectic. "He is a shallow fucking wannabe. He tried to join the SAS, but failed. Somebody has to quiz him about capabilities. . . . We would like to divest ourselves of the wannabes, and Tim is right at the head of the queue."

Members of the private security industry usually keep quiet with regard to criticisms of other companies and operators, believing that less public spotlight on the failures of individuals benefits the group. One of Richard's most pointed criticisms of Spicer reflects this tight-lipped environment as he says, "He made things worse by taking his case to the press. It's not done that way."

Considering the circle-the-wagons impulse of the industry, George's continuing response to the mention of Tim Spicer is remarkable, even given Spicer's obvious faults. "Tim is a scurrilous wanker, a lightweight. He has never succeeded as an adult. His impact on our industry has been profound." He shakes his head in disgust.

The gentlemanly Richard restrains his comments on Spicer but still expresses disdain at the media's reporting that Spicer was a member of the SAS. "Tim had failed selection for the SAS, and although well-respected in the UK military, was not considered someone who did well in the field."

Richard's more forgiving view of Spicer perhaps comes from his past acquaintance with the man. "He is a hard-working fellow. When Spicer was asked to join Executive Outcomes and Sandline, he talked to me. I warned him that once you go down that path, you cannot come back."

Erik is enamored with the mystique of mercenaries, private military corporations, and men like Richard and George—men who have chased pirates in Somalia, advised potentates in Oman, fought terrorists on the streets of Belfast, and guarded the royal family. For their part, Richard and George like Erik's boundless enthusiasm and unabashed American patriotic zeal, a stark contrast to the cool, reserved style of former SAS commanders. Richard and George are fascinated by the massive amounts of American money being spent in Iraq to reinvent the wheel. They see the Americans trying to fight a counterinsurgency, protect the reconstruction of infrastructure, and keep foreign workers and government employees alive while advancing the nation's business interests—something soldiers, colonial administrators, and privateers of the former British Empire did for hundreds of years.

The British historical memory of the use of mercenaries and privateers is very different from the Americans'. The English tradition of private military companies reaches as far back as the Crusades, when wealthy patrons raised private armies to fight for the Holy Land. Later, heroic, colorful privateers like Sir Francis Drake and royal charter companies would employ indigenous soldiers to open up new territories for the British

Empire. In the English tradition, "mercenary" evokes a dashing "boy's own" aura. In America, the term has an ugly feel to it, recalling the brutal reality of Angola, Nung tribesmen, Contras, and Latin American death squads. The irony of America and their new partner Britain hiring privateers in Iraq and Afghanistan does not escape those within the private security industry. While the American government does have a limited history of employing mercenaries abroad on an ad hoc basis through the CIA, the war in Iraq has introduced a modern justification for formalizing the system—something the Brits learned generations ago.

One of the reasons for this meeting between HART and Blackwater is that the two groups want to see what kind of synergy they can develop. HART hopes to integrate the long British historical experience and conservative style of using indigenous talent commanded by first-world officers with Blackwater's aggressive American entrepreneurialism. Their first joint venture ended up a success with the client choosing HART as the lead contractor. Now Erik is looking to expand utilization of his company, and HART is looking to export its low-key SAS culture of assimilation into the brash, almost xenophobic, Navy SEAL–oriented Blackwater culture.

Erik mentions that he wants to create a peacekeeping and intervention force for Africa, particularly focusing on the Darfur region of southwestern Sudan. George and Richard express frustration at the complete lack of interest by governments and aid organizations in utilizing the experience of a private army to solve major security and stability problems in Africa. George's new focus is the Congo, a place where millions have died without attracting much meaningful attention from the international community and where a long-running UN peacekeeping mission has made little difference in the suffering of the people.

"The Congo contains all that is evil about social disintegration—AIDS, child soldiers, disease, warfare, crime, the list goes on. Everything in every segment of scientific and human studies is abused in this massive region. Yet a small peacekeeping force could fully protect the tiny population per mile with little trouble," George asserts.

Erik also sees governments and the UN renting armies as the ultimate evolution of his corporate investment in Blackwater, a rapidly growing organization that is fully prepared to capitalize on the Bush administration's privatization of the War on Terror. Lest I forget Blackwater's mantra, Erik reminds me again: "We are ready to field a battalion anywhere in the world."

As an offshore company with sophisticated financial and government contacts around the world, HART could bring much to the bold red, white, and blue culture of Blackwater. George recounts for Erik the most important lesson he learned during his years in the SAS: "To defeat your enemy, you don't have to kill. There is negative impact. Even when we did our ambushes in Northern Ireland, the aim was to arrest, not kill. The experiences of an SF soldier at that moment is critical. It's instinct. That's what we bring to this world. It's abhorrent to shoot a warning shot. It's never nice to discharge your weapon."

Prince wants HART to help develop his knowledge and hone his skills in operating in foreign territories, something that would greatly benefit his latest business endeavor—Greystone. Greystone is a departure for Erik, since it is not an overtly American entity, but rather an offshore private military company that would employ locals in the English tradition— a foreign legion modeled after Executive Outcomes, Sandline, Erinys, and HART.

Erik is particularly excited because he's planning a big reception to roll out the idea of Greystone in a couple of weeks. The party will be held at the Ritz-Carlton in Washington, DC, and Prince expects to entertain a long list of diplomats representing a broad spectrum of nations, along with oil company execs, financial experts, gun manufacturers, and others who could use the services of an armed force. Cofer Black, former ambassador for counterterrorism at the State Department, former director of the CIA's Counterterrorism Center, and now vice chairman of Blackwater, will give the keynote address.

It doesn't seem like a very subtle message that Greystone will be available and capable, just as EO and Sandline were, to solve security problems worldwide. For now, the immediate goal will be to provide static security when budgets do not allow for the cost of an American or Brit. Former

U.S., British, or South African military can be hired for between $400 and $600 a day, but Gurkhas, Chileans, and ex-soldiers from developing nations are thrilled to make half to a tenth of that. Although the market for the high-end operators may be running short, there are plenty of rank and file available. The black-tie audience listening to Cofer Black's pitch will include government representatives from the Philippines, Yemen, Indonesia, Angola, Russia, Kenya, Tunisia, and numerous others. Their need combined with Erik Prince's love of covert paramilitary operations, his hawkish and conservative ideology, and his entrepreneurial and expansionist business philosophy may allow Greystone to push the boundaries of privatized security.

The Greystone brochure and website offer the expected services of training, security assessements, and protection options. A quick scan by a disinterested outsider might miss an innocuous but carefully worded paragraph:

Proactive Engagement Teams:

Greystone elements are prepared to configure capabilities to meet emergent or existing security requirements for client needs overseas. Our teams are ready to conduct stabilization efforts, asset protection and recovery, and emergency personnel withdrawal.

In short, Greystone will be selling the same services offered by Executive Outcomes and Sandline. EO's first operations were essentially the use of mercenaries in "asset recovery" of Tony Buckingham's oil-drilling equipment; their second job was the massive offensive campaign to push back the rebels of UNITA, masked as a training operation; and their third project was the "stabilization effort" in Sierra Leone. Depending on the contract opportunities presented to Greystone, the future may see a further blurring of the fine line between privatized security and privatized military operations. It's impossible to predict exactly where the industry may lead Prince's army, but for foreign leaders it will certainly provide a legitimate and credible enhancement to traditional military or clandestine operations.

It becomes clear to me during the meeting that there remains a very high wall between the HART's very English view of security and Blackwater's view of a brave new neocon world. While Erik's dreams of fielding a private army have yet to be realized, the principals of HART have already been down that road. Their military careers in places like Oman or Afghanistan put them in charge of large "levees" or local troops. Richard as an SAS captain and George as the regimental sergeant major for 22 SAS have developed over decades hard-won skills in dealing with insurgencies, dirty wars, and covert operations. While Prince paints a picture of a flashy, high-tech, road-warrior-style military company that could solve any client's problem by application of sheer brute force and advanced weaponry, Richard and George calmly promote the idea of low-key and culturally integrated solutions. One more time before the meeting breaks up, George repeats his mantra for Erik: "It's the application of minimum force."

CHAPTER 12

The Bight of Benin Company

"We should expect bad behaviour; disloyalty; rampant individual greed; irrational behaviour (kids in toyshop type); back-stabbing, bum-fucking and similar ungentlemanly activities."
— SIMON MANN IN HIS BIGHT OF BENIN COMPANY PLAN

"It may be that getting us out comes down to a large splodge of wonga."
— SIMON MANN IN LETTER FROM PRISON

The afternoon attack on the northern Liberian town of Voinjama begins with the booming sound of RPGs being fired from the surrounding jungle followed by the dut-dut-dut of AK-47s. The LURD rebels grab their weapons and begin running toward the sound, while the tattered child soldiers of the Small Boys Unit jump around singing and chanting. The terrified villagers quickly bundle up their goods up in colorful fabrics and start to flee the village.

My security man, Niek du Toit, a forty-six-year-old mercenary and ex–32 Battalion colonel from South Africa, is annoyed at the disturbance interrupting his leisurely reading on the veranda of our dilapidated house. The broad-shouldered hulk of a man with light brown, shortly cropped hair and crooked nose looks necessarily imposing as a bodyguard should, but his appearance contrasts with his easygoing nature and quiet demeanor.

Seeing me head toward the action with my camera, Niek begrudgingly puts down his book and picks up his AK to follow. As we reach the contact point, the LURD rebels are cheering over a prone body. They thrust the freshly severed head toward me, mocking the fate of the poor man and making faces for the camera. It didn't faze Niek to watch the rebels celebrate their victory, since he had probably seen much worse in his more than two decades of bush wars. Later that day, the rebels show up at our house and offer us the head as a souvenir, now fitted with a wire handle conveniently attached to the ears. Niek doesn't even look up from his book this time.

That evening in the summer of 2002, Niek would tell me about an upcoming gig—something big. The candlelight of our electricity-free house gave our conversation a conspiratorial air as he described a plan to lead a hundred men by boat across a lake from Bujumbura, Burundi, into the eastern Congo to start a war with the Rwandans who had occupied the region. The flare-up would give the Congolese government army justification to enter the UN-controlled area and take back the lucrative diamond fields. Niek was to bring out a stash of diamonds and share the proceeds with the junior Kabila, the U.S.-backed president of the Congo. Under different circumstances, the story could be written off as the delusions of an aging mercenary, but we were in the jungles of Africa, and this was Niek du Toit.

Niek had his coming-of-age, so to speak, as a commander in the South African Defence Force (SADF) and its 32 "Buffalo" Battalion, running long-range missions into Angola to fight against Communist-backed insurgents from the midseventies through the eighties. Niek had gone on to become a professional mercenary, working a variety of different gigs, including time with Executive Outcomes. I casually mentioned that he should contact me if his gig ever got off the ground. When I left Liberia, I wasn't sure if I would hear from or ever see Niek again, but his turn of fortune eventually had me seeking him out four years later. In March 2004, Niek was arrested, tried, and convicted for attempting to overthrow the president of Equatorial Guinea. In the spring of 2006, President Obiang finally granted me permission to visit him.

Obiang has had the old, infamous Black Beach prison on the island of Bioko destroyed and has built a new higher-security facility specifically for Niek and the other mercenaries arrested with him. Waiting at dusk at the gates of the new Black Beach prison on the outskirts of Malabo, I can see an emaciated, gray-haired old man in shackles shuffling up the hill toward me. I recognize the broken nose and thick Afrikaner accent, but this is a very different Niek. The shackles around his ankles that have become a permanent fixture have chunks of foam rubber to prevent the skin from being rubbed raw. He says it's the first time he has been out of his cell in six months. One of his men, Gerhard Mertz, has already died in captivity—reportedly of cerebral malaria—and "Bones" has prostate cancer. The rest all have malaria. At age fifty Niek has thirty more years of his sentence to serve out in this fetid prison, but from the way he looks, it's unlikely he will last that long. His capture in Equatorial Guinea brought an inglorious end to his career and taught me sobering lessons in my exploration of the crossover between privatized security and mercenary actions.

In the current debate over whether security contractors are mercenaries, those left of center typically insist that "private security contractors" in places like Iraq are mercenaries, while the political right insists that "mercenary" is a pejorative term and only applicable in the most obvious use of ex-soldiers for hire in foreign conflict. The more simplistic dividing line is simply offense versus defense, but the contractual nature and financial need for ex-soldiers to earn a living makes the concept of moving in and out of both worlds not only feasible, but increasingly common. Niek has jumped back and forth between the two separate, but not very distinct, career choices. He was my private security contractor while planning to lead a phantom army into the Congo. He also reportedly had worked on a contract training the Equatoguinean military before trying to overthrow the government. Niek du Toit shows that mercenary and contractor can be one and the same.

One interesting facet of the coup attempt in Equatorial Guinea is that the conspirators involved clearly saw a parallel between their plans, hatched in early 2003, and the invasion of Iraq. After all, the claims of the looming threat of Iraq's alleged WMDs had fallen apart, and the Bush administration fell back on the argument that Saddam was a brutal tyrant who tortured and killed his own people and needed to be stopped. Like the Bush administration, the backers planned a public relations campaign that would spin the coup as the elimination of a tyrant who'd brutalized his own people, playing down the embarrassing questions of impartial evidence, international legality, and popular support. The backers of the coup in oil-rich Equatorial Guinea espoused a high purpose, though it would eventually be exposed that they sought money, not the protection of humanitarian ideals, and viewed the violent, illegal overthrow of a dictator as the most expedient way to control the country's petrodollars.

Equatorial Guinea

The minuscule country of Equatorial Guinea (EG) consists of two separate pieces of land tucked into the armpit of West Africa. The mainland is a rectangular chunk of fetid coastal mangrove and jungle sandwiched between Cameroon and Gabon, while the government and business center occupies the volcanic island of Bioko.

Equatorial Guinea gained independence from their Spanish colonial authorities in 1968, and the first ruler, the self-proclaimed "Unique Miracle" Macías Nguema, quickly assumed the mantle of a stereotypical brutal African dictator. In the eleven years of Ngeuma's rule, fishing was banned, slavery was reintroduced to keep the cocoa plantations producing, foreigners like the Spanish and Nigerians were expelled, and a long list of members of his government were executed after failed coups and suspected plotting. During his reign, fifty thousand of his subjects were estimated to have been killed and over a hundred thousand fled the country, further weakening any attempt at creating a viable economy.

In 1979, thirty-seven-year-old Teodoro Obiang Nguema Mbasogo, then the governor of Bioko Province and Nguema's nephew, overthrew his uncle's regime. Obiang's new administration only took four days to try, convict, and execute Nguema. Obiang inherited what was then the poorest country in Africa, but the change in leadership seemed initially cause for optimism as he set about stimulating small-business growth and bringing back foreign investors. Obiang's treatment of his people was an improvement over the brutality of his uncle, but he did preserve absolute control over the country's anemic economy and ruled with a tight grip through his own family and tribal group.

Under pressure from the international community, Obiang offered a referendum in 1991 to see if his loyal subjects wanted a multiparty system. Only eighteen hundred of the one hundred forty-eight thousand who voted were against it. The new pluralist constitution in 1992 conceded to allow political organizing, though Obiang has resorted to regular crack-downs on opposition parties to maintain his tight hold on power. EG was subsisting on handouts from aid organizations and sympathetic nations, until one by one they all abandoned the country because of the rampant theft by Obiang and his cronies. In 1993, even the World Bank stopped giving money to the rapacious dictator.

EG's first major resource find was in 1984 when the natural gas was discovered offshore. The Alba field went into production in 1991, mark-ing the beginning of a change in fortunes for the cash-strapped nation. The Zafiro offshore oil and gas field was discovered in March of 1995. Output from the Zafiro and other fields exploded over the next decade from 17,000 barrels per day to 371,000, ultimately capped at 350,000 bar-rels today. EG has 1.28 billion barrels' worth of proven reserves with more exploration under way. The current leases expire in 2007, at which point the oil companies will have been reimbursed for their development costs, putting EG in a position to negotiate a higher percentage of future earn-ings. The country will also begin to sell its own oil, dramatically adding to its wealth. Its current oil-related revenue is $1.5 billion per year and is only expected to increase. Although geographically small, Equatorial Guinea is slated to be the next big oil and gas powerhouse in Africa after troubled Nigeria.

The oil industry knows the potential of the vast unexplored sub-terranean world under the Gulf of Guinea in EG's EEZ, or Exclusive Economic Zone. Oil-starved European nations like Spain and France un-derstand the benefit of controlling oil-rich nations, but Obiang has chosen to look to America and not its former colonial master, Spain, to develop its fields. It is not surprising that the U.S. market consumes three-quarters of Equatorial Guinea's output, and thus should have a vested interest in the country's stable output of this precious resource. In the early 2000s, U.S. oil companies kept finding new offshore fields. Houston-based Hess and Marathon Oil as well as Triton Energy, Exxon-Mobil, GE Petrol, and a smattering of resource companies from other nations are quickly turning Equatorial Guinea into the "Kuwait of West Africa."

To understand the relative scale, EG has one-fiftieth the population of Iraq and consumes the minuscule amount of two thousand barrels a day, though it produces roughly a quarter of the crude that Iraq does. The oil that flows from the offshore rigs is also sweet crude—making it easily refined—and takes a shorter distance to transport to the East Coast of the United States. Today, oil fields in West Africa (EG, Nigeria, and others) provide roughly 15 percent of America's oil and are expected to exceed imports from Saudi Arabia in a few years.

As it became clear that EG sat on huge untapped resources, the country's rapidly enriched leadership became a more valuable target for overthrow. Not surprisingly, Africa is the most volatile continent on earth—a place where it is actually more likely that a government will change by coup than by any other means. Between 1956 and 2001, the continent saw 80 coups, 108 known failed coups, and 139 reported coup attempts. Only three countries have not experienced a coup: Botswana, Cape Verde, and Mauritius. In 2003, France allegedly backed an attempt in EG to further the interests of French energy company TotalFinalElf, and to bolster a dispute over French-backed Gabon's claim to Mbagne Island and the associated oil leases. Today Obiang employs a Moroccan praetorian guard to lessen the chances that his enemies will infiltrate his personal ring of security, but they would be a minor barrier if outside intervention was intent on Obiang's demise.

The Conspirators

Fifty-eight-year-old Eli Khalil understood the value of West African oil. Born in Kano, Nigeria, as part of the great Shia diaspora from Lebanon,

Khalil knew the ways of West Africa and had made big money as a middleman—a type of post-colonial bagman who makes introductions, pays bribes, and closes deals between Western businesses and African rulers. A healthy percentage of the payments would also stick to the fingers of the middleman, making people like Khalil very wealthy men. Though customary in Africa, the practice smacks of corruption to Western sensibilities, and in 2002 Khalil's profession landed him in trouble. TotalFinalElf (TFE) had hired Khalil to handle oil contracts with former dictator Sani Abachi of Nigeria. In 2002, the French government arrested Khalil in Paris for his oil lease kickbacks between Nigeria and TFE. Though the French released Khalil while the investigation proceeded, they froze his assets, making money tight. Flagged as a dirty dealer and with his lucrative deal with Nigeria under pressure, Khalil turned to a bigger, more insidious way to make money.

The plan sounded simple: overthrow President Obiang and install an acceptable ruler who would give Khalil access to riches without the responsibility of running a country. To enact his plan, Khalil needed three basic elements: a pliable and acceptable ruler, a small, disposable army, and the quiet influx of funds from big-player investors interested in reaping the wealth of Equatoguinean resources. Khalil found the first ingredient in Severo Moto Nsa, a former seminary student and Fang tribesman from EG.

Moto had been living in exile in Madrid for almost a decade, hiding out to avoid punishment for his first attempt to overthrow Obiang. Specifically, Angolan authorities had picked up Moto off the coast of northern Angola in a Russian fishing trawler loaded with weapons and mercenaries and headed toward his homeland. After being ejected from Angola, Moto fled to Spain and applied for political asylum to keep himself safe from imprisonment. In 1995, an Equatoguinean court sentenced Moto in absentia to 101 years in jail for high treason and plotting to kill the president.

Since about twenty anti-Obiang political parties made Spain their base of operations, Moto quickly settled into the life of opposition from afar. From his gilded perch in Madrid, Moto regularly railed against Obiang on the radio and created a website describing Obiang as an "authentic canni-bal." Moto declared that if he returned to Equatorial Guinea, Obiang would "eat my testicles." Khalil began to finance Moto's activities in July of 2002, and Moto used the funds to create a "government in exile" in Spain.

Khalil found the second ingredient for his coup in Simon Mann. Simon had a proven history with Executive Outcomes and knew the dangerous business of hiring, deploying, and extracting mercenaries in covert operations. Although he came from privilege, Simon Mann did not come from money. Educated at Eton, with military service in the Scots Guards and coming out as a captain in the SAS, Mann never really adapted to civilian life. Mann had made $60 million from Executive Outcomes's contract in Angola, but his lavish lifestyle—or rather his wife's—threatened his nest egg. If Mann had succeeded in the operation, his total personal profit would have been $15 million, enough to keep him and his wife comfortable for some time.

Mann had serious expenses: a country estate in England, a town house in Chelsea, and an opulent rented house in South Africa just down the street from Margaret Thatcher's son and Obiang's son in an upscale suburb of Cape Town. Mann and his wife, Amanda (nicknamed "the Duchess"), held lavish dinner parties three times a week catered by a now-famous chef, bought designer clothes, vacationed in the south of France, and lived the life of upper-class English gentry. Mann had made South Africa his primary residence in 1998 when the British government turned up the heat after Sandline's exploits in Sierra Leone and Bougainville. Many of the investments he made in mining and oil had not done so well, and his fortunes had begun to wane.

Friends have said that by 2002, Simon needed to make a big hit not only to maintain his financial status, but also to keep his hand in the game. Mann had big plans, and big plans need big money. Simon had never given up on the idea behind EO and Sandline, and had spent the previous years looking at the map of Africa with an eye toward reshuffling and reshaping some oppressive and underperforming regimes. Mann loved to fly, and from thousands of feet above, he would look down on the beauty of an Africa without borders and the lush potential of a land yet to be "civilized."

Mann says in his statements after his arrest that his wife's real estate agent, Gary Hersham, introduced him to Khalil in January 2003. At that meeting, Mann responded to Khalil's plan to depose Obiang with full support, although much of the language of violence would be couched euphemistically. According to Mann, Khalil asked him to "help escort Severo Moto home at a given moment, while simultaneously there would be an uprising of both military and civilians."

Simon initially estimated it would cost $2.5 to $5 million for an Executive Outcomes–style operation in which a group of men would enter, subdue, and hold a small territory until the "cavalry" arrived. According to Mann's later confession, Khalil confided in him that the Spanish government had promised Moto that they would have troops standing by to pacify both the island of Bioko and the mainland government seat of Bata. Though no conclusive evidence—other than the statements of coup plotters—has been uncovered to prove the backing of the Spanish government, changing the leadership in EG would have been in their strategic interests. Spain has a growing demand for oil, and it would have thus brought great economic benefits if they'd been able to reassert their influence over the former colonial holding. The number of dissident exile groups based in Spain also indicates that the Spanish government had a pretty strong opinion about Obiang's leadership of the country.

Even if he truly had the Spanish prepared to provide backup after the coup, Simon knew he would also need people inside Equatorial Guinea laying the groundwork far in advance of the operation. He needed a coordinator on the ground, someone who could keep his mouth shut and who had experience with mercenary actions. For that, he turned to Johan Sevrass Nicholas du Toit.

Niek had known Mann since he had approached Simon regarding an investment in a Congo diamond mine back in 1989. Niek had also worked for EO in Angola and Sierra Leone. Conflicting stories have circulated about when, how, and to what level Niek got involved in the EG plan. One source in the Equatoguinean government told me that Niek first came to the country in 2003 for a stint training the military, but Niek refused to answer questions about that, possibly to protect the contacts he had cultivated at that time. What is known for certain is that Niek relocated to EG in 2003 and began setting up what on the surface looked to be a legitimate commercial enterprise. In the confession he signed after his arrest, Niek conceded that he had come to EG with the purpose of setting up a front company that would arrange logistical support in advance of the coup—an assertion that correlates with what Simon Mann also admitted in his confession. However, Niek now maintains that his business venture was an aboveboard undertaking funded with insurance money he had received from a business partner's death in a plane crash. He claims that he knew nothing of the coup until Greg Wales first outlined the plan to him in a meeting at a South African hotel on January 3, 2004. However, Logo Logistics bank records indicate that Mann started transferring funds into Niek's new business, Triple Options Trading, in June 2003. Since one of the partners in Niek's company was Armengol Ondo Nguema, Obiang's half-brother and head of security who ended up returning to government service after a very brief postcoup detention, Niek has good reason not to come completely clean about the initial planning phase. With the possibility of being silenced hanging over his head, Niek may not want to upset his still-powerful former partner.

The earliest documentation to have surfaced about Mann's part in the coup preparations comes from the notes of a February 12, 2003, meeting between Simon and his accountant, friend, and business advisor Greg Wales. It is clear from the notes that Wales and Mann had a long list of things to go over. They needed to develop a code for discreet communications, "pre and post" contracts for the coup, and maps of oil blocks in Equatorial Guinea. They even discussed concerns about "what gets the marines coming in" and whom to hire to do PR in Washington. The document also indicates that Wales intended to attend a November 19, 2003, meeting of the International Peace Operations Association (IPOA) in Washington, DC, in order to put out feelers about support for the impending coup. The IPOA is an organization of private military companies and security contractors who had a special interest in privatized force being used in Africa for peacekeeping or interventions.

When he attended the conference, Wales was there to meet Theresa Whelan, the U.S. deputy assistant secretary of defense for African affairs, and hear her speak about the U.S. military's use of contractors for logistics and training support under an AFRICAP version of LOGCAP. In her closing remarks, Whelan stated, "I think that from our perspective, contractors are here to stay in supporting U.S. national security objectives overseas and really in the aggregate we think that they add considerable value to the process by bringing a dimension of flexibility that we really didn't have before and that we desperately need now as things in the world are so fluid and changing." Her comments seemed terribly naïve, considering that the whole purpose of IPOA was to promote the idea of companies like Executive Outcomes and Sandline for use in intervention and peacekeeping operations.

Attendees recall seeing Wales chatting with Whelan at the conference. Though there are no indications that Wales raised the subject of the upcoming operation in Equatorial Guinea, he did try to cultivate Whelan as a professional contact—interesting for someone who was supposed to be an accountant and financial advisor. Bank records released by Equatorial Guinea after the coup indicated Mann paid Wales $8,000 in November of 2003, presumably for expenses related to the trip. Simon must have liked what Wales had to report after returning to the UK, since he asked Greg to make another trip and made a second $35,000 deposit to Wales's Sherbourne Foundation in January 2004.

Wales returned to the United States in February for a scheduled appointment with Whelan on the nineteenth, the exact date the coup was initially supposed to occur. In a statement released after the coup, the Pentagon said that though Wales and Whelan had a wide-ranging discussion about many issues related to Africa, there had been no specifics discussed regarding EG. One U.S. official privately recounted that Wales wrote down more information than he provided.

During his February trip, Wales also took steps to ensure that Moto would have an opportunity to solidify his relations with the U.S. government after the coup. He offered $40,000 to a former senior State Department employee turned lobbyist named Joe Sala to set up a four-day program to introduce the soon-to-be-installed Moto to Congress, think tanks, academics, and the media. During Sala's first meeting with the State Department, an official told him that Moto had been there the year before with Khalil as sponsor and had been given a cool reception. Sala claimed he hadn't known about Moto's main backer but learned quickly that Khalil and Moto wouldn't be welcome in Washington. His efforts on Moto's behalf petered out, and Sala claims he was never actually paid any money by Wales. Mann never heard that Moto and Khalil were *persona non grata* in DC or that Wales had never clearly made his case or obtained the slightest indication of approval from the U.S. government.

As Wales worked to make contacts in the United States, Mann worked to raise the money for the operation. To handle the business aspects of the plan, Simon would use Logo Logistics, a company he had set up in October 2000 one month after Tim Spicer left Sandline. The initial fund-raising did not go as smoothly as planned, and Mann struggled to convince people to put in money, even though he expected they would receive a fivefold return on their money. According to a source close to Mann, Simon had to sell nearly a half million dollars' worth of diamond concession shares in order to have his own investment staked in the operation. Like any troubled business venture, the dreams of finding a single backer devolved into half-million-dollar shares; then each shareholder resorted to raising smaller pieces to make up their shortfalls. What should have been a tight-knit, tight-lipped group of half-million-dollar men became a huckster cluster with nickel and dime shares.

Though Khalil had initially promised Simon $1.8 million, he later complained that the French government had frozen most of his assets. Khalil was only able to scrounge up $750,000 but did refer Mann to friends who could be approached for more. On November 15, 2003, Logo Logistics signed an investor agreement with a Lebanon-based company named Asian Trade and Investment Group SAL, run by Karim Fallaha, a friend of Khalil's. The half million from Fallaha was reportedly collected from smaller investors, though there is no indication they had any idea to what end their money would serve.

Big investors who had allegedly pledged or given up to a half million included David Tremain, a South Africa–based businessman who reportedly represented a number of smaller investors; David Hart, a former advisor to Margaret Thatcher; J. H. Archer, a disgraced politician turned author of potboiler novels; and Gary Hersham, the director of a London real estate brokerage who had introduced Mann to Khalil. Afterward, all of these men would provide denials and alibis, and none would be charged with any crimes. Hersham says he only introduced Mann to a mortgage broker so he could mortgage his million-dollar-plus home on Portobello Road in Notting Hill. Wales later claimed that he was simply acting as middleman for Eli Khalil and/or that he had been discussing multiple possible projects with Mann, though nothing coup-related had been raised. Wales had known Mann for years, and even back in the days of Sandline would reportedly hang around the company's Chelsea offices "to catch scraps off the table," as one associate remembers.

The two investors who actually suffered serious consequences for their involvement in the venture, James Kershaw and Mark Thatcher, both fell under the jurisdiction of South Africa's recent antimercenary legislation. Kershaw, a twenty-four-year-old accountant and computer expert in South Africa, invested only a measly $90,000 of his own money, but also took on the role of being essentially the office manager for the plan—arranging payment for the foot soldiers and other contingencies.

Thatcher is the investor who has drawn the greatest amount of public scrutiny, since his mother is the former prime minister of England. Thatcher paid his half million in two installments, though would later claim that he had been contributing to the purchase of an air ambulance. Thatcher's cover story stretches credulity, since he and Simon Mann were friends and neighbors, and bank records indicate some of the supposed air ambulance money took a circuitous route into Logo Logistics.

The only son of Margaret Thatcher, Mark studied accounting but failed the licensing exams three times. At Harrow, he earned the nickname "Thickie" and has been described by those who know him as "not very bright." During his stint as a dilettante racing driver, he somehow managed to get himself lost for six days during the Paris-Dakar.

In 1981, Mark had worked as a rep for a British construction company and pushed for a $600-million university construction contract in Oman while his mother was there on a trade promotion trip. His role as middleman in another $25 billion arms deal to Saudi Arabia earned him $15 million while his mother was still in office. Separately, he also brokered an arms deal with the sultan of Brunei. His numerous business dealings and peddling of influence drew enough public criticism to be considered a minor scandal in the UK, though he was never brought up on any charges of impropriety. Regardless, Thatcher clearly had no problem in making his money in creative and slightly questionable ways.

Neither Mann nor Thatcher were really part of polite society in the UK, but in South Africa they were minor local celebrities—Mann for his life as a mercenary, and Thatcher for his jet-setting days as racer, pilot, bon vivant, and famous son. The two had much in common, including their love of flying, and over many neighborly dinners they would discuss their adventures and business ventures. Though Thatcher has publicly maintained he had no foreknowledge of the coup, it is inconceivable that they did not have discussions about Mann's upcoming gig in Equatorial Guinea, particularly considering how many times Thatcher met with others involved.

Thatcher met with Simon Mann and Niek du Toit at Lanseria airport near Johannesburg in July of 2003, ostensibly to discuss Thatcher's purchasing two of Niek's Russian-made Mi-8 helicopters for a mining operation in the Sudan. Niek was to meet Thatcher four times over the months leading up to the coup but claims to have never specifically discussed the planned operation with him. In December 2003, Mark Thatcher met with Greg Wales and coup pilot Crause Steyl at Lanseria airport, and later with Simon Mann and Crause Steyl in Constantia, South Africa. According to Thatcher, he eventually agreed to invest in Triple A Aviation Services (the

"AAA" comes from "Air Ambulance Africa"), and funded the purchase of a French-made Alouette III helicopter that could double as an ambulance or a gunship for the coup.

Triple A Aviation, with Crause Steyl as one of the owners, was set up in January 2004 to hold Thatcher's contribution and to act as a buffer against his exposure if the plot was discovered. Thatcher transferred $275,000 to Triple A on January 8, and the final payment of $255,000 was deposited on January 16. Bank records show that $100,000 was transferred on March 2 from Triple A to Mann's Logo Logistics, essentially creating a pass-through to the coup investment.

After the exposure of the conspiracy, Thatcher claimed he had no knowledge of the coup plot and insisted that he only intended to con-tribute funds for purchase of an air ambulance. It could almost be plausi-ble that Mann, Wales, and Steyl kept Thatcher uniformed about the actual final destination of his investment, if memos seized from James Kershaw's computer after the coup didn't express concern that "MT" might be dis-covered as a backer and insist that all precautions be taken to protect his involvement.

It is unclear why Mann continued to seek Thatcher's money, since by the time Thatcher had decided to put in his half million, Simon had al-ready received a $5 million promise from a Verona Holdings of Vaud, Switzerland. He may have worried about the other investors actually following through with their deposits or have been planning other uses for future endeavors. The five-page Verona Holdings contract outlines how Logo intends to develop potential projects in the fields of mining ex-ploration, commercial fishing, aviation, helicopter charter, and commer-cial security in the following countries: Guinea Republic, Sierra Leone, Liberia, and Angola. Equatorial Guinea is not mentioned. Simon's signa-ture is clearly legible on the last page of the document, but that of his new business associate appears as nothing more than a scribbled line with a bump at the end. Thus far, the person or people behind Verona Holdings have yet to be identified.

With the money finally coming in, things were finally looking up for the conspirators. To end the year on a good note, Mark Thatcher threw a big Christmas bash, held at his home in Constantia. Mark flew his seventy-year-old mother down for the occasion, and Simon, Greg Wales, and other coup plotters were in attendance. Guests at that party recall Wales and Mann discussing the idea for the coup as casually as if it were a horse race.

The Best-Laid Plans

Any good conspiracy requires multiple layers of cover stories and intrigue, and Mann had experience creating credible diversionary tales from his experience with Executive Outcomes and Sandline. For all public purposes, Mann's Logo Logistics activities were part of a mining security contract in the Congo, and versions related by different backers were mostly variations on this same story. Even the mercenaries hired for the job were told they would be guarding a Congolese mine.

Mann may have told a variety of cover stories, but the July 22, 2003, document titled "Assisted Regime Change" makes clear the intent of the plotters. The document is one of a number that have surfaced through the legal proceedings against those charged for the coup attempt. They all sound like accurate representations of the conspirators' plans, but since they were slipped to the prosecution by a journalist and not all seized directly from Mann, it must be mentioned that there is the slightest possibility one or all could be forgeries.

The Assisted Regime Change document lists as its number-one objective: "To replace, in the shortest possible time, the controlling unit of a country." The four-page plan outlines the most important steps to quickly replacing all the existing power structures of a country, and recommends a functional PR program to market the new and improved leadership domestically and abroad, a disinformation campaign to discredit the old regime, and a formal pogrom against the previous supporters—all to begin within twenty-four hours of a coup.

Another July 22 document crudely lays out a two-part contract between "Mr. M" and "Captain F." Mr. M is clearly Severo Moto, and Captain F is former SAS captain Simon Francis Mann. The copy of the contract I viewed had Simon's signature but not Moto's, and it established the intended business arrangements and cash bonuses to be given by the leader of the provisional government to the backers and executors of the plot. By signing, Moto would agree to pay four unnamed participants (possibly Crause and Neil Steyl, Niek du Toit, and Simon Witherspoon) $1 million each, six men would get $50,000 (the advance team with Niek), and seventy-five men $5,000 each (foot soldiers). Captain F was slated to earn a generous $15 million for his role. If the coup was successful, each would also be given EG citizenship, passports, letters saying they were members of the armed forces, and immunity from extradition. Captain F would also be contracted to become the new president's personal security contractor and would be given a diplomatic passport, any rank of his choosing, and controlling interest of a "newco." A common name used to describe a yet-to-be-formed business entity, the newco would handle much of the business deals to be redirected to the benefit of the coup backers. Moto probably did not realize that if he agreed to give Captain F the right to hire, train, and command his bodyguard, he would have literally signed his life away. Another document that purportedly originated with Mann indicates that after the coup, the power behind the new EG president would not hesitate to dispose of Moto if he turned out to be less than completely pliant.

The "Bight of Benin Company" (BBC), written in the archaic British schoolboy style typical of Simon Mann, is a Machiavellian plan laced with paranoia and greed. The document lays out a plan to turn EG into something resembling the British East India Company. It details the coup backers' intent to claim the sole right to make agreements and contracts with the newly installed government—essentially becoming a board of directors that would dictate the decisions and actions of whoever ruled Equatorial Guinea. The BBC makes it abundantly clear that Moto is disposable and that his main backer, Eli Khalil, was not to be trusted.

The document lists nine reasons why the backers should not count on Moto, ranging from the interference of tribal supporters "who are desperate to get their noses in the trough" to concern that "he may die, or be incapacitated, at an inconvenient moment." The document then goes on to list ten remedies, the first being that the same forces that brought Moto to power could be used to bring the new dictator down. They would also insulate Moto from getting any opportunity to gain public support, keeping him under twenty-four-hour surveillance and gathering or making up information that could be used for blackmail or negative publicity. Plans to groom the newly installed dictator's successor were also critical to Simon Mann's thinking.

Moto is not the only one who has a noose and a trapdoor carefully prepared for him. The BBC document also voices much concern about how closely "E. K.," or Eli Khalil, must be managed. The planner's criticism ranges from "may have exaggerated view of his level of control over 'M'" to may have "ulterior motives." The suspicion was that Khalil could be secretly "working for the French, being part of the usual Lebo [Lebanese] conspiracy, which includes diamond trading, money laundering and . . . an exaggerated view of extent to which oil companies can be screwed for more money, actually the thing most likely to get the USG pissed off." As a well-documented "middleman" for French and Nigerian oil interests, if the coup had been pulled off as Khalil had wished, he could have become a major player in pushing the country's upcoming negotiations of oil leases from the Houston cabal toward TotalFinalElf. Just as Lebanese businessman Hassan Hashem is currently the éminence grise for President Obiang, Khalil would have advised Moto from the shadows. His first piece of advice would probably have been to arrest and/or expel the mercenaries and to shift the balance of favor toward the French in granting new leases and security partnerships.

In this document it appears that Simon Mann does not even trust Niek du Toit. "NDT" comes under suspicion as possibly working for Obiang, or even having his own plans. Since du Toit was partnered with Obiang's half-brother and national security advisor, a man reputed to have his own ambitions for the top post in EG, it's entirely possible Niek could have cut his own separate deal that would have included booting Moto, Mann, and everyone else.

In any conspiracy involving vast sums of money, the deceit involved stirs intense paranoia as each conspirator jockeys for the best position to promote their own selfish interests. Until the coup went down, however, everyone involved had to continue to maintain a façade of trust and cooperation.

Mann had always tapped into the same people to run his operations, and this time he enlisted the help of former leaders of the 32 Battalion and ex-EO hands like Simon Witherspoon and pilots and brothers Neil and Crause Steyl. Those three and Niek were referred to as the "Million-Dollar Men" because each stood to gain a million dollars from the operation— Niek for his role inside EG and for using his contacts with the Zimbabwe Defence Industries (ZDI) to arrange for a weapons purchase, Simon for leading the mercenaries during the ground operation, Neil for flying the fighters into EG, and Crause for flying Moto from Spain to Malabo. Mann also quickly put together the by-now-standard EO-style complement of Ovambo gunmen from Pomfret, South Africa, recruited by Niek du Toit and handled by twenty-four-year-old accountant and computer programmer James Kershaw. Recruiting a mercenary army wouldn't be a problem in a place like Pomfret, an abandoned military base and home to ex-members of 32 Battalion. Anyone with enough money could easily raise a thousand-man army in twenty-four hours, making the desolate village a favorite of EO and Sandline in the days when they required manpower.

According to Crause Steyl, who had been hired to coordinate the air logistics, Simon's original plan was laid out in his meetings at a resort near Pretoria, South Africa, between Greg Wales, Steyl, and Niek du Toit. As part of his new venture, Niek was to lease two Armenian-crewed cargo planes. They would be painted blue and white with the logo "PANAC," short for Pan-African Cargo. One was a twenty-passenger Antonov prop plane, the other an Ilyushin 76, a massive four-jet engine overhead wing cargo plane.

On the night of the coup, rebels would attack and take control of an airfield in the Kolwezi region in the Democratic Republic of Congo (DRC). Two DC-3s would fly the sixty or so men and mining security equipment from South Africa to a staging area in Ndola, Zambia, first, and then on to Kolwezi when the signal came that the landing strip was secure.

The old Antonov was supposed to fly first from Malabo to Harare, Zimbabwe, to load in the wooden cases of ammunition and weapons, and then on to Kolwezi at the appropriate time. While the plan sounds somewhat convoluted, it was designed to avoid being seen anywhere respectable while loading a weapons cache onto a plane with a small army of obviously irregular soldiers. When the DC-3s and Antonov arrived, men and weapons would all load onto the massive Ilyushin cargo plane.

The Ilyushin would be carrying a cargo more interesting than even a load of armed men. A collection of luxury SUVs would also be on board and used as an enticement to bring Obiang out to the airport. The president would be invited to accept these as a gift from Niek and his partners. Once on the tarmac, the president and his Moroccan security detail would be overpowered and "detained."

Once the airport was secured, the men were to use the SUVs and the minibuses from Niek's local taxi service to move the mercenaries to secure the military base and police stations. The helicopter paid for with Mark Thatcher's investment in Triple A Aviation would already be on the island and used as a gunship to deal with rebellious units and as an air ambulance for any wounded in the action. With only about five dozen mercenaries planning to subdue an army of a few thousand Equatoguinean troops and police, the plotters were either naïve, overly optimistic, or more likely had set up a network of local co-plotters who could ensure they would expect little resistance.

Meanwhile, as the coup was occurring, Severo Moto would be traveling with Greg Wales, David Tremain, and Karim Fallaha in Simon's South African–registered Beachcraft King Air plane flown by Crause Steyl to Bamako, Mali, from the Canary Islands. Once they got the signal, Moto and the entourage of investors would fly in about thirty minutes after Obiang was neutralized. If everything went smoothly, the Equatoguineans would awake to a new era of enlightened and mercenary-installed leadership.

According to Khalil, an initial contingent of six hundred Spanish soldiers would be waiting off the coast to be landed by ship as an advance group of three thousand Spanish peacekeepers Moto planned to invite in to help "restore law and order." Moto would declare a new era of human rights and democracy, while Eli Khalil and his cohorts would become stunningly rich from leasing lucrative oil plots to oil companies.

Mann was inspired by the beautiful simplicity and profitability of the plan, and quickly expanded the initial idea into a much bigger vision of how Africa could be changed by a small private army. There is a detailed intelligence report by Johann Smith, a former South African intelligence officer, indicating that at one point the conspirators may have been planning a coup hop—starting by taking out the leadership of São Tomé before moving on to EG. Early on, there had also been discussions at Mann's house with financial advisor Greg Wales and real estate broker Gary Hersham about Sudan and Gabon—both oil-producing countries with upside potential for an aggressive investor with a private army. Mann had actually met with someone to discuss filming the coup with an eye toward a PR program to benefit his future plans.

Before he could move on to other countries, Mann would have to pull off the EG gig, and there was at least one man who was going to try and throw up roadblocks. Johann Smith, former 32 Battalion officer and contemporary of du Toit, was based in Malabo and considered EG his turf. He had often touted himself as security advisor to President Obiang, though Obiang denies such claims. Smith is one of the many South Africans who hover on the fringe selling their skills to the highest bidders, and he initially learned about Mann's operation when two other 32 Battalion vets complained to him that they had missed out on a well-paying mercenary job. Smith told the men that if they could try again to get themselves hired, he would pay them for any information they could feed back to him.

The men managed to pass on enough details for Smith to discover the involvement of Niek, a friend and SADF contemporary. Smith actually confronted du Toit to warn him that the gig was up. Although Smith's warning gave Niek serious cause for reflection, he and Simon still decided to proceed. Perhaps the decision would have been made differently if the conspirators had known that Johann Smith was assembling a detailed dossier on the impending coup, which he began to forward to what he thought were interested countries. According to Smith, he forwarded a detailed report to government officials in the United States and the UK, including Pentagon official Michael Westphal. The report outlined preparations for the coup, listed the backers (including cell phone numbers), and estimated a date of mid-March 2004.

On January 29, the British government received Smith's report, which ended up in the hands of foreign secretary Jack Straw. Straw said later in an official statement, "It was not definitive enough for us to conclude a coup was likely or inevitable. It was passed by another government to us on the normal condition that it not be passed on. . . . I considered the case and agreed the [Foreign Office] should approach an individual formerly connected with a British private military company, both to attempt to test the veracity of the report and to make clear the [Foreign Office] was firmly opposed to any unconstitutional action such as coups d'état." Since the coup plan as outlined had all the hallmarks of an Executive Outcomes or Sandline operation, it's not surprising that Jack Straw called Tim Spicer for more information. According to the British Foreign Office's official account of the meeting, "the individual concerned claimed no knowledge of the plans." While the exact level of Spicer's involvement in the coup is unknown, and there is no evidence he actually was involved, people who know both Spicer and Mann find it highly unlikely that two people with such aligned interests, social contacts, and financial interests did not talk about such a major opportunity. And it surprises no one in that circle that the first person Jack Straw called was Tim Spicer.

In Straw's official recounting of the meeting, Spicer was told to notify his long-time friend Simon Mann of the FO's displeasure and disapproval. However, a source close to Simon Mann recollects being briefed on a different exchange. In this version, Spicer told Mann that he had laid out the full details of the coup and described Straw as pleased: "When Spicer met Simon in February last year, just after he had met the FO, reports are that TS and SM had a good meeting and that SM was not in the least discouraged by TS's FO meeting, and whatever TS had to say to him put him in a good mood." Spicer denies briefing Mann after the meeting.

Jack Straw had initially claimed that the UK government had no fore-knowledge of the coup, but a year of media coverage made that position unsustainable, and Straw finally admitted he'd known of the plans five weeks prior to the coup. He had even set up an emergency evacuation plan for UK citizens from the island of Bioko in preparation for any fallout from the coup.

Someone had given Mann the impression that the UK government had tacitly assented to the coup plot, which buttressed the same sentiment associate Greg Wales had already informed him would be coming from the U.S. government. If any major government had informed Mann's cabal not to go ahead with their plans, it would have been clear that there would have been no benefit from continuing with the coup. The truth is that no one took any concrete steps to interfere, and the U.S. and UK governments may have simply sat back to watch with interest. Once the operation had succeeded, the PR component would have made it very difficult for anyone to reinstall Obiang or argue that Moto was not a better ruler. After all, the coup was being presented as a persecuted and enlightened government-in-exile mounting a return by humanely deposing one of Africa's most brutal oppressors. No government could oppose that. Mann kept close the secret that the plot was really about a group of private investors hiring security contractors to take over an oil-rich country.

By January of 2004, Mann had most of his investors lined up and had received or had pledges for the required funds. Khalil was pressuring Mann to schedule the coup for the third week of February 2004, lest the impending democratic process disrupt their carefully laid plans. There were upcoming elections in Spain, and the plotters discussed the possibility that they would lose Spanish support if the conservative prime minister, Jose Maria Aznar, lost his bid for reelection. Also, imminent elections in EG could potentially install a new, democratically elected leader, which would make it more difficult to put a positive PR spin on the coup. Further, December had seen yet another coup attempt against Obiang, this one staged by General Agustin Ndgong Ona, the president's half brother and commander of the army. Obiang's premature death or overthrow could shut out Moto's chance at leadership. Mann determined the third week of February would be the target date for the coup and went to work formulating the operational plan.

The First Attempt

By late January, fifty-five men had been hired and were doing house clearing and small squad tactics training at a farm in South Africa. They practiced shooting and breaching doors with wooden rifles in groups of five or so. The training may have seemed a little rigorous for the mining security operation they had been told they would be doing, but the soldiers might not have questioned it for fear of losing the work.

In early February of 2004, Mann and du Toit traveled to Harare to purchase a stock of weapons. ZDI officials would later say that the men had raised suspicions because their business cards showed the same address—Mann's for Logo Logistics and du Toit's for MTS, or Military Technical Services, a company he had started in 1989. Further, it seemed curious that the men would purchase arms from Zimbabwe, since their businesses were based in South Africa—a much larger supplier of weapons—and MTS was a legally licensed dealer. The officials may have not really believed that the men intended to help President Robert Mugabe seize valuable diamond areas in the Congo's Kolwezi region, but arms dealers aren't known to ask too many questions. ZDI obviously didn't care enough about Mann and du Toit's motivations to refuse $180,800 in exchange for sixty-one AK-47 assault rifles with 45,000 rounds of ammunition, twenty PKM light machine guns with 30,000 rounds of ammunition, a hundred RPG anti-tank launchers with 1,000 rockets, five hundred hand grenades, ten Browning pistols with 500 rounds of 9-mm ammo, and two 60-mm mortar tubes with 80 mortar bombs. James Kershaw flew in from South Africa the next day with $90,000 to make the first payment. The entire shipment was supposed to be ready within a week.

Niek and Simon arrived at the Harare airport on February 18 with the final $90,800 payment for the weapons cache. They were supposed to pick up the weapons and then rendezvous with the mercenaries to combine forces and commence the coup, but the planned operation hit an insurmountable snag. The plane carrying the mercenaries had hit a bird and broke its nose wheel, leaving the plane a motionless hulk of metal in Ndola. The fifty men who had flown up to Ndola from Wonderbroom Airport in Pretoria were stranded and had to make their way back home. Simon Mann had to put a hold on the weapons, fly from Harare to Ndola to drop off money for the plane repair, and return home in a funk. Agitated by the setback and blaming Crause Steyl for the excessively complicated plan, Mann sidelined Steyl and hired Ivan Pienaar, a South African pilot and former mercenary for UNITA, to develop the new aviation logistics. It was a decision that likely cost Mann dearly, since it would be this new plan that would be leaked directly to the highest level of the Angolan government, leading to the exposure of the coup.

Second Attempt

Mann wanted the plan simplified, and Ivan Pienaar did just that—no fancy ruses with luxury cars and no multiple flights and connections. They would use only one aircraft, which would stop to pick up the mercenaries in South Africa, then Simon and the weapons cache in Harare, and then on to Malabo for the coup. Instead of inviting Obiang to the airport, Niek—through his partner, Armengol—would invite Obiang to dinner on the night of the coup. Obiang would be forcibly held until the mercenary army arrived a few hours later to take over.

Without the luxury cars, they wouldn't need the massive Ilyushin cargo plane for transport, and the Antonov was too small for all the weapons and men. Simon made some urgent phone calls and finally located the classic choice for mercenary operations at Dodson Aviation in Kansas—a forty-year-old 727-100, which had been converted from a civilian airliner for use by the U.S. Air National Guard. The converted 727 was complete with a pressurized cargo hold and could carry twice the capacity of the Antonov with a range of three thousand miles. It even had a U.S. flag on its tail.

Mann bargained hard with Dodson Aviation and agreed in the first week of March to buy the plane for a price of $400,000. Dodson arranged for a U.S. crew to deliver the plane to South Africa. The white plane arrived at Wonderbroom Airport just north of Pretoria at 8:00 A.M. on Sunday, March 7, where the U.S. crew deplaned to go into town, and the mercenaries immediately started loading up. What they did not know was that someone with excellent and exact knowledge of their aviation activities had already contacted Angolan president Eduardo dos Santos on March 4 with explicit details of the coup. On Friday, March 5, Angolan intelligence contacted the minister of the interior for EG and told him to come to Luanda immediately. Manuel Nguema Mba, who has since been promoted to Obiang's minister of national security, chartered a Falcon jet and flew down for a briefing on the coup plot by dos Santos. Manuel urgently began relaying the information back to Malabo. Even if the mercenaries had managed to make it into EG, they now would have met fierce and violent resistance.

Back in South Africa, the mood was cheerful. First on board the new 727 was pilot Neil Steyl, an old Executive Outcomes hand and one of the "million-dollar men." Hendrick Hamman took the copilot's seat, and Ken Payne was the engineer. The flight crew would be transporting sixty-four men, a pile of supplies, $30,000 in cash for fuel, and $100,000 for expenses. After loading the cargo, the mercenary army took their places in the hold. Altogether there were twenty-three Angolans, eighteen Namibians, twenty South Africans, two Congolese, and a Zimbabwean.

One South African contractor on board had just finished a gig in Haiti and had only been back for two days. Raymond Stanley Archer, a former EO hand, was working for the Steele Foundation when President Aristide was deposed on February 28. He had been part of the security detail that had escorted Aristide into exile in the Central African Republic. After his arrest in Zimbabwe, Archer stated in court that he had arrived home in Johannesburg on March 4 and was having lunch with his ex-wife three days later when James Kershaw contacted him on his cell phone. "He said if I could get to the airport within an hour, I could have the job." When security contractor Archer boarded the plane, he recognized ten of the men on board. It looked like a reunion of South Africa Defence Force vets from the old Executive Outcomes days.

The fighters did not know they were heading to Equatorial Guinea via Zimbabwe, but it was not the first time mercenaries and contractors working for Mann were not told their ultimate destination. Although the group had been training for combat operations and house clearing—neither related to guarding mines—the contractors were happy not to know too much. They would be briefed just before the plane landed.

Meanwhile, Simon Mann, Lourens Horne, and Jacobus "Harry" Carlse had arrived in Zimbabwe to make sure the weapons were ready. The South Africans, Horne and Carlse, were part owners of Meteoric Tactical Systems, a private security company with contracts in Iraq—one to guard the Swiss mission and another to train the Iraqi army. The two had taken off from Iraq, telling their clients that they were taking two weeks to go buffalo hunting in South Africa. Instead, they ended up spending their "vacation" in a Zimbabwean jail.

At 7:30 P.M., the unmarked 727 touched down at Harare and taxied to the military side of the airport to refuel. The pilot's manifest said they had three pilots and four loaders on board and were refueling on their way to Bujumbura, in Burundi, and Mbuji-Mayi in the Congo.

According to statements by the Zimbabwean government immediately after the incident, a curious airport guard had wondered why all the aircraft's oval windows were shuttered. When the soldier asked to look inside, he was rudely rebuffed. He and a cohort told their commander and the plane was then boarded by armed men. The mercenaries and flight crew were immediately arrested. A few minutes later, the Zimbabweans took Mann, Horne, and Carlse into custody as well. A television crew was invited to board the plane and film the "military cargo."

Though the initial reports of the capture of Mann and his mini-army made it seem like a case of serendipity, Zimbabwean officials would later insist that it had been part of an orchestrated sting operation set up after they had been alerted of Mann's intentions by South African intelligence. While conceivable, it also seems possible the Zimbabweans were just trying to cover the embarrassment of having their own state-owned defense industry selling weapons for a coup in Equatorial Guinea, and rebels in the Congo.

Before he was arrested, Mann managed to make a sat phone call or text message to tell Niek: "It's necessary to cancel the operation due to last-minute difficulties." He also quickly sent a text message to the others in the twin-engine plane with Moto waiting on the tarmac in Bamako, Mali. Mann and his crew were taken to Chikurubi Prison just outside Harare. The mostly black team of mercenaries was packed in eight to a cell, while Mann was put in solitary confinement.

That was enough to scatter the wild geese. Moto and his contingent flew back to the Canary Islands, where they were briefly detained and questioned by immigration officials early on the morning of March 8. It seems Crause had somehow entered Spain from South Africa without even a passport, but even so, the entire crew was released once a member of the Spanish intelligence force arrived, adding to the suspicion of Spanish complicity in the plot.

On Tuesday, March 9, Niek and fourteen men were arrested in Equatorial Guinea and dragged to the Black Beach jail. Two of the men say they were tortured and beaten by being hung upside down and shocked with electricity. The next day, Niek was paraded on TV with his confession. Suddenly Africa's two most reviled and ignored dictators, Zimbabwe's Robert Mugabe and Equatorial Guinea's Obiang Nguema, became the saviors of post-colonial Africa.

The participation of so many players from previous Executive Outcomes business made it seem like a tired, worn-out plot. Many media reports drew parallels between the coup attempt and the 1974 book *The Dogs of War* by Frederick Forsyth. Forsyth had written the bestselling book in the Hotel Bahia on a hook of land overlooking the city of Malabo, and his fictional country of Zangaro was indeed based on Equatorial Guinea. His characters Cat Shannon and his backer Sir James Manson were based on real people who had attempted to overthrow the previous Macias Nguema regime in 1972. According to Forsyth's fictional account, a group of business interests had gotten together to mount a coup in order to control EG's precious mineral resources—an interesting analogy to the

modern attempt to dominate the oil industry. In that attempt, the mercenaries had taken a fishing boat from Spain via Lansarote in the Canary Islands toward Equatorial Guinea. Due to the security leaks and the
incongruous sight of foreigners sailing from Spain in a trawler, the ship
and crew were arrested upon arrival. Forsyth, now a shareholder in Aegis,
was implicated as a backer of the 1972 coup in the media, though he has
always denied the charges.

The trials in Zimbabwe and Malabo were a foregone conclusion. In
Zimbabwe, the mercenaries from Pomfret were given twelve-month sentences for immigration violations, and returned home shortly after the
coup attempt. Members of the flight crew were sentenced to sixteen
months but were also released early. Charged again in South Africa, Neil
Steyl paid a $25,000 fine and agreed in his plea bargain to assist in the
investigation.

Mann was convicted on two weapons charges on July 22, 2004, and
given seven years, though the Supreme Court in Zimbabwe later reduced
it to four with a third of his sentence reduced for good behavior. According to a source close to Mann's family, the Zimbabwean government had
offered to allow him to pay a massive fine in exchange for his release. His
freedom would have required he unload one of his houses, but Simon's
wife, Amanda Mann, thirty-nine and pregnant at the time with their sev-
enth child, refused to sell.

A couple of weeks after his arrest, Simon Mann wrote a letter to his
wife that was intercepted by South African intelligence and eventually
leaked to the media. The letter, written in Etonian schoolboy slang, appealed for a big "splodge of wonga" to be spent on his release. He insisted
that he had been tortured and that his confession had been coerced. The
"Smelly" and "Scratcher" mentioned in the letter were crude codes for Eli
Khalil and Mark Thatcher. Mann wrote his wife to forcefully demand a
promised $200,000 from Gianfranco Cicogna, another $200,000 from
"Scratcher (he of the Scratcher Suite)," and the remaining $500,000 from
Greg Wales. Mann wrote, "Do they think they can be part of something
like this with only upside potential—no hardship or risk of this going
wrong. Anyone and everyone in this is in it—good times or bad. Now it's

bad times and everyone has to F-ing well pull their full weight. GW's was for the last resort and this *is* the last resort."

The scandal sparked by the letter only served to cement the divide between the backers and those in prison. In a later affidavit, Mann would try to distance himself from his former supporters, saying, "It is a matter of great regret to me that some of my friends and acquaintances, such as Sir Mark Thatcher, Eli Khalil and Tony Buckingham, have been accused . . . of conspiring with me. . . . I maintain there was no plot or understanding or conspiracy in which I was involved."

Despite his long association with Mann, Greg Wales has sought to distance himself from the plot, as he told the British press, "Whatever Simon was doing, he was incredibly stupid. Finding yourself in Harare with a bunch of blokes, an aircraft, and buying lots of kit—if you think you can do that without a problem, you are a bit naïve." Wales has never been arrested and denies any involvement, though he had enough inside information to have written a yet-to-be-published book about the coup called *Power and Terrain.*

On August 25, South Africa's Scorpions arrested Mark Thatcher as he was preparing to fly to Dallas for the beginning of his children's school year. James Kershaw had also been arrested but negotiated himself a reduced sentence and fine by becoming a witness for the prosecution of Thatcher. Mark pleaded guilty to a reduced charge and was given a four-year suspended sentence and had to pay a fine of half a million dollars.

In Equatorial Guinea, Niek du Toit was sentenced to thirty-four years, an effective death sentence for a forty-eight-year-old. He complained before his trial that they had been abandoned by all the big players behind the coup plot, and said, "I feel bitter more than anything."

The six Armenian airmen arrested with Niek were sentenced to between fourteen and twenty-four years in jail but were mysteriously pardoned a year later and flown home. Four other South Africans were given seventeen-year sentences.

Severo Moto was not charged with anything by Spain but was ejected from the country. He was also sentenced in absentia to sixty-five years (on top of his previous 101-year sentence) in Equatorial Guinea. Moto has suggested that Obiang is attempting extrajudicial means to extract revenge and has claimed to have barely escaped an assassination plot by Balkan hit men paid for by Obiang. Though there is no verification of his story, it's entirely possible that Obiang would want to neutralize Moto as a threat before he returns for a third try at the presidency. Even with Moto gone, Obiang rule is likely not long for this world. No one that vulnerable can sit on a pile of resources that valuable indefinitely. Niek tells me there have been at least six coup attempts since he has been in prison.

The End

If there is a lesson in all of this, it is that once the security business is un-hitched from established corporate or government clients, its proponents can quickly turn it into the insecurity business. Mercenaries are above all opportunistic businessmen. It is completely logical, and perhaps necessary, to ask where these men will find the same income and sense of mission once Iraq and the War on Terror gold rush end. Just as an army could be raised with two phone calls to the pool of unemployed ex-soldiers in Pom-fret, South Africa, the next generation of mercenary may be found in the bars of security shows in Texas, or even on websites where the guns-for-hire network looks to find the next opportunity.

If Erik Prince convinces the U.S. government that his private army can bring peace to war-torn regions, the private military contractor could be-come a profession as respected as medic or teacher. If private backers ex-ploit the large pool of available talent for self-serving deeds, then the world may see more "Bight of Benin" companies and 727s full of armed men. The ultimate direction of these nearly converging paths of the pri-vate security contractor and mercenary could closely resemble a combina-tion of both.

What I learned from Niek is that in the debate between contractor and mercenary, it will always come down to the individual. When Niek du Toit was my security man, I knew him as an upstanding, loyal, dependable provider of security in what was at the time the world's most dangerous place. Now, four years later, he is a criminal behind bars for what appears to be the rest of his life.

In Black Beach prison, I ask him why he does not take a plea bargain deal offered for him and Simon Mann. In order to take the deal, Niek would likely have to turn and testify against all the planners and financial backers. Despite having signed a confession before the trial, Niek now sticks to his original story—that he is a businessman and knew nothing of the coup. He insists he has no knowledge of a possible plea deal and is not even allowed South African embassy visits and mail.

When the light begins to fail and his jailers begin tapping their watches to let me know I have had enough time with Niek, I begin to pack up. I leave Niek with some minor gifts and a stern admonishment to the guards to allow him and the others fresh fruits and vegetables, time outside, and shackle-free ankles. Outside the prison in the stifling heat, the attorney general, who had escorted me to the prison, shakes his head and wonders aloud why Niek sticks to his story. I tell him that Niek is a soldier, a professional, and will remain loyal to his own credo to the end.

Epilogue

Picturesque beach cottages dot the California coast just south of Santa Barbara—the former weekend getaways for people of moderate means decades ago have become $1-million, thousand-square-foot primary residences for double-income middle-class families. Every turn takes me down yet another exceedingly quaint street lined with brightly painted bungalows, sometimes color-coordinated with their neatly manicured landscaping. As I pull up in front of my destination, I have a moment of incongruous revelation when confronted with the Stateside reality that one of the "shit hot" badasses I rode back and forth with on Baghdad's Route Irish actually lives in a cute little house with a picket fence. As if he has been watching for my arrival, "Miyagi," the former LAPD cop and leader of the Mamba team, comes out to greet me.

Miyagi gives me his typical "Hey, bro" handshake but his grip is weaker now. A fresh pink quarter-inch jagged scar with industrial-sized

334

stitch marks runs down the inside length of his forearm, but that wasn't his worst injury. "I still have a hole in my ass," he tells me, tracing the point where a piece of shrapnel ripped a fist-sized hole in his right buttock and exited his crotch, seriously nicking his penis. A close call, though Miyagi's doctors expect a full recovery. "They told me my boy is going to be fine. Man, I shoulda got the five-hundred-dollar upgrade," he laughs. He further describes the trajectory of the bomb blast to explain how that same shard of flying metal then sliced a furrow in the back of Tool's hat and finally became embedded in the steel wall of the Mamba.

The day of the attack, April 21, 2005, Miyagi took the lead gunner position in a convoy of three Mambas and one truck heading toward Ramadi. "We were driving down the road, and there was a parking area on our right, people just hanging around outside their cars. I was looking through the AimPoint on the PKM. We were doing eighty to ninety kilometers an hour. My attention was towards two cars that came off a dirt road. I was thinking, 'Gosh, I feel like they are slowing us down.' Tool blew the air horn two to four times. Those dudes wouldn't turn around, and within seconds—BOOM—an IED went off. I knew they were slowing us down, boxing us in.

"The Mamba came to a complete stop because the air line had been hit. Tool got on the radio and asked the second Mamba to push us out of the kill zone. They came up and tried to push. We didn't know that once the air line was gone, the wheels lock up. It's some safety feature.

"I knew my right hand was totaled, but I was waiting for secondary fire. My legs were on fire. I did a quick check. I could feel it was hot. I kept flexing my right hand. I remember pulling the trigger with my left hand and yelling, 'Hey, fucker, I can still fight!' Tool was cussing the entire time and he looked at me and said, 'How ya doing?' I was bleeding. I said, 'I can still fight. I got one good hand.' Then I ducked down and looked in the back. Shit, Sparky was on top of the other guys just laying there. He was just laying on top of the other two guys just dying. I didn't see any marks on his face and chest. He was hit in the groin, and it blew out his femoral artery. He got it from the knees up." In an all-too-familiar twist of fate, Sparky

wasn't supposed to be in the convoy that day. He had actually been scheduled to fly home for a few days, but the boredom of repeated delays had
him volunteering for the run. Miyagi remembers, "Sparky was a great gun
guy, fabulous worker, real nice guy—one of the 'dudes.'" Two other contractors in the back of the Mamba had also suffered shrapnel wounds:
"The back of the Mamba was like Swiss cheese. Whatever was in that
bomb just blew through all that armor."

Sitting amid the wreckage of one destroyed vehicle, Miyagi started
getting the ominous feeling that the insurgents might come back for
more. "Traffic behind us had been stopped by the rear guy. In the distance
I saw a kid running at about two hundred meters ahead, carrying a big
white flag. If you looked further down you could see traffic stopped. I remember seeing that kid in his late teens. I yelled, 'We need to get off the
X.' From the time we got hit to the time we started moving—we were
gone, vehicle torched, and reloaded in less than fifteen minutes."

Miyagi describes the fortunes of his survival as simply "blessed, bro."
His wife appears more distraught than he is about his near-death experience, and the most supportive superlative she can come up with to describe his most important success in Iraq is to call him "the most messed
up contractor that didn't get killed." Miyagi escaped the attack with his life
intact, but he has no illusions about how close it came. "If Tool would've
been leaning back one inch, he would have been dead. If I'd been turned
an inch either way, it would have taken out my femoral." As he talks, he
rhythmically squeezes a rubber ball painted with the cartoon face of a
baseball player. "The worst part was when I got home, my youngest saw
me with my arm all messed up and he started crying. He said, 'You promised you would throw a baseball with me.' That hurt."

Miyagi is about as philosophic as he ever gets about the risks of his
chosen profession. "Call it faith. Call it what you want. You know going
into it." Despite his serious wounds and the deaths of many friends,
Miyagi still plans a comeback as a security contractor. "Either you love
what you do or you don't. I love what I do. It keeps my wife from working
full-time. We want to do a room addition. I don't want her to work so she
doesn't have to bust her ass. She is a court reporter. She was stressed. My

wife grew up here—a town of fourteen thousand people a quarter of a mile from the beach. My son can ride to the beach, my nine-year-old. This is like Mayberry RFD with a beach." It is a common refrain I have heard repeated so many times during the past few years. Though critics have accused security contractors of working "for the money," in my journey I have found it would be more precise to describe a good majority as working "to support their families." Miyagi likely wouldn't be able to afford his mortgage payments if he rejoined the LAPD on a beat-cop's salary. However, he knows his skills are in high demand on a global scale, though it remains to be seen where exactly he will work next.

Though they lost one man and one Mamba in the attack on Miyagi's convoy, it wasn't the deadliest encounter Blackwater had that day. Insurgents shot down—reportedly with missile fire—an Mi-17 transport helicopter leased by Blackwater, killing all except one on impact. The attackers had their propaganda tool at the ready and began filming the aftermath. When they discovered the one survivor, the pilot, they forced him to stand before executing him in a barrage of bullets, making for another very vivid and public broadcast of the fate that may befall a security contractor in Iraq. Six American Blackwater contractors, along with three Bulgarian crew members and two Fijian security guards, died in the Mi-17 attack. In total, on April 21, 2005, Blackwater Security suffered a loss of seven employees, four wounded, one torched Mamba, and one downed transport helicopter.

By scouring the media for accounts of attacks like April 21, icasualties.org had come up with an unofficial count of 314 contractors killed in Iraq by the spring of 2006. The Department of Labor has had more than 400 death-benefits claims filed for Defense Bases Act insurance. This higher number also includes claims from the surviving members of Iraqis who had been employed by American companies, but likely also indicates that not all contractor deaths garner mentions in the press.

It should not be surprising that neither the American nor Iraqi government keeps an official count of the number of contractors killed, since they can't even seem to estimate the number of security companies now operating in the war zone or the number of contractors they employ. In the spring of 2006, 730 members of the Iraqi government alone required the services of private security details—all operating without direct control from either the occupying regime or the beleaguered Iraqi government. The proliferation of armed civilians providing security and the lawless environment in which the business has expanded have resulted in a flourishing of private militias, many of which double as death squads.

To counter this trend, an organization called the Private Security Company Association of Iraq (PSCAI) has been established to try to organize the legitimate companies and to push for legislation to rein in the illegitimate ones. The problem the PSCAI has encountered is that the government of Iraq is simply not capable of or willing to regulate the contractors. Confidential PSCAI internal documents from early 2006 outline the response of the ministry of the interior after the first batch of security companies attempted to register with the MOI. Fifty of those who submitted the paperwork to the MOI either received no response or were rejected, while forty-eight were still waiting for their weapons permits four months after they had applied. The MOI had also admitted that there were at least fifty-four armed private "security" companies about which they had no information. A more disturbing revelation can be found in the notes of a PSCAI meeting, where discussion centered around their determination that 14,600 unregistered individual Iraqi members of armed personal security details were operating in Iraq, who therefore exist completely outside the boundaries of the current modicum of regulation now in place. Adding to that the additional 19,120 unregistered foreign security operators makes for an estimate of more than 33,720 men with a license to kill in Iraq. Another PSCAI internal document, discussing the accountability of those unregistered entities, states, "Each PSD is effectively its own entity, and subject to the perceived power of those whom they protect." The implication is that the security situation is driving the country toward a kind of neo-warlordism. The PSCAI best estimate is that there are more than 70,000 privately armed men in Iraq, not including insurgents or militias.

While waiting at BIAP with the Mamba team during my November 2004 visit, I chatted with two American security contractors working for one of Iraq's largest employers at the time. They seemed freaked out and told me that their Kurdish owner would routinely leave their secure compound to extract payback for the death of family members during the Saddam era. "We have caught him more than once outside the wire before dawn," they confided in me. Though it would be difficult, if not impossible, to verify their account, if true it would be entirely in line with everything I have learned in my journey about the lawless environment in which security contractors are operating in Iraq.

An American partner in an Iraqi security company told me that his firm gave up on the Western-style PSD after finding it more effective for the security of their operations to hire Iraqi Sunnis from Saddam's former elite guards. He told me that the effect of this shift in human resources recruitment policy is that "you shoot at us or cause a problem, and the solution is taken right down to the family level." While he wouldn't go into exact details of what that might entail, it suggests that his new contractors are using revenge as a tool aimed at preventing future attacks. The Iraqi security company al-Rawafid also employed many Sunni ex–security forces from the Saddam era and is owned by a prominent Sunni sheik and member of Parliament. In March 2006, armed men wearing Iraqi police uniforms abducted fifty employees of al-Rawafid. The ministry of the interior said that the attackers were insurgents with stolen uniforms, though al-Jazeera reported that Iraqi police had long-held suspicions about al-Rawafid's manner of providing security. In Iraq, it is becoming increasingly unclear who is working for whom and to what end exactly.

The one thing that has become clear is that Western contractors fire at or into Iraqi vehicles on a regular basis. The controversial Aegis video—taken out of context and judged by a public with a limited understanding of standard operating procedures and the working environment for security convoys—gave the impression that PSDs randomly shoot at Iraqis with the same restraint as a fourteen-year-old playing a violent video game. In reality, the video more likely portrayed an inexperienced and terrified contractor uncertain whether cars behind the convoy were friend or foe. A comparison could be drawn with the issues raised in the United States after an accidental shooting by police officers. Police have to make split-second decisions of life and death, and if they're in what they feel is a dangerous situation, the heightened tension makes an irreversible mistake more likely. The most dangerous environment an American police officer might encounter, multiplied by a hundred, may begin to give a sense of the pressure under which PSDs working in Iraq must operate. Mistakes happen, but the lack of accountability for even justified accidental shootings makes abuses more likely.

Neither the Pentagon nor the Iraqis keep statistics—at least publicly—on the number of civilians injured or killed by contractor shootings. However, in early 2006, the Pentagon did release a cache of four hundred serious incident reports that spanned nine months of 2004–2005. In analyzing the documents, Jay Price of Raleigh-Durham's *News and Observer* determined that contractors in Baghdad had reported shooting into sixty-one vehicles during that nine-month period. Of those, only seven incidents involved the targets shooting back, threatening violence, or conducting threatening activities. In most cases, the contractors fled the scene after the incident.

The four hundred reports represent only a portion of the actual incidents. Contractors are supposed to file an account about the reasons for every single weapons discharge, including warning shots. However, during my time with contractors in Iraq, I never saw a single report filed, even though gunfire against civilians was an everyday event, possibly to an average of three to six warning shots per run. I must add, however, that I never witnessed any of the men I rode with acting outside the bounds of the standard rules of engagement, but then again, none of the Iraqis they fired on were insurgents but normal commuters.

When I ask Shannon, a Blackwater contractor with many tours of duty in Iraq, how extensive he thinks the problem of civilian casualties may be, he replies: "Contractors shoot at people all the time, but we don't stop to see if anyone was killed or injured." When I press him for more information on his memory of any specific incidents, the usually loquacious Shannon remains uncharacteristically circumspect. Shifting angles, I ask him what he views as the worst-case scenario for the security industry in Iraq, to which he offers: "The FBI showed up once looking for a rogue group. And no one knows if the USIS rumors about contractors doing offensive operations in Fallujah are true. There are plenty of stories from Iraqis about drive-by shootings, but the fact is that there are plenty of white SUVs used by insurgents." As a member of the close-knit, self-protective tribe of security contractors, it may be difficult for Shannon to acknowledge that his own contemporaries may actually represent a larger problem than any rogue group. Or he may just be putting a positive spin on the practices of his chosen profession.

Most contractors I have asked about this issue have responded with a chuckle or a sarcastic remark, and the general consensus has been that the most serious incidents—the ones in which civilians were likely killed—are the least likely to be reported. The only negative elements of the security industry Shannon would comment on were two items that have already been reportedly resolved: "We had a problem with black-market weapons, but that got shut down. There was the whole steroid thing, but State clamped down on that." Though I have spent years traveling with and talking to contractors and have made many lasting and meaningful friendships through the experience, it is obvious that on many levels their world will remain a closed society—even to me. But even as simply a close observer of the standards and practices of private security in Iraq, two critical issues have become glaringly obvious. They are that some Iraqi security companies are very likely operating as private militias, and that there has yet to be an accounting of deaths caused by contractors—men who for now still operate with a license to kill.

As of spring 2006, there has not been a single contractor charged for any crime that occurred in Iraq, though hundreds of soldiers have been court-martialed for offenses ranging from minor violations of military code to murder. Even if a particularly negligent or intentional attack on civilians was publicly exposed, it is unclear what legal avenues would be used to hold the perpetrators accountable. The only contractor who has been charged with a crime during the War on Terror will be tried for a violation of the Patriot Act, even though the incident in question occurred in

Afghanistan: David Passaro, an independent contractor working a covert paramilitary job, allegedly assaulted a prisoner in detention. He now awaits trial in his home state of North Carolina.

It is evident that the depth and breadth of this problem has yet to be fully explored, though there is a clear need to understand the impact that hired guns have on the people and environment in which they operate—not just for today's War on Terror, but also for the future.

The rise of the private security company in war zones and high-risk areas has created a new breed of private soldiers, armed mercenaries, security guards, and companies who have the license to resort to full-scale violence if attacked—a potential freelance warrior class that operates under murky legal restraint. The commercial provision of an armed force has become a standard way of doing business, as well as a supplemental tool of foreign policy. The thing to watch in the future will be whether or not armed men hired on a contract basis become an integral tool of foreign policy.

Some of the khaki-clad legions in Iraq do a ninety-day tour and realize that their life is worth more than $500 a day. Others will develop an addiction to the lifestyle and a dark craving for being "in the game." The war against the Russians in Afghanistan drew legions of mercenaries to fight jihad, creating an army of thousands of trained, seasoned private soldiers with a tight network of contacts with aligned ideologies and capabilities. After the Russians withdrew, leaving the jihadis unemployed, some of them went home, but many ended up joining al-Qaeda and/or moving on to fight other Islamist insurgencies. Working in violent areas and being given a license to kill can be frightening to some and an addictive adrenaline rush to others. It is impossible to predict how successfully the thousands of security contractors now working in Iraq will integrate back into a normal civilian life after their wellspring of employment dries up.

Examining the coup attempt in Equatorial Guinea provides a good model of how private military forces can be harnessed by well- or ill-intentioned wealthy patrons for their own personal and financial designs. Established military powers have little to fear from the designs of a few dozen men winging their way on a 727, but had the coup been successful in Equatorial Guinea, America would have had to protect its oil interests from being sold off or diverted to the highest or most corrupt bidder. A small group of men with experience as hired guns could be exponential in their influence, given the right opportunity. Just as Billy Waugh was sent in to train and hire foreign legions in Southeast Asia in the 1970s and more recently in Afghanistan, it would take only a limited number of willing participants to act as the catalyst for a much broader military action.

Loosely organized old-boy networks and their financially motivated players have a proven ability to operate within clearly defined loopholes and then vanish when the gig is done. Even the more visible proponents of the soldier-for-hire club like Simon Mann, Tim Spicer, even Keith Idema, can relabel and reposition themselves as the times and opportunities dictate. The business has scurry holes where an egregious abuser can disappear, only to reappear with a different corporate label and purpose a few months later. I have met former Apartheid-era enforcers, dictators' bodyguards, bounty hunters, and mercenaries working as contractors for large Western security companies. I have also met seasoned cops, decorated veterans, and highly educated intellectuals working on the same teams. The first set would likely not hesitate to take a gig like Equatorial Guinea, but it will be interesting to see if any "normal" Western contractors will take money to make a big jump to the dark side.

In my years of travels among guns-for-hire, I have never seen an example of a clearly evil person deliberately doing evil things as a contractor. All have their own moral, professional, and emotional rationale for what they do. Their tribal nature forces reprobates out and word travels quickly. Many of the more recent initiates see their calling as identical to what they did in the military or police. Many switch back and forth seamlessly, such as the two men arrested in Zimbabwe with Simon Mann while they were on a "hunting vacation" from their jobs in Iraq. The more experienced ones see that times and rationale can change quickly, turning the savior into the demon.

President Obiang's lawyer, Henry Page, has spent quite a bit of time pondering the moral dilemma of employing a PMC to effect "regime change." He has his own opinions about the future of the private security industry, and contrasts the post-9/11 "license to kill" to a passage from *A Man for All Seasons* in which Thomas More stands by the letter of the law against the wishes of the king, who wants to bend the rules to divorce his wife. In his terribly posh British accent, Page paraphrases, "If the laws protect you like trees from the devil, and you cut them down to get to the devil, what will protect you when the devil comes after you?"

GLOSSARY

ABC—American Broadcasting Corporation

AIC—Agent in charge

AK-47—Avtomat Kalashnikov Model 47, a Soviet-designed assault rifle that fires heavy 7.62-mm rounds, developed for Russian motorized infantry in 1949

AN/PRC 112—A palm-sized, 28-ounce survival radio/GPS for locating downed air crews and combat patrols

ANC—African National Congress

ASIS—American Society for Industrial Security

BBC—British Broadcasting Corporation

BBC—Bight of Benin Company

BIAP—Baghdad International Airport

Blackside SF—Covert Special Forces

Blue Badger—Full-time CIA employee

BMW—Bavarian Motor Works

CAC—Common access card issued to contractors

CACI—California Analysis Center, Inc

CAMCO—Central Aircraft Manufacturing Company

CASA 212—The newest version of Spanish-made short takeoff and landing transport aircraft, which can carry twenty-five equipped paratroopers or 6,500 pounds of payload

CAS—Close Air Support, now called TAC-P, Tactical Air Control Party

CAT—Counterassault team

CCB—Civil Cooperation Bureau

CDI—"Chicks Dig It"

CEO—Chief executive officer

345

CH-47—U.S. twin rotor workhorse helicopter that can transport forty-four troops or lift up to 26,000 thousand pounds by sling

CIA—Central Intelligence Agency

CIDG—Civilian Irregular Defense Group

Clandestine—Actions done in secret, often in order to conceal an illicit or improper purpose

CNN—Cable News Network

Covert—Activities conducted, planned, and executed so that any U.S. government responsibility for them is not evident to unauthorized persons and that if the activities are uncovered, the U.S. government can plausibly disclaim any responsibility for them

CPA—Coalition Provisional Authority

CQB—Close-quarter battle

CRG—Control Risks Group

CRM—Crisis and Risk Management

DBA—Defense Base Act Insurance

DC—District of Columbia

DCI—Director of Central Intelligence

DEVGRU—Development Group (SEAL Team 6), short for United States Naval Special Warfare Development Group

DIA—Defense Intelligence Agency

DoD—Department of Defense

DPG—Defense Planning Guidance

DSL—Defence Systems Limited

DSS—Diplomatic Security Service (U.S. State Department)

EEZ—Exclusive Economic Zone

EKG—Electrocardiogram (EKG comes from the German name Elektrokardiogramm)

EO—Executive Outcomes

ESS—Eurest Support Services

FLIR—Forward-looking infrared

GAO—Government Accountability Office

GC—Governate coordinator

GMC—General Motors Corporation

GMSSCO—Global Marine Security Systems Company
GPS—Global Positioning System
Green Badger—Freelance CIA contractor
Green Zone—Ten-square-kilometer fortified area along the banks of the Tigris chosen as the U.S. occupation center in Baghdad
H&K—Heckler & Koch
HVT—High-value target
IC—Independent contractor
ICDC—Iraqi Civil Defense Corps
IED—Improvised explosive device
IPOA—International Peace Operations Association
ISI—Inter-Services Intelligence
JDAM—Joint Direct Attack Munition
JSOC—Joint Special Operations Command
JSOTF—Joint Special Operations Task Force
KAS—Kilo Alpha Services
KBR—Kellogg, Brown and Root
KIA—Killed in action
KPD—Karzai Protection Detail
K-Town—Khartoum, Sudan
LOGCAP—Logistics Civil Augmentation Program (U.S. Army)
LURD—Liberians United for Reconciliation and Democracy
M4—The M4 carbine, a more compact version of the M16A2 rifle with a shorter barrel and a telescoping four-position buttstock
M16—The standard-issue U.S. rifle
MACV-SOG—Military Assistance Command Vietnam–Special Observation Group
MI6—UK Military Intelligence Section 6
MiG—Russian aircraft designers Mikojan & Gurevich
MNF—Multi-national forces
MP—Military police
MRE—Meals ready to eat
MTS—Meteoric Tactical Services
MTS—Military Technical Services

MVM—Marquez Vance Marquez
NA—Northern Alliance
NBC—National Broadcasting Company
NGO—Nongovernmental organization
NOC—Nonofficial cover
NVA—North Vietnamese Army
NVGs—Night-vision goggles
ODA—Operational Detachment, Alpha
OGA—Other governmental agencies
Ops—Operations
ORHA—Office of Reconstruction and Humanitarian Assistance
OSS—Office of Strategic Services
PBS—Public Broadcasting Service
PCO—Project and Contracting Office
PKM—Pulemyot Kalashnikova Modernizirovanniy, the standard general-purpose machine gun adopted in 1961 that fires the heavier 7.62 × 54 R bullet
PMC—Private military company
PNAC—Project for the New American Century
PNG—Papua New Guinea
PNGDF—Papua New Guinea Defence Force
POW—Prisoner of war
PRS—Primary ring security
PSC—Private security company
PSD—Personal security detail
R & R—Rest and relaxation
REMFs—Rear-Echelon Mother Fuckers
Red Zone—Baghdad outside the Green Zone
RFP—Request for proposal
ROWAL—Ranger Oil West Africa
RPG—Rocket-propelled grenade
RSO—Regional Security Officer
RTI—Research Triangle Development, Inc.
RUF—Revolutionary United Front (Sierra Leone)

SAD—Special Activities Division (CIA)

SADF—South African Defence Force

SAS—Special Air Service (UK)

SAW—Squad automatic weapon

SCI—Sensitive Compartmented Information above "top secret," an access restriction applied to information that could cause exceptionally grave damage to the national security

SCG—Smith Consulting Group

SEAL—Sea, air, land (U.S. Navy)

SF—Special Forces (U.S. Army)

SOAR—Special Operations Aviation Regiment

SOCOM—Special Operations Command

SOFLAM—Special Operations Forces Laser Marker

SUV—Sport utility vehicle

TAC-P—Tactical air controller party

TCNs—Third-country nationals

TF—Task force

TFE—TotalFinalElf

UAV—Unmanned aerial vehicle

UN—United Nations

UNITA—União Nacional para a Independência Total de Angola

USAID—United States Agency for International Development

USIS—United States Investigations Services

Vanilla SF—Overt Special Forces Groups

VBIED—Vehicle-borne improvised explosive device

VIP—Very important person

VP—Vice president

ZDI—Zimbabwe Defence Industries

ACKNOWLEDGMENTS

I'd like to express my profound gratitude to the countless people who've helped me in my journey, especially my agent, Paul Bresnick, for his vision and commitment; my unflagging editor, Christina Davidson, for her patience and care; and Chris Jackson and Rick Horgan at Crown, who saw the reason why this book should be brought to market. As with all my books, *Licensed to Kill* would be nothing without the extraordinary trust, assistance, and insight from individuals, groups, and organizations that agreed to let me into their world. To these named and unnamed people in this book who share my devotion to the truth, I thank you.

INDEX

Scurka, Gary, 230–38
SEALs, 31, 53, 57, 124, 125, 167, 188, 221
 DEVGRU, 71–72, 73, 78, 178, 184, 211
Secret Service, 74
security companies, *see* private security companies; *specific companies*
security contractors:
 assassination ban and, 27, 114
 enlisted in search for bin Laden, 31
 enlisted in War on Terror, 36
 Church-Pike investigations and, 25
 clothing of, 188–89, 196, 202–3
 in combat situations, 149–65
 cost benefits of using, 121
 creed of, vii
 culture of, 196
 death of, 218
 insurance for, 122, 137, 138, 139, 176, 218,
  337
 in Iraq, *see* Iraq, security contractors in
 laptops used by, 196, 199
 in MACV-SOG, 23–24
 mercenaries vs., 5–6, 109, 304, 332
 motivations for, 95
 nicknames given to, 196
 pay rates for, 95, 121, 197, 219–20, 337
 pecking order among, 178
 professional career, 95
 rules of engagement for, 149, 153–54,
  340
 see also personal security details; private security companies
security convoys, *see* convoys, security
security equipment, 89, 95–96
September 11 attacks, 28, 29, 31, 41, 69, 98,
 99, 275, 294
Services Bureau (Maktab al-Khadamat), 46
Shah-i-Kot Valley, 61
Sherzai, Gul, 71–72
Shim, Jorge, 248
Shinseki, Eric, 102–3
Shkin, 38–39, 40, 43–44, 49
Sierra Leone, 261–63, 265, 266, 268, 270–72,
 275, 285, 290, 300, 309, 310, 316
Simm, George, 287, 288, 290–92, 296–99,
 301
Singarok, Jerry, 268–69
Singer, Peter, 107–8, 214, 296
Sites, Kevin, 236, 237
60 Minutes, 231–32
Sloan, Alfred, 2

Slowe, Richard, 269, 273, 274
Smith, Jamie, 36–40, 41
Smith, Johann, 322–23
Soldier of Fortune, 229, 231, 245
Solomon Islands, 99
Somalia, 101, 136, 140, 290
Soviet Union, Afghanistan and, 44–48, 50, 61,
 63, 97, 342
Spain, 310, 324, 329, 331
Spann, Johnny Micheal, 69, 243
Sparky (contractor), 335–36
Special Forces (SF), 20–21, 25, 31, 52, 97, 169,
 188, 221
 CIA and, 20–21, 22
 Idema and, 241–42, 243, 244
 MACV-SOG and, 23, 24
 SEALs vs., 31
 Walther in, 75–76, 77
 Waugh in, 18, 19, 20–23
Special Forces Operations Exhibition, 4
Spicer, Timothy, 252, 254, 257–58, 264–69,
 270–83, 285, 296–97, 313, 323, 343
Spielberg, Steven, 230
State Department, 74, 76, 82, 110, 123, 208,
 209, 215, 234, 292, 295
 Aegis and, 277–83
 Aristide protection and, 83, 84, 85
 Diplomatic Security Service of, 94
 Karzai protection and, 77–78, 82, 110
 Najaf siege and, 153
 rules of engagement for personal security
  detail, 111
Steele Foundation, 83, 84, 85, 90, 93, 327
Steiner, Rolf, 253
Steve (pilot), 12, 144, 146–47, 153
Steyl, Crause, 315–16, 318, 320, 321, 326, 329
Steyl, Neil, 262, 318, 320, 327, 330
Stirling, David, 288, 289
Stout, Don, 175–76
Strasser, Valentine, 262, 263
Strategic Technical Directorate Assistance
 Team 158, 23
Straw, Jack, 323–24
Sudan, 27–29, 44–45, 285, 286, 322
suicide bombers, 200–201
Sundberg, Olle, 288

Taliban, 30–34, 36, 44, 45, 51, 53–56, 58–60,
 69, 97, 98
 'dog' hits by, 74
 fall of, 70, 76, 97, 98